4-a-03 ~~DATE DUE~~

APR 1 6 2003
APR 1 6 2003
APR 2 3 2003
JUN 1 1 2003

MISSISSIPPI LAW

Forbids the retention without authorization or mutilation of
library materials. This is a misdemeanor punishable by a fine
not to exceed $500 or by imprisonment in the county jail not to
exceed six months or both.

Operation Pretense

MID STATE PIPE & SUPPLY

608 Hwy. 16 West • Carthage, MS 39051

Bus. (601) 267-8840
Res. (601) 992-2494

JERRY JACOBS

Operation Pretense

The FBI's Sting on County Corruption in Mississippi

James R. Crockett

University Press of Mississippi   Jackson

www.upress.state.ms.us

This volume is supported in part by the University of Southern
Mississippi and its College of Business Administration and School of
Accounting and Information Systems.

11 10 09 08 07 06 05 04 03 4 3 2 1

∞

Library of Congress Cataloging-in-Publication Data

Crockett, James R.
    Operation pretense : the FBI's sting on county corruption in
Mississippi / James R. Crockett.
        p. cm.
    Includes bibliographical references and index.
    ISBN 1-57806-496-1 (cloth : alk. paper)
        1. Misconduct in office—Mississippi—Case studies.   2. Political
corruption—Mississippi—Case studies.   3. Local
government—Mississippi—Corrupt policies—Case studies.   I. Title.
JK4645 .C763 2003
364.1'323—dc21   2002006153

British Library Cataloging-in-Publication Data available

People need heroes, and even forty-five-year-old men need new heroes. I was fortunate enough to gain one at that age when I became a colleague of Jerold J. Morgan in 1987. This work is dedicated to the memory of Jerold J. Morgan, Ph.D., CPA, founding director of the School of Professional Accountancy in the College of Business Administration at the University of Southern Mississippi. Dr. Morgan was a great and good man whose influence within the academic accounting community continues through the lives of his many protégés. Dr. Morgan's integrity stands in sharp contrast to that of the public officials who were convicted and pleaded guilty as the result of Operation Pretense.

Contents

Acknowledgments

For two of the four-plus years consumed by this project, I was the Jerold J. Morgan Distinguished Professor of Accountancy at the University of Southern Mississippi. The professorship provided the majority of the funds needed to conduct the underlying research. I thank all of those, especially Dr. Morgan's family, whose generous contributions made the Morgan professorship possible.

I thank the College of Business Administration and School of Accountancy and Information Systems for supporting the research for this book and its publication. I also thank the University of Southern Mississippi for granting me a sabbatical to get the project started and for providing monetary support of the book's publication.

It is not possible to thank all of the many people who encouraged me in this project and provided important information and research support. However, the vital contributions of three people must be acknowledged:

Dorothy Crockett, my loving wife, served as the first reader and made numerous corrections and helpful suggestions. She also humored me during a long period of time when Operation Pretense was never completely out of my thoughts.

Charles Jordan, professor of accountancy and valued colleague at the University of Southern Mississippi, served as the second reader and made many corrections and helpful suggestions.

Tyrone Black, professor of economics and former dean of the College of Business Administration, served as the third reader and made many invaluable contributions to the readability of the manuscript.

Introduction

Operation Pretense was a 1980s Federal Bureau of Investigation (FBI) undercover investigation of corruption in county purchasing in Mississippi. The investigation resulted in 56 of the state's 410 county supervisors either being convicted by a jury or pleading guilty to various felonies. County supervisors, a county road foreman, and corrupt vendors were indicted as the result of the investigation. Collectively they became known as "The Highway 70."

Fifty-seven supervisors from twenty-six counties were charged under Operation Pretense. This total includes two supervisors from Rankin County who were indicted on state charges. Forty-six supervisors pled guilty in federal court. Two supervisors pled guilty in Rankin County Court. Six supervisors were tried and convicted in federal court. One supervisor was tried in federal court and found not guilty. One supervisor was found mentally incompetent to stand trial. One supervisor died shortly after being indicted. Thirteen vendors were charged under Operation Pretense. Twelve vendors pled guilty in federal court or cooperated in the investigation to the extent that charges were dropped. One vendor went to trial and was convicted in federal court on 241 counts.

Nearly all of Mississippi's counties operated under the antiquated "beat system" of county government that almost invited corruption. Under the beat system, the five members of the board of supervisors were in charge of all activities related to building and maintaining roads in their individual districts (beats). There was a lack of even rudimentary controls over purchases made with tax monies and essentially no planning and control over roads at the county level. Supervisors exercised almost unlimited power over county employees and expenditures for their beats. Corrupt supervisors often displayed unmitigated gall, and county citizens seemingly accepted the status quo.

The primary purpose of this book is to provide a detailed account of Operation Pretense and some related instances of corruption in Mississippi state and county government. The focus is on the causes and results of the

FBI investigation and sting. Conditions that allowed elected officials and unscrupulous vendors to commit thousands of crimes over many years are described. The charges filed against individuals are summarized, along with how the individuals were prosecuted and the extent to which those convicted were punished.

Chapter 2 of the U.S. Justice Department's manual *Prosecution of Public Corruption Cases* is entitled "Corruption in Government Contracts: Bribery, Kickbacks, Bid-Rigging and the Rest." Written by John R. Hailman, the chapter is actually based on Operation Pretense, and in it Hailman provides an informative perspective on five types of governmental corruption disclosed in Operation Pretense:

1. Extortion in government contracting involves a vendor unwillingly giving a gratuity or other type of undeserved reward or benefit to a government purchasing agent, usually in cash or kind, whether personal property, fuel, equipment, free labor, free trips, tickets to sporting events, or other desirable things of value. Extortion is often successful because the victim fears economic loss or being shut out of a lucrative but relatively closed market where everybody is making payoffs. However, because extortion involves a readily identified victim, it is rarer in local government contracting than is bribery.

2. Bribery involves one party soliciting a payment or offering to pay another party to enter into a transaction; the process is completed when the other party agrees, the transaction is consummated, and the payoff is made. Bribery benefits the bribe-taker, who gets the payoff, and the briber, who gets the business, often at the expense of more honest competitors and ultimately the public. The briber and the bribe-taker are in a real sense partners in crime; consequently, neither has incentive to inform on the other. Moreover, either party can initiate the offer, and if the transaction is not consummated, there is little chance that one will turn informant. Unfortunately, "no harm, no foul" is the way bribery attempts are often viewed by the public and jurors.

3. Kickbacks are probably the most common form of corruption after bribery. In government contracting, kickbacks usually involve purchase contracts for which the vendor gives, or "kicks back," to the government purchasing agent or other official either cash or something else of value. In some cases, the kickback is a fixed percentage of a given series of contracts, such as 10 percent on culvert pipes (in Operation Pretense, the preacher's 10 percent supervisors expense), 12 percent on gravel, and

15 percent on equipment repairs. In other cases, the "thing of value," which may be given weekly or monthly, is not cash but such gratuities as trips, use of hotel suites or expensive condos, and liquor.

4. Busted invoices involve payments for undelivered items. Sometimes competing vendors offer higher and higher kickbacks to obtain government contracts. Thus, prices can become so high that they arouse public or media attention. When this point is reached, bolder vendors approach government purchasing agents and suggest a step up the ladder of corruption—use of the "phantom" or "busted" invoice, which involves the vendor submitting fictitious invoices for materials not delivered or services not rendered. This practice gives rise to terms like "invisible pipe" (a term coined by FBI special agent Jerry King during Pretense) and "phantom employees." In such cases, either the vendor or the corrupt government purchasing agent will suggest that if the items on the invoice are only partially delivered, or not delivered at all, the vendor can split the unmerited profit on the deal, usually fifty-fifty, with the purchasing agent. This practice is the most lucrative situation for the crooks and the most costly for the taxpayers—the crooks get higher payoffs, but taxpayers get less than they paid for or nothing at all.

5. Bid-rigging schemes involve collusion among vendors to divide government business, usually geographically or for defined periods of time, in order to avoid competition and to inflate prices. Suppliers may meet and agree on how much each will bid on governmental requests to supply certain types of materials. Participants agree never to underbid the others, and each is guaranteed to "win" one or more contracts, usually at exorbitant prices. Bid rigging may also occur when companies compete for service or commodity contracts using copies of competitors' letterhead stationary. This practice allows a single company to submit multiple "bids" to the government agency on other companies' letterhead, thus assuring success for the company making the multiple submissions. The privilege of making multiple bids is rotated among conspirators. Another version of bid rigging involves competitors submitting "complimentary" high bids, and asking the same courtesy on their next bid, thus passing jobs around the group at inflated prices. A major legal defense of bid rigging is that there was no real financial loss to the government, only a theoretical one. This theory can usually be rebutted with proof of the lower prices the government unit should have been paying.

The body of the book is divided into three sections. Part I consisting of chapters 1–8, is designed to give the reader an overall understanding of the how and why of Operation Pretense. It begins with a chapter that explains the conditions that spawned the FBI investigation and outlines the scope and nature of Operation Pretense. The other chapters deal with counties that had one or more supervisors actually go to trial on Pretense-related charges. Extensive use is made of materials taken directly from trial transcripts to show how the FBI's sting actually worked, and sworn testimony is used to depict the conditions and mores that allowed corruption to flourish.

Part II, which includes chapters 9–12, deals with matters related to Operation Pretense. Chapter 9 is devoted to the Mississippi Department of Audit, the way it has evolved, its involvement with Operation Pretense, and with the fallout from the investigation. Chapter 10 describes the political struggle for the unit system of county government and the momentum given it by Operation Pretense. Chapter 11 deals with state highway commissioners who were investigated by the Department of Audit and the FBI's Operation Pretense team and pleaded guilty to major crimes involving bribery and kickbacks. Although Operation Pretense did not directly affect Madison County, Chapter 12 outlines some curious developments in that county that involve the county's board of supervisors and a vendor who pled guilty to Pretense-related charges to further illustrate the depth of the problems in county government in Mississippi.

Part III focuses on supervisors who pled guilty to Pretense-related crimes without going to trial and vendors who were implicated in Pretense but did not go to trial. In seven of the eight chapters in this section, counties are grouped by geographical area, and cases against their corrupt supervisors are summarized. The final chapter deals with vendors who were implicated but did not go to trial. Drawing from newspaper articles, interviews, and court records that include arrest warrants, informations, indictments, plea agreements, orders, and petitions, Part III captures in some detail the extent of illegal behavior perpetrated by these individuals and their efforts to prevent or limit the resulting punishment.

Operation Pretense left in its wake devastated lives, lost political careers, significant reforms in county government, and changes in the day-to-day operations of county government. However, the reforms resulting from Pretense were far from perfect. My goal was to document the important details of Operation Pretense and related matters in one place and to demonstrate that vigilance is necessary to prevent a similar scandal in the future. It is hoped that the book will serve as a reminder of the conditions that allowed corruption to flourish and that it will prod the citizens of Mississippi to continue the reforms that Operation Pretense spawned.

Timeline of Significant Events Related to Operation Pretense

1984

January—Ray Mabus becomes state auditor.

March—The Reverend John Burgess begins cooperating with a federal investigation of corruption in county purchasing. Mid-State Pipe Company is opened as an FBI front for an undercover sting, and Operation Pretense is born.

July—Neshoba County Board of Supervisors votes to transition from the beat to the unit system of county government.

1985

February—The FBI takes over all undercover operations. FBI special agent Jerry King, working undercover as a salesman for Mid-State, meets Ray Davis, owner of Davis Chemical Company, who will soon become a key figure in the investigation.

1986

June—Ray Davis is co-opted by the FBI, and he begins to cooperate in the investigation. The FBI front, now Mid-State Pipe and Supply Company, is shut down.

1987

February—The first Pretense-related indictments are handed down by federal grand juries in Jackson and Oxford. Bobby Dean Stegall, supervisor of Pontotoc County's district five, becomes the first supervisor to plead guilty as a result of Pretense.

March—Lauvon Pierce of Green County's district five is the eleventh supervisor charged by federal authorities as a result of Operation Pretense. Pierce is "flipped" by the FBI and becomes an invaluable asset to the investigation

June—Perry County district four supervisor Trudie Westmoreland is the first supervisor tried and convicted as a result of Operation Pretense. By the time of Westmoreland's conviction, thirty-one supervisors had been indicted, and six had pleaded guilty. Billy Lott, a salesman for Puckett Machinery, is given the first prison sentence imposed as a result of Operation Pretense, six years.

July—Wayne County supervisors Jimmy Duvall and Alfred Revette are tried and convicted.

August—Lamar County district five supervisor Kermit Rayborn becomes the fourth supervisor to be tried and convicted.

November—Wayne County district five supervisor William Hutto is tried and convicted as a result of Operation Pretense. Ray Mabus is elected governor, and Pete Johnson is elected state auditor. Former Copiah County district one supervisor Thomas M. Heard is sentenced to ten years in prison. Ten years turns out to be the longest prison sentence imposed as a result of Operation Pretense. Lauderdale County district five supervisor Billy Joe Harris is the fifth supervisor sentenced to prison. His six-year sentence proves to be the longest prison sentence imposed on any supervisor who pleaded guilty.

1988

February—Claiborne County district one supervisor Albert Butler is tried on Pretense-related charges and found innocent. The Operation Pretense jury trial score after this verdict stood at five convictions and one innocent verdict. Butler proved to be the only supervisor charged under Pretense who was found innocent in a court of law.

March—Marion County district two supervisor Sim Ed Moree is convicted of obstruction of justice charges.

Jasper County district three supervisor John Robert Ulmer becomes the first supervisor who pleaded guilty whose sentence does not include time in prison.

April—Winston County district four supervisor Larry Miller is the sixth and last supervisor tried and convicted.

Southern District highway commissioner Bob Joiner pleads guilty to federal corruption charges.

May—"The Preacher and the Sting Man" airs on CBS's *60 Minutes* and introduces the nation to Operation Pretense.

August—Governor Mabus calls a special session of the legislature that approves a bill that requires counties to choose between the beat and unit systems of county government in a November referendum.

September—Bobby Little, president of North Mississippi Supply Company of Rienzi in Alcorn County, is convicted on 241 Pretense-related counts.

November—Forty-six of Mississippi's eighty-two counties opt for the unit system of county government in the mandated referendum.

1989

February—Central District highway commissioner Sam Waggoner pleads guilty to federal corruption charges.

May—Copiah County district three supervisor Sidney Thompson pleads guilty in the last Operation Pretense case prosecuted.

October—The forty-six counties that voted for the unit system in the November 1988 referendum are supposed to have implemented it.

Part I.

The Operation Pretense Investigation and Related Trials

1. A License to Steal

Friday, the thirteenth day of February 1987, was a very bad day for many of Mississippi's county supervisors. An FBI undercover investigation into corrupt county purchasing practices hit the media on the thirteenth after nine indictments had been handed down by federal grand juries in Jackson and Oxford. The three-year investigation was revealed at news conferences in Jackson and Oxford while state auditors seized financial records in many of the state's eighty-two counties. The indictments charged nine supervisors with bribery, extortion, and mail fraud for allegedly accepting kickbacks, rigging bids, and billing counties for goods never delivered.

Speaking in Jackson, George Phillips, U.S. attorney for the Southern District of Mississippi, said, "There are many more indictments to come and a number of supervisors and vendors alike will be the subject of many, many cases. We just can't handle them all right now, but we intend to work the cases through the grand juries for a number of months to come." State Auditor Ray Mabus asserted that the Department of Audit's actions were "taken in cooperation with the FBI." Phillips's words proved to be prophetic, as the maelstrom that was to become known as Operation Pretense was unleashed with these first nine indictments. Among Pretense's immediate effects were renewed emphasis on reforming the state's purchasing laws and calls for mandating the unit system of county government.

Each of Mississippi's counties is divided into five districts commonly called "beats." Each beat elects a supervisor, and the five supervisors constitute the board of supervisors that operates the county government and is responsible for all of the county's business except for public schools. In 1987, most of the counties operated their road programs on the beat system, under which supervisors had complete control over all road work in their districts. Operation Pretense resulted in criminal charges against 57 of the state's 410 county supervisors and one district road foreman. Corrupt vendors and sales representatives doing business with corrupt supervisors made payoffs in the form of cash, property, fuel, equipment, free labor, free trips, and tickets to sporting events. Fourteen vendors and sales representatives were also charged in Operation Pretense.

Attala County supervisor Robert Ellard was one of the first nine supervisors indicted in Operation Pretense. The *Star-Herald*, Kosciusko's weekly newspaper, published an editorial on February 19, 1987, related to Ellard's arrest and the system that allowed supervisors to steal. While incomplete, the editorial's description of the system captured the essence of a statewide problem—supervisors had a license to steal.

> In Attala, and probably most counties of Mississippi, each supervisor is a one-man business. He makes the purchases, signs the receiving slips, and authorizes payment. In cases of purchases of under $500 no paperwork is required in making the buy. While a purchase order is required in cases over $500 only the person placing the order knows the whole story. He can sign the purchase order, the receiving slip and the order for payment. The chancery clerk is only responsible for issuing the check authorized by the official.

Federal authorities had heard numerous complaints about corrupt supervisors. When such complaints came from credible sources and were documented, they become a form of "predication" (indications that supervisors were predisposed to engage in illegal activity) that is required by federal guidelines for an undercover investigation. Based on such complaints, U.S. Attorney George Phillips and Weldon Kennedy, special agent in charge of the FBI in Mississippi, were formulating plans for an undercover investigation targeting county supervisors when, according to Phillips, "manna from heaven" arrived in the form of a preacher.

John Burgess, a Pentecostal minister and businessman from Carthage, was a key figure in Operation Pretense. In fact, Pretense stood for the "Preacher's Ten-Percent Supervisors Expense." Burgess learned about kickbacks in 1982 when he invested in Polk Concrete, a pipe manufacturing company just south of Jackson. He learned that the company's sales representatives had to pay kickbacks to supervisors to sell their product to counties. Burgess contacted the FBI by phone and told them that doing business with supervisors required paying kickbacks to these elected officials. Nothing came of this for some time.

Under pressure from other owners, Burgess soon left the failing business, which had filed for bankruptcy. In 1984, the FBI investigated alleged hiding of assets in the company's bankruptcy filing and sent an agent, Keith Morgan, to interview Burgess. Burgess told the agent that he knew nothing about an expensive forklift that had supposedly disappeared but that he did know about county supervisors taking kickbacks. This time the FBI took notice.

Burgess told the federal authorities what he knew, and they persuaded him to cooperate in the planned undercover investigation. Burgess owned a building supply company in Carthage, and he agreed to open an FBI front named Mid-State Pipe Company in a building next to his business. Beginning in 1984, a wired Burgess taped conversations that took place as he paid kickbacks to secure business from several county supervisors. Burgess ultimately testified against supervisors before several grand juries and in two criminal trials. Mid-State became the business that provided cover to launch a broad investigation of county purchasing practices that became a very successful sting operation. The FBI placed undercover agents at Mid-State as sales representatives and as the office manager. The agents ultimately took control of the entire Mid-State operation as Burgess stepped aside with the story that the salesmen were purchasing the business from him. The FBI took over all of the undercover work in February 1985 and used Mid-State as a front until July 1986, when the company was closed.

Rev. John Burgess was presented the Louis E. Peters Memorial Award by the Society of Former Special Agents of the FBI at the society's October 1991 meeting in Honolulu. Named for a California automobile dealer who helped the FBI expose organized crime figures who attempted to buy his business, this annual award is given to a citizen "who, at great personal sacrifice, gave unselfishly of themselves to serve their community and nation." Commenting on the honor, Wayne R. Taylor, special agent in charge of the FBI in Mississippi, said, "The whole basis of the award is to emphasize the fact that each of us can make a difference. Each of the recipients identified a problem, stood up, and said, 'This is not right. I can do something.'" Burgess said, "I didn't know the FBI had to have help. When I saw the job had to be done and I had to do it, I did it. . . . Those that were affected by it didn't like it of course. Most everybody else commended me for what I did. The business community commended me."

Alvin M. Binder, a defense attorney who represented several of the indicted supervisors, criticized Burgess for accepting $40,000 from the FBI over a two-and-a-half-year period, claiming that he cooperated for the money. "He tried to imply that his motive was pure and that he was doing it for America. But he did it to line his pockets with gold," Binder said. Burgess calmly replied, "I could have made that much money in my building materials business in one year. I doubt if the attorneys took one case and got less than that." Burgess claimed that the $40,000 was to pay the costs of travel, fuel, meals, and other expenses. He indicated that if he had worked for the money, "I wouldn't have done it for $400,000, much less $40,000. . . . I didn't do it for the money, I lost money. I wouldn't have jeopardized the safety of me and my family." Special agent Wayne Taylor said, "What Burgess enabled us to do was to have an impact. He didn't do it for the FBI; he did it for everybody."

FBI undercover agents Jerry King and Cliff Chatham assumed the aliases Jerry Jacobs and Cliff Winters, respectively, to play their parts as Mid-State sales representatives eager to make sales and willing to buy business with kickbacks. Another agent, Roger White, alias Roger Bennett, joined the sting as office manager for Mid-State. The sales representatives told supervisors that they had recently invested in Burgess's Mid-State and were eager to expand the business. The agents became proverbial backslappers as they bought lunches and hosted parties for supervisors and picked up tabs at conventions to gain their confidence while always hawking their products. Numerous newspaper articles, court records, and transcripts of undercover FBI tapes demonstrate how effective the FBI agents were, especially the colorful Jerry King, a former athlete and football coach from Arkansas, in playing the part of the corrupt businessman. At the trial of Perry County supervisor Trudie Westmoreland, King testified that for delivered materials, the salesmen paid supervisors 10 to 12 percent of the purchase price. Sometimes special deals were tailored to meet supervisors' specific requests. For example, a deal was struck with Greene County Supervisor John Crocker on February 19, 1985, to pay the $200 that Crocker had specifically requested.

Ray Davis, owner of Davis Chemical Company of Hattiesburg, was another key figure in Operation Pretense. He began cooperating with the FBI in June 1986. Jerry King first met Ray Davis in the home of a Wayne County supervisor as they were both doing business with the supervisor. The two hit if off personally and, noting that they were not selling the same commodities and were not in competition, Davis asked King to come to his business in Hattiesburg to talk with him about cooperating. They soon began to cooperate by selling each other's wares and sharing information about corrupt supervisors. King took the list of members of the Mississippi Association of Supervisors and went over it with Davis, as they told each other which supervisors they had paid kickbacks. Later, the federal authorities "flipped" Davis and persuaded him to cooperate in the investigation by confronting him with evidence of his illegal activities.

Davis, who eventually pleaded guilty to federal mail fraud charges, claimed to have arranged fraudulent deals with officials from at least seventeen Mississippi counties. According to U.S. Assistant Attorney Nicholas Phillips, Davis's detailed knowledge of county purchasing practices was invaluable in the indictments of several supervisors. Phillips said, "I consider Davis to be an invaluable asset statewide in the prosecution of corrupt supervisors." In his work for the FBI, Davis recorded conversations that concerned many illegal transactions. Davis was mentioned in several indictments as a source of kickbacks, and he testified before grand juries and trial juries.

Stewart Murphy, a native New Yorker, headed up the FBI's Operation Pretense investigation from its Jackson office. Murphy retired in October 1989 after nine years in the Jackson office. Speaking of Pretense, he commented, "It was an interesting experience, supervising Operation Pretense. It ran from March 1984 to 1987 and it was very difficult. There were a lot of obstacles and there was concern about the exposure of undercover agents working in the rural areas." Jerry King said that he had been concerned that he might be robbed. While traveling the back roads of Mississippi, King had carried large amounts of cash to be used as payoffs.

John Hailman, assistant U.S. attorney and chief of the Criminal Division of the Northern District of Mississippi, described Burgess's part in Operation Pretense and explained the success of the investigation: "He introduced three undercover agents from Arkansas, Alabama, and Louisiana who had the appropriate accents and 'good ole boy' demeanors to be accepted as crooked local salesmen. They wore caps saying Mid-State Pipe and chewed liberal amounts of tobacco." Mid-State initially advertised "covert pipe" to supervisors, but this was wisely deemed too risky a "gotcha," according to Hailman. The assistant U.S. attorney also noted that even when Pretense was in its third year and many indictments had been returned and trials were taking place, supervisors were still asking for and taking payoffs. Although becoming somewhat more cautious, several supervisors continued their corrupt practices even after having been indicted.

It had been widely rumored long before the FBI's investigation that many county supervisors were on the take, but county sheriffs, county prosecuting attorneys, and district attorneys had little stomach for pursuing supervisors. Such reluctance is not surprising given that boards of supervisors approved the budgets of the sheriffs and county prosecutors. Furthermore, the Mississippi Attorney General had no subpoena power, which made it almost impossible for that official to investigate rumored corruption. Consequently, U.S. attorneys and the FBI were probably the only law enforcement agencies that could have effectively investigated supervisor corruption.

Legislation passed in the mid-1980s made it easier for federal officials to prosecute corruption in state and local government. In the 1992 U.S. Department of Justice manual *Investigating and Prosecuting Public Corruption*, James B. Tucker, chief assistant of the Criminal Division of the U.S. Attorney's Office of the Southern District of Mississippi, explained the significance of the anticorruption legislation:

> In 1984, with the passage of (Title 18 United States Code (U.S.C.) Section 666) Congress provided federal prosecutors and agents with an effective additional tool (supplementing the Hobbs Act, Travel Act, RICO, and Conspiracy) for combating corruption by state and local officials. The stated purpose of the legislation was ". . . to augment the ability of the United States to vindicate significant acts of theft, fraud and bribery involving federal monies that are distributed to private organizations or State and local governments pursuant to a Federal program." 1984 U.S. Code Congressional and Administrative News 3182, 3510–3511. This discussion primarily addresses application of the statute to corrupt payments to State and local government public officials and the usual attendant fraudulent conduct as proscribed by Section 666(a) (2) for the supplier.
>
> Quite simply, Section 666 reaches out to State and local public officials by virtue of the giving of benefits by Uncle Sam to the local governmental agency. If the State or local agency received the statutory requisite of federal funds ($10,000 within a year), the officials or agents of that agency are "federalized" in regard to those transactions meeting the statutory requisite minimum ($5,000). The concept is one that career federal prosecutors fantasized over for years when faced with allegations of corrupt local officials. No longer must there be pleading and proof machinations to fit plain old "good ole boy" kickback schemes by public officials and suppliers, into interstate extortion and bribery schemes, or essential mailings, of defrauding the citizenry of good and faithful services.

Tucker went on to explain that federal authorities must prove five general elements to successfully prosecute under Title 18 U.S.C.:

1. The defendant was an agent of a state or local government or an agency thereof.

2. The state or local government or agency thereof received, in any one year period, benefits in excess of $10,000 under a federal program.
3. The defendant corruptly solicited or demanded for the benefit of any person [or accepted or agreed to accept] anything of value from any person.
4. The defendant did so, i.e., solicited, demanded, accepted or agreed to accept the thing of value, intending to be influenced or rewarded in connection with any business, transaction, or series of transactions of the value of $5,000 or more to the government or agency thereof.
5. The defendant acted so knowingly.

To be successful, Operation Pretense almost had to be an undercover operation involving a sting. Supervisors could ensure that the paperwork was in order to support the chancery clerk's payment of invoices for quantities of materials not delivered and invoices on which they were to receive kickbacks. For routine purchases of materials used on the road programs in their beats, supervisors legally controlled the purchasing activities, from initiation to payment approval. They could also easily manipulate the system by rigging bids on most purchases that they could not control directly. In addition, the law did not require counties to keep records of inventories or other assets. This made tracking items that had supposedly been purchased difficult if not impossible. Thus, supervisors had to be caught taking payoffs on county business, which is precisely what the FBI designed the sting to do.

Agents acting undercover as salesmen for the front company, Mid-State Pipe, tape recorded illegal deals with supervisors. The FBI also used "flipped" vendors and supervisors, who were under indictment for paying or taking bribes, to tape similar illegal dealings. The resulting chain reaction ran from a compromised supervisor who, under a plea agreement with a U. S. Attorney, would implicate vendors and other supervisors on whom the FBI would then operate its sting. Those caught in this manner would implicate other supervisors and vendors under similar plea agreements, and the process would continue. The FBI would not sting a supervisor or vendor unless it had evidence that the person was predisposed to engage in illegal activity. This strategy was essential to prevent those who would succumb to a sting from successfully using the "entrapment" defense. The necessary predication (documentation of predisposition) was provided by vendors who had attempted to do business with supervisors, compromised vendors, and supervisors who were working with the FBI under plea bargains.

One reason corruption flourished in Mississippi was that the very structure of county government was basically flawed. Under the beat system, the board of supervisors performed both the legislative and executive functions of government. It levied taxes and approved each district's road budget, while individual supervisors directed the day-to-day roadwork in their beats. Other contributing factors were the lack of elementary internal controls over purchases and poor accounting practices related to inventories and other assets. The Department of Audit failed to deter or detect corrupt purchasing practices because audits were often performed years after the fact, and they usually did not include analytical procedures that would have highlighted suspicious purchasing practices. Even if the auditors had uncovered suspicious purchasing patterns, there was usually insufficient evidence to prosecute a corrupt supervisor. The Trudie Westmoreland case chronicled in chapter 2 shows that supervisors sometimes after the fact manufactured the paperwork necessary to support fraudulent transactions.

Under state law, supervisors could make purchases of up to $500 without competitive bids. Purchases between $500 and $2,500 required two bids or quotes, but the supervisors did not have to advertise for bids. Advertising for competitive bids was required for purchases costing more than $2,500. Splitting purchases to avoid the dollar limitations was illegal. Keeping accounting records for equipment or supplies inventories was not required. Theoretically, all county purchases had to be made through the Mississippi Office of General Services at state contract prices. There were, however, exemptions and exceptions that could be construed to cover almost any purchasing situation. For example, "All agencies shall purchase commodities at the state contract price from the approved source unless approval is granted from the Office of General Services to solicit competitive bids . . . provided, however that prices accepted by the agency shall be less than the prices set by the state contract." Commodities were defined as "goods, merchandise, furniture, equipment, automotive equipment of every kind, and other personal property." The law exempted the purchase of culverts and required competitive bidding for all purchases of culverts. Specifically excluded from the bidding requirements were purchases of repairs to equipment, gravel and fill dirt, motor vehicles purchased from a state agency at auction, perishable supplies of food, sole source items, solid waste disposal facilities, data-processing equipment, energy efficient services and equipment, insurance, coal, and natural gas. These conditions provided an open invitation for corruption involving the purchase of materials and services related to county road work.

Court records clearly show how common bribery, extortion, bid rigging, and purchase splitting were and how easily such practices were accomplished. Vendors would offer to "kick back" to supervisors in cash a percentage, ranging from about 10 to 20 percent of the purchase price of materials, if they would buy from the vendors. Actually accomplishing such a scheme constitutes bribery and the acceptance of a bribe. The reverse of this, where supervisors would approach vendors and threaten not to do business with them unless they made kickbacks, is extortion, and it, too, was a common practice. Bid rigging and purchase splitting simply facilitated breaking state law to accommodate those vendors and supervisors involved in bribery and extortion.

It was very easy to engage in such activities on purchases of under $500 where supervisors controlled both ordering and receiving. It was only slightly more complicated for purchases of between $500 and $2,500 where two bids or quotes were required but where there was no requirement for advertising for competitive bids. In such cases, supervisors and vendors often conspired to arrange for "complimentary" bids or quotes. This involved a vendor agreeing to submit a bid higher than the known bid of another vendor with the expectation that the other vendor would return the favor in the future. Bid rigging was more complicated when advertisements for bids were required because more potential sellers were involved in the open process that was required. Specifications were sometimes written to assure that the favored vendor would be the only one to qualify for the purchase contract (in one case the serial number of the equipment to be purchased was included in the specifications), or the low bid was sometimes rejected for spurious reasons.

Some of the most egregious crimes perpetrated by supervisors involved busted invoices. As an example, a supervisor would agree with a vendor to order thirty culverts with the understanding that the vendor would deliver only twenty. The supervisor would process the paperwork to have the county pay for thirty culverts, and the vendor would kick back cash to the supervisor, usually half the purchase price of the ten undelivered culverts. The undelivered culverts were jokingly referred to by those in the know as "invisible pipe." While such practices were bad enough, the invoice busting often defrauded the county of everything on the busted invoice. For example, a vendor would agree with a supervisor to send the supervisor an invoice for certain items with the understanding that actually nothing would be delivered. The supervisor would process the paperwork to have the county pay the invoice, and then the vendor would kick back half of the invoice price to the supervisor.

The very day the first Pretense indictments were handed down, a supervisor attempted to cancel an order with a vendor with whom he had conspired to bust an invoice on the purchase of antifreeze. His explanation was, "The weather has changed in Pontotoc County." Unfortunately for the supervisor, the vendor was working with the FBI. In fact, this particular supervisor had already been stung; he was even then caught in the maw of Operation Pretense. The weather had indeed changed in Pontotoc and in all other Mississippi counties—it had become hotter for corrupt county supervisors.

As Operation Pretense was winding down in November 1988, the FBI indicated that it would refund to nineteen counties about $53,000 collected by the FBI in corrupt transactions. Nearly bankrupt Greene County, one of the poorest counties in the state, was to receive the biggest windfall—$17,186. According to Wayne Taylor, "These are taxpayers' funds. It's a bonus for the counties." All of the illegal payoffs to supervisors had been made with the FBI's money. The FBI had some the counties' money because the agency had kept the payments made to Mid-State by counties on busted invoices in a separate non-interest bearing account. Thus the FBI refunded to the counties monies that had been paid for things never delivered to the counties. Taylor indicated that the FBI had completed all of the cases where its agents had paid kickbacks to supervisors, saying, "It's the only money we'll be giving back."

Two of the counties that received the FBI refund payments, George and Marshall, never had a supervisor charged as a result of Pretense. U.S. attorneys scrutinize evidence and evaluate the potential for conviction very thoroughly before they ask a grand jury to charge anyone. As a general rule, federal prosecutors will not charge anyone with a crime based solely on the testimony of an FBI agent or someone who is cooperating with the investigation as part of a plea bargain. Corroborating evidence such as the testimony of others or taped conversations is usually required. Apparently, federal authorities lacked sufficient evidence to feel confident in charging any supervisor in either George or Marshall County.

The extent of public corruption in Mississippi and the federal government's efforts to stamp it out were captured well in a front-page article in the January 17, 1989, issue of the *Clarion Ledger*:

> State FBI 2nd in corruption convictions—Only the New York City office topped Jackson's last year.

The FBI in Mississippi ranked second in the nation in the number of public corruption investigations that resulted in convictions obtained last year, the agency's top state official said Monday.

Despite the fact that the Jackson office ranks fourth to the last in size of 59 FBI offices, "Mississippi had more convictions in the public corruption area than anywhere but the New York field office (in New York City)," said Wayne R. Taylor, special agent in charge of the FBI in the state. . . .

"Whether it's Pretense or whatever, those who go to trial have been convicted," said the 46-year-old Taylor. "And the juries have not been out long."

He credits the achievement to agents' experience in the area, the cooperation of state and federal agencies and the expertise of the U. S. attorney's offices in Jackson and Oxford. . . .

U.S. Attorney Robert Whitwell attributed the large number of convictions to the FBI's work and Assistant U.S. Attorneys James Tucker and John Hailman.

"I feel they are the two top public corruption experts in the nation as far as assistant U.S. attorneys," Whitwell said. "They were instrumental in writing the (U.S. Department of Justice) manual on public corruption in the U.S." . . .

The question of whether the Magnolia State is more corrupt than other states continues to haunt Taylor after each speech the agent gives.

"I'm repeatedly asked, 'Do we have a greater problem in Mississippi than in other places?' I've avoided that answer because I don't know," he said. "Per capita, you might make a case for one period of time."

Whitwell said it is difficult to tell whether the state has more corruption, but "we're constantly working against some type of public official—sheriff, mayor, supervisor. There always seems to be one or two." . . .

Taylor believes that citizens' attitudes have begun to change, citing last November's vote by 48 of 82 counties to switch from the traditional beat system to the unit system.

"I think people are aware the victims of these problems are the people of Mississippi," he said. They're the ones paying excess amounts of money for automobiles through odometer rollbacks. They're the ones who are paying in Pretense on county funds, which are tax funds." . . .

"We can't be successful unless the public wants a change. That's the key to the drug war," he said. That's the key to Public corruption. The whole thing will continue in society until society decides to do something about it."

Jerry King retired from the FBI in 1989. In the summer of 2000, King told the author that he was proud of his work in Operation Pretense, that it served a useful purpose for the taxpayers of Mississippi, and that he would do it all again in "a New York minute." He reflected on Operation Pretense as follows:

> One sad fact about this case was that the supervisors as a whole were pretty good folks. They were good family heads, and they were not involved in burglaries, robberies, arsons, etc. Their families were surely punished for the supervisors' actions and that bothered this undercover agent. The supervisors were just thieves in a system that was a way of life in Mississippi politics. The supervisors were paid poorly for their positions, and a lot of the public knew that they were making money on the side but turned their heads to this. Of course, some of the supervisors got very adept at abusing the system when they got into the area of busting invoices, which was out-and-out theft. They justified the ten percent kickbacks on delivered products as being expenses of the salesmen, not even taking into consideration that the product price was elevated by ten percent or more.

2. Perry County

The First Trial

Perry County was established by the Mississippi legislature in 1820 and named after Oliver Hazard Perry, a naval hero in the War of 1812. The western part of Greene County was partitioned to form Perry County so that the people in that area would not to have to cross the Leaf River to conduct county business. Richton, Beaumont, and New Augusta, the county seat, are the only towns in the county located in the long-leaf pine belt of southeast Mississippi. Perry County had a total population of fewer than 11,000 according to the 1990 census. The county had a population of 14,682 in 1900; the decline reflects the decreased need for labor in timber and agriculture, the county's economic mainstays.

In the late 1980s, three of the county's supervisors were indicted as the result of Operation Pretense and subsequently pleaded guilty or were convicted of federal crimes. The cases of supervisors George F. "Junie" Mixon Jr., William F. Bowen, and Trudie Westmoreland reflect the depth of corruption in county government. The cases also illustrate defense strategies of accused supervisors and their attorneys and the procedures used to prosecute Pretense cases. Having pleaded guilty to Pretense-related charges, Mixon died while facing sentencing; Bowen was ruled mentally incompetent to stand trial; and Trudie Westmoreland's case eventually made its way to the United States Supreme Court.

An indictment lists formal charges prosecutors have presented to a grand jury that concluded there was enough evidence supporting the charges to bring the case to trial. Junie Mixon had been supervisor of district one for nineteen years, and he was president of the Perry County Board of Supervisors when he was indicted April 7, 1987, on two counts of extortion, one count of bribery, and twenty counts of mail fraud. The charges against the seventy-one-year-old farmer resulted from stings by the FBI and evidence provided by a cooperating vendor, Ray Davis of Davis Chemicals Company. Mixon pleaded guilty on August 21, 1987, to two counts of mail fraud involving his acceptance of an $80 kickback from FBI agent Jerry King, who was posing as a salesman for Mid-State Pipe and Supply Company. Mixon resigned from office and did not seek reelection. U.S. District Judge William H. Barbour Jr. sentenced Mixon on November 23, 1987, to one year in prison and five years' probation, fined him $20,000, and ordered him to pay restitution of $680 to Perry County and $240 to the FBI. A special condition imposed on the probation was that Mixon not seek or hold public office. The judge imposed a heavy fine and a relatively short prison sentence because of Mixon's poor health. Mixon died in Methodist Hospital in Hattiesburg on December 11, 1987, having not served any time.

The guilty plea that Mixon entered was the result of a plea bargain with the U.S. Attorney who required him to cooperate with the government in its investigation and prosecution of corrupt county officials and vendors. Count two of Mixon's indictment included the following statement: "The defendant would and did propose with Mid-State that another Supervisor in Perry County was willing to enter into similar false and fraudulent arrangements as described in subparagraphs (a), (b) and (c) herein and offered to assist in accomplishing such arrangements." These paragraphs describe schemes with Mid-State and Ray Davis to bust invoices and defraud the county by having it pay for items never received and rigging a quote to be submitted to the Perry County Board of Supervisors for the purchase of culvert pipe. While Mixon actually pleaded guilty to only counts sixteen and eighteen of the indictment, his cooperation in the investigation implicated at least one fellow supervisor.

William F. Bowen, a sixty-six-year-old Richton banker and district three supervisor, was charged with two counts of extortion, one count of bribery, and three counts of mail fraud on March 9, 1987. The charges against Bowen involved taking $2,542 in kickbacks on county purchases from L&M Equipment Company of Pearl and Holiman Equipment Company of Jackson. Bowen faced maximum penalties of fifteen years' imprisonment and $300,000 in fines. He was also charged with three counts of filing false and fraudulent income tax returns for 1980, 1981, and 1982. At the time of the indictment, Bowen was hospitalized in New Orleans, but he later pleaded innocent to all charges. He was hospitalized again during April in Hattiesburg.

The Perry County Board of Supervisors removed Bowen from office in June when his family began chancery court proceedings to appoint a conservator to take care of his personal business affairs. Bowen previously had stepped down as an officer of the Richton Bank, where he had served as a vice president and loan officer.

In late September 1987, U.S. District Court Judge Tom S. Lee ordered Bowen committed to a federal prison psychiatric hospital. The judge indicated that Alzheimer's disease and arteriosclerosis had rendered Bowen, at least temporarily, mentally incompetent to stand trial. Mental health officials at the hospital were to determine whether his mental condition was likely to improve so that he could stand trial later. Dr. Franklin Jones, a Hattiesburg psychiatrist who had treated Bowen, testified that improvement was unlikely. "My prognosis is that this will get progressively worse, not better. I don't believe Mr. Bowen could testify accurately if his life depended on it about things that happened a year or two ago. Exactly what happened six months ago or two years ago is totally out of this man's grasp." The judge's order resulted in Bowen undergoing evaluation for about two months at the U.S. Medical Center for Federal Prisoners in Springfield, Missouri.

At a February 1988 hearing before Judge Lee, there was conflicting testimony from psychologist David Reuterfors and psychiatrist Franklin Jones about Bowen's mental competency to stand trial. Reuterfors, who had evaluated Bowen at Springfield, maintained, "Mr. Bowen does have a mental defect, but not of severity that he would not be able to understand and work with his attorney. I feel that Mr. Bowen has a pretty good understanding that he's in trouble right now. I think Mr. Bowen is trying to do the best he can to get out of this mess." But under cross examination from attorney James Kitchens, the psychologist admitted that Bowen "might have some problems remembering some things." Dr. Jones testified that "we have seen a progressive deterioration in this man even since April," and he indicated that Bowen suffered from a form of dementia or impairment of mental powers, resulting in loss of memory, personality changes, and lack of concentration. Under cross examination from U.S. Attorney Frank Violanti, the psychiatrist stated, "If he was a physician, I would not let Mr. Bowen operate on me right now." The case was eventually closed based on an order made public on March 23, 1988, in which Judge Lee ruled that Bowen was too mentally ill to assist his attorneys in a trial.

Trudie Westmoreland, district four supervisor, was arraigned before a U.S. magistrate in Jackson in early March 1987 on six counts that alleged bribery, aiding and abetting mail fraud, mail fraud, and extortion. The thirty-six-year-old first-term supervisor was accused of extorting $2,202 from Mid-State and Davis Chemicals . She pleaded innocent to all of the charges. The first woman elected supervisor in Perry County, Westmoreland had won the post in a special 1985 election after serving one term as a justice court judge. She owned a restaurant, convenience store, and auto parts store in Beaumont. Westmoreland was the first supervisor actually tried on Pretense-related charges, and her case proved to be pivotal in that it demonstrated the strength of the government's cases.

The indictment alleged that beginning prior to February 1986 and continuing to about July 1986, Westmoreland

> devised and intended to devise a scheme and artifice to defraud the citizens of the State of Mississippi, Perry County, the offices of the Board of Supervisors and the Chancery Clerk of Perry County, the State Auditor, and all persons desiring to engage in the business of the sale of materials and supplies to Perry County in a legitimate manner, and to obtain money and property from the State of Mississippi and Perry County by means of false and fraudulent pretenses, representations and promises, and in furtherance thereof did use and cause to be used the United States mails for the purpose of executing the scheme.

As part of the scheme and artifice to defraud, Westmoreland proposed:

(a) to use her position as supervisor to cause and arrange for various items to be purchased by the county from Mid-State in return for her being paid a cash kickback for some purchases;

(b) to submit busted invoices to the Perry County Board of Supervisors and the Perry County chancery clerk by mail and otherwise for purported sales by Mid-State to Perry County of grader blades, metal pipe, and other items;

(c) to falsely and fraudulently charge the county for materials and supplies not delivered to the county and receive a percentage of the warrant/check to be issued and mailed by the state of Mississippi, Perry County, to Mid-State in payment for the materials and supplies not delivered;

(d) to "split" invoices on orders of pipe and supplies for the County from Mid-State; "split" invoices being false and fraudulent invoices depicting more than one purchase and false dates in order to avoid the lawful advertising requirement; and

(e) to obtain false and fraudulent high-price quotes from other companies to be submitted to Perry County in connection with the purchases from Mid-State.

It was further alleged that Westmoreland proposed to cause and arrange for various items to be purchased by the county from Davis Chemicals in return for her being paid a cash kickback for such purposes. The following charges were contained in the indictment:

(a) between February 1986 and June 1986, Westmoreland approved approximately ten Davis Chemicals invoices to the Perry County supervisors for which she received cash payments from a representative of Davis Chemicals;

(b) on February 5, 1986, Westmoreland approved several false and fraudulent invoices to the county for approximately $5,680.92 and received $760 in cash;

(c) on March 18, 1986, Westmoreland approved false and fraudulent invoices to the county for approximately $4,444.20 and received $600 in cash; and

(d) on June 27, 1986, Westmoreland received $342 in cash for having previously approved a false and fraudulent invoice to the County for approximately $683.80.

Westmoreland was also charged with using the U.S. Postal Service to mail county checks to vendors in payment of the fraudulent invoices listed above. In addition, she was charged with having discussed with Mid-State whether other supervisors in the county were willing to enter into similar false and fraudulent arrangements. Finally, the indictment charged that from February 1986 through July 1986, Westmoreland obstructed, delayed, and affected commerce and the movement of articles and commodities in interstate commerce by extortion. That is, she knowingly and willfully obtained cash in the sum of $500 from, and with the consent of, a representative of Davis Chemicals and also received cash in the amount of $1,702 with the consent of a representative of Mid-State, wrongfully under cover of official right, which monies she was not entitled to obtain.

Westmoreland was tried by a jury in the U.S. District Court of the Southern District of Mississippi in Hattiesburg from May 27 to June 2, 1987, with Judge Tom S. Lee presiding. Assistant U.S. Attorneys James B. Tucker and Ruth Harris prosecuted the case, and attorneys Alvin Binder and Lisa Binder Milner represented the defendant. According to State Auditor Ray Mabus, who had been cooperating with the FBI in its investigation, the defense attorneys for several indicted supervisors wanted Westmoreland to be the first supervisor tried because they thought she would be a sympathetic figure that a jury would find difficult to convict. The government was understandably not eager for a woman and a first-term supervisor to be the first person to face trial as a result of Pretense. Both sides believed that this case could well be a harbinger of things to come.

The prosecution built its case around testimony by Ray Davis, the owner-salesman for Davis Chemicals, and testimony by FBI special agent Jerry King, along with tape-recorded dealings between King and the defendant. The transcript of Westmoreland's trial vividly depicts how supervisors and vendors were defrauding counties all across Mississippi and how the FBI's sting worked.

The prosecution summarized its case well in its opening statement to the jury:

> You will hear a tape of the particular meeting, of the first meeting between Agent King and the Defendant Westmoreland. Agent King goes into the defendant's place of business in Beaumont, Mississippi, introduces himself as the person that got the grader blade bid for the county and asks her if she wants any grader blades. I want you to listen carefully to the defendant's voice at the beginning of this very first tape. Her tone of voice, she first tells Agent King, "No, we don't need anything. I'm sorry, we just don't need anything. We have plenty." Agent King says, "Okay, thank you," and starts to leave, and he actually says goodbye and he is leaving the building. And as he is leaving, he happens to mention, "Well, Junie Mixon," who is another Supervisor in the same county, "mentioned your name to me."
>
> Again, I want you to listen carefully to the tape and to the defendant's tone of voice, which I submit to you will hear it changes, and all of a sudden she says, "Wait a minute. Would you like a cup of coffee?" And agent King comes back; she actually has him come back sit down and have a cup of coffee and she starts a conservation with him. And it's that first meeting where the first kickback transaction is completed.
>
> They sit there and they discuss how the transaction is to be worked out. The defendant wants several invoices, or several invoices are made out to keep the price of the order that she's going to place with Agent King under $1,500 so that she won't have to advertise for bids. Also, the dates on the invoices are staggered so it won't look obvious when they are submitted to the county for payment that they were all made on one day, as part of keeping the county from knowing that these are false of fraudulent invoices. The dates are staggered and the amounts are staggered on several invoices.
>
> Also, arrangements are made during that first meeting for—even though

the amount is under $1,500, you have to have two price quotes—and arrange-
ments are made for another company to send in another high quote so that
Agent King and Mid-State Pipe and Supply will have on record with the
county a lower price quote. You will actually hear this tape and hear the
kickback transaction as it takes place.

Listen carefully, again I ask you to listen carefully to the tape and to the
words of the language that the defendant uses. On the first transaction she
tells Agent King that you have to be careful, basically, when you do stuff like
this. And she assures him that she is a careful person. And in her words she
tells him, "Momma didn't raise no fool," assuring him that she's not going
to, you know, let this particular situation get out.

She also tells Agent King during this very first transaction that "If you
don't put the word out on me, I won't put the word out on you," saying
basically, "If you don't tell on me, I won't tell on you and everything will be
cool."

The next transaction we will submit evidence on is February 10th, 1986,
which is a $60 kickback from Ray Davis of Davis Chemicals. The next one
will be February 19th, 1986, only nine days later, another $60 kickback from
Ray Davis to the Defendant Westmoreland, and this is in connection with
the purchase of what's called Permabond which is a substance that's used to
help repair roads and was sold by Ray Davis as part of his business at Davis
Chemicals.

The next transaction involves again Special Agent King it's March 18, 1986.
The defendant—it's again a meeting between the Defendant Westmoreland
and Agent King, and involves the defendant making a purchase of pipe from
Mid-State Pipe and Supply Company and receiving another 12 percent kickback on the total purchase price of that invoice. On that date, she receives a
cash kickback of $600.

On that date, the defendant also orders some supplies that are not even
to be delivered at all, that she's going to get the county to pay for; this is
the busted invoice. Again, the meeting is tape recorded, you will hear the
conversation as it actually occurs. You will hear her discuss the transaction
itself, and then you will also hear her discuss with Agent King how she
checked him out with Ray Davis, again showing what a careful person she is
and doesn't want to get caught in this type of situation; how she checked
with Ray Davis to make sure that Agent King could be trusted.

You will hear Agent King testify how, when he made this particular cash
kickback payment to the defendant, how he got—he initially was standing in
front of the door of the building that they were in, and he had to go back to

the back of the room and turn his back on the door and makes the cash kickback to be sure nobody walking by could see it, and they sort of laugh and joke over that, you know, about how they have to be careful when he is actually dishing out the money to her. You will also here the defendant tell Agent King how she knows that for every rule there is, there is two ways to break it.

After that particular transaction on March 18, we will have evidence, present evidence, we expect, that from March 1986 to June 1986, Ray Davis paid the defendant eight more times, ranging from $30 to $60, cash kickbacks, eight more times during these few months.

Then we get to June of 86. During that period of time, June 24, 1986, the defendant placed an order of grater [sic] blades with Mid-State Pipe and Supply Company but she does it through Ray Davis. You will hear testimony that Jerry King, acting as Jerry Jacobs, knew Ray Davis and they had agreed that sometimes Ray Davis would take orders for Mid-State Pipe and Supply Company if Jerry was not around and able to do it and he ran into a Supervisor that wanted to order stuff that Davis Chemicals didn't sell.

Well Westmoreland orders some grater [sic] blades through Ray Davis. She was ordering them, but she didn't want any of them delivered to the county, she just wanted to bust the invoice and get her kickback. You will hear testimony that the order was for 40 grater [sic] blades, which are a type of blades that go on a piece of equipment, and that none were to be delivered. For this particular busted invoice transaction, the defendant received $342.00 in cash from the undercover agent, and as a part of his helping the agent, Ray Davis was paid $171.00, half of the half is what it amounts to. In between, during the situation, you will hear taped telephone conversations between the defendant and the agent, making arrangements for this particular busted invoice deal.

Basically, that's just a general overview of what we expect the evidence to show.

In his opening statement, defense attorney Binder vividly depicted the defense strategy:

May it please the Court. Ladies and Gentlemen of the Jury. As you can see from the opening remarks of the Government, these lawyers and I are not unprejudiced witnesses, and as the Court told you, what we say to you is not evidence, but I want to acquaint you with what our view of this case is.

We want you to listen to the tapes too; I'm not going to zero in on any particular portion of it. Our view of the case is different because until about March 9 of this year, when Trudie Westmoreland was Indicted, she had never been convicted of a crime, she had led a hard life, she was raised with 15 children, she was the 13th of the children, I think she had eight brothers. You're going to find that her father farmed, and that she did a man's work beside her brothers, and that she talks the language of men, and that she was a good person.

I think that you are going to find that she was elected a public official running against five men. She was the first woman ever elected Supervisor in Perry County Mississippi. There was a woman who was appointed right before her to serve a short time at the expiration [sic] of the death of her husband. We believe the evidence will show that will be important to you.

We believe that the evidence will show that Mrs. Westmoreland's first contact with the Federal Bureau of Investigation was about February 5, 1986. She had just taken the oath of office two and a half months before. We believe that the evidence will show that unlike most jobs in Mississippi, that there is no instructions offered by the State of Mississippi or any other portion of the state on how to be a supervisor. Even Justices of the Peace have seminars now where you can learn the job, but there is no instruction to teach this person, we believe the evidence will show, on how to be a Supervisor.

On February 5, a fellow came to see her who was an FBI agent. As counsel opposite just told you, he posed as a man named Jacobs. Jacobs. Jacobs. Jerry Jacobs. He in fact was an FBI agent. He told her, as counsel opposite just told you, we believe the evidence will show that he had just won the low bid on grater [sic] blades and that he was a salesman for Mid-State. We believe the evidence will show that she immediately told him that she had 13 sets of grater [sic] blades and she didn't need any.

We believe the evidence will show that at this point in time she didn't know much about being a Supervisor. We believe the evidence will show, contrary to just what was told you, that a fellow named Ray Davis never sold her until after she first met FBI Agent King who is really named Jacobs.

We believe the evidence will show that in the early part of 84 or 85 the United States attorney's office in conjunction with the FBI, the United States Justice Department in Washington and others, decided to put a sting operation in Mississippi and they called it operation pretense. And we believe the evidence will show that several of these FBI agents worked down here in Mississippi for over a year and a half pretending that they were real salesmen and representing an alleged real company.

And we believe the evidence will show that they were put here with the prime purpose to entice elected officials, particularly Supervisors, to do a wrong. And we believe that the evidence will show that this officer of the law posing under the name of Jerry Jacobs has a sole purpose to lure and entice Trudie Westmoreland into doing a wrong. And listen to how he talks on that tape, we pray, and you listen to how he approaches her, and you judge whether he is persistent or not in his persuasion.

We believe that the evidence will show that at the time she didn't know it, but in his pocket he had from the vaults of the United States Treasury FBI money, and that he would convince her that she ought to have some of that. And you watch his words, leading her to believe all the time that she was buying less than the state price, less than the advertised price.

In the beginning of the conversation of these first tapes that you hear, listen carefully, and when throughout all this discussion with her, he tells her how she's not going to get into trouble if she'll do his will. You listen and see who approaches who in this case. Did she send for him or did he go to her?

We believe the evidence will show that there were several bizarre transactions, and that unknown to her he was taping her with an electronic surveillance device wired to his body. We believe the evidence will show that you will see from this witness stand that alleged sting operation that your Government took part in, and we hope that it will be of interest to you as you investigate this case.

We believe the evidence will show that Mr. Jacobs, and I agree with counsel opposite, was acting undercover, and that he was acting pursuant to a book that the FBI publishes telling him how to be a sting operator. We believe the evidence will show that Jacobs attempted to involve her, and taunted her, lured her if you will, into a wrong, and that his temptations and reassurances commenced in an unceasing invitation every time he was with her to get her to do a wrong, by insuring her all the time that if she came below the bid law of the State of Mississippi, that, quote: Nothing would happen to her. See if he doesn't say that to her, or words to that effect.

And then after they gave her this money and created this wrong, they came over here to the Grand Jury, and you are going to hear some of the things they told that Grand Jury that brought the Indictment, and you measure that against what you hear on the tapes, and you are going to be shocked. We believe the evidence will show that.

We believe the evidence will show that he went into a Grand Jury in the State of Mississippi to bring this Indictment in this court, and told that Grand Jury things that she said but in fact he said to her, and they brought an Indictment down. We believe the evidence will show that King was reassuring to her in how she would benefit and how her county would benefit, and that she was getting this low price.

And we believe the evidence will show, if you listen to these tapes until the mountain rings, you will never hear Trudie Westmoreland ask this fellow King for one nickel. If I have lied to you, then I have told you wrong, but I don't believe that she ever asked him for anything.

You are going to get a chance to see what the agent said, and I think that you are going to find out that the agent had no knowledge whatsoever that this woman was predisposed to do a wrong. She certainly hadn't been a Supervisor but two and a half months. We believe the evidence will show that she is going to get on the witness stand and tell you what he gave her and admit that he gave her some money, and she is going to explain her words and what she said and give you the reasons for, and I beg that you wait and listen until you hear her before you make up your minds, like I told you in voir dire. We believe the evidence will show that they've got a witness named Davis that counsel opposite was talking about, and you are going to have a sharp divergence in proof on him. . . .

Our position is that he sold himself to the United States Government and would agree to anything to help save himself. I suggest that you are going to have to be the real investigator in this case. You are going to have to judge the motives of people in this case. We believe at some point in this evidence that you are going to have to make a decision whether Federal Government should be allowed to do what it did to this defendant. . . .

We are going to suggest to you, and the evidence will show, that she agrees with some of the things they say and violently disagrees with others. Now you are going to have to decide at the end of this case whether the Federal Government ought to be able to do this kind of stuff to folks in Mississippi or anywhere else. Trick somebody, and then the defendant is going to allege from the witness stand that she was overreached, that the wearing of these wires is wrong, and our case is going to be that we shouldn't allow this kind of stuff in the United States.

We are going to allege that if the scheme was a scheme, it was produced by the United States Government, our Government, that encouraged the breaking of this law and then they bring an Indictment after they create the offense and want you to put her in jail. Now that's what we are in and about in this case. . . .

We believe the evidence will show that King, and all of those who worked with him, created the breaking of a law where none ever existed, nor was one intended. In fact, in the first conversation which lasted quite a long time, you won't get to know how long it stated because certain parts of the tape have been deleted, but believe me you will hear from the witness stand it lasted a long time.

You will find how she reacted in the beginning of the tape, and then how she reacts at the end of the tape as he overcomes her and her resistance to what—half the time she doesn't know a grater [sic] blade from a culvert. But you will find that she was going by a list of what she needed made up by her county engineer, and you are going to hear that county engineer testify in this case and tell you how he took this little lady the first month and a half she was elected and told her what she needed for the spring rains.

And we are going to contend that every piece of that culvert came to Mississippi, and you are going to hear witnesses and pictures of every piece of that culvert in the ground. And you are going to hear that we dug up the ground the day before the trial started and got the last picture of the last piece of culvert that was delivered so you can set your eyes on it yourself. . . .

I believe that you will withhold your judgment until our case comes before you, you'll get a better picture of what's going on here. You are going to hear some evidence from the witnesses in this case about the character of Mrs. Westmoreland. We're going to put on some evidence about how long the investigation lasted. We believe that the defendant will charge and come forth with enough evidence to satisfy you that any normal, law abiding person, especially in this case a woman, would be susceptible to the fast talking, brilliant Agent King. You are going to have to judge at the end of this trial whether the conduct of the Government in this type of situation is wrong or whether you condone it. If you condone this type of activity, you must find the defendant guilty.

But at the end of this trial, I'm going to agree with the counsel opposite, I'm going to get to talk to you one more time, and I'm going to tell you that I believe, considering all of the evidence that you are going to hear, that this woman was entrapped, and I'm going to tell you to send a message to Washington as a citizen of this country, that it's wrong and that you won't have anything to do with that. And I thank you.

Alfred Lott, the Perry County chancery clerk, and Mary Shows, the purchases clerk, testified as to the authenticity of the paperwork supporting county disbursements that had been introduced as evidence. Shows testified about the five documents that were required before issuing a check to pay for any of the purchases included in the charges: (a) a claims summary, which had to be filled out and signed by the supervisor of the district for which the merchandise was purchased; (b) an invoice signed by the supervisor or the person receiving the goods; (c) the purchase order—in this case Shows said that she prepared the purchase order based on information on a Mid-State invoice; (d) the purchase requisition, a form that states that a supervisor or department head had requested that the items be ordered; and (e) a receiving report which must be signed by the person who received the goods. Shows indicated that she filled out all of the reports (after the fact, based on an invoice), but they were signed by others as required. Shows also testified that although it was her responsibility as purchase clerk to secure two quotes for purchases between $500 and $1,500 as required by law, she had not personally secured the quotes from Mid-State and Central Culvert and Pipe, supporting the transactions in question. She testified that to her knowledge Perry County had never done business with Central Culvert or Mid-State before the first transaction in question. She also testified that any purchase over $1,500 would require advertising for bids, and that if the three invoices for culvert purchases from Mid-State introduced into evidence for $1,020, $1,050, and $1,170 were negotiated on the same day, the transactions would not be legal. In regard to the transactions with Davis Chemicals, Shows testified that for purchases under $500 only an invoice signed by the person receiving the goods and a claims summary were necessary before payments could be made.

Ray Davis testified that he paid kickbacks to Westmoreland as outlined in the prosecution's opening statement. Under examination by the prosecution Davis revealed why he had paid the kickbacks.

Q. Mr. Davis, why, why did you make these cash kickbacks to the Defendant Westmoreland?

A. I found that it's easier to sell a product if you do have a little gratuity going along with it in many cases. And it helps me sell, it helped me make a living, it helped me make money, and if this was what it took, then I was willing to do it.

Q. When you say, "this is what it took," what do you mean?

A. Kickbacks, the payoffs.

Q. But this is what it took to do what, is what I'm asking?

A. Well, I felt that I would make more sales and get better orders by giving a kickback when I did make a sale, and I felt like this was an encouragement to get people to buy more.

Q. And what basis, if any, did you have for that feeling?

A. Previous, previous experience with other people that I dealt with and, of course, the fact that I had been dealing with Mr. Mixon, he was conducive to this, and I felt like it would certainly help me with Mrs. Westmoreland in enticing her to buy products. . . .

Q. Why did you pay these kickbacks to the Defendant Westmoreland?

A. I felt like Mrs. Westmoreland would buy more products if I paid the kickback and, possibly, not get any or very little business without doing this. I felt like this was necessary for me to sell products.

The testimony of Jerri Purvis, the secretary for Central Culvert and Pipe in Preston, Mississippi, revealed how "complimentary quotes" were secured.

Q. For what reason did Mr. Winters and Mr. Jacobs come to Central Pipe? [Winters and Jacobs represented the FBI front, Mid-State.]

A. At the time Supervisors for the State of Mississippi in the county had to have two quotes in order to purchase a culvert, and we were to quote quotes for them and they gave us quotes for our customers.

Q. Is that called complimentary quotes?

A. Yes, sir.

Q. Explain to the jury in regard to obtaining business with the county how it works.

A. At the time the State required that you had to have two quotes to purchase a pipe, and of those two quotes the lower price was the one you were to purchase.

Q. And what was the arrangement, as you understood it, that Central Pipe had with Mid-State in regard to the submission of quotes?

A. We were to give high quotes to their customers, in turn they would give high quotes to my customers.

Q. That means that if Mid-State wanted to sell to Perry County, they would contact Central and get a higher quote for the particular product they wanted to sell?

A. Right.

Q. If Central wanted to sell to another county, they would reciprocate?

A. Right.

Q. Did you personally discuss this with Mr. Barrett? [Barrett owned Central Culvert and Pipe. He would later plead guilty to Pretense-related charges.]

A. Mr. Barrett instructed me to do this.

FBI special agent Jerry King testified basically as the prosecution had indicated he would in its opening statement. His testimony was vital in refuting the entrapment defense. He testified as follows:

Q. Did you have anything to do with the original proposals or initiation in regard to that undercover operation? [Pretense]

A. No, sir.

Q. And as you understood your assignment when you came to start, what were you supposed to do?

A. I was to be a salesman in a culvert company and to attempt to do business with County Supervisors.

Q. At that particular time, according to the original instructions that you had, were you targeting any particular Supervisors?

A. Yes, sir. The agents that were in charge of the case would advise me as to whom they had received predisposition on, and that would allow me to make a contact with that particular Supervisor to see if he would engage in transactions with me.

Q. So that the jury understands, what does predisposition mean?

A. Predisposition, in an undercover case, is the set of facts that would indicate that an individual would be willing to take a kickback along the lines with his, his or hers [*sic*] duties as a County Supervisor.

Q. Talking plain, Agent King, does that mean that somebody had to have a complaint about that particular supervisor?

A. Would be a myriad of reasons. Sometimes it would be a complaint, a series of complaints. Sometimes it would be another vendor telling us that he knew that that person would take a kickback. Someone had said that they would be willing or had taken kickbacks.

Q. Was that a very strict requirement in regard to this undercover operation?

Mr. Binder: We object to this type leading, your Honor. This is crucial.

The Court: I'll sustain the objection to the leading question.

Q. What significance, if any, to your daily work was this particular requirement?

A. I was prohibited from contacting any individual or Supervisor that I didn't have that predisposition on.

Q. Okay. Then let's go specifically to the case in issue, during some point in your investigation, did you have opportunity and occasion to go to Perry County, Mississippi?

A. Yes, sir, I did.

Q. At some point did you have the opportunity and occasion to come in contact with a person known as Mrs. Trudie Westmoreland?

A. Yes, sir, I did.

Q. Would you give us the background on that? How did you come to Perry County?

A. I had been in touch with another Perry County Supervisor.

Q. What was his name?

A. Junie Mixon, M-I-X-O-N.

Q. As a result of you coming into contact with Junie Mixon, what did you do?

A. I advised him that I would be willing to pay him kickbacks for any orders that he would give me—

Mr. Binder: We object to this type of testimony and ask that you tell the jury to disregard; we are not charged with any crimes of a Supervisor named Mixon; improper to put that before the jury. We object to it.

The Court: The witness can testify as to the basis for his initiating an investigation or what was motivating him, so I'll overrule your objection.

A. Mr. Mixon and I had discussed the fact that I didn't know any of the other

Mr. Binder: We object, your Honor, on the grounds of hearsay. I don't have Mr. Mixon, as counsel opposite knows well, to cross-examine, and here this Agent is sitting up here telling me what Mr. Mixon says and that's hearsay, your Honor. You have indicted Mr. Mixon and I don't have him here to testify.

The Court: Inadmissible hearsay is that which is asserted for the truth of it. Mr. Tucker, what do you say in response to the objection?

A. We are not asserting it for truth at this time, your Honor, only his background information.

The Court: I'll overrule the objection.

Q. [should read A] We discussed that I didn't know any of the other Supervisors, and he and I reached a meeting of the minds that he understood what I meant when I was talking about kickbacks. And then I asked him, I said, "Do you know of anyone else that I might could contact or, you know, that I could talk to?" And then on a second meeting or subsequent meeting with him, I asked him, "have you had time, you know, to talk with the others?" And he said, "Well, no one," and then he went into, "except I did talk to Trudie and you can contact her."

Q. Give us a time frame, Agent King.

A. This was in early 86, like in January, and I said, "Is she all right?" And he said, "Yes, she's"

At this point the defense objected, and the court sustained the objection. King continued his testimony without giving any more specifics about that conversation with Mixon.

At another point in Agent King's testimony, commenting on what the jury had just heard from a tape and read from a transcript of the tape, he explained that invoice "splitting" was designed to fool the state auditors who were usually powerless to do anything about it.

Q. Okay. Now what are y'all talking about there, Jerry?

A. We are talking about the situation that, since there was such a short time gap between the invoices and the similar pipe and it could be obvious to the State Auditor that it was all ordered on the same day and we broke it up in separate invoices to bypass the advertising law requirement, that it may be suspicious, and we were just discussing that.

Q. Backing up several lines there where Special Agent King says, "And, and, all they can do is to tell you not to do it any more," who is the "they" you are referring to?

A. State Auditor's office.

Q. And when Mrs. Westmoreland then on down says, "I'll just act so dumb," who is she talking about that she'll act dumb to?

A. The State Auditors, if they do inquire about these invoices.

Under redirect examination, King testified further about Westmoreland's desire to conceal certain facts from the state auditors.

Q. What did—so everybody is clear, Agent King, what did Mrs. Westmoreland ever say, if anything, during the course of your conversations with her, that indicated that she wished to conceal from the State Auditor's office what she was doing with you?

A. I—three things come up to my mind specifically over all of those conversations. One, told me to bill them out differently; one, "Don't screw up my paperwork;" and, thirdly, "For every rule they make up there, there is two ways to get around it," something to that effect. I know that's not verbatim.

Q. They make up where?

A. The State of Mississippi.

Under cross-examination, the defense attempted to show that King had taken advantage of a woman with only two and a half months of experience as a supervisor. But under redirect examination the prosecution asked King about Westmoreland's previous government experience, and it was revealed to the jury that she had served as a justice court judge for eight years before she became supervisor.

Westmoreland testified that FBI agent Jerry King led her down "a one way street" when he paid her kickbacks on purchases of culverts and grader blades. She said, "He tricked me, cajoled me, assured me. He wouldn't shut up. You couldn't get your head straight. . . . Most of the time, I'd be concentrating on my order. This man talked non-stop. I thought if I said 'uh-huh or yea' he'd slow down so I could check if my order was correct." King had testified he spent about an hour and twenty minutes with her on February 5, 1986, and at that time he gave her a $760 kickback based on 12 percent of her order. The meeting had been taped, and the jury heard portions of the tape, including Westmoreland agreeing that 12 percent was all right. She testified that she thought he meant that he was going to give the county a 12 percent discount and that she had no idea that he meant anything else. She said the February 5 meeting lasted more than two hours. "I thought that he'd never leave. He talked and talked. He figured and figured. He wrote my order wrong twice. It was a mess."

Westmoreland contradicted King's testimony concerning a June 1986 order for grader blades that were never delivered, creating a busted invoice. King said that he paid Westmoreland $342, half of the grader blade purchase price. She said "I don't know exactly what he was doing on these grader blades. When I was indicted, I realized they thought I didn't get those grader blades. They must have screwed up their paperwork. . . . Every man who works for me saw the grader blades. I don't know whether they intended to ship them or not, but they did."

She also contradicted Davis, who had testified that he gave her about $500 in kickbacks, usually $30 or $60 at a time. "He told a lie. Ray Davis never gave me a kickback" she said. She also said that Davis was lying about a mid-July 1986 meeting after Davis began cooperating with the FBI. Davis said that Westmoreland wrote him a note saying that she knew about his cooperation and that she would not discuss business with him in case he was wearing a tape recorder. She said, "That's the biggest lie he's told yet. I deny that. I continued to buy from him until January 1987. If I had known he was working for the FBI, trying to tape me, I wouldn't have had anything to do with him." Davis said that he paid all the kickbacks directly to Westmoreland with the exception of one $60 payment that he left at her auto parts store in Beaumont. "For sure, there was $110 in that envelope," she said. She claimed she did not know why Davis left the money, "I been waiting on him to explain it but he's never mentioned it."

One part of Trudie Westmoreland's testimony illustrates the defense strategy, as her lawyer leads her to explain her acceptance of the $760 the first day she met agent King and some comments that had been caught on tape.

Q. Now the day came at the end of your final conversation there with Mr. King when he handed you the $760.00; do you acknowledge that he did that?

A. Yes, sir, he gave me $760.00.

Q. Tell this jury, when he pulled out the $760.00 or whatever and counted that money out to you, what went through your mind right at that moment, if you can remember?

A. I remember that I was shocked. I didn't want to let him know that I was shocked, I wanted to hide that from Jerry Jacobs. In private business, salesmen or vendors will give you a ham or a cake or something like that at Christmastime, but I had never seen anyone give cash before in my life.

Q. Was it a sizable amount of cash to you?

A. It was a large amount of cash to me, Mr. Binder, and I was tempted and I took it.

Q. Okay.

A. It was wrong, but I took it.

Q. Okay. Do you remember telling Jerry King toward the end of that conversation words to the effect, "Well I'll tell you one damn thing, I wasn't going to approach you"?

A. Yes, sir, I remember that.

Q. Tell the jury what you meant by those words at that time.

A. I suppose that I was trying to act like a big shot Supervisor, that I could hold my own with him, that it didn't scare me and that I knew exactly what was going on, and he seemed as though that what we were doing wasn't wrong.

Q. Tell the jury whether or not, were you frightened or not at that time?

A. Yes, sir, I was scared.

Q. Tell the jury, when you said the words "Momma didn't raise no fool," in what vein was you saying that to Jerry King at the time?

A. Blowing smoke. I was in a pickle and I didn't want him to know it. I was going to try to act like something I wasn't, that like I was maybe like from New York City, that I wasn't a little ole country girl from Perry County.

Westmoreland claimed that she had second thoughts about accepting the payoff she had received from King and that she attempted to contact the district attorney about it.

Q. Tell the jury, at the end of that conversation you told King words to the effect "If you don't put the word out on me, I won't put the word out on you," tell them what you meant at that time.

A. I had taken his money, I had fell in his trap, I was afraid that he would get out here and tell people that he had given me $760.00 and he would get me in trouble or blackmail me or whatever. I didn't know.

Q. Okay. And you tell this jury, after Jerry King went to your office or wherever you were that day, what did you do, did you think about after he left?

A. Mr. Binder, he left that money on the corner of my husband's desk, and I set there and I stared at it.

Q. Were you upset or not?

A. Mr. Binder, the more I looked at that money the more afraid I became. I finally got up the nerve to call our District Attorney, Glen White.

Q. Did you call him?

A. I called him, but he wasn't in and I didn't leave my name and number, and I decided that I better keep my mouth shut or I sure enough would be in trouble.

Q. Did you ever talk to him about this?

A. No, sir, not ever.

Westmoreland's testimony concerning invoice splitting is also revealing.

Q. Tell the jury, what did Mr. King say to you that the jury heard in this courtroom that day about splitting invoices?

A. That it was all right, that there was nothing wrong with it, that I couldn't get into any trouble, and he knew how to do the paperwork so well and so knowledgeable, I went along with it, I thought everything he was doing was right.

Q. Did you think that as long as you ordered on an invoice less than $1,500 at that time that you could get in trouble?

A. No, sir. He assured me that was the correct way, I guess, to legally avoid the State bid law, was what he was talking about.

Q. Okay. Now at the end of that day, you had a conversation with him after that, I believe, where you said you'd play dumb if the State Auditor's office came down and investigated you?

A. Yes, sir, I did. I played into his hands again Mr. Binder.

Judge Lee allowed the prosecution to present testimony about an investigative audit that the Department of Audit was in the process of conducting in relation to funds collected by Westmoreland while she was justice court judge. Sheila Patterson of the Department of Audit testified that "our investigation is not complete. So far, we have $9,506.95 in funds that were not turned into the county." Patterson testified that no demand for repayment had been sent to Westmoreland because the investigation was not complete. She noted that Westmoreland was aware of the investigation that began after state auditors referred her books to the investigative auditors in 1984. Judge Lee told the jurors they could draw inferences about Westmoreland's motives from the testimony. In the prosecution's proffer before Judge Lee asking that Patterson be allowed to testify before the jury, Patterson said that in 1979, while Westmoreland had been a justice court judge, an audit demand had been made on her and that she had repaid those funds.

Several character witnesses testified for Westmoreland, including vendors who said that she had never asked for a kickback and that they had never paid her one. The prosecution countered these character witnesses effectively by simply asking them if they had any direct knowledge about Westmoreland's conduct regarding the transactions cited in the indictment. None of them did. Alfred Lott, chancery clerk of Perry County, who had testified as to the authenticity of documents introduced and as to the process for payment, was one of the character witnesses. He said that Westmoreland's reputation for truth and honesty was good and that "I would think that she would tell the truth under oath."

Closing arguments focused on the defense's claim that Westmoreland had been entrapped by the federal government. Binder criticized the government for running a sting operation. "It's not proper for law enforcement people to use excessive persuasion. It's the duty of law enforcement, as I understand it, to detect criminals, not to create them," he said. "Trudie, you, I, a lot of folks in this world aren't made of steel. If you don't take the bait, they'll come at you another way, upside down or some way." Binder told the jury that doubt is "an uneasiness that flows through your mind and heart as you think about a case." "I pray your conscience won't let you convict this woman. She's an average person, I don't think that they have proven her a criminal. I don't think they went about it the right way," he said.

Assistant U.S. Attorney James Tucker called Binder's argument "gibberish." "That man talked about 40 minutes about something that doesn't amount to a hill of beans," he said. He also told the jurors that they would be instructed that King's undercover role and the use of a body recorder were "necessary and permissible." "How could we ever have caught her if Jerry hadn't worn a wire?" he asked. "There's only one way we can do it. Sometimes you have to do a wrong to do a greater good." He also reminded the jury that Davis did not begin cooperating with the FBI until July 1986 and that he testified that he gave Westmoreland ten payoffs before then. "The proof is in the pudding," he said. "She took that money. If she took the money and spent it, she's guilty. It's no defense to say that Ray and Jerry tattle-taled on me."

The prosecution's overall strategy is easily summarized. The case was built primarily on the tape-recorded transactions that Trudie Westmoreland, as Perry County district four supervisor had entered into with Jerry King representing the FBI front, Mid-State Pipe and Supply Company, and King's testimony concerning those transactions. This was supplemented by Ray Davis's testimony concerning kickbacks that he had made as a representative of Davis Chemicals to Westmoreland as supervisor. Finally, the testimony of Shelia Patterson, the investigative auditor, buttressed the prosecution's case by showing that Westmoreland had a history of not handling public funds properly.

The defense's strategy was to admit to the facts concerning the transactions caught on tape, attempt to mitigate Westmoreland's behavior in regard to those transactions, and to deny everything else. Thus, Westmoreland was depicted by the defense as an innocent who had been entrapped by the wily FBI agent King. The fact that Ray Davis was himself charged with wrongdoing under the Pretense investigation and was cooperating with the prosecution under a plea bargain agreement was perceived as a weakness in the prosecution's case. Davis had been indicted the same day as Westmoreland, and the transactions that he testified about occurred before the indictment and had not been taped. For these transactions, it was her word against his, and she simply denied that she had agreed to take kickbacks associated with them. Westmoreland also denied busting invoices and claimed that she received all of the grader blades that had been ordered. Since grader blades were considered "consumables" and there were no related inventory records or controls, it was not possible to demonstrate that any were actually missing. The auditor's testimony about the unfinished investigative audit was countered very weakly by simply showing that the state auditor had not made a demand for the $9,506.95 in question.

Judge Lee's instructions to the jury explained "entrapment" in the eyes of the law:

> When a person has no previous intent or purpose to violate the law but is induced or persuaded by law enforcement officers or their agents to commit a crime, he is a victim of entrapment, and the law as a matter of policy forbids his conviction in such a case. On the other hand, where a person already has the readiness and willingness to break the law, the mere fact that Government agents provide what appears to be a favorable opportunity is not entrapment. For example, it is not entrapment for a Government agent to pretend to be somebody else and to offer either directly or through an informant or other decoy to engage in an unlawful transaction.

In his instructions to the jury, Judge Lee also explained how they should weigh the testimony of someone, such as Ray Davis, who was cooperating with the prosecution under a plea bargain:

> An alleged accomplice, including one who has entered into a plea agreement with the Government, does not thereby become incompetent as a witness. On the contrary, the testimony of such a witness may alone be of sufficient weight to sustain a verdict of guilty. Such plea bargain, as it's called, has been approved as lawful and proper and is expressly presently provided for in the rules of this court.

In another important part of his instructions to the jury that related to Shelia Patterson's testimony, Judge Lee stated:

> If the jury should find beyond a reasonable doubt from other evidence in the case that the accused did the act charged in the Indictment, then you may consider evidence as to an alleged act of a like nature in determining the state of mind or intent with which the accused did the act charged in the particular count. And where proof of an alleged act of a like nature is established by evidence which is clear and conclusive, you may, but are not obliged to, draw the inference and find that in doing the act charged in the particular count under deliberation, the accused acted willfully, and not because of mistake, or accident or other innocent reason.

On June 2, 1987, the jury rendered its verdict of guilty on all six counts of the indictment. Judge Lee set sentencing for August 3 in Jackson and directed the probation service to conduct a presentence investigation and make a report to the court. Judge Lee indicated that their report would have a significant bearing on the sentence that he would impose. Westmoreland faced maximum penalties of sixty-five years in prison and fines of $1.5 million. The now-convicted felon was allowed to remain out of jail until the sentencing date on the same $5,000 bond that she had originally posted.

After the verdict, Assistant U.S. Attorney Tucker said, "We are extremely pleased. I will not comment specifically to Trudie, but we believe the verdict verifies the public approves of Operation Pretense and what the federal government and state auditor's office are trying to expose in regard to corrupt county officials." He also indicated that the conviction might persuade twenty-four other supervisors who had pleaded innocent to similar indictments to change their pleas. "We think the first jury verdict heralds the outcome of the other Operation Pretense cases," he said. "I think this will stimulate those who have been hesitant to come forward." Westmoreland was the first of thirty-one supervisors who had been indicted on Pretense-related charges to stand trial. Six of those indicted had already pleaded guilty.

Defense attorney Binder said the conviction would probably be appealed. He also indicated that he thought the defense was going well until Shelia Patterson said that the state auditor's office was not through checking into Westmoreland's financial dealings as a justice court judge. She had testified that almost $10,000 collected from 1981 to 1983 was unaccounted for. Binder said that was "devastating" and that "it's hard to overcome that sort of testimony."

Less than a week after her conviction, Trudie Westmoreland resigned as district four supervisor, giving no reason. Her attorney indicated that Westmoreland planned to appeal her conviction to the U.S. Fifth Circuit Court of Appeals. He said, "Until the case is heard on appeal, these questions [of honesty] remain." The Perry County Board of Supervisors immediately appointed Westmoreland's brother, Phillip Pittman, to replace her as supervisor. In another of the many ironic twists associated with Pretense, one of the supervisors who voted on the appointment was Junie Mixon. It had been his talks with Agent King that had led to Westmoreland being subjected to the FBI sting, and at the time of the appointment he was under indictment as a result of Pretense. On the very day Westmoreland resigned, June 5, 1987, Pittman qualified to run in the August primary for supervisor of district four. Pittman finished third in the six-candidate August Democratic primary.

In pleading for leniency at the July sentencing hearing, defense attorney Binder told Judge Lee that his client was only following long-established political tradition accepted by the public. Binder's comments reflect an interesting perception of what had gone on in the state for years. "The people of Mississippi are partly to blame in these supervisors' cases. The real truth is that the focus of these investigations has been only on the supervisors. The people of Mississippi have been harmed and the system should be changed. But the light also should focus on the voters of Mississippi. They escape punishment." He said that county supervisors traditionally "covenant" illegally to put gravel in residents' driveways, and candidates couldn't be elected if they didn't make promises to break the law. "That's been our way of life since I can remember. It's wrong, but the people of Mississippi expect that covenant from their supervisors," Binder said. Assistant U.S. Attorney Ruth Harris had a different perspective. In recommending a ten-year prison term and restitution, she said that Mississippi voters "expect honesty, and do not expect corruption from their public officials. Sometimes the old adage that crime does not pay must become a reality."

The judge seemed to agree with the prosecution. On July 13, Judge Lee imposed a sentence of nine years in prison, imposed a $10,000 fine, and ordered Westmoreland to make restitution in the amount of $1,702 and to pay a court fee of $300. The maximum sentence could have been sixty-five years' imprisonment and fines of $1.5 million. Westmoreland was allowed to remain free on bond until October 19, 1987, when she reported to the Federal Correctional Institute at Fort Worth, Texas.

On March 23, 1988, the U.S. Fifth Circuit Court of Appeals affirmed the district court's ruling in all aspects. The court held: (a) the federal statute prohibiting theft of bribery concerning programs receiving federal funds does not require direct involvement of federal funds in allegedly corrupt transactions; (b) the testimony of the state investigative auditor concerning discrepancies in Westmoreland's financial records from her prior term as justice court judge was admissible; (c) the evidence established that Westmoreland was predisposed to take kickbacks on purchases of county material and that she was not entrapped into committing the charged crimes.

Through her attorney, Westmoreland filed a Motion for Admission to Probation, For Reduction of Sentence, or for Sentence Under Title 18, U.S.C., Section 4205(b), on April 5, 1988. In this filing, she noted the ill health of her husband, that she had been imprisoned since October 1987, that this was her first conviction, that her sentence had been very harsh when compared to other supervisors in like circumstances, that the imposition of her sentence had helped the government in plea bargaining with other supervisors, and that she was repentant. She claimed, "The reality of being incarcerated is both an interior and exterior stigma which will never leave Trudie P. Westmoreland's heart and mind." The court was requested to consider other options, such as immediate release with a requirement of defined community service, house arrest, probation, reduced sentence, or reduced sentencing under Section 4205 (b) Title 18, U.S.C., specifying that she become eligible for parole at such time as the board of parole might determine. On April 19, 1988, Judge Lee issued an order denying the motion.

One paragraph of Westmoreland's Motion captures the importance of her conviction.

> Defendant feels that it would be safe to say that the imposition of such a sentence as hers had the beneficial effect of aiding and assisting the United States Government in obtaining plea bargains and induced counsel through the State to heartily recommend to their supervisor clients to enter pleas and not face trial, resulting in a considerable savings to the United States Government.

This observation is no doubt true. As noted previously, defense attorneys thought that Westmoreland would present a sympathetic figure that a Mississippi jury would find difficult to convict. The overwhelming evidence produced by the FBI's professionally handled sting was able to overcome any sympathy that the jurors might have had. When the strength of the government's cases became evident as a result of the Westmoreland trial, attorneys began to advise their supervisor clients to make the best plea bargain possible. The resulting plea bargain agreements invariably included cooperating in the investigation, thereby adding to the momentum of Pretense.

Westmoreland's attorneys appealed the Fifth Circuit's decision to the U.S. Supreme Court. In early October 1988, the Court without comment refused to hear the case and thereby let stand the conviction and sentence.

In late November 1988, responding to another Motion for Reduction of Sentence, Assistant U.S. Attorney James Tucker recommended that Westmoreland's sentence be reduced to a term in the range of six to seven years. The reason given was that sentences imposed in other Operation Pretense cases subsequent to that of Westmoreland's indicated that a reduction of sentence would be appropriate and fair. On November 29, 1988, Judge Lee issued an order that reduced her prison sentence to six years but left all other aspects of the sentence unchanged. Westmoreland was actually paroled on October 17, 1989, after having served only two years.

The Westmoreland case came before the court again in July 1991 when Alvin Binder filed a Motion to Set Aside Interest on Fine. Westmoreland had been fined $10,000 with interest to run at 18 percent beginning with the date of her confinement. The motion requested an order setting aside the interest, or that the interest be suspended for the time period that she was incarcerated. After two related filings by the government and one by the defendant, Judge Lee issued an order on August 6, 1991, denying Westmoreland's motion.

3. Wayne County

Two Trials and *60 Minutes*

Wayne County, which borders Alabama in southeast Mississippi, has a population of about 19,500 and only two towns of any size, Waynesboro and State Line. The county was named after Revolutionary War hero General Anthony "Mad Anthony" Wayne, who in 1783, with his small army, liberated Georgia from the British. The county seat, Waynesboro, derives its name from the county itself. Wayne County captured the nation's attention in 1988 when the country's most watched television program, CBS's *60 Minutes*, ran a segment entitled "The Preacher and the Sting Man."

The *60 Minutes* segment vividly described how the FBI stung two Wayne County supervisors as a part of Operation Pretense. However, the television show hardly captured the full extent of the corruption of Wayne County politicians in the 1980s. Three of the county's five supervisors were eventually convicted on federal charges as a result of Operation Pretense. In fact, three of the seven supervisors who actually went to trial on Pretense-related charges were from Wayne County. Another of the county's favorite sons, Bob Joiner, a state highway commissioner and former Waynesboro mayor, pleaded guilty to federal charges of extortion and income tax evasion based on the work of the state Department of Audit and the FBI's Pretense team. The highway commissioner's story is told in Chapter 11.

In April 1987, Alfred Grant Revette, district one supervisor, and Jimmy T. Duvall, district three supervisor, were indicted together on a total of seventeen counts. They were charged with one count of conspiracy, two counts of bribery, ten counts of mail fraud, and four counts of extortion. The sixty-four-year-old Revette was charged with taking $2,820 in kickbacks, and the sixty-three-year-old Duvall was charged with taking $1,840 in kickbacks. Both men pleaded innocent to all charges, and both faced maximum penalties of eighty years in prison and fines of $2.25 million. Several of the charges against Revette and Duvall involved busting invoices with Mid-State Pipe Company. The indictment contains a good illustration of why invoice busting flows from the practice of paying and taking kickbacks and how it disrupts legitimate commerce.

Paragraph ten under "OVERT ACTS" in the indictment read: "On December 30, 1985, a Mid-State representative told Revette that Mid-State was going to bid low to get a grader bid and that he wouldn't be able to pay the 12% 'kickback' (previously agreed to) but that they could make money by 'shorting' their orders. Revette agreed to this proposal and agreed to discuss the proposal with Duvall."

Duvall and Revette were tried before a jury in Meridian during July 1987, with U.S. District Court Judge William H. Barbour Jr. presiding. Alvin Binder and Dan Self served as defense attorneys. Theirs was the second Pretense-related case that actually went to trial. By the time this trial began, eighteen supervisors, three salesmen, and a county road foreman had already pleaded guilty.

Appearing as a character witness for Revette, Raymond Luke Newell, a salesman for Puckett Machinery Company, testified that Revette never demanded cash in return for his business. Under cross-examination, Assistant U.S. Attorney Ruth Harris asked Newell if he had paid former Lauderdale County supervisor William C. Brown $100 during the Mississippi Association of Supervisors convention in 1985. Newell denied making any such payment and further denied making payoffs to any other supervisor. Brown had resigned as supervisor of Lauderdale County district two earlier in the month and pleaded guilty to Pretense-related charges based on a plea bargain.

Revette denied participating in a bid-rigging scheme that involved a plan to bust invoices rather than to take percentage kickbacks. However, the prosecution introduced into evidence a conversation taped by the FBI, which refuted his testimony. Revette could be heard on the tape agreeing to a plan suggested by FBI special agent Jerry King who was posing as Jerry Jacobs, a salesman for Mid-State. The plan involved Mid-State submitting a low bid for culverts and making up for the loss of kickbacks to the supervisor by busting invoices. The busted invoices involved billing the county for more goods than were actually delivered, with the supervisor and salesman dividing the invoiced price of the undelivered goods. Revette admitted to taking payments from King, and when asked why he never said no to King, he replied, "He'd pressure me and pressure me." King testified that he saw Revette taking a payoff from Ray Davis on April 17, 1985. Revette denied taking any such payoff.

In a June 18, 1985, telephone conservation between Revette and King that the FBI agent taped, Revette said that fellow supervisor Fred Andrews was "all right" after King asked if he could "take care" of Andrews, too. Revette denied that he had recommended Andrews as another supervisor who would take kickbacks. He said, "I didn't mean it that way." He indicated that of course he would say that because "Fred is not a bad person." Revette claimed he thought that the payments he took from King were coming out of the salesman's commission. He admitted to taking $850 but claimed he thought that he was saving the county money. "I didn't figure I was beating the county out on one nickel," he testified. Revette agreed with codefendant Duvall's claim that the FBI agent's personality was overwhelming and persuasive. He said that a person could walk into a store wanting dress shoes and that "he could have you walking out in a pair of tennis shoes." The jury laughed at this remark.

In the defense's closing arguments, Binder compared his clients to his mother who had only a third grade education; they were not sophisticated enough to resist the smooth King. "You are not a match for their brother King," he told the jury. Actually, Duvall had graduated from high school, and Revette had completed the eleventh grade. Binder also called Ray Davis, who had testified against his client, "a bald-faced liar." Dan Self argued that the defendants were not predisposed to accepting bribes. He accused the government of creating the crimes, while noting that entrapment is a legitimate defense, not a lawyer's daydream. The prosecutor, Assistant U.S. Attorney Richard Starrett, countered that using undercover agents is not wrong. He called the entrapment question a loophole. "A supervisor taking money for approving an invoice is wrong," he said.

After about six hours of deliberation, the jury had claimed to be deadlocked, but Judge Barbour would not accept that and told them that they would be sequestered if necessary. On July 30, the jury convicted both Revette and Duvall on three of the seventeen counts; both were convicted on count one for conspiracy, Duvall was convicted on count two for bribery, and Revette was convicted on count three for bribery. Sentencing was set for September 16 in Jackson. Each man faced maximum penalties of fifteen years' imprisonment and $500,000 in fines. They remained free on $5,000 bond awaiting sentencing.

Duvall and Revette said that they did not plan to resign and that they were going to appeal their convictions. Both planned to stand for reelection, and they remained on the August 4 Democratic primary ballot. The two attended a board of supervisors meeting on August 3 and conducted business as usual. Meanwhile, the Mississippi Attorney General's Office prepared to file suit to remove the convicted felons from office. State law required removal from office of any public official convicted of a state felony. "Should the federal court order adjudicating guilt not disqualify the supervisors, the attorney general's office is prepared to file a motion in Circuit Court to have them removed and their offices declared vacant," said Assistant Attorney General Sam Keys. Keys noted that such a motion could be filed before any appeals were resolved. On August 5, 1987, attorney Dan Self filed a motion in federal court on behalf of Duvall and Revette seeking to "arrest" the judgment against his clients and seeking a new trial. This motion was denied.

Despite their recent convictions, the two supervisors fared well in the August 4 Democratic primary. District one citizens gave Revette a victory over challenger James E. "Jimmy" McCaa by a vote of 814 to 689. Duvall was not quite as fortunate. Although he led a field of five district three candidates with 603 votes, Duvall was faced with a runoff against Robert "Bobby" Reynolds who garnered 587 votes.

At the initial sentencing hearing, Duvall was sentenced to six years in prison on count one, while Revette was sentenced to seven years on the same count. Duvall was to serve five years of probation on count two and pay a fine of $10,000. Revette was to serve five years' probation on count three and pay a fine of $10,000. Both men were ordered to report to federal prison prior to October 19, 1987.

It turned out that parts of these sentences were improper, even illegal. The prison sentences had been imposed for conspiracy under count one of the indictment. The maximum prison sentence for the section of the U.S.C. under which this charge was made was five years. The judge had meant to send both defendants to prison under the bribery charges contained in counts two and three for which the applicable law allows the sentences imposed. Judge Barbour corrected this situation at a second sentencing hearing on September 30. This was accomplished by simply changing the count numbers in the sentence to reflect that the prison sentences were on counts two and three while the probation sentences were on count one. At this sentencing, the judge also imposed restitution of $4,042 on Revette and $2,247 on Duvall. The judge allowed the defendants to remain out of prison on bail pending the outcome of their planned appeals.

As in the Trudie Westmoreland case, the defense strategy had been to deny everything not caught on tape and admit everything that had been taped but claim entrapment as a defense. The defense attorneys said that an appeal would be filed for both supervisors. "This is a very confusing verdict," Binder said, while noting that the jury had exonerated the supervisors on charges that were part of the conspiracy indictment. Binder also claimed that Operation Pretense had not been successful in this case and that it had hit a bump in the road. Self indicated that the jury accepted the defense's claims of government responsibility. "I think the entrapment defense got it," he said.

In September, the Wayne County Board of Supervisors appointed Jewell Revette and Marguerite Duvall to fill their convicted husbands' unexpired terms. Fred Andrews, district two supervisor, said that board members believed appointing the women was their best option. Bobby Reynolds, who defeated Duvall in the Democratic runoff in August and didn't face opposition in the November general election, wanted to wait until January to assume office, so Marguerite Duvall was appointed for the remaining months of her husband's term. Andrews further explained, "In beat one, we've got an election coming up so we didn't really know what to do with that situation. We felt like, to keep it from interfering with any other candidates that were running [appointing Jewell Revette] would be the best thing we could do."

Alfred Revette remained a candidate in the race, and he was scheduled to face his cousin, Republican Clyde Revette, and Independent E. W. Douglas in the general election. Andrews noted that the county's budget and millage for the upcoming year had been set and that the women would have the same road crews that had worked in the districts under their husbands. He also said that other supervisors had offered their assistance if the women "get into a problem they don't understand and need our advice." While acknowledging that some county residents objected to the appointments, Andrews said that three out of four people he discussed it with were "in favor of it." Kathlyn Rainwater, a resident of district three, said that she and her husband, George, disapproved. "It sure doesn't seem like they should serve after their husbands were convicted," she said. Rainwater indicated that "everybody was real happy after Duvall was defeated until this came up." "We just want honest government. We work hard for our living."

The convictions were appealed to the U.S. Fifth Circuit Court of Appeals. The appeal challenged omission of instructions to the jury concerning the possibility of a "gratuity" defense (no bribe, and no monetary effect on the county), admission of tape recordings into evidence (supposedly the tapes were made without sufficient evidence of predisposition to commit a crime), the sufficiency of the evidence to sustain the jury's verdict, and the judge's supplemental instructions to the jury regarding the entrapment

the judge's supplemental instructions to the jury regarding the entrapment defense (the judge explained that entrapment could only be accomplished by the government, not a private citizen such as Ray Davis).

The CBS television program *60 Minutes* ran a feature entitled "The Preacher and the Sting Man" in early May 1988. The program focused on the roles of the Reverend John Burgess and FBI special agent Jerry King in the Pretense investigation. Mike Wallace interviewed Duvall and Revette for the program, and they claimed that they had been entrapped by King. Both of the supervisors and the federal officials who prosecuted them agreed after the program aired that it had portrayed their roles and Pretense accurately. Revette said, "I think they were real fair. I was pretty well pleased with it. I think they did a real good job." But he added that the supervisors' side of the story "certainly hasn't been told. All of it wasn't told."

Duvall said that he was disturbed by Burgess's actions on the show because he laughed throughout his interview. "I can't see how a man of God seeing this was so funny. I know I sinned and done wrong, but I don't see anything funny about it." He said rather than offering bribes "it looks like he'd rather be praying that I wouldn't do it. If he was really a man of God, he wouldn't want to create a crime for me to do." Burgess, whose congregation had been unaware of his role with the FBI, was preaching the Sunday night that CBS aired the *60 Minutes* program.

The Monday after "The Preacher and the Sting Man" aired, newspapers reported that Duvall was abandoning his appeal. He was quoted as saying, "I've been under arrest the last year. The pressure has been so bad that if I got to go and pay the debt, I'd rather do that and live the rest of my life in peace. I think I'd feel better. I've never been a person to put things off." Duvall reportedly said that spending time worrying about appeals was "worse than the actual time" in prison. Later that same week, Duvall claimed to have been misquoted about abandoning his appeal and stated that it would not be dropped. His attorney, Alvin Binder, said, " I'm told he said if he was unsuccessful in his appeal to the Fifth Circuit, he was not going to the U.S. Supreme Court." Binder added that he was sure that the inaccuracy was the result of a "misunderstanding." Duvall confirmed Binder's version, saying, "That's right. I said I wasn't going any further than the court that we're in now." Revette, whose conviction and appeal were associated with Duvall's, was noncommittal. He said, "I just don't know. I'll have to wait till that time comes."

As members of the former supervisors' families looked on in tears, on May 20 Judge Barbour ordered both Duvall and Revette to report to prison on June 13. They had been free on bond pending the outcome of their appeals. Barbour explained his order, "I have no choice today but to deny bail pending appeal." No substantial question existed "likely to result in a reversal or a new trial." The judge noted that the two men posed no threat to society and that they had conducted themselves well while free on bail. Barbour had ruled the past September that they could remain free on bond because no appeals court had decided whether federal officials had the authority to prosecute under a 1984 bribery statute concerning involvement of federal funds. The U.S. Attorney had appealed that decision to the Fifth Circuit. In upholding Trudie Westmoreland's conviction on March 23, the Fifth Circuit ruled that prosecutors were not required to prove that federal money could be traced directly to a bribe. A month later, the Fifth Circuit vacated Barbour's earlier ruling that had allowed Duvall and Revette to remain free on bond and ordered a new hearing. The Court of Appeals affirmed the lower court's verdict in all respects on May 24, 1988.

Forty-eight-year-old William H. Hutto, district five supervisor, was arrested on August 9, 1987, on Pretense-related charges. He was charged with one count of extortion, one count of bribery, one count of conspiracy to commit bribery, and three counts of mail fraud. The indictments charged Hutto with submitting fraudulent bills for materials and supplies to the Wayne County Board of Supervisors, busting invoices as a part of a deal with an undercover FBI agent, and accepting kickbacks of at least $200 from the FBI agent. Hutto, who was completing his third four-year term, had not stood for reelection in the August 4 primary.

Hutto went to trial on November 16, 1987, in Meridian, with Judge Barbour presiding. He was charged with extortion, bribery, conspiracy to commit bribery, and mail fraud for allegedly receiving $900 in kickbacks. He faced up to fifty years in prison and $1.5 million in fines. He was charged with scheming with employees of Holiman Equipment Company of Jackson to bust invoices and to take kickbacks on sales to Wayne County between November 1985 and August 1986. The charges included conspiring with Max Gilbert, part owner of Holiman, and salesman Pete Dacus to receive a $600 kickback on the county's purchase of a $11,654 mower. Hutto was also charged with conspiring with Mid-State Pipe Company to bust invoices and with taking illegal kickbacks from Mid-State.

In his opening argument, Hutto's attorney, Rex Jones, claimed that his client never committed a crime. "He had no intention to violate the law," Jones said, but he "knew something was not right." Jones claimed that FBI special agent King brought up the subject of busting invoices and on May

29, 1995, offered Hutto a 12 percent kickback, which he refused. The next day, Hutto told County Attorney Charles Leggett that King was "a crook," Jones claimed. "He told all the board members to leave him alone." Continuing, Jones said that, on February 11,1986, King put $200 in Hutto's pocket. Hutto then wrote in a notebook that King "paid $200 for grader blades." In fact, the indictment states wrongly that only $100 was involved, Jones said. The lawyer maintained that when the FBI came to arrest him, Hutto said, "Wait a minute, that indictment contains something that's not true. When he actually gave me the money, he gave me $200."

Assistant U.S. Attorney Richard Starrett contradicted Jones's version of how the subject of busted invoices came up. Maintaining that Hutto brought up the subject, Starrett quoted the supervisor as telling King that his predecessor had been caught on a $13,000 busted invoice because he had, "simply been too greedy."

FBI agent Glen Breedlove testified that when he arrested Hutto on August 10, 1987, Hutto asked permission to return to a bathroom to destroy a record of kickbacks. He said that Hutto asked to return to the bathroom a second time and that the request was again refused. "How about going back to get rid of the book?" Breedlove quoted the supervisor as saying. The agent claimed he refused, and then Hutto asked, "How about getting rid of these three pages?" The agent said that he then seized the book, which contained notations on alleged kickbacks, and that "when I took the book, he seemed upset."

Other testimony involved a June 26, 1986, shrimp and liquor party that had been partly funded by the FBI. Agent Jerry King testified that at the party, Hutto once again indicated that he would like to receive a kickback as a part of a busted invoice. Max Gilbert of Holiman Equipment testified that he made kickbacks to a number of supervisors, including Hutto. "I done my share of it. We didn't feel like we could carry our business without them," he said. He testified about approaching Hutto May 10, 1985, about receiving a bid on an $11,654 power mower, and promising a kickback. "He didn't do anything . . . he just got quiet. . . . I told him our deal was 5% of the purchase price." Pete Dacus, a former salesman for Holiman, testified that he delivered the $600 kickback to Hutto in a white envelope. Ray Davis of Davis Chemicals testified that his company made four or five payments to Hutto for buying their products. Dacus, Davis, and Gilbert all faced federal charges for making kickbacks to supervisors to obtain business. All three testified that as a part of their plea agreements the government had promised to recommend prison terms of not more than three years and probation for five years.

Hutto, the lone defense witness, testified that he didn't take money from agent King; he claimed that King had put it in his pocket. Starrett asked Hutto if he had the money now, and Hutto replied, "Yes, sir, you want to see it?" as he produced four $100 bills from his pocket. "I still got the money; I did not intend to spend the money," he said. Regarding the notebook notations of the three alleged kickbacks, Hutto testified, "I wanted to keep myself clear. I'm not a crook." He disputed claims that on February 11, 1986, he accepted a $100 kickback from King. He said that King put $200 in his pocket. Reading from his notebook, he testified that a kickback that allegedly took place on July 9, 1996, actually took place on June 27. In his closing argument, the prosecutor said that Hutto came up with amounts and dates from invoices before his arrest. This led to making mistakes such as drawing the date from the June 27 invoice, which was two weeks before the actual kickback took place.

After deliberating just two hours, on November 19 the jury returned guilty verdicts on all six counts. Sentencing was scheduled for January 8, 1988, and Hutto was to remain free on bond until that time. Speaking of the verdict, prosecutor Richard Starrett said, "The message is clear to supervisors and public officials: We won't put up with the wrongdoing." He called Hutto's claim that he accepted the money but wasn't guilty "simple but unbelievable." Hutto was the fifth supervisor to be convicted by a jury as the result of Pretense. Jones also said that he was discussing a possible appeal with his client. Starrett commented that recent criticisms of the length of Pretense were unwarranted. "We have heard some comments that perhaps Mississippians are tired of Operation Pretense. I think this verdict shows that they're not tired of Operation Pretense but of the corruption it's uncovered. I frankly believe that Mississippians will always speak out against corruption in all its forms." Defense attorney Rex Jones noted the prosecutors perfect court record and said, "Because of public officials and public opinion on Operation Pretense, it's a snowballing situation. It's a situation that makes it very difficult to try one in Mississippi, even though jurors are not influenced." With this verdict, the Pretense running count stood at forty-eight supervisors charged in twenty-three counties (with thirty-four guilty pleas and five convictions before juries) and nine salesmen and one road foreman charged (with guilty pleas from the road foreman and five of the salesmen).

Hutto was sentenced by Judge Barbour on January 8, 1988, to six years' imprisonment, fined $10,000, ordered to pay restitution of $900, and ordered to serve five years' probation after release from confinement. Assistant U.S. Attorney Nicholas B. Phillips had told Barbour that Hutto had not cooperated with the investigation, and Phillips had requested that the judge impose a substantial period of incarceration. In imposing the sentence, the Judge said, "Regrettably you have fallen into the same situation others have—you have breached the trust, stolen from the county. You're going to have to pay for it." Hutto was ordered to report to a federal prison by 9 A.M. on January 28.

4. Lamar County

Campaign Contributions

Named for L. Q. C. Lamar, U.S. senator from Mississippi and justice of the U.S. Supreme Court, Lamar County was established in 1904 in the south-central part of the state. According to the 1990 census, Lamar County had 30,424 residents. Purvis, with a 1990 population of 2,256, is the county seat. The extreme western part of Hattiesburg is in Lamar County, and the bulk of the county's population resides in the city or its western suburbs. Hattiesburg is the home of the University of Southern Mississippi and a large medical community, as well as several manufacturing plants, including a world-class Sunbeam facility. The city is also the banking, retailing, and financial services center of South Mississippi. Hattiesburg prospered greatly in the 1980s and 1990s, and Lamar County benefited from Hattiesburg's growth. The county is home to several of the city's most affluent suburbs, including Canebrake, which has been featured twice in *Southern Living* magazine.

Lamar County government was rocked by scandal in 1987–1988. Two of its five supervisors, Kermit Rayborn and Pascal Lott, were indicted as a result of Operation Pretense, and two of the other three supervisors were implicated in corrupt practices in a Pretense-related trial.

Lamar County District Five Supervisor Kermit Rayborn was indicted by a federal grand jury in early May 1987 on four charges, and on May 5 he was arrested and arraigned before U.S. Magistrate John R. Countiss III. The fifty-three-year-old Sumrall resident pleaded innocent to all four charges and was released on a $5,000 personal recognizance bond. Rayborn, a first-term supervisor, was charged with scheming to accept and accepting $1,200 in kickbacks from Holiman Equipment Company on a series of county transactions that occurred from about December 1985 until January 1987. He was also charged with extorting the payments from Holiman Equipment Company and with using the U.S. mails and aiding and abetting mail fraud in perpetrating the schemes.

The indictment charged Rayborn with: (1) using his position as Lamar County district five supervisor to cause and arrange for various items to be purchased by Lamar County from Holiman Equipment Company in return for cash kickbacks; (2) proposing with Holiman to submit fraudulent bills for materials and goods to be furnished by Holiman to the county and with actively assisting in accomplishing these activities; (3) proposing with Holiman that other supervisors within the county were willing to enter into similar false and fraudulent arrangements and assisting in accomplishing such arrangements; and (4) proposing with Holiman to falsely and fraudulently document fraudulent transactions to avoid detection by the state auditor and others.

Specifically, the indictment charged that in December 1985, Rayborn ordered an A-Boom mower attachment from Holiman Equipment Company, and assisted Holiman in securing orders for similar and related equipment from other Lamar County supervisors, Joe Bryant and R. E. "Pug" Easley, in exchange for promised kickbacks from Holiman Equipment Company. Later, Rayborn approved a Holiman Equipment Company invoice in the amount of $11,654 for a TK A-boom mower attachment for the county. During March 1986, Rayborn obtained a kickback of $600 from Holiman on the order and obtained an additional kickback of $200 from Holiman for his efforts in helping secure related sales to Bryant and Easley. In December 1986, Rayborn ordered from Holiman a TK 72-inch versa side mount mower attachment for the county. Later, he approved a Holiman Equipment Company invoice in the amount of $6,390 for a TK 72-inch versa side mount mower attachment for the county. In January 1987, Rayborn obtained a kickback of $400 from Holiman on the order.

Despite the fact that he was under indictment and about to go to trial, Kermit Rayborn ran for a second term in the August 4 Democratic primary. He led three other candidates and was to face Jesse Douglas in the August 25 runoff; the winner would have no opposition in the November general election.

At the late August trial, Max Gilbert, vice president of Holiman Equipment Company, testified that he had approved an extra kickback to Rayborn, in addition to two already paid, for Rayborn's help in arranging deals with two other supervisors. Gilbert testified, "He said he thought he should get an additional $200 for his influence with the other supervisors. I told him he could have the extra $200 if he could make good, get the other two folks." Bryant and Easley were identified as the other two "folks." The fifty-six-year-old Easley, president of the Lamar County Board of Supervisors, had died of cancer in May 1987.

Gilbert, who was under indictment and was cooperating in the Pretense investigation based on a plea bargain, explained how his company got involved with the kickbacks. He testified, "We did [pay] only if the supervisor asked for it. If a supervisor asked for a kickback, we would obligate five percent of the bid price for the kickback." Gilbert said he first met Rayborn when Holiman salesman Pete Dacus was attempting to sell the supervisor an $11,654 A-boom mower. He and Dacus met with Rayborn at a county shop in October 1985, and that day Gilbert authorized the additional $200 payment. "I authorized Mr. Dacus to go ahead and finish the transaction in Lamar County," he said. Gilbert indicated that Dacus paid the kickback from his own pocket and was later reimbursed by the company. He also said that Easley came by the shop that day but that no business was conducted at that time. Dacus was also under indictment and was cooperating with the Pretense investigation.

Dacus testified that he paid Rayborn a $600 kickback on the December 1985 purchase of the A-boom mower and $200 for his influence with two other supervisors. The $800 payment was made in a Lamar County courthouse bathroom, according to Dacus. "I caught him out in the hall and said that I needed to see him. He said, 'come in here.' We went in the bathroom. I gave him eight $100 bills. He put it in his pocket and he walked out." Dacus also claimed there was an additional $400 kickback on a November 1986 purchase of a side-mount mower. In his opening statement, defense attorney Rex Jones claimed that Rayborn had not taken any kickbacks, but he had accepted $400 as a campaign contribution. He also said that Rayborn "found" $700 in his coat pocket, but that he had no memory of how the money got there.

During the trial, a tape recording of a conversation between Rayborn and Dacus was introduced as evidence. The recording was made on January 15, 1987, in the driveway of the supervisor's Sumrall home.

Part of the conversation went as follows:

> Dacus—"It's coming up on election year, right?" (something garbled) begins counting and then says, "350. Is that what we agreed on?"
> Rayborn—(garbled) Then, "I thought it was going to be $400."
> Dacus—"Is that what I told you? Hey, we do what we said."

Testifying in his own defense, Rayborn admitted taking $400 from Dacus but denied accepting kickbacks. He testified, "I knew I received the money as a campaign contribution." He claimed that he and Dacus had discussed a $400 campaign contribution in late December 1986. Rayborn claimed that Dacus said, " 'Well I want to do something for you, give you some money.' " "I said, 'What do you mean money?' He said, 'I don't want to get you in trouble. . . . I can give you $400 as a campaign contribution, and it won't get you in trouble.' " Rayborn claimed that the salesman had mentioned the proposed contribution again at the supervisors' convention in Jackson in early January. "He called me off to the side and said, 'Don't worry, I'll take care of what we talked about. It'll be a campaign contribution.' " Rayborn also denied ever getting $800 from Dacus. He claimed to have found $700 in the right-hand pocket of a coat ten days to two weeks after a March supervisors' meeting. "Some of it I spent for charity," he said.

Under cross-examination by Assistant U.S. Attorney James Tucker, Rayborn said he did not think about why the Jackson salesman would be interested in the Lamar County supervisor's race. He said, "I didn't take that into consideration. I didn't see any reason anybody couldn't give a campaign contribution." Rayborn agreed that the $400 "contribution" was the only one listed on his June 10 campaign finance contribution form. He said that the other nine contributions he received ranged between $10 and $200 and that they were not required to be reported. Rayborn said, "I was told I didn't have to report anything except $400 or above." Claiming that he had been given that information by Lamar County deputy circuit clerk Katie Strahan, Rayborn testified, "I may have made a mistake, but if I did, it was honest." Contributions of $200 or more were required to be disclosed under state law.

Dacus testified that he also paid kickbacks to Bryant and to the Easley. During cross-examination, defense attorney Rex Jones called attention to Dacus's dealings with Easley. "Is it not true that when Pug Easley was lying in the hospital dying of cancer, you went up there and stuck money in his pocket, trying to set him up too?" Jones asked. "No sir," Dacus replied. "He asked for it." Dacus claimed that Easley later telephoned him and that he went to Easley's home and took the money back.

During cross-examination of Rayborn, Tucker asked how he and Jones came to know about the Easley incident. Rayborn answered, "After this indictment happened, I asked some of the other board members what they knew about this Pete Dacus." He said Patricia Easley, who had been appointed by the board of supervisors to serve out her husband's unexpired term, told board attorney Kent Hudson that "she knew when her husband was in the hospital in February, the salesman came down and put an envelope in his pocket." Rayborn claimed that Patricia Easley said that when her husband found the money in the envelope, he had Dacus come get it. Dacus was called and went back to get the money after Operation Pretense became public knowledge in mid-February.

The closing arguments in the trial revealed a lot about the whole nature of Operation Pretense. Defense attorney Rex Jones attacked the testimony and character of both Gilbert and Dacus. "Those two in the operation remind me of fat ticks on the sleeping dog of county government," Jones said. He labeled Dacus the "head drum majorette," who enjoyed his role as "hero" of Operation Pretense. Jones argued, "All his life he has dealt in deception. Now Dacus, he wants to live in the highlands when he's spent all his life in the marshes. . . . I just have a problem with a man like Dacus, turning him loose to roam this state with a body bug."

Prosecuting attorney James Tucker countered that neither Dacus nor Gilbert were in the highlands. He said, "They're both in the marshes. This was a dirty, nasty business. They wallowed in it. Who did business with these men? Kermit Rayborn did business with these men. We're not vouching for Pete Dacus. We're not vouching for Max Gilbert. We're asking you not to vouch for Kermit Rayborn. . . . This man has admitted, with twisted interpretations, everything that's in the indictment. . . . He is absolutely, by his own mouth, guilty." Prosecuting attorney Richard Starrett addressed the defense's claim that the $400 was a campaign contribution. He said, "When you listen to the tape there's not a shred of discussion about campaign contributions. Mr. Rayborn made that up. It's insulting to you to get up here and ask you to believe that's a campaign contribution."

On August 26, 1987, after a trial that lasted more than twenty-five hours, a jury convicted Rayborn on three of the four counts in the indictment. The jury had deliberated its verdict for almost six hours. Rayborn was convicted on one count each of bribery, mail fraud and aiding and abetting mail fraud, and extortion. He was found not guilty of count two, which, along with count three, alleged mail fraud and aiding and abetting mail fraud. He faced maximum penalties of thirty-five years' imprisonment and fines of $750,000. Rayborn remained free on bond, and the judge ordered a presentence report.

It is not difficult to discern the jury's reasoning in rendering a not guilty verdict on count two of the indictment. The count alleged mail fraud and aiding and abetting mail fraud in connection with Rayborn's acceptance of a $600 kickback on the county's purchase of the $11,654 A-boom mower attachment from Holiman Equipment Company. No tape-recorded evidence was introduced during the trial regarding this transaction. However, the prosecution did present evidence that the defendant induced Lamar County to pay Holiman Equipment Company's invoice by mail, but the only evidence concerning the kickback was the testimony of Pete Dacus, who was himself cooperating with the prosecution based on a Pretense-related plea bargain agreement.

Pete Dacus testified that district four supervisor Joe Bryant accepted a kickback from him, but Bryant was never charged under Operation Pretense. Bryant was re-nominated in the August Democratic Primary and reelected supervisor in the November 1987 general election. Patricia Easley lost her race for her deceased husband's district two post in the August 4 primary.

U.S. District Judge William H. Barbour Jr. passed sentence on Kermit Rayborn on October 23, 1987. Assistant U.S. Attorney Richard Starrett recommended a ten-year prison sentence. Rayborn was sentenced to six years in prison on the extortion count, fined $10,000 and placed on five years' probation on the bribery count, and placed on five years' probation on the mail fraud count. Rayborn was also ordered to pay $1,200 in restitution to Lamar County. The two probation terms imposed were to run concurrently and were to begin at the time of release from incarceration. Rayborn was to report to prison on November 16, 1987. The judge recommended that Rayborn be assigned to the federal correctional facility at Eglin Air Force Base in Florida.

There was an interesting exchange between Judge Barbour and Kermit Rayborn at sentencing. Judge Barbour told the defendant, "You have directly stolen from the people of your county. The supervisors who have been prosecuted are being made an example of." With a shaking voice, Rayborn asked for mercy and told the judge that he and his family had already suffered a lot because of the charges brought against him and the subsequent convictions. Rayborn said, "I've been through a lot, and I do have remorse." Judge Barbour, citing letters that had been sent to him and other court officers by friends and supporters of Rayborn, said that Rayborn's "record up to this time has been exemplary. It's obvious to the court that you and your wife have expended your life in service-oriented jobs. I am very sympathetic to you. On the other hand, you occupied a position of trust. The people voted for you." But the judge also told Rayborn that he believed that the supervisor had lied during his testimony.

While his trial was in progress, Rayborn lost to Jessie Douglas in the August Democratic runoff election. Neither his conviction nor sentence necessitated that he immediately resign from office. But at the time of his October sentencing, Rayborn's attorney indicated that his client would probably step down soon; he had to report to prison on November 16.

Defense attorney Rex Jones of Hattiesburg indicated that Rayborn would not appeal the conviction and that he had asked that he be assigned to the correctional facility at Eglin because he had relatives who lived nearby. Jones indicated that an appeal would probably be a waste of money. He said, "I don't think there was any error in the trial. I think he will be better off to get his time over with and get his life back together, get back to his family. We took our best shot, we lost. I'm just glad the judge didn't punish my client for exercising his constitutional right to a trial. We got the same sentence that some of them who have pleaded guilty have gotten."

By the time Operation Pretense had run its course, Jones's assertion about the comparability of Rayborn's sentence to those of supervisors who pleaded guilty would prove to be very wide of the mark. Rayborn was the fourth supervisor who was convicted in a jury trial, while thirty-one supervisors had previously pleaded guilty. However, only a few of those who had pleaded guilty had actually been sentenced. Most were in the process of cooperating with the investigation, and their cooperation invariably led to shorter prison sentences. In fact, most supervisors who pleaded guilty and cooperated in the investigation received two- or three-year sentences, and some were sentenced to only six months' prison time.

Pascal Lott, district one supervisor, was indicted by a federal grand jury in Jackson on November 8, 1987. Lott, who was arrested and arraigned before U.S. Magistrate Countiss on November 10, was charged with one count each of conspiracy to commit bribery, bribery, and extortion. He pleaded innocent to all charges and was released on a $5,000 personal recognizance bond. The felony charges against Lott carried maximum penalties of thirty-five years in prison and $270,000 in fines. The fifty-eight-year-old Lott was charged with conspiring with a representative of Holiman Equipment Company to accept and with actually accepting a $350 kickback on Lamar County's November 1986 purchase of a 72-inch mower. He was also charged with extorting the $350 kickback and thereby obstructing, delaying, and affecting interstate commerce.

Lott and his attorney, William E. Andrews III, entered into a Memorandum of Understanding with Assistant U.S. Attorney Starrett on February 9, 1988. This plea bargain called for Lott to plead guilty to the bribery and extortion counts. Upon tender of the guilty pleas, the U.S. attorney was to recommend acceptance of the pleas and a suspended sentence and five years' probation on the extortion count. The government was to make no recommendation as to sentence on the bribery count and to recommend that the conspiracy count be dismissed. The government was also to recommend that if probation were imposed, it should begin after release from any confinement that might be ordered and that Lott be prohibited from seeking or holding public office during any probation. Lott had not run for reelection in the 1987 primary. Maximum penalties for the two counts to which Lott agreed to plead guilty were thirty years in prison and $500,000 in fines. The plea bargain did not require Lott to cooperate in the ongoing investigation.

On March 22, 1988, Judge Barbour accepted Lott's guilty pleas under the terms of the plea bargain agreement. Judge Barbour sentenced Lott to five years in prison with four and a half years suspended, fined him $5,000, and ordered him to pay restitution to Lamar County in the amount of $350. He also imposed two five-year terms of probation, both of which were to start with the ex-supervisor's release from incarceration. The judge recommended confinement in the Federal Correctional Institution at Eglin Air Force Base. However, Lott was assigned to the Federal Prison Camp at Maxwell Air Force Base in Alabama; he reported as ordered April 11, 1988.

At the time, Lott's sentence was the lightest that had been imposed as the result of a Pretense conviction. Lott himself had suggested a two-year prison sentence and a $5,000 fine in a federal probation presentence report. At sentencing, Judge Barbour remarked, "I will quite frankly tell you that is the first time I have ever seen an offender recommend jail time in that portion of the probationary report, other than a probationary sentence. From that, I read that you are indicating to this court you are sorry for what you have done and are facing up to what you have done by pleading guilty." However, the judge also had some harsh words for Lott. Referring to the trust that the voters of his district had placed in him by electing him supervisor, Judge Barbour said, "You breached that trust, and the court feels you must be punished for that offense." Lott's attorney expressed the defense's feelings with, "We're happy!"

5. Claiborne County
A Not Guilty Verdict

Claiborne County, located in the southwestern part of Mississippi, has the Mississippi River as its western border. Its population of fewer than 12,000 was 82 percent black in the 1990 census. When the Yankee general Ulysses S. Grant passed through the county seat during the War between the States as he approached Vicksburg from the south, he declared Port Gibson a "city too pretty to be burned." The general's words are still on signs that welcome visitors to the city. In the 1980s, Claiborne County became the home of the very controversial Grand Gulf nuclear power plant that is located along the Mississippi River.

Unfortunately for its citizens, during the 1980s and 1990s Claiborne County government was plagued by corruption on an almost unbelievable scale. In the 1980s two supervisors were charged with federal felonies as a result of Operation Pretense. One of the supervisors pleaded guilty, and one went to trial and was found not guilty.

Eddie Burrell was district four supervisor and president of the Claiborne County Board of Supervisors when he was charged on May 15, 1987, with one count of mail fraud. He was charged in an information, a document prepared by prosecutors that includes charges the government is prepared to present to a grand jury in seeking a formal indictment. Burrell waived indictment and pleaded innocent to the charges in Jackson before U.S. Magistrate John R. Countless III. Burrell indicated that he would change his plea later and cooperate in the Pretense investigation. U.S. Attorney George Phillips said, "He is obviously cooperating with the government and is going to be extremely valuable to Operation Pretense and not limited just to Claiborne County. Things are happening. New cases are still being made." Burrell, the thirty-seventh person charged in the Pretense investigation, was accused of using his position to cause Claiborne County to buy items from Mississippi Road Supply in return for being paid a cash kickback. He was said to have arranged for the county to mail $88,500 to Mississippi Road Supply as part of the scheme.

Burrell pleaded guilty to two counts of mail fraud on June 16, 1987. According to the charges, Burrell met with Bill Anderson, a representative of Mississippi Road Supply, in April or May 1985 at Burrell's home and accepted $3,000 in cash in return for his role in arranging for the county to buy a piece of road equipment for $92,934. In August 1986, Anderson met with Burrell again and paid him $4,000 in cash after the supervisor agreed to buy a road grader for $88,500. Two county checks totaling $88,500 associated with these purchases were mailed to Mississippi Road Supply in August 1986. The supervisor was also charged with accepting $3,500 from Johnny Williamson of Tubb Williamson and Company in July 1984 after the Claiborne County Board of Supervisors had agreed to buy another piece of road equipment for $85,700. Payment on this purchase was mailed by the county on July 12, 1984.

The plea agreement called for the government to recommend a suspended sentence of not more than three years, fines at the judge's discretion, and five years' probation, during which time Burrell would not seek public office. He had faced maximum penalties of five years in prison and a $250,000 fine on both counts. Burrell resigned from office June 7 and did not seek reelection in the August primary. He cooperated in the Pretense investigation, and his sentencing did not take place until March 31, 1989. At that time, Judge William H. Barbour Jr. sentenced him to five years in prison with four and one-half years suspended. The judge also placed Burrell on probation for five years, with the probation beginning with his release from incarceration, and he was prohibited from seeking public office during the time of probation. He was also fined $5,000 and ordered to pay $12,100 in restitution to Claiborne County. The former supervisor reported to the Federal Prison Camp at Maxwell Air Force Base in Alabama on May 1, 1989.

Claiborne County district one supervisor Albert Butler was arrested and indicted on September 11, 1987. The forty-year-old Butler was charged with one count of conspiracy to commit mail fraud and three counts of mail fraud. The popular supervisor, who had just been nominated for a second term in the August Democratic primary, pleaded innocent to the charges, which carried maximum penalties of twenty years' imprisonment and fines totaling $1 million. Despite the indictment, Butler defeated independent candidates, Calvin E. Reed and W. L. Thompson, in the November 1987 general election. Butler garnered more than twice as many votes as the two independent candidates combined.

Butler went on trial in Jackson in February 1988. Max Gilbert, sales man-

ager and vice president of Holiman Equipment Company of Jackson, testified that Butler had twice purchased parts for his personal car and had
them billed to Claiborne County. Butler's wife had been involved in an
automobile accident in October 1986. Butler went to Holiman Equipment
Company in December and told Gilbert that he needed parts for the dam-
aged car and that he had been told Gilbert could help him. According to
Gilbert's testimony, "He came in two weeks later and asked me if we could
still help him with the parts, and I told him we'd be glad to." The prosecution showed that Holiman bought the needed car parts for $1,197 from
Flower Buick GMC, Inc. in Jackson during January and gave them to Butler. Holiman then sent Claiborne County a fraudulent bill for $4,043 for
the car parts. The bill itemized equipment the county never received. According to the indictment, Butler authorized payment, and the county actually paid the bill on February 5, 1987.

Alvin Binder, who represented Butler, asked Gilbert under cross-examination whether Butler had ever asked for a favor or kickback before the
January 1987 incident. Gilbert replied, "He was one of the finest supervisors
I knew. He never asked for anything before this point." Gilbert himself was
under indictment for making payoffs to supervisors, and he was cooperating with the government in the Pretense investigation. Under questioning
by Assistant U.S. Attorney Nick Phillips, Gilbert said that Butler was "now
just as guilty as I was for doing the transaction." Gilbert testified that he
assigned parts manager Andy Goolsby the task of helping Butler with the
car parts. Goolsby, who was also cooperating in Pretense, testified that Gilbert "just told me to fix the customer up," which to him meant "bill it to
the county." According to Goolsby, Butler signed an incomplete delivery
ticket for the parts. The delivery ticket was incomplete because Goolsby did
not know how much the parts would cost. A former employee of Holiman,
Brent Bowman, testified that he received the car parts from Fowler Buick,
loaded them into Butler's vehicle, and took the invoice to Goolsby. According to Goolsby, two days later, he arranged to get more parts for Butler.
Goolsby testified that he completed the delivery ticket when Fowler Buick's
invoice was received listing parts that would fit the type of county equipment the supervisor used.

Court testimony showed that Butler went to Holiman later, possibly in
March after Operation Pretense became public, and asked Goolsby if he
could pay for the parts. Goolsby testified that "I told him to go see the
bookkeeper." But under Binder's questioning, Goolsby said that, when But-

ler asked to pay for the parts, he told him that the FBI had taken the company's records.

Butler testified that he never asked Holiman employees to bill Claiborne County for parts for his wife's car. The Port Gibson resident stated, "I never asked them for anything." Butler admitted seeing the $4,034 invoice from Holiman but maintained that he never signed it. He claimed to not have realized the invoice, which listed a hydraulic motor and other items, was actually for the parts for his wrecked car. He said, "I had no idea they were Buick parts. . . . I just knew that they didn't have anything to do with my personal automobile." He said that he received the parts in January and that he saved $300 by getting them wholesale through a Holiman official. "He [the Holiman official] told me he'd let me get the parts at cost." Butler also said, "The first time I realized I didn't get an invoice was in the later part of February." Butler also testified that when he approached Goolsby in March about paying the invoice "He [Goolsby] told me to come outside. He said he didn't have the invoices because the FBI had come and picked them up." Claiming that Goolsby "was a little upset," Butler said, "[h]e couldn't tell me how much I owed because he didn't have an invoice." Butler also denied that he had ever spoken to Gilbert about the car parts.

In his closing argument, defense attorney Binder asked the jury, "Who in this room, including you, hasn't asked a friend to get him a good price on something wholesale? If you are going to steal some parts from the Buick place are you going to go down and sign your name to it? If you are going to do something wrong, are you going to leave the cops a note with your name on it, say, come arrest me?" Assistant U.S. Attorney Phillips countered that Butler had made no effort to pay for the parts until after he learned of the Pretense investigation. Phillips told the jury, "If this wasn't a scheme to defraud, I don't know what is."

On February 19, after about two hours of deliberation, the jury returned an innocent verdict on all charges against Albert Butler. After the verdict, Butler hugged defense attorneys Alvin Binder and Lisa Binder Milner and said, "I'm glad it's over. It's been a lot of pressure on myself and my family. The Lord works in mysterious ways." James Tucker, the assistant U.S. attorney who led the prosecution, said the verdict should have no effect on future Pretense trials. Tucker maintained that this was not a traditional Pretense case. What distinguished Butler's case from the others was that the accused supervisor had not received any money. However, the lead defense attorney said that prosecutors had claimed the charges against Butler were a direct result of Operation Pretense. Alvin Binder said, "This is what they said in the opening arguments, let the headlines come out screaming. I think the jury believed Albert Butler."

The Operation Pretense jury trial score after this verdict stood at five convictions and one innocent verdict. Butler proved to be not only the first, but the only supervisor charged under Pretense who was found innocent in a court of law. Thirty-six supervisors, five salesmen, and a road foreman had pleaded guilty of Pretense-related charges at the time of the Butler verdict. Additionally, two of the indicted supervisors had died, one had been ruled incompetent to stand trial, and charges against one salesman had been dismissed. Nevertheless, one wonders why the federal prosecutors ever brought this case to trial. This is especially true if they could not show that Butler signed the invoice. As Assistant U.S. Attorney James Tucker said, this case was different from the others because no money had changed hands. There was apparently no predisposition and therefore no sting or tapes involved. The case seems to have been built almost entirely on the testimony of the two Holiman officials who were under indictment themselves and were cooperating with the government. They did not claim that Butler actually asked them to bill Claiborne County for the car parts.

6. Winston County

"I Didn't Know What a Kickback Was"

Winston County was established in 1833 under the Choctaw Cession of 1830. The county boasts a famous Choctaw Indian mound, Nanih Wayia, which is about 35 feet high, 60 feet wide, and 100 feet long. A natural geological formation called the Nanih Wayia Cave Mound located a mile and a half east, is 80 feet high and 180 by 340 feet at the base. Both mounds are in the Nanih Wayia State Park sixteen miles southeast of Louisville. The legendary birthplace and capital of the Choctaw Indians, Nanih Wayia has been called the "Mother Mound" of the Choctaws, and the area around it is believed to have been occupied by the Choctaws about the time of Christ. The mound itself was probably built around A.D. 500 At least three different legends relate how the mound came to be and why the Choctaws occupied the land around it.

The county is named for Louis Winston (1784–1824), a native of Virginia who came to the Mississippi Territory and became a prominent lawyer and colonel of a regiment of militia. Winston served as secretary of the state constitutional convention of 1817 and as a judge of the Mississippi State Supreme Court from 1821 until his death. Located in the eastern part of north-central Mississippi, the county had a 1990 population of 19,433. Its county seat, Louisville, which was also named for Louis Winston, had a 1990 population of 7,323. Operation Pretense ended the political career of one of the county's supervisors far short of that of the county's illustrious namesake.

Winston district four supervisor Larry Miller was indicted on five counts in Oxford on February 10, 1987, by a grand jury of the Federal Court of the Northern District of Mississippi. The thirty-two-year-old Louisville resident was one of the first supervisors indicted under Operation Pretense. Miller was arrested February 13 and released on a $25,000 bond. Miller was arraigned before U.S. Magistrate Norman L. Gillespie in Oxford on February 20 and was represented at the arraignment by attorney Johnnie Walls of

Greenville. Trial was scheduled for April 6 in U.S. District Court in Aberdeen.

The indictment alleged that during the period March 1985 until February 1987 Miller took $907 in kickbacks on Winston County purchases of $7,169.92 from Mid-State Pipe Company. He was charged with using the U.S. mails to help carry out the scheme. Four purchases of culvert pipes were cited in the indictment along with purchases of antifreeze and shop towels. The invoices from Mid-State for antifreeze and shop towels were alleged to have been busted, with the county receiving only seven of the ten cases of antifreeze and only one of the two cases of shop towels it paid for. Maximum penalties for the five mail fraud charges were $5,000 in fines and twenty-five years' imprisonment.

Following a court motion, the case was transferred to Judge Neal B. Biggers Jr.'s courtroom in Oxford on March 13. Based on a motion by the defendant, Judge Biggers granted a continuance of the case on March 31. Trial was reset for July 20, but on June 17, Judge Biggers granted another continuance.

In mid-March, Miller had announced that he would run for a second term as supervisor of district four. The March 18 *Winston County Journal* quoted Miller as follows:

> I seek your support and vote for re-election of District Four. In the last two years I have worked toward the improvement of roads, hospital, taxes and all aspects of the county. I sincerely thank each of you for allowing me the opportunity to serve as your supervisor for the past two years. If re-elected, I promise to continue to serve you to the best of my ability. I will still promise to be a 24 hour-a-day supervisor with an open door policy, available to discuss your needs and concerns, and that together, hopefully, we can arrive at an agreeable solution to our districts and county problems. I challenge the voters of district four to let my work speak for me. I ask you, district four voters, to re-elect me for your supervisor. Your support and vote is needed.

Miller won the August Democratic primary despite being under indictment at the time of the election. Three other candidates, Brady Dawkins, Silas Dempsey and John Arthur Young, received a total of 975 votes, while Miller received 981. This six-vote majority assured Miller's reelection in November because there was no Republican opposition.

A Superseding Indictment dated August 27, 1987, added bribery and extortion to the five counts of mail fraud against Miller bringing the total to seven counts. Miller now faced maximum penalties of $1.75 million in fines and fifty-five years in prison. The defendant pled not guilty to the new indictment and remained free on bond. Trial was set for October 5. However, Judge Biggers granted another continuance on September 21. Later, a trial date was set for January 25, 1988.

On January 4, 1988, Miller filed a motion with the court for an Order Transferring Trial. Paragraphs three and four of the motion are of particular interest in light of Miller's reelection:

> Defendant would respectfully show unto the Court that there exists in the district where his prosecution is pending (Oxford Division) and in the Aberdeen Division so great a prejudice against the defendant, as an "Operation Pretense" indictee that the defendant can not obtain a fair trial at any place fixed by law for holding court in either the Oxford Division or the Aberdeen Division. Since the initial indictments under the "Operation Pretense" investigation there have been a number of indictments returned against members of the various county boards of supervisors within the Oxford and Aberdeen Division, there has been a tremendous amount of publicity surrounding the said indictments, and there have been either guilty pleas and/or trials in said districts which have greatly publicized throughout said districts the facts and circumstances surrounding the indictment herein and other "Operation Pretense" indictments. Because of the extensive pretrial publicity, defendant does not believe that he can obtain a fair and impartial trial held either in Oxford or Aberdeen.
>
> Defendant would respectfully show the court that there have been virtually no indictments to his knowledge against members of boards of supervisors in any counties that comprise the Delta Division or the Greenville Division of this court, and that there has been no publicity regarding local public officials in those divisions which would tend to prejudice juries drawn from these divisions for a trial of an indictee under the "Operation Pretense" investigation. Consequently, defendant believes that in order for him to receive a fair trial in the Northern District of Mississippi, his trial should be held in the Delta Division or the Greenville Division.

Judge Biggers denied the motion in an order dated January 15, 1988:

> After considering the motion and the knowledge of the court that several trials involving the Operation Pretense cases have been conducted in the

Southern District of Mississippi without any changes of venue taking place and in consideration of the paucity of publicity concerning the defendant herein, it is the opinion of the court that the motion to change the place of trial should be and is hereby DENIED.

Despite Miller's victory in the primary election, it is not difficult to understand the strategy of Miller and his lawyers in requesting the change of venue. Larry Miller was the first elected black supervisor in Winston County's history. The Oxford and Aberdeen divisions from which the jury pool would be drawn were predominately white. Conversely, the populations of the Delta and Greenville Divisions were overwhelmingly black.

Miller's trial began in mid-April 1988, about three months after he had been sworn in for a second term. During the trial, Miller claimed that he took cash gifts, not kickbacks, and that he had been entrapped by the FBI. He testified, "I never asked anybody for a kickback. In a sense, I didn't even know what a kickback was until Pretense." He claimed to believe that it was acceptable to take money from Mid-State salesmen because he did it before the county paid Mid-State for the supplies ordered. He maintained that had the company wanted to wait until after the county had paid he would not have accepted the cash. Miller said, "The money I got came out of his [the salesman's] pocket." He claimed the payments were like commissions for giving business to Mid-State.

The prosecutor, Assistant U.S. Attorney John Hailman, questioned the defendant about the legality of the deals. "You're sitting here telling this jury with a straight face that was an honest transaction?" Hailman asked. Miller replied that he never sought kickbacks. Hailman then said, "You never asked for them, but when they were offered you took them." "I never took kickbacks," Miller replied. Hailman retorted, "It's just a matter of words. You took the cash didn't you." "I took the cash," Miller replied.

Rev. John Burgess, the instigator of Operation Pretense and the nominal owner of Mid-State Pipe Company, testified against Miller. He told the jurors that he went to lunch with Miller in March 1985 wearing a tape recorder. Burgess said that when he approached the supervisor in an attempt to sell him supplies, Miller told him that he was getting 8 percent cash kickbacks from other salesmen. Burgess said that he offered him 12 percent and that Miller agreed to take it. Miller then placed an order for six culverts and accepted $105, or 12 percent of the invoice amount, according to Burgess.

The jury heard several taped conversations that caught Miller discussing "invisible supplies" (busted invoices) and taking kickbacks from undercover FBI investigators. Most of the conversations were between Miller and Clifton Chatham, an FBI agent who posed as a salesman for Mid-State. Chatham, who during the investigation used the name Cliff Winters, testified that Miller accepted kickbacks from him on purchases of various supplies and authorized fraudulent invoices for items not received by the county. Chatham testified that in July 1985, he approached Miller about submitting a fraudulent invoice and asked whether the supervisor thought anyone would check. Miller was caught on tape saying, "I don't really think they'd check if [it] was a small order." Chatham then told Miller that he would bill the county and split the profit. During the same meeting, Chatham is heard giving Miller a $175 kickback on a $1,459 purchase of metal culverts.

In another taped exchange, Miller was heard telling the agent that he needed some roofing tin and lumber to build a barn for himself. "You want to charge the county for it . . . and not let them know it?" Chatham asked. "Yeah," Miller replied. Miller was also taped agreeing to buy ten cases of antifreeze and have seven delivered and agreeing to buy two cases of shop towels and have one delivered. Chatham testified that Miller signed two fraudulent invoices totaling $368 and accepted $87 in cash for his split of profits from the invisible supplies paid for by Winston County but never delivered. In his testimony, Miller said that he expected all the items that he had ordered to be delivered. He also said that he considered the Mid-State salesman a "pest." Prior to Miller's testimony, Winston County supervisor Devon Thomas testified that Miller was never trained in the duties and responsibilities of the office. He also said that Miller had been under tremendous pressure as the first black member of the board of supervisors.

Defense attorney Johnnie Walls argued in his closing statement that Miller had been entrapped. He said the case was not about Miller but about a government that makes crooks and puts them in jail. He claimed that his client was "a victim of corruption" and that the government put the idea of taking cash in his head. He described a system that turns out inexperienced supervisors with taxpayers' money and says, "If you fail, we're going to put you in jail." Co-counsel Tyree Irving pointed out to the jury that Miller had won reelection after he had been charged and asked, "If he was stealing them blind, is everybody in district four a fool?"

Assistant U.S. Attorney Hailman told the jurors that many of the state's supervisors "are stealing us blind, and Mr. Miller is a typical example." He said, "They think they can beat the Legislature. They think they can beat everybody. It makes honest people not want to run for office." Hailman called Miller's defense the "dumbness defense" and said, " But Mr. Miller is not dumb. Taking payoffs is illegal, and Miller didn't have to go to school to learn that."

When the case went to the jury for a decision, Judge Biggers gave the jurors two separate instructions concerning the entrapment defense. Instruction No. D-17 included the following:

> As used in the law "entrapment" means that law enforcement officials, acting either directly or through an agent, induced or persuaded an otherwise unwilling person to commit an unlawful act. On the other hand, where a person is predisposed to commit an offense, that is, ready and willing to violate the law, the fact that the government officials or their agents merely afforded opportunities for him to do so does not constitute entrapment.
>
> Inducement by law enforcement officials may take many forms including persuasion, fraudulent representations, threats, coercive tactics, harassment, promises of reward, or pleas based on need, sympathy, or friendship. A solicitation, request or approach by law enforcement officials to engage in criminal activity, standing alone is not an inducement. Law enforcement officials are not precluded from utilizing artifice, stealth and stratagems, such as the use of decoys and undercover agents in order to apprehend persons engaged in criminal activities, provided that they merely afford opportunities or facilities for the commission of the offenses by one predisposed or ready to commit them. . . .
>
> In summary then, if you find no evidence that the government induced the defendant to commit the crimes, with which he is charged here, there can be no entrapment. On the other hand, if you find some evidence that the defendant was induced to commit the acts with which he is charged, you must then go on to consider if the defendant was predisposed to commit such acts. Only if you find beyond a reasonable doubt that the defendant was predisposed to commit such acts can you find that the defendant was not a victim of entrapment. However, if the evidence in the case leaves you with a reasonable doubt whether the defendant was predisposed to commit the charged acts then you must find him not guilty.

Instruction No. D-18 contained the following:

> Entrapment occurs when criminal conduct was the product of the creative activity of law enforcement officials or their agents, that is, if they initiate,

incite, induce, persuade or lure an otherwise innocent person to commit a crime and to engage in criminal conduct. If that occurs, the government may not avail itself of the fruits of this instigation. . . .

If you find no evidence that the government agent or the informant directly or indirectly induced Larry D. Miller to violate the law, there can be no entrapment. However, if you find that there is some evidence that the government agent or informant induced Larry D. Miller to commit the crimes charged, the government must prove beyond a reasonable doubt that the inducement was not the cause of the crimes, that is, that the defendant was ready and willing to commit the offenses charged.

To sustain the burden of proof the government must satisfy you that its agent and informant have not seduced an innocent person but that the inducement, which brought about the offenses charged was but another instance of the kind of conduct which Larry D. Miller was prepared to engage in if offered an opportunity.

The jury returned guilty verdicts on all seven counts on April 11, 1988. Miller was the sixth and last supervisor convicted by a jury as a result of Operation Pretense. Given the judge's instructions, the jury must have concluded that the testimony of both Burgess and Chatham and the taped conversations were supported by solid evidence of predisposition. Perhaps the predisposition was supported by an informant who was a vendor or another supervisor cooperating with the investigation based on a plea bargain agreement. After the trial, Hailman said that it had been a very interesting trial that showed a lot about how the supervisor system worked. He said, "I think it is very important that so many citizens from Winston County attended the trial. Because of the problems in Winston County, it was important that the black citizens saw that Miller got a fair trial."

On August 1, 1988, Judge Biggers sentenced Miller to a total of six years in prison and three years' probation upon completion of incarceration. Miller was also ordered to make restitution to Winston County in the amount of $1,051.40. Judge Biggers noted that Miller was the only supervisor charged in the Northern District of Mississippi who had denied his guilt. The judge said, "It's almost an insult to the intelligence of the jury and the judicial system for you to say that you are not guilty. You admitted you took the money, you just said you didn't do anything wrong." The judge went on to say, "If stealing from county taxpayers is doing a good job, then you did a good job."

7. Marion County

Pretense Plus

Located in south-central Mississippi along the Louisiana border, Marion County was named for Frances Marion, a general in the Revolutionary War. Columbia is the county seat and the only city of any size in this county that had a 1990 population of 25,544, the thirty-first largest in the state. The late Chicago Bears running back Walter Payton, the leading rusher in National Football League history, played high school football at Columbia High. While the county could take pride in the accomplishments of native son Walter Payton, one of its elected supervisors' antics in the 1980s proved more than a little embarrassing.

Forty-six-year old Sim Ed Moree, supervisor of Marion County's second district, was arrested on October 8, 1987, and charged with accepting a sawmill in exchange for approving fraudulent invoices and accepting kickbacks on county purchases. When Moree was arrested at his sawmill in Goss, he was serving his second four-year term as supervisor. Moree had won nomination for a third term in the recent Democratic primary and faced no opposition in the upcoming general election. In a five-count indictment, Moree was charged with conspiracy, bribery, and extortion. U.S. Magistrate John R. Countiss III postponed arraignment until October 13 because Moree did not have a lawyer to represent him. He was released on a $5,000 personal recognizance bond. Moree requested a court-appointed lawyer, but Countiss refused, saying that the defendant wasn't poor enough to qualify.

The October 7 indictment charged that in November or December of 1984, Moree agreed to accept from Holiman Equipment Company a schematic drawing of a sawmill and the parts for building the sawmill, with a total value of about $3,000. According to the charges, Moree agreed to approve invoices from Holiman Equipment to Marion County for parts and services that were never provided. During the period from January through April 1985, Holiman Equipment delivered the drawings and parts to Moree and mailed fraudulent invoices for about $4,600 to the county for parts and services never delivered. According to the grand jury indictment, in December 1984 J. H. Holiman Sr. told equipment salesman Pete Dacus to make the drawings for Moree's sawmill, using parts available from Holiman Equipment. Holiman vice president Max Gilbert and Dacus allegedly met with Moree on December 26, 1984, and discussed the sawmill to be provided. Later, Holiman told company parts manager Andy Goolsby that the company was building a sawmill for Moree and instructed him to prepare invoices to Marion County for $3,000 for parts and services that would not be delivered. Moree was also charged with accepting $900 in kickbacks from Davis Chemicals Company from October 1982 to February 1987.

At his October 13 arraignment, Moree pleaded not guilty to all charges. No charges were filed against J. H. Holiman Sr., whose company was cooperating in the investigation. The week before Moree's arrest, Pete Dacus and Max Gilbert had pleaded innocent to Pretense-related charges, and both were cooperating with the investigation. Charges against parts manager Goolsby had already been dropped. Ray Davis of Hattiesburg, who owned Davis Chemicals, had pleaded guilty to Pretense-related charges and was cooperating in the investigation.

At the request of the U.S. Attorney's Office, the charges against Sim Ed Moree were unaccountably dropped in early December 1987. Assistant U.S. Attorney Don Burkhalter would not explain why the charges were dropped, but he did indicate that Moree might be reindicted later. While he was still under indictment, Moree had won the November general election in which he was unopposed; he was scheduled to take the oath of office for his third term in January 1988. However, Moree was unable to take the oath of office on January 4, 1988, with other elected county officials because he had not obtained the surety bond of about $200,000 required by state law. Moree later posted a property bond and was duly sworn into office.

January 4, 1988, was indeed an eventful day for Moree. On that day, Moree met with Southern District highway commissioner Bob Joiner, a defendant in a pending criminal case, and indicated that for $160,000 he could arrange for a substantially reduced sentence. The next day he met with Joiner again and accepted $50,000 in cash; moreover, Joiner promised to deliver another $30,000 in the future. Moree was arrested on January 5, 1988, and charged with obstruction of justice for promising a criminal defendant that he could get him a shorter federal sentence for a payment of $160,000. In an affidavit, FBI Special Agent Jerry D. Marsh stated that he personally monitored the second meeting's conversation electronically and that he observed Moree leaving the meeting with the $50,000. After his arrest, Moree appeared before U.S. Magistrate Countiss, waived a preliminary hearing, and was bound over to the grand jury. He was released on a $25,000 bond.

On January 7, two days after his latest arrest, Moree was reindicted on Pretense-related charges. This six-count indictment charged him with one count of extortion, two counts of conspiracy to commit mail fraud, and three counts of mail fraud. The charges in this indictment involved the sawmill and Moree's dealings with Holiman Equipment. Moree pleaded innocent to these charges on January 8, and U.S. District Judge Tom S. Lee set March 7, 1988, as the trial date for all charges against Moree, who faced up to fifty-five years' imprisonment and $2 million in fines.

Hattiesburg television station WDAM revealed on January 7 that Moree had just met with Commissioner Bob Joiner when he was arrested January 5 at a Columbia motel. Joiner, who was under federal indictment, had pleaded innocent December 17 to eleven counts of extortion, bribery, and tax evasion. Joiner had allegedly extorted more than $238,000 in kickbacks since 1980 from four contractors doing business with the Highway Department.

U.S. Attorney George Phillips indicated that Moree used the fact that the original Pretense-related charges against him had been dropped as a ploy to claim that he could fix the case against Joiner. Phillips said, "By showing his indictment had been dropped, he could say, 'the proof is in the pudding.' " Moree's first indictment on Pretense-related charges had been dismissed because of a technical problem. Jim Dukes of Hattiesburg, one of Joiner's attorneys, said that Moree's upcoming reindictment was common knowledge. According to Dukes, "When Moree's indictment was dropped, it became generally known that the indictment was dismissed for a technical reason. He knew he was going to be reindicted. His attorney [Stephen L. Beach of Jackson] knew it. I knew it." Phillips said that, even though Moree knew that he would be reindicted, he nonetheless set up the highway commissioner to shake him down for $160,000. Moree had told Joiner in late December that he paid $25,000 to unnamed co-conspirators to get the charges against him dropped and that for $160,000, half to be delivered up front, he would get these people to arrange a substantially reduced sentence for Joiner. While he would not name the co-conspirators, Phillips indicated that the U.S. Department of Justice Office of Public Integrity was investigating the involvement of some other people.

In the December meeting, Moree refused Joiner's request to meet with the people who were supposed to be able to accomplish the fix, and Moree instructed Joiner not to tell Dukes about the offer. Nevertheless, Joiner told Dukes, and Dukes contacted the U.S. attorney's office. This led to Joiner's cooperation with the FBI in a sting operation designed to gain evidence against Moree.

On December 31, Moree told Joiner that the co-conspirators had set January 4 as a deadline for Joiner to make the first payment. On January 4, 1988, Joiner and Moree met in a Columbia motel room, where Moree said that his people would agree to accept $80,000 initially and another $80,000 later. The next day, the two met again at the motel, and Moree accepted $50,000 in cash from Joiner, with the remaining $30,000 to be paid in three days. Joiner used money provided by the FBI, and he was wearing a wire that allowed the FBI to monitor and tape the conversations from the motel room next to where the meetings took place. Moree was arrested as he left the motel room, and the money was seized.

At Moree's trial, which ran from March 7 to 12, FBI special agent Jerry King outlined for the jury the events that led to Moree's arrest outside the Columbia motel in January. The co-conspirators were not named in the indictment or the trial. King said that he was unable to find out who the unnamed co-conspirators were. Under cross-examination from defense attorney Stephen Beach, King said, "I never found out—you'll have to ask Mr. Moree." King testified that he did not find any evidence that any judge, U.S. attorney, or defense attorney had been approached to fix Joiner's case or had been threatened in any way. King also testified Moree's brother, Ben, had accompanied Moree to the Western Motel on January 4 and 5 to meet Joiner. Ben told the FBI agent that he was there at his brother's request to perform surveillance and that he had followed Joiner at a distance when the highway commissioner left the motel on January 4.

Bob Joiner testified that Moree had offered help in getting his sentence reduced. Joiner said Moree claimed that for $180,000 he could arrange a three-year sentence with only nine months to a year of actual prison time plus a $25,000 fine if Joiner would plead guilty to the charges. The money was supposed to go to four men who could make the arrangements. Joiner testified that Moree said he had paid $25,000 to two men to get the original Pretense-related charges against him dropped. U.S. Attorney Richard Starrett said that the real reason the original charges were dropped was that the prosecutors had discovered evidence of additional wrongdoing by Moree and wanted to add those charges to the indictment.

Hancock County supervisor Sam Perniciaro, who had been indicted in the Pretense investigation, testified that Moree visited him on December 14, 1987, at his towing service and that they went to the place where wrecked cars were stored behind the building. Moree took off his clothes to show that he wasn't wearing a wire and offered to help Perniciaro avoid a jail term on the charges against him in exchange for $55,500. Perniciaro, who was awaiting sentencing, had reached a plea bargain with the government, resigned from office, and pleaded guilty on November 16, 1987, to one count each of extortion and mail fraud. He turned down Moree's offer and reported it to the attorney for the Hancock County Board of Supervisors. Perniciaro testified, "He said to me, 'All my charges have been dropped, I can get yours dropped too.' I told him that I'd take my chances with the federal government."

The defense called only one witness, Assistant U.S. Attorney Richard Starrett, the prosecutor handling the Pretense-related charges against Moree. He testified that the original Operation Pretense charges against Moree had been dropped in December solely because federal officials had developed additional information and wanted to secure a more extensive indictment. He said he knew of no effort to fix Moree's case and that Moree had been reindicted in January.

More tellingly, however, the tapes containing conversations between Joiner and Moree spoke for themselves. Prior to playing the tapes for the jury, Assistant U.S. Attorney Patricia Bennett told them, "There's not going to be anything for you to guess or speculate about in this case; it's all on tape."

The jury of nine women and three men rendered a guilty verdict against Moree on March 11, 1988, after deliberating for less than two hours. He was found guilty of obstruction of justice and conspiracy to obstruct justice and faced maximum penalties of five years in prison and $50,000 fines on both charges. Moree was freed on a $25,000 bond and ordered to appear before Judge Lee for sentencing on May 20, 1988.

Faced with overwhelming evidence against their client during the trial, defense attorneys claimed that Moree was innocent of obstruction of justice because he didn't have any way to actually influence the outcome of Joiner's case. Attorney Sebastain Moore told the jury, "You're going to have to ask, 'Where's the obstruction? Where's the beef?' " After the trial, one of Moree's attorneys contended that Moree was innocent of obstructing justice and that he simply designed a scheme to get money from Joiner. Stephen Beach said, "Mr. Moree did not contest any of the facts or the proof presented by the government. We feel that Mr. Moree did not act in a proper way or a bad way, but that this was not the proper forum nor the proper charges to try him on."

On April 25, 1988, Moree pleaded guilty to the Pretense-related corruption charges. He had reached an agreement with the government to plead guilty to one count each of mail fraud and extortion, resign from office no later than May 9, and cooperate in the ongoing investigation. Under the agreement, he faced maximum possible penalties of twenty-five years in prison and $500,000 in fines. As a result of the plea bargain, sentencing on both the obstruction of justice and conspiracy conviction and the guilty plea to the Pretense-related charges was delayed to allow Moree to cooperate with the continuing investigation.

In mid-May 1988, district three's John Glen Stringer recommended that the board appoint Sim Ed Moree's wife, Sylvia Moree, to replace her husband as supervisor. At a later meeting of the board of supervisors, district one's Hoy Stringer made a motion, seconded by district five's Lloyd Johnson, that she be appointed to the post. Then Billy Ray McKenzie of district four and the other three supervisors voted for the appointment, which would make Sylvia Moree supervisor of district two until a special election could be held in November. The appointee's paid work experience consisted of several years in the Moree family-owned hardware and sawmill business.

The *Sunday Mirror* published in Columbia ran an editorial pointing out how the appointment left the county open to criticism. A bond of more than $200,000 was required, and Joe Shepard, Sylvia Moree's attorney, said, "It's hard to find a bonding company to write a supervisor's bond these days." He noted, however, that two companies were considering writing Sylvia Moree's bond and that, if those companies refused, she planned to put up property for a personal bond. Sim Ed Moree had been sworn in for his latest term based on a property bond.

Commenting on the appointment, Columbia resident Homer Pope said, "I think it's disgusting really. While there is nothing wrong with an honest man being replaced by his wife, for one to go out under these circumstances, it doesn't look to me like it's right. I haven't found anybody yet that approved of it. The deal with that bunch (the supervisors) is they think they are a law unto themselves."

Sylvia Moree failed to post the required bond and withdrew her name from consideration on June 15. Subsequently, Landis Herrin was appointed by the board of supervisors to complete Sim Ed's term. After approval of a surety bond of $208,135, Herrin took office in late July 1988. He was to serve until the special election scheduled for November 1988.

Moree was sentenced on both cases on May 8, 1989. Judge Lee sentenced him on the Pretense-related charges to five years in prison, with five years' probation upon release from custody, and imposed restitution of $4,084.31 to the county and $120 to the FBI. A special condition of the probation was that Moree not seek or hold public office during the period of the probation. The other charges resulted in a twenty-one-month prison sentence and three years' probation, during which 400 hours of community service were to be performed during the first two years. Seeking or holding public office during this probation was also prohibited. Incarceration was to run consecutively to the sentence imposed for the Pretense-related charges. Moree was ordered to report to federal prison on March 6, 1989.

Moree faced possible fines of $2 million, but the judge did not impose any fines. The 400 hours of community service were imposed instead of fines because the presentence report submitted to Judge Lee indicated that Moree had a negative net worth of $374,216.85 (Moree claimed that it actually was $425,000). At his original arraignment on Pretense-related charges, Moree had requested a court-appointed lawyer. U.S. Magistrate Countiss refused, saying that the defendant was not poor enough to qualify. At sentencing, Judge Lee advised Moree of his right to appeal and that, if he were unable to pay the cost of appeal, he could do so in forma pauperis.

Moree appealed his conviction and sentence related to the obstruction of justice and conspiracy charges to the U.S. Fifth Circuit Court of Appeals. The court of appeals affirmed the conviction but concluded that the district court had erred in applying sentencing guidelines; it vacated the sentence and remanded the case to the district court for sentencing. The U.S. Court of the Southern District of Mississippi then sentenced Moree in absentia to two concurrent sixteen-month terms on the charges. This sentence was appealed to the U.S. Fifth Circuit Court of Appeals. In 1990, the court concluded that the district court had erred in acting as if its action was a reduction in sentence (rather than resentencing) and that the new sentence should not have been imposed without the defendant being present and being allowed to speak. On March 28, 1991, the appeals court vacated the sentence and remanded the case to the district court for resentencing.

On August 8, 1991, Judge Lee resentenced Moree to concurrent sixteen-month terms on the two obstruction of justice charges. The sentence was to be served after completion of the five-year Pretense-related sentence. He was also ordered to complete 400 hours of community service. Moree was out of prison by the summer of 1995; he was killed in a logging accident on September 27, 1995.

In late May 1988, a federal grand jury indicted Larkey Wilburn Broome of Marion County and Donald Frank Gowen of Rankin County on six charges of obstruction of justice, extortion, and making false statements to the FBI. They had allegedly extorted $21,000 from Sim Ed Moree and promised to fix the indictments against him. They were also accused of attempting to extort money from supervisors Sam Perniciaro of Hancock County, Sidney Thompson of Copiah County, and Southern District highway commissioner Bob Joiner by promising to fix their indictments or sentences. In addition, the pair was charged with lying to federal agents by claiming that they had paid money to federal officials to fix a pending federal criminal case, "when in truth and in fact the defendants well knew that no such monies had been paid by them to or exacted from defendants by any such federal officials."

According to one of Moree's attorneys, Stephen Beach III, when the original Pretense charges against Moree were thrown out, Moree was convinced that the payments he had made to Broome and Gowen had influenced that outcome. When he was unable to pay all the $25,000 they had asked for (he paid $21,000), Broome suggested that Moree could make up the difference by convincing Joiner and Perniciaro that he could help them.

At the time of his May 11 arrest, Broome, who was related to Gowen, was out of prison on probation from a 1984 mail fraud conviction. He was arrested in Marion County three days after federal authorities began seeking to revoke his probation based on the new allegations, and he was retained in custody. The two eventually entered into plea agreements with the federal authorities and pleaded guilty to reduced charges.

Larkey pleaded guilty to two counts: obstructing justice in the Sim Ed Moree case and making false statements to the FBI about paying money to federal officials to obstruct justice. He was sentenced to a total of seven and a half years in prison and two years' probation after release from prison; he was also fined $4,000. The newly imposed prison sentence was to run concurrently with that of the sentence that had been revoked when he was arrested. Gowen pleaded guilty to a charge of making false statements to the FBI. He was sentenced to five years' probation and fined $5,000. The probation carried thirteen specific conditions, one of which was that he had to reside in the Jackson County Treatment Center for two months.

8. A Vendor's Trial

Bobby Little Never Busted an Invoice

On November 19, 1987, a grand jury in Oxford indicted North Mississippi Supply Company of Rienzi in Alcorn County and its president, Bobby R. Little. The fifty-two-year-old businessman was a member of a very prominent politically connected family. His father was a former Alcorn County supervisor, and a brother was serving as an Alcorn County supervisor at the time of Little's indictment. Little pleaded not guilty on November 20 to a 310-count indictment charging him and his company with mail fraud, bribery, and conspiracy; his company also pleaded not guilty through an attorney. Little was released on a $50,000 bond. In the 327-page indictment, Little was charged with mail fraud involving a series of transactions with seven former North Mississippi county supervisors. The government alleged bribery of the supervisors in exchange for orders from his company during the period 1974 through June 1987. The charges included 298 counts of mail fraud, 7 counts of conspiracy, and 5 counts of bribery. The mail fraud charges resulted from Little's company mailing allegedly fraudulent invoices to the counties involved.

Because of technical problems associated with the first indictment, Little was reindicted in August 1988 in a superseding indictment on a total of 264 counts involving bribery, mail fraud, aiding and abetting bribery and mail fraud, and conspiracy. The charges carried maximum prison sentences of 1,345 years and fines of $66 million against Little and $132.5 million against his company.

The former supervisors who had allegedly accepted bribes from Little were Bobby Dean Stegall, Grady O. Baker, Theron Baldwin, O. L. Finley, and Talmage M. Nix of Pontotoc County and Leonard G. Faulkner and John A. Cockerham of Monroe County. Assistant U.S. Attorney John Hailman indicated that each of these former supervisors had pleaded guilty to Pretense-related charges and that all of them had agreed to cooperate with the investigation. The seven supervisors were alleged to have been paid kickbacks—Stegall, $3,100 on sixty-two transactions; Baker, $2,505 on thirty-nine transactions; Baldwin, $2,600 on fifty-seven transactions; Finley, $2,100 on fifty-one transactions; Nix, $2,445 on fifty-seven transactions; Faulkner, $1,115 on forty-three transactions; and Cockerham $950 on fifteen transactions.

The indictment, which alleged that the supervisors received secret cash payments in return for doing business with North Mississippi Supply Company, included the following wording: "Defendants would and did conceal the existence of the cash gratuities from the counties by causing the omission of all mention of them on every invoice, purchase order, and other documents relating to the transactions." Testimony of supervisors in Little's September 1988 trial revealed the extent of corruption in county purchasing. Under direct examination, Assistant U.S. Attorney Hailman had Stegall explain how he got started taking payoffs from Little and how long the practice continued.

Q. Do you recall how this began, Mr. Stegall, and how it happened and how you learned that he would do this [make payoffs] or how it got started?

A. Well, I remember the first time I went up [to Little's office, approximately 60 miles from Stegall's district] after I was on the board [of supervisors]—I don't recall exactly the date—but I went up with another supervisor, Mr. (Theron) Baldwin. . . .

Q. All right, so you went up with Mr. Baldwin to see Mr. Little. How did you learn there was going to be cash given to you? What was the first notice you had that this was going to happen?

A. Well, Mr. Baldwin indicated that he would help you out a little, you know.

Q. And based on your dealings as a supervisor, when somebody says they are going to help you out a little, what does that mean?

A. That means they are going to give you some money.

Q. And how long did that practice of cash payoffs to you continue, Mr. Stegall?

A. The whole time I was in office, each—everything that I purchased.

J. P. Coleman, former governor of Mississippi and former justice of the U.S. Fifth Circuit Court of Appeals, was one of Little's attorneys. The distinguished politician and judge found himself arguing that his client had not helped violate a statute he had signed into law as governor. The law required that employees of the state or its agencies receiving gratuities from those doing business with the state or a state agency give the money to their employer. During the direct examination of Finley, Coleman addressed the court:

> Your Honor, may I point out—I'm hoarse. I'm trying to talk so the jury can't hear. This statute cited in this Indictment, it turns out, I had forgotten all about it. In the past when I was Governor of Mississippi in 1958 I of course signed it into law in May of 1958. I didn't know anything about it until this case came up. The whole point, though, is that the statute does not prohibit a vendor from making a gratuity. It simply says if he makes one that those who receive it must turn it over to the county.

The prosecution's argument was that the payments were bribes, not gratuities that were to be returned to the county.

In his closing remarks to the jury, Hailman told the jurors how the illegal conspiracies worked and their devastating effects.

> Now a conspiracy, as the judge will tell you, is an agreement, or it's like a plan or a scheme. Now it's usually, as Mr. Stegall told you, one of the best descriptions I have ever heard by a witness, is it's an unspoken agreement. Because a conspiracy is a criminal contract, you don't write it down. Usually you don't even talk about it. You simply do it. Usually, in most bribery cases you will see the first transaction is simply the first of giving a bribe, walking up, and the other person is standing there, he puts it in his pocket. After that he doesn't need to tell him anything. He knows the next time that man comes he's going to put that money in his pocket. It's like giving a dog a bone. You do it a few times, next time you come that dog expects a bone. That's what Mr. Little was doing to these supervisors. He was rewarding their behavior in buying from him, and he was encouraging their behavior in the future to buy from him again. That's what's corrupt about it. That's the essence and nature of the scheme, and it's the essence and nature of conspiracy. That's what you have here.
>
> Of course, his scheme didn't work without supervisors willing to be corrupted. Now what they did was they took the money, which should have gone to the county. It should have been a discount that went to the county. The county didn't ever get five percent off. The county every time paid the full price. The county should have had a great savings through all these cases. And if you multiply this times how many times that happens and all these other items like heavy equipment or motor graders or all the other things

you heard these men plead guilty to taking bribes on, you multiply that by every county in the state and every supervisor in every county, you got a tremendous amount of money. Maybe we wouldn't be in such bad shape if we could get this problem cleaned up.

The trial ran for four days in U.S. District Court Judge Glen Davidson's court. All seven supervisors named in the charges testified that Little had given them payoffs. On September 15, 1988, after only five hours of deliberations, a federal jury in Oxford found Little and his company guilty of 241 counts of mail fraud, bribery, and conspiracy. Twenty-three counts of the superseding indictment were dismissed due to either insufficient evidence to support the charges or technical errors.

On January 9, 1989, Little was sentenced by Judge Davidson to six years in prison. He was also ordered to pay a $25,000 fine. North Mississippi Supply Company was ordered to pay concurrent $50,000 fines on all counts. Notice of appeal was filed, and the defendant remained free on bond.

Little and his attorneys appealed the case to the U.S. Fifth Circuit Court of Appeals. In a brief filed with the court, U.S. Attorney Robert Q. Whitwell and Assistant U.S. Attorney Hailman summarized the essence of the case against Little very succinctly.

Summary of Argument

I. County supervisors who receive and conceal secret cash kickbacks from suppliers on county contracts defraud their counties of both the amount of the cash, which under the applicable Mississippi statute they had to turn over to their counties, as well as economic information, which still constitutes "property" after the Supreme Court's decisions in *McNally* and *Carpenter*, *infra*. Therefore the appellant-suppliers below were properly convicted of aiding and abetting those frauds.

II. Under 18 U.S.C. 666 it was an offense to give secret, cash kickbacks to county officials in connection with county purchases where the evidence showed the payoffs constituted bribes intended either to reward the officials for past purchases or to influence them favorably to make future purchases from appellant-suppliers, and the mere fact that the corrupt supervisors claimed they were not influenced thereby did not preclude the jury from concluding that defendants, who did not testify, intended to reward and influence the public officials.

In the twenty-one-page argument that followed, Hailman cited case decisions and statutory law to strongly buttress two points:

I. Appellants defrauded two Mississippi counties by making secret cash payoffs to seven powerful county officials in connection with county purchases.

II. Appellants committed bribery in violation of 18 U.S.C. Section 662(a) (2) by making secret cash payoffs to officials of counties receiving federal funds with intent to influence or reward those officials either for having made purchases from appellants in the past or to influence them to continue making such purchases in the future.

In late November 1989, the court of appeals affirmed the district court's judgment, stating:

Little also argues that the federal bribery statute should not apply in this case absent proof that the corruption cost would have to be replaced by federal funds. That is, Section 666 applies only where the agency involved receives benefits in excess of $10,000 under a Federal program" in any given year. But this Court in *U.S. v. Westmoreland* rejected that argument in another prosecution under "Operation Pretense." There the Court held that if the agency received $10,000 in any given year, then the agents were subject to Section 666. There is no requirement that the particular program be the recipient of the federal funds. . . .

This Circuit's construction of *McNally* defines "property" to include economic information, such as that denied Pontotoc and Monroe counties in this case. Further, future convictions under Section 1341 will no longer require a substantive "property" loss, so we see no reason to change our Circuit precedent to require one for this case alone. For these reasons and those stated above, Little's conviction is in all things AFFIRMED.

J. P. Coleman's petition for a hearing before the U.S. Supreme Court during its October 1989 term was unsuccessful. Subsequently, Little reported to the Federal Corrections Institute, Pensacola, Florida, on February 20, 1990.

After several postconviction motions, the judge ordered that the period of incarceration be reduced to the time Little had already served, approximately twenty-one months. Prior to this order, Little had been transferred to a Community Correction Center in Tupelo, Mississippi, and he was permitted to work in Corinth during the day. In January 1994, Little had still paid only $3,000 of the $25,000 fine.

Part II.

Related Matters

9. The Auditors

Ray Mabus was elected state auditor in 1984, and he was serving in that office when Operation Pretense broke in February 1987. Under Mabus, the Department of Audit had been cooperating with the FBI investigation for more than two years before any indictments were handed down. When the first indictments were made public on February 12, 1987, Department of Audit personnel were in counties across the state copying public records that might be needed in the investigation. Before Mabus became its head, the Department of Audit had long been politicized and was simply not a professional audit organization. The state auditor is an elected official in Mississippi, and the office of state auditor is potentially one of considerable power. The reform-minded Mabus used the position as a springboard to the governor's office in 1988. Mabus's accomplishments as state auditor and governor will forever be linked with Operation Pretense, and rightly so.

Syndicated columnist Bill Minor described some of the pre-Mabus problems in the Department of Audit in a July 1983 column. Minor claimed that seventy-three year-old Hamp King, who had held the office unchallenged for twenty years, was attempting to anoint longtime associate Mason Shelby as his successor. Citing a "good ole boy" system that handed down the position from one insider to another, Minor noted that only one outsider had been elected state auditor in the past forty years. Before a constitutional amendment was adopted in the 1960s to allow the auditor to succeed himself or herself, an auditor could serve only one four-year term. The last elected noninsider was Boyd Golding, who had served from 1960 to 1964. King had been elected five times to four-year terms, beginning in 1964. Minor reported that Shelby had been picked by a committee of the Department of Audit as their candidate. Supposedly, at a two-day meeting of department personnel at a Biloxi hotel in December 1982, a strategy had been worked out to elect Shelby. The strategy was said to include a suggestion that each employee contribute 2 percent of his or her salary for the campaign. Shelby ran against Ray Mabus and Murray Cain, a former radio station operator and a state employee during former governor Bill Finch's administration.

Minor noted that nobody had ever accused the old-school politician King of being dishonest. However, he went on to write, "but being naive is quite another matter, and being cozy with county politicians subject to close scrutiny is still another. Citizen delegations who came to King to report suspicions of chicanery on the part of county officeholders often found that before they reached home, word of their visit to King had already gotten back to the county officials."

During the 1983 campaign for auditor, Cain and Mabus attacked Shelby for some of the antiquated procedures used by the Department of Audit and its "good ole boy manner" of dealing with malfunctioning county governments. Shelby remained silent while King sent a six-page, single-spaced letter to Mabus with copies to newspapers and journalists throughout the state. The letter that was designed to deny Mabus's charges of foot-dragging in conducting county audits and in collecting misappropriated funds actually raised more questions than it answered. King maintained that audits were only one year behind, whereas Mabus had claimed that they were two to four years behind. In fact, six counties had recently lost their bond ratings because of the absence of current fiscal information. The legislature had not funded enough audit positions, and some legislators were not bothered by the situation since they were protective of county politicians. Moreover, the legislature had passed a bill in the early 1970s during Bill Waller's administration to bring the state auditors under legislative control. Governor Waller wisely vetoed that legislation.

King called on the legislative Performance Evaluation and Expenditure Review Committee (PEER) to conduct an investigation to prove how wrong Mabus was about conditions in the Department of Audit. Entitled "A Management and Operational Review of the Mississippi Department of Audit," the PEER report, which was not issued until December 1983, after Mabus had been elected state auditor, showed that the Department of Audit's operations were even more sloppy and further behind than Mabus had said.

The summary of the PEER report notes:

> The Department of Audit is responsible for annually post-auditing a total of 340 governmental entities. To perform these audits for FY 1982, the department currently has a staff of 122 auditing accountants located throughout the state and has received $5,285,987 in general and special funds.
>
> PEER found that the department's systems and procedures for management and quality control are inadequate to promote efficient and effective operation; consequently, the department is not current in conducting audits

of entities under its purview. As of September 15, 1983, only 44 (12.9%) of the
340 entities had been audited every year through FY 1982. The department is
delinquent for 581 fiscal audit years. Also, audit fee limitations set by the
statute, and ineffective billing and collecting procedures, deprive the department of the timely use of non-state, local funds. Finally, the department is
not consistent in complying with generally accepted audit standards.

The report went on to recommend statutory, organizational, and proce-
dural changes to improve the efficiency and effectiveness of the department.
It also recommended that the department's annual general fund appropriation be reduced by approximately $1 million.

Ray Mabus, who holds degrees from the University of Mississippi, Johns
Hopkins, and Harvard, got his start as one of the bright young members of
Governor William Winter's staff who were labeled "The Boys of Spring."
While working on a project for Governor Winter in 1982, Mabus requested
the last three audit reports on Hinds County. The Department of Audit
sent him the three reports, the latest of which was for 1977. Thinking that
there had been a mistake, Mabus contacted the Department of Audit and
reiterated that he wanted copies of the audit reports for the last three years.
He was informed that the 1977 report was the latest and that all audits were
running five years behind. At that time, the politically ambitious Mabus
was considering seeking political office for the first time. Noting that there
was an obvious problem with the Department of Audit, he researched the
laws under which it operated and found that state auditor was a powerful
position.

When Mabus took office as state auditor, he found the Department of
Audit in total disarray. It was hundreds of fiscal years behind in audits of
state agencies, and there was no filing system. The first day on the job he
found a shoebox in his office containing checks for $330,000 that repre-
sented payments from counties, cities, and state agencies for audit services.
Mabus convinced the legislature to allow him to contract with CPA firms
to perform audits, thereby enabling the Department of Audit to catch up
on over 500 fiscal years of required audits within two years.

Early in his administration, Mabus discovered that the condition of accounting records in some counties was such that the auditors would have
to construct the accounting records before audits could be performed.
Counties found it less costly to pay the Department of Audit $25 a day for
audit time than to maintain current accounting records. When auditors
attempted to construct accounting records five years after the fact from

source documents filed in haphazard fashion, they often found essential records missing. Little had ever been done to correct this situation, but Mabus understood that not keeping records was a means of preventing fraud detection. He took some actions that very quickly improved accounting at the county level. For example, he required the counties to keep current accounting records, and he began charging $100 per day for audit time, although it actually cost $200 per day to keep an auditor in the field. Mabus also appointed the first official head of an enhanced investigative division within the auditor's office.

In a speech to the Mississippi Association of Supervisors, Mabus informed supervisors that he intended to enforce the law strictly and that he would not allow deviations from purchasing laws, graveling private driveways, installing county-owned culverts on private property, or opening graves with county labor and equipment. That sent shockwaves through the supervisors' ranks. But Mabus didn't just threaten supervisors, he reached out to them in two very important ways. He established a technical assistance unit within the Department of Audit, and he visited the board of supervisors of each of the 82 counties. The technical assistance unit's charge was to provide advice on legal and accounting matters before the fact, as questions arose in any county or other unit of state government. Mabus's visits with the supervisors were designed to deal with potential problems beforehand, if at all possible, and to communicate both what state law actually required and what his expectations were as state auditor.

The public had been registering complaints about known and suspected corruption of public officials with the state auditor's office for years, but usually little came of these complaints. Mabus facilitated such complaints by establishing a hotline to the Department of Audit, and complaints poured in. Complaints about county supervisors were many and varied. Among the more frequent complaints were graveling private driveways, digging graves, misusing county-owned culverts, busting invoices, paying people who did no work, using county equipment and labor on private property, extorting payments from contractors, allowing private use of county vehicles and gasoline, dealing with companies owned by county officials, accepting bids improperly for products and services, favoring individuals and companies on taxes, writing specifications on bid invitations so that only one company could qualify, giving away county funds to charity, giving county-owned materials to family members, and appropriating county-owned materials for personal use. One person actually complained that a supervisor had refused to put a driveway on his private property even though the county had already built a road on the complainant's private property.

Early in his tenure as state auditor, Mabus began cooperating with the FBI in the Pretense investigation. This required secrecy as the FBI accumulated allegations of wrongdoing and operated its sting. The federal prosecutors and the FBI were hesitant to bring the Department of Audit into the investigation because of the department's reputation for being cozy with county politicians. It is doubtful that the Department of Audit would have been included in the investigation if Mabus had not been elected state auditor. Complaints against county supervisors became a politically sensitive issue for Mabus, who had been elected on a reform platform. Operation Pretense took a long time, and the first indictments and arrest did not take place until three years after Mabus took office. Some who had complained to the Department of Audit accused Mabus of being just like old-line politicians and not acting on complaints. But by the time Pretense had run its course, several supervisors against whom complaints had been registered with the auditor's office had been convicted of various crimes as the result of Pretense.

Bill Minor predicted in a September 1984 article that the thirty-six-year-old Mabus would run for governor as early as 1987. In retrospect, parts of that column stand out:

Taking over one of the most antiquated bureaucracies in state government, Mabus has toppled some of the sacred cows in the state, mainly the illegal graveling of private roads and driveways which county supervisors have done as a political favor to constituents since year one. . . .

. . . When he first clamped down on the promiscuous use of gravel, the howl could be heard from the cupola of every courthouse in the state, and it appeared the Legislature would teach Mabus a lesson—that he couldn't mess with the spoils system. A remarkable thing happened: Lawmakers saw public sentiment shift dramatically in favor of what Mabus was doing, and they backed off.

Now many county supervisors are grudgingly admitting that Mabus actually relieved them of a big headache, and the savings thus far in graveling and labor alone in eight months run into the millions of dollars.

When the first Pretense-related indictments were announced in Jackson on February 12, 1987, by Roger T. Castonguay, FBI special agent in charge for Mississippi, he said that State Auditor Mabus had cooperated throughout the investigation working with agents in "sensitive" areas involved in the investigation and assisting in other areas. Later that day, Mabus issued a statement saying that the indictments pointed out a continued need for the legislature to pass stronger laws affecting spending of tax dollars by county government. He added, "Over the last two years, we have stayed in close contact with the federal officials working on the case. We have provided them with information during the course of the investigation, and we will continue to cooperate with them as the case progresses." Mabus went on to say that the findings demanded a quick response by the legislature to require all counties to adopt the unit system of government; require that all counties use a full-time professional administrator to manage the financial, purchasing, and administrative affairs of the county; and require improved record-keeping by the counties. Mabus also recommended legislation that would prohibit state officials convicted of a federal crime from ever holding public office and bar vendors convicted of crimes from doing business with state and local governments. He also advocated establishing a white-collar crime unit within the state attorney general's office. Mabus had taken these positions during his tenure as auditor, and he would stress them again in his soon-to-be-announced campaign for governor.

Prior to February 1987, only Ray Mabus and Louisa Dixon, director of the Investigative Audit Division of the Department of Audit, were aware of the details of the statewide scope of the FBI investigation. The investigation had taken more than two years, and "leaks" were always a possibility. In June 1987, Dixon announced that her division was putting new investigations on hold to assist in Operation Pretense. She said, "We've had some audits before that were very complicated, but I think this is the most far-reaching effort." While declining to discuss specifics of the auditors' work with the FBI, she noted, "There are a number of matters which the state auditor's office looks into in the course of audits that may well be prosecuted in federal court. It is possible and certainly probable, that if any of our investigators uncovers anything that could be brought to federal court, we will." The Department of Audit's work in the investigation mainly involved securing needed documentary evidence related to specific purchases, and much of it was done after the undercover sting was completed.

As detailed in chapter 2, in early June 1987 the importance of the Department of Audit's role in Pretense had become very evident in the trial of first-term Perry County supervisor Trudie Westmoreland. In the first Pretense-related trial, U.S. District Judge Tom S. Lee allowed the prosecution to present testimony about an investigative audit that the Department of

Audit was in the process of conducting in relation to funds collected by Westmoreland while she was justice court judge. The auditor's testimony allowed the prosecution to establish the fact that Trudie Westmoreland was predisposed to engage in corrupt practices. Without the investigative auditor's testimony, the prosecution's task of convincing the jury that Westmoreland was predisposed to commit crimes would have been much more difficult. Westmoreland's defense attorney, Alvin Binder, indicated that he thought the defense was going well until Shelia Patterson said that the state auditor's office was not through checking into Westmoreland's financial dealings as a justice court judge. Binder said that Patterson's testimony was "devastating" and that "it's hard to overcome that sort of testimony."

It is difficult to overstate the effect of Trudie Westmoreland's conviction on the subsequent developments surrounding Operation Pretense. The decision was appealed to the U.S. Fifth District Court of Appeals, which sustained the verdict; then it was appealed to the U.S. Supreme Court, which refused to hear the case. However, long before the U.S. Supreme Court closed the book on the case in October 1988, its impact on other Operation Pretense cases had been established. When other indicted supervisors and their attorneys learned that a Mississippi jury would convict a first-term female supervisor based on the type of evidence developed by the FBI's sting and that federal judges would impose long prison sentences, plea bargains became very attractive. The investigative auditor's testimony was crucial to this entire set of events. Overall, the Department of Audit under Ray Mabus played a relatively small but critical role in the Pretense investigations and resulting prosecutions.

On February 16, 1987, Ray Mabus announced that he would be a candidate for governor in the upcoming Democratic primary. With Operation Pretense unfolding daily as the August election approached, Mabus's position on reform in state and local government resonated with voters throughout the state.

In a July 1987 syndicated column about the race for governor, Sid Salter wrote that a yet-unmeasured backlash against Mabus had evolved from the Pretense scandal. He claimed the scandal had sent a goodly number of the courthouse gang into active opposition. Salter wrote that, for good or evil, the aftershocks of Pretense had cost Mabus several percentage points. In the August Democratic primary, Mabus led runner-up Mike Sturdivant, a wealthy planter and motel chain owner, by 170,000 votes. Bill Minor noted that as state auditor Mabus had tightened the reins on the politically powerful county officials. The conventional wisdom had held that if Mabus should ever run for governor, the county courthouses would "fix his wagon." Minor noted that the time for "wagon fixing" had come in the August 4 primary and that Mabus seemed to come through it nicely. Minor attributed Mabus's showing to the fact that voters liked anticorruption politics. He noted that during the last three weeks of the campaign, Mabus's television spots had emphasized corruption with a "stop the stealing" pitch.

After Mabus had been elected and sworn in as governor, former undercover agent Jerry King put another slant on the subject. King claimed that supervisors actually wanted Mabus to be elected governor. He said, "Every day I dealt with the supervisors they would bring up Mabus' name. They'd say, 'We got to get him elected governor and get him out of the state auditor's office.'" Transcripts of King's recorded conversations with supervisors strongly support what King said. Supervisors simply detested Mabus as state auditor.

In late August, Mabus registered 65 percent of the vote in the Democratic run-off election. This reversed a trend in which leaders in the first Democratic primary for governor had regularly been defeated in run-offs. Mabus defeated the Republican nominee, Tupelo businessman Jack Reed, in the November general election by a 53 to 47 percent margin. In a December 1987 column, Sid Salter captured the change in Mississippi's political landscape and the parts played by Ray Mabus and Operation Pretense:

> Few years have marked greater political upheaval and change in Mississippi than did 1987. . . . Not since Reconstruction have more widespread abuses of public political power been exposed than during this year. What began as a little-known investigation, code named "Pretense" snowballed to become a household word that struck fear in the hearts of one of the state's most exclusive clubs—county supervisors. "Pretense" changed, perhaps forever, the way the average Mississippian perceived political power. Suddenly, the previously untouchable became fair game for federal investigators. Arguably, the exposure of public corruption can be credited to the phenomenal success enjoyed by State Auditor Ray Mabus in his quest for the Governor's Mansion. In 1988, the Mississippi Legislature will likely mandate at least a modified county unit system on a statewide basis. "Pretense" indictments will continue as the corruption investigation widens. . . . In matters dealing with public corruption, Mabus will be able to call his own tune among the lawmakers.

Ray Mabus was sworn in as Mississippi's forty-ninth governor on January 12, 1988. As governor, Mabus continued his crusade against corruption in county government by pushing for and eventually getting a unit bill through the legislature. This effort was indeed helped by the steady flow of Pretense-related indictments in 1988, but it wasn't as easy for Mabus to call the tune as Salter had expected. As reflected in chapter 10, the unit and central purchasing legislation that became law in 1988, while representing significant progress, left much to be desired.

Pete Johnson, elected state auditor in the fall of 1987, succeeded Mabus on January 7, 1988. Johnson was from a family that had already produced two Mississippi governors. Paul B. Johnson was his grandfather, and Paul B. Johnson Jr. was his uncle. Pete Johnson proved to be politically ambitious himself.

Early in Johnson's term, he seemed to have picked up where Mabus left off in enforcing the law and rooting out corruption in county government. In late March, the Department of Audit sent out letters to boards of supervisors in nine counties advising supervisors to stop graveling private driveways and roads or collect fees for the work. According to Donald O'Cain, chief of the audit department's investigative division, "This is our first step toward bringing this to their attention—more or less putting them on notice. We are hoping we will get results on this. I mean we are being nice to them." He noted that the letters had resulted from complaints in some counties and from some supervisors admitting that they were using county equipment to work on private driveways and roads. The nine counties involved were Attala, Covington, Lincoln, Madison, Marshall, Neshoba, Simpson, Wayne, and Winston. The president of the Madison County Board of Supervisors, J. S. Harris, said that he was not aware of any complaints in his county. He went on to add, "I can tell you what I did when Mr. Mabus was elected auditor and announced no gravel on private driveways—I quit [doing the work]."

In mid-April, Johnson issued a letter to the Rankin County Board of Supervisors demanding that they repay $115,059.62 for expenditures that had been deemed to be in violation of the state purchasing laws. In early May, Johnson seemed to have changed his approach. He announced that except for the most blatant cases, he would stop asking public officials to repay public funds that had been spent illegally until legal questions surrounding the state purchasing laws had been resolved. All five of Rankin County's supervisors had recently been indicted on charges of violating the state purchasing laws. The supervisors maintained that the purchasing violations were merely technical errors and did not involve their own personal gain.

The problem with Johnson's new stance was captured in an editorial that appeared in the *Meridian Star* on May 7, 1988: "The course the state auditor has decided to follow, though based on legitimate concerns, is not a good one. The court process is simply too lengthy. Mr. Johnson should pursue the misspent money, then comply with the courts when—and if—they rule on his concerns. Up to now he has taken a tough stance on corruption by public officials. This is not the time to weaken."

When he became governor, Ray Mabus immediately began to push for legislation to mandate the unit system for all counties. He strongly believed the unit system, which involves central management and better control over purchasing and building and maintaining roads, would help combat the corruption, mismanagement, and inefficiencies that he had become concerned about as the results of Pretense and his term as state auditor. Mississippi's lurching movements toward the unit system are chronicled in chapter 10.

Pete Johnson's role as state auditor in the unit system saga was controversial. He suggested at the May 1988 Mississippi Association of Supervisors convention that supervisors voluntarily adopt central purchasing systems for their counties. Twenty-one counties had followed his suggestion by mid-July, when a special session of the legislature was considering unit legislation. At that time, Johnson said twenty-five other counties had some form of central purchasing. Johnson denied that his call for voluntary central purchasing systems was designed to blunt Mabus's call for a more complete unit system. Of course, the major problem with Johnson's suggestion was that central purchasing would be voluntary and could be changed at any time by a board of supervisors.

While the special session was considering unit legislation, Johnson furnished a letter at Senator Ollie Mohamed's request estimating the total cost of statewide conversion to the unit system at $36.1 million. Called on to defend his estimate before a House committee, Johnson called it a "worst-case scenario." When asked about the details of his projections, it became obvious that the cost projections were considerably overstated.

A modified unit bill finally passed the legislature and was signed into law by Governor Mabus. It mandated central purchasing and called for a county-by-county referendum to be held in November on whether to adopt the unit system for road building and maintenance and other county activities. The bill also allowed supervisors to develop estimates of costs associated with transition to the unit system. The estimates could be submitted to the state auditor for his certification. In September, Johnson and other

Department of Audit personnel met with boards of supervisors' presidents and chancery clerks to discuss the format and procedures to be used in developing the cost estimates. By September 25, the state auditor had received cost estimates from forty-seven of eighty-two counties. The estimates ranged from $500 to $1.48 million, and these figures did not include any expected savings from administrative changes. Johnson said he would verify each county's estimate.

In the heat of the campaign for and against the unit system, Johnson issued a statement saying the unit system was not needed to address corruption in county purchasing. Johnson called for a "cessation of hostilities" in the debate between Mabus and county officials about the upcoming referendum: "The Legislature did an excellent job of providing safeguards for county purchasing." Johnson's statement disputed comments by federal officials who had been involved in Operation Pretense as well as by state officials who had prosecuted corruption in county government. Although Johnson described himself as a supporter of the unit system, he would not give a "yes or no answer" as to whether he supported the question on the November ballot. Johnson said, "To say that the unit system is good for everybody is like saying that ice cream is good for everybody."

In mid-October, Johnson released figures that estimated the cost to convert fifty-three counties then operating on the beat system to the unit system at $19.5 million. The figures did not include any estimated cost savings. Johnson said, "The problem we're having is documenting them. We don't have a constant we can apply. The savings will vary relative to how inefficiently they're operating now." The Department of Audit had pared down the counties' estimates by eliminating costs associated with central purchasing, which was required by the law even if the unit system was defeated by the voters. Mabus immediately challenged the numbers in a statement released from his office. He said, "At worst they contribute generously to a campaign of disinformation and distortion designed to discourage voters from supporting the unit system on November 8." He added that Johnson's figures "don't pass the straight face test."

The *Meridian Star* summed up what was happening as follows in another editorial: "State Auditor Pete Johnson, while saying that he favors the proposed changeover, is acting strangely like a man who is attempting to shoot it down. Voters have serious cause to wonder about this fellow."

In the November 8, 1988 referendum, forty-six of the state's eighty-two counties voted for the unit system. According to the law, these counties had to be operating under the unit system by October 1, 1989. The law gave the state auditor the responsibility for checking on compliance and the authority to cause state funds to be withheld from counties that were not in compliance. As the deadline approached for full implementation, Johnson sent a message to supervisors in unit counties:, "We are hearing widespread reports that are disturbing us in that a number of supervisors are saying they are going to continue to operate as they have. It would not surprise me if one or more counties tested our resolve. We don't want to be put to the test, but if they don't comply with the law, I will shut their money off so quick it will make their heads swim."

Johnson was correct about being tested. As outlined in chapter 10, the Tallahatchie County Board of Supervisors balked at fully implementing the unit system, and the Department of Audit made the moves necessary to shut off state funds. The action showed the state auditor's resolve and quickly brought the county into line. No doubt it prevented future problems, as supervisors saw that the Department of Audit would enforce the law.

The entire time he was state auditor, Pete Johnson had his eye on the governor's mansion. He ran against Fordice in the 1991 Republican primary and lost. Surely, his political ambition explains some of the positions he took as auditor. He lived in the shadow of Operation Pretense and Mabus's accomplishments as state auditor. He had to distance himself from Mabus, make his own mark, and establish a reputation in a way that he thought would benefit him politically. His strategy did not work, and he was succeeded as state auditor in 1992 by Steve Patterson, who won election as a Democrat. Patterson had served as an aid to former Governors William Winter and Bill Allain and former U.S. Senator John C. Stennis and had chaired the Mississippi Democratic Party from 1984 to 1987.

During Patterson's first term, he appeared to be following in the wake of the reforms that flowed form Operation Pretense and the efforts of Ray Mabus, who lost the governorship to Republican Kirk Fordice in 1991. Patterson often got his name in the newspapers by making demands on public officials and threatening to hold college presidents personally responsible for missing equipment. He announced that he was going to run for reelection shortly after releasing a report on a performance audit of state government in February 1995. The $500,000 audit was a joint effort of Peat Marwick consultants and members of the Department of Audit's newly formed performance audit staff. Patterson claimed that it contained recommendations that could save the state $650 million by the year 2000. The performance audit report was very critical of the operations of some state agencies, and it was attacked by officials of those agencies. Neither the Republican governor nor the legislature, which was controlled by Democrats, paid much attention to the report, which contained many excellent recommendations for improving state government.

In late July 1996, Patterson's career as state auditor began to unravel. Danny Banks, who headed the Department of Audit's investigative audit unit from 1992 until January 1996, was indicted on state charges that he embezzled $102,412 from the Mississippi Association of Chiefs of Police. Banks, a former Itta Bena police chief, had left the Department of Audit after being appointed sheriff of Carroll County. He was a lifetime member of the Mississippi Association of Chiefs of Police and had begun a term as secretary-treasurer in April 1995. While investigating Banks, the attorney general's office learned that Steve Patterson had used a forged letter to avoid paying taxes when he purchased a license plate for a personal vehicle in 1995.

Ryan Hood, Patterson's opponent in the 1995 general election, raised the car tag issue during the campaign when he charged that Department of Audit investigators placed investigative tags issued to the Department of Audit on their personal vehicles. The Department of Audit and the State Tax Commission believed that using investigative tags on personal vehicles during investigations was legal if the investigators had also purchased a proper tag for their personal vehicle. The Department of Audit did not own vehicles. The practice of using "undercover" tags during investigations went back to Mabus's days as state auditor when he requested the plates so that investigators could not be traced. When Hood's charges came to light, Deputy Tax Commissioner Lester Herrington said, "The tags can't be placed on vehicles that don't belong to the agency. Even though the tags may be properly used for investigative work, there is not a provision for it under current regulations." The Tax Commission asked the Department of Audit to return sixty-two car tags.

During February 1995, Patterson paid $238 for a new tag for his 1988 Range Rover. He also submitted a letter and an affidavit to Hinds County tax collector Glenn Pepper stating that the vehicle "was not operated on the streets or highways of this state" since its old license plate expired at the end of October 1993. Under state law, owners are not required to pay taxes on vehicles that do not travel public roads. When the issue came to light, Patterson claimed the vehicle had been used by Banks in undercover work and that a Department of Audit registered license plate had been used on it. In early December 1994, Patterson's wife, Debbie, had been involved in an accident while driving the Range Rover; it bore a Department of Audit tag at the time. Apparently, it took until late February 1995 to get the vehicle repaired. When questions arose concerning the Range Rover's tag, Patterson paid $733 that included back taxes and penalties. But the investigation of Banks revealed that the letter that accompanied Patterson's February affidavit was a forgery. The letter, which was on Gatco Fire Apparatus stationery and purportedly signed by its president, Charles Gatlin, stated that the Range Rover had remained at the Greenwood business for eighteen months awaiting parts.

By August 1996, Patterson was being investigated by the state attorney general, the state highway patrol, and the FBI. The investigations involved the car tag caper and his dealings with Banks, including a trip to Colorado with Banks that was apparently financed by embezzled funds. Also under investigation were contributions Banks had made to Patterson's 1991 campaign and Patterson's possibly profiting from his former business partner Randall F. Aldridge's illegal dealings with the Federal Home Administration. In mid-August 1996, Attorney General Mike Moore said that he would present the tag matter to the Hinds County grand jury scheduled to meet in early October.

Patterson put on a happy face. At an August 19 meeting of the Jackson Rotary Club, he downplayed his problems and emphasized the accomplishments of the Department of Audit under his leadership. He was especially proud of the performance audit and its recommendations and indicated that he wanted such an audit because he wanted to serve as governor. He also vowed to remain in his position saying, "I'm going to continue being an aggressive state auditor." The happy face and grandiose plans did not last long. On October 12, the day investigators from the state attorney general's office were scheduled to appear before the Hinds County grand jury to seek a felony indictment against him, Patterson announced that he would resign from office and plead guilty to a misdemeanor charge related to his attempt to avoid paying taxes on a motor vehicle. Patterson issued a statement saying, "Much controversy has plagued me, my family and my administration concerning my car tags. Today I am hopefully putting an end to this controversy." He also submitted a one-sentence letter to Governor Fordice that read, "With this letter I am rendering my resignation as state auditor, effective November 1, 1996, at 5:00 P.M."

Patterson pleaded guilty to the misdemeanor charge before Hinds County judge William Barnett October 18, 1996. The judge imposed a fine of $1,020, twice the amount of taxes owed, but gave Patterson credit for

$506 that he had paid for renewing the license plates. Interest and penalties had raised the total to $733 by the time Patterson had paid the taxes in the fall of 1995.

Patterson became the first statewide elected official to resign in modern Mississippi history. So ended a sorry episode in the history of the Department of Audit. However, Steve Patterson made at least one contribution that was very positive and continuing. He gained legislative approval to conduct performance audits of state agencies and to make recommendations designed to improve efficiency and effectiveness of operations. Prior to this approval, the Department of Audit had conducted only financial and compliance audits designed to make sure that the accounting was proper and that laws and regulations had been adhered to. Performance auditing has a rich history that has proven its value, and the state stands to reap continuing benefits from the process in the years to come.

Governor Fordice appointed Republican state representative Phil Bryant of Brandon to complete the remaining three years of Patterson's term. Bryant pledged that he would dig up wasteful spending and pursue wrongdoing "without regard to political party, position or association. Our standard will be a total commitment to honesty." Fordice said he had sought someone with "absolute honesty and integrity and hopefully a background in investigations. Phil Bryant comes close to being the ideal candidate for this job." Bryant had fifteen years' experience as an arson investigator with a private firm, and he had served in the Hinds County Sheriff's Department as a patrol officer, as an investigator, and as chief of detectives. The appointment won praise from both Democrats and Republicans. Bryant was elected to a four-year term as state auditor in the fall of 1999. His performance in the office through the summer of 2001 can be characterized as reassuring and without controversy.

10. The Unit System

Slow Progress

Richard S. Childs was quoted in the Brookings Institution's 1932 *Report on a Survey of the Organization and Administration of State and County Government in Mississippi* as follows:

> The county is of all units of government the most unprogressive and corrupt, the most neglected by citizens, press, and reformers. It is the very citadel of political bossism. Reform waves and improvements in governmental structure have made machine rule precarious in cities, and state governments are the scenes of vast renovations, but county government is in structure as it was in the stage-coach days when it was designed. . . . Deeds that would shock the modern city hall are still respectable in the county courthouse.

For the 52.9 percent of Mississippi's population still living in rural areas as late as 1990, the most visible government services were those provided by counties. And to rural citizens, the most important county services are building and maintaining roads and bridges. Because these services are so vital to rural constituents, they have always dominated the politics, organization, and functioning of county government. Therein lies a fascinating tale about why Mississippi enters a new millennium with almost half of its counties operating under an antiquated, corruption-prone beat system for providing these services. The story of county government in Mississippi involves an ongoing struggle to combat corruption and improve effectiveness by converting to a more efficient unit system of county government. Although there have been ongoing attempts since the 1930s to convert all counties to the unit system, politics has prevented a complete transition. During the 1980s, Operation Pretense played a pivotal role in the struggle that continues into the new millennium.

Prior to 1988, nearly all Mississippi counties operated under the beat system that evolved in a time when communication systems and modes of travel were primitive. Then it was efficient to have regionalized outposts of county government to keep roads passable and otherwise attend to the needs of the people. From a management and political perspective, supervisors needed to respond to only one-fifth of a county. Under the beat system, individual supervisors are in complete charge of construction and maintenance of roads and bridges in their districts. Supervisors are allocated a portion of the county's road and bridge budget based on a formula devised by the board of supervisors. Usually, the road budget is simply split five ways among the supervisors or is allocated based on the road miles in each of the five beats. In essence, there are five separate and duplicative construction and maintenance operations for road and bridgework. All other county functions are addressed by the board of supervisors, which acts as a policy-making body for the county and decides the activities to be undertaken by county government. In most cases, supervisors also act as executives and implement the policy decisions of the board. A county administrator may oversee the functions not related to any specific beat, while individual supervisors maintain executive control over activities in their own beats.

The unit system is characterized by centralized management of governmental services and functions. This centralization includes road and bridge maintenance and construction and maintenance of equipment and buildings. Centralized administrative functions include personnel matters, purchasing and inventory control, financial management, risk management and insurance, economic and industrial development, recreation, emergency services, and those other areas in which county involvement is authorized. Authority for implementation of policies established by the board of supervisors is vested in an administrator or manager who is appointed by and serves at the will and pleasure of the board. In 2001, forty-four of Mississippi's eighty-two counties operated under the unit system, a dramatic increase from the days before Operation Pretense.

During the early 1980s, in nearly all counties the board of supervisors performed both the legislative and executive functions of government. The boards levied taxes and approved each beat's road budget, and the individual supervisors directed the day-to-day roadwork in their beats. In most counties there was a lack of elementary internal controls over purchases and poor accounting practices related to inventories and other assets. Supposedly, counties had to employ well-designed purchasing procedures, with chancery clerks in each county making authorized disbursements. Before payments were submitted to the board of supervisors for approval and disbursements actually made, properly approved purchase orders, receiving reports, and vendor invoices were required. In practice, there were major flaws inherent in the systems, including no requirement for inventory records and controls. Moreover, supervisors could initiate purchases, falsify (or pressure employees to falsify) receiving reports, and approve payments. For busted invoices, the falsified receiving report was the key. In the case involving Perry County supervisor Trudie Westmoreland, court testimony revealed that the required forms were often completed after the fact by an employee in the chancery clerk's office, with all of the required information being taken from a vendor's invoice submitted by a supervisor.

The state legislature authorizes the formation of counties, delegates to them certain powers, and establishes parameters under which counties must operate. In 1930, the state legislature established the Research Commission of the State of Mississippi that contracted with the Institute for Government Research of the Brookings Institution to perform a survey of the administrative structure of state and county government. The institute issued its 971-page report in 1932. This well-reasoned, fact-based document contained many astute observations concerning the problems associated with county government in Mississippi and offered more than a hundred recommendations for reform. While politics prevented implementation of most of the recommendations, reviewing some of them proves enlightening.

> Any step from beat administration toward county-wide administration should be viewed in Mississippi as an advance in the right direction.
>
> In many, perhaps most, counties this [county highways] is the field where the greatest waste and most serious maladministration exists.
>
> County districts or beats should be abolished as political subdivisions and road districts and supervisors should be elected on an at large basis from the county as a whole.
>
> All county officers should be appointed except the board of supervisors and the county school board.
>
> The board should be assigned and should exercise only the functions of supervision, control, appointment, and removal. The board should be relieved of all direct administrative work.
>
> Functions of the board of supervisors relative to highways should be confined to general supervision and control.

During the 1940s, a few members of the state legislature and the Mississippi Economic Council (MEC) pushed for legislation to mandate the unit system in all counties. Anticipating the introduction of such legislation in the 1948 legislature, the Mississippi Association of Supervisors (MAS) published an article in its November 1947 journal attacking the unit system. The closing paragraph reflects the view of beat supervisors,

> Older members of the legislature need no advice on what to do with the unit system bill, which is sure to show its head early in the January session. New members would be wise to consult their own supervisors before arriving at conclusions as to the merits of the measure. After all, supervisors are closest to the taxpayers, and the taxpayers want, demand, and will get action from their supervisors, so long as they are not hamstrung, hog-tied, and hopelessly encumbered with laws which come between the taxpayer and his official.

In the mid-1950s, the MEC published a pamphlet that contrasted the beat and unit systems, stressed the advantages of the unit system, and advocated public involvement to pass unit system legislation. The pamphlet reported on studies of the implementation of the unit system for county roadwork in four counties in nearby states, three in Alabama and one in Texas. The studies showed that under the unit system, roadwork was much more efficient and economical and that taxpayers were pleased with the results. As with its preceding attempts to change to the unit system, this MEC effort bore no fruit.

Bill Minor, then a reporter for the *New Orleans Times Picayune*, wrote in late 1961 that federal bankruptcy proceedings involving Southern Equipment Sales, Inc. implicated county officials in a long-running system of kickbacks on purchases of road machinery. An attorney for the company testified that it had been making rebates for nineteen years. The system involved mythical sales commissions that actually went to public officials as kickbacks. Reacting to these revelations, the state legislature appointed a committee consisting of three members from each chamber to investigate the scandal and make recommendations. The Joint Investigation Committee uncovered evidence of corruption, which it presented to grand juries in three counties. The commission also made recommendations for legislation to counter the rebating practices. This episode eventually led to the strengthening of the antibribery laws, but no one was ever indicted or convicted. Legislation was not passed to address the structural problems in county government that allowed the scandal to develop in the first place.

The MEC published another pamphlet in 1965 entitled "Proposed Statute for County Unit System of Road Administration in Mississippi." The MEC noted that in 1960 the legislature had authorized expenditure of $250,000 to survey Mississippi's highway needs and to outline a plan of operation for securing a well-balanced, efficiently operated, and soundly financed highway system. The proposed legislation was designed to implement one of the resulting recommendations, which called for "all counties [to] consolidate their highway activities under a board-engineer management plan." The MEC explained that this was a call for a county unit system under which one road department serves the needs of an entire county.

In 1973, Bill Minor uncovered and reported another major kickback scandal involving the purchase of culverts. From discussions with a Lauderdale County supervisor and a Waynesboro culvert salesman, as well as a review of official records, Minor reported that of the $4,275,000 that Mississippi supervisors spent on culverts in 1972, at least $1,000,000 was padding of prices to cover kickbacks and cushy profits for suppliers. The going rate for kickbacks was 22 percent of the purchase price. Minor noted that the culvert market was dominated by a few Mississippi manufacturers and suppliers who bid almost identical prices. Minor pointed out that a Mississippi company bid 40 percent less in Louisiana than in Mississippi, and a Louisiana company entered bids in thirty-six Mississippi counties that averaged 37 percent below the Mississippi competition.

In June 1973, the legislature became involved again when an official of a Louisiana company testified about bid rigging and kickbacks before the Mississippi legislature's Performance Evaluation and Expenditure Review Committee. The official said that boards of supervisors had given "all kinds of reasons that don't make any sense at all" for rejecting his firm's low bids. The Hancock County Board Of Supervisors told him that he "didn't use the right stationery" to submit his bids, which he maintained were 30 percent less than the other bids. He said he was later told by a Hancock County man, "The front door was locked but that he had a key to the back door."

Some boards of supervisors were frustrated with the 1973 battle over culverts at the state level. The Leflore County board had requested help from state officials in 1969 according to a Leflore supervisor, James Hooper. Some boards, including Leflore's, balked when they received identical bids from several companies, and they tried to put an end to the practice. Hooper said, "Our hands were tied. Periodically we'd reject all bids and readvertise, hoping it would bring some relaxation in [the bidders'] policy. Of course, they would just send the same thing back in." In July 1969, the Leflore County board wrote a letter to Governor John Bell Williams complaining of a lack of competition. Copies of the letter were sent to the attorney general, the state auditor, and members of the Leflore County legislative delegation. "We resent the fact that we received no answer or acknowledgment to our letter or copy of our letter from any person receiving them," Hooper said. Within a month after Leflore's board sent its letter, Tunica County's board filed a federal lawsuit that accused four culvert dealers of price-fixing. That suit was dropped in January of 1970 after the culvert dealers submitted bids with differing prices.

The Mississippi legislature enacted legislation in 1981 that supposedly mandated the unit system for all counties. However, the law contained a provision that allowed boards of supervisors to vote to exempt individual counties from the "mandatory" system. By the summer of 1983, 79 of 82 boards of supervisors had voted to exempt their counties. The only virtue of this legislation was that it forced the supervisors to take a public stand on the unit system every four years.

A 1981 opinion by the Mississippi attorney general highlighted a practice of self-dealing that supervisors had engaged in for years. An incoming supervisor would lease land to the county on a short-term basis, use county funds to build a beat barn (maintenance and storage facility) on the land, and eventually leave office with the county-financed building increasing the value of his or her property. Based on state law allowing supervisors to use county funds to lease or purchase property or buildings for storing and maintaining county equipment, the attorney general's 1981 opinion allowed supervisors to donate land to the county for barns and to place barns on private property as long as the supervisors did not receive payment for it.

In February 1986, the House Constitution Committee approved a proposed constitutional amendment that would mandate the unit system for all counties. The legislation would have required a statewide referendum on the issue in November 1986. The bill was introduced by Representative James D. Price, who had introduced similar bills for the past five years only to see each of them fail. The MAS opposed the bill, maintaining that the unit system was no better than its management and that it would cost taxpayers more in counties that did not want it. The president of the MAS, Robert Earl Claton, expressed fears that voters in larger counties would dominate a statewide vote. Bob Pittman, president of the MEC, supported a statewide referendum, but remarked that he would prefer that the unit system be mandated by legislation. He opposed a county-by-county vote, noting that DeSoto County voters had overwhelmingly approved a change to the unit system in the early 1970s but the board of supervisors simply did not implement the change. The DeSoto County supervisors claimed that the whole county had not been represented because less than 20 percent of the registered voters had cast ballots. Unfortunately, Price's bill was again defeated in the Legislature.

In early February 1987, the first Pretense-related indictments brought immediate calls from several prominent officials for legislation mandating the unit system. At the time, only 16 of Mississippi's eighty-two counties operated on some form of the unit system. Referring to the beat system under which the other counties operated, U.S. Attorney George Phillips, said, "The system almost invites corruption and is not built to protect itself from corruption." Governor Bill Allain, Attorney General Ed Pittman, and State Auditor Ray Mabus all called for legislation to require the unit system. According to Mabus, "The unit system saves money, provides better service, and is harder to abuse. Other than that there is no reason to adopt it." He argued that the beat system made it too easy for county officials to steal. "You have five different governments in each county and no one person responsible for county finances. From a practical side, it would be easier to keep an eye on 82 people than 410. There is no such thing as a little corruption. What is killing Mississippi is the little things—$100 here, $200 there— that when they occur day-after-day, county-after-county, add up to a very serious problem."

These events marked the beginning of a protracted political battle over the unit system that was punctuated by heated rhetoric, opportunism, turf protection, and an eventual compromise that allowed one of the worst features of the beat system, separate road districts, to continue in some counties. The battle lines were clear. Officials elected by a statewide vote, federal officials, the MEC, prominent businesspeople, and legislators from urban counties generally supported the unit system. The MAS and legislators from rural counties generally supported the beat system. Newspapers began to run stories, columns, and editorials almost daily about problems and scandals in county government. The editorials and opinion columns strongly supported movement to the unit system based on legislation making such a system mandatory in every county or on a statewide vote.

The legislature was in session when the first Pretense arrests were made. Representative Bennett Malone, who had introduced a bill to allow voters in each county to decide whether they wanted a unit system for road construction and maintenance only to see it die in committee, expected a push to get the rules suspended so that his bill could be brought to the floor. While he supported a voter referendum on the county unit system, Senator

F. M. Smith Jr. did not believe the House could garner the two-thirds' vote required to bring to the floor either Malone's bill or a similar one introduced again by Representative Price. Smith favored giving the state attorney general a white-collar crime unit, which lawmakers had voted down in the past. Smith said, "We have a tendency to sit back and wait for things to happen and let the 'feds' catch our people instead of doing it ourselves."

The MAS flexed its political muscle and put pressure on legislators to kill any chance of a unit system bill in the 1987 legislative session. However, 1987 was an election year and a continuing flow of Pretense indictments kept the beat system controversy in the limelight. Several Mississippi peculiarities help explain what happened in the 1987 elections, the two legislative sessions of 1988, and a special election in 1988. First, most supervisors are elected from rural districts, and control of road building and maintenance in rural areas gave supervisors political capital; that is, the ability of supervisors to dispense favors and patronage gave them great visibility and political clout in their beats. The situation is similar to Huey Long's Louisiana, where roads that passed the property of the governor's political enemies did not get paved. Furthermore, a Mississippi law prohibited persons convicted of state felonies from holding public office, but it was silent as to federal felonies. Consequently, several supervisors who were under federal indictment as a result of Pretense ran for reelection in 1987 and won. Thus, the plea bargains that U.S. attorneys struck with the indicted supervisors usually included a provision that the supervisors would resign and not seek election to public office during any probation time imposed by the courts.

Even after the Pretense revelations began, those who supported the beat system continued to reason in a manner conveyed by the *Mississippi Supervisor* in a reprinted article that had originally appeared in the *West Point Daily Times Leader*.

> Our district or "beat" system supervisors are being assaulted on all sides. My (your) supervisor is the only truly personal political representative that I've (you've) got. Allow this representative to be destroyed, or gutted of political clout, and you and I are out in the cold with nobody to turn to when we need a little relief. . . .
>
> There are those who will argue that your county could be managed more efficiently and less expensively if you would just install something called a county unit system. Appoint a manager, they tell you. Place your county affairs in the hands of a university-trained auditor. You'll get more bang for your buck, so to speak. . . .

But try calling that county manager on the phone and asking him for some relief for a special problem of yours. He's busy? He'll call back?

Try calling your newspaper editor or favorite columnist who touted you on to the unit system and ask him for relief. How do you spell your name? Would you like to put that in writing so it can be published as a "Letter to the Editor?" Sure. That'll help.

Relief? You won't get it from your district supervisor because you just emasculated him of all his power—all his clout—by placing the real management of your county's affairs in the hands of a well-educated stranger who doesn't care how you voted in the last election or whether or not you vote in the next election.

But, of course, you'll save a dime here and there. It'll take a few saved dimes to pay his salary.

Your supervisors may not necessarily provide the cost efficiency you'll get from the county management system. They may not even provide for you the specific relief you look for at the time you want it. But at least you've got an ear to the message. You've got hope. That's worth something.

By the way that's what is called representative government.

On the other side, the MEC strongly supported the unit system and encouraged the electorate to vote for supervisor and legislative candidates who favored it. Almost as one voice, the newspapers in the state editorially decried the faults of the beat system and trumpeted the merits of the unit system, while encouraging readers to vote for reform-minded candidates for all state and local offices. As noted in chapter 9, Ray Mabus rode a reform campaign to victory in the 1987 gubernatorial election.

The year 1988 brought new hope to unit system advocates who watched a continuing flow of Pretense indictments. In addition, the state had a newly elected legislature and a reform-minded governor. Governor Mabus submitted a plan to the legislature to mandate the unit system. The plan would make boards of supervisors policy-making bodies and called for construction and maintenance of roads on a countywide basis. Mabus also wanted to require the hiring of a county administrator and to separate the functions of purchasing, receiving, and disbursing money. While the MAS would have preferred no new legislation, facing the reality of the public's demand for some kind of reform, it backed legislation that would allow each county to vote on the matter.

Advocates of the unit system had gained a powerful weapon in the form of a report published by Mississippi State University. The report, entitled

Converting to the Unit System: The Neshoba County Experience, is actually a case study of one county's conversion from the beat to the unit system, tracing the process used to convert Neshoba County from a beat to a unit system and detailing the savings and other positive changes accruing to Neshoba County. The author, political science professor Dr. William "Marty" Wiseman, had directed the university's project that provided assistance to Neshoba County in making the conversion. As shown in chapter 14, the report used data for fiscal year 1985–1986 and three months annualized data for 1986–1987 to make several comparisons. Projecting an overall 38 percent savings under the unit system, the report concluded that the unit system had brought advantages to Neshoba County in the form of efficiency in existing operations, monetary savings, capable professional administration, economic development, increased policy-making capabilities, and overall expansion of county government capacity. For fiscal year 1986–1987, Neshoba County was able to implement a tax cut of about 15 percent. Wiseman's report was cited many times in discussions of the two systems and in newspaper articles and editorials about the controversy.

Pete Johnson had been elected state auditor in the 1987 election. Prior to taking office, Johnson appointed a Committee on Reform of County Government in Mississippi and named Wiseman its chairman. The committee produced a position paper on the restructuring of county government, which contained recommendations for reform that Johnson embraced. The position paper clearly outlined the problems that existed with the beat system and the need for structural reform. It also provided a framework for conversion from the beat to the unit system and made recommendations for new legislation to effect the needed restructuring of county government.

Unfortunately, however, in late 1987 and early 1988 conditions in Neshoba County took a turn for the worse. Three of the five Neshoba County supervisors who had implemented the transition to the unit system were indicted by federal authorities and eventually pleaded guilty as a result of Pretense. Moreover, soon after taking office in 1988, Neshoba's new board of supervisors began to dismantle the unit system. Among the first acts of the new board was to purchase new pickup trucks for themselves. They also voted to relieve the road foreman of his duties and return those responsibilities to the individual supervisors. Wiseman was quoted as saying, "It boils down to where four men have essentially taken control of the government, like in a banana republic. They want to return to the beat system because that's the way it has always been done. And the people are the ones who will pay for it." The board of supervisors and its newly appointed attorney, State Senator Terry L. Jordan, strongly denied the charges. Two of the supervisors also disputed Wiseman's 1987 report, claiming that the cost savings estimates were exaggerated.

Facing public pressure to take action on the unit system issue, the Senate passed a very weak bill that required all counties to be operating on what could only loosely be described as the unit system by October 1. The House passed a much stronger bill, but it required a county-by-county referendum on the issue. Both bills mandated central purchasing. The MEC lined up on the side of the House bill, while the MAS backed the Senate version. Governor Mabus preferred the much stronger bill approved by the House. A six-member committee of House and Senate representatives could not negotiate an agreement reconciling the different versions of the unit legislation before a time limitation expired. Thus, in early June Governor Mabus announced that he would call a special session to consider unit legislation.

In a related legislative development, the legislature had passed a bill giving supervisors a 20 percent pay increase. One of the justifications of the proposed pay increase was that low salaries were a factor in the corruption revealed by Pretense. Using corruption as an excuse to raise salaries while failing to pass reform legislation showed the extent to which legislators were influenced by the supervisors. The situation also reflected the power struggle between a reform-minded governor and the powerful old guard combination of supervisors and legislators. A paragraph from Governor Mabus's April 30 veto message gave his reasoning and demonstrated that he would not be easily dissuaded: "I cannot in good conscience, sign an increase in salary for county supervisors as long as county reform goes unaddressed. In the wake of investigations of county officials over the last four years, in the wake of the Pretense operation, and in the wake of recent problems with purchasing by county supervisors, we in state government have an obligation to the taxpayers of Mississippi to enact improvements in the organization and operation of county government."

The MAS offered a plan endorsed by the state auditor that called on its members to establish central purchasing systems in all counties voluntarily. Governor Mabus said, "The greatest danger of all is that some people might believe that voluntary centralized purchasing eliminates the need for a mandatory statewide unit system bill." Central purchasing alone would eliminate only one of the many flaws of the beat system. It would leave intact most of the beat system's inefficiencies associated with running five small government units in a single county. Also, central-purchasing systems established by the voluntary actions could be abolished at any time by the board of supervisors. The MAS plan was a transparent effort to head off meaningful unit legislation.

The MEC continued its strong support of a mandatory unit bill and put forward an estimate that if all counties changed to the unit system, the state could save approximately $30 million annually. Newspapers across the state had been pushing the unit system in numerous editorials for more than a year, and the MEC had been raising money to purchase television time to extol the benefits of the unit system. At an MAS meeting in Jackson, an advertising campaign was proposed to tell the other side of the story, which would be that costs would increase and taxes would have to be raised if the unit system were mandated. The MAS claim that taxes would have to be increased was based on increased personnel costs associated with hiring a county administrator and building central county barns. The supervisors asserted that the unit system was not appropriate for rural counties or the rural districts of counties with large urban districts.

At the MAS convention in late July, Governor Mabus and editorial writers across the state were denounced in scathing terms by supervisors, State Senator Terry Jordan from Neshoba County, and former governor Bill Allain. Speakers claimed that by supporting legislation mandating a strong form of the unit system, the governor and editorial writers showed that they did not really understand the issues or the will of the people. Jordan claimed that Neshoba County's much-trumpeted plunge into the unit system had actually been an unreported disaster. U.S. Senate candidates speaking at the convention, Trent Lott and Wayne Dowdy, avoided any mention of the unit system while praising local government.

Absent an agreement with legislators, Governor Mabus called for a special session to convene on August 10, 1988. Some legislators expressed skepticism about the prospects of passing a bill that the governor would accept and criticized him for not having put together a package that he knew would win approval. Addressing a joint session of the House and Senate, Mabus said he hoped his version of the unit proposal would pass, but he recognized that "negotiation and compromise" would probably be required to pass a bill. He attacked the beat system primarily on purchasing and the appropriation of funds. He called Pretense a "tragedy" and indicated that the unit system would reduce the opportunity for graft. The governor called the beat system an "archaic system of county government [that] has made stealing too easy and too tempting." He also noted that dividing county funds equally among five districts with varied needs was inefficient and that the unit system would result in more equitable use of county money.

The governor's proposed legislation would also put an end to the practice of putting county barns on private property. It would allow supervisors to buy land for the county or lease land on a long-term lease for no more than fair market value. At this time, there were at least 145 county barns on private property, 95 of these on property owned by individual supervisors. Counties operated anywhere from one to five barns; in five counties, all of the barns were on property owned by supervisors. In another county, four barns were on supervisors' property and a fifth on property owned by a supervisor's father.

On August 15, House and Senate negotiators hammered out a tentative agreement and sent it to both chambers. On August 16, the House and Senate approved the bill by votes of 111 to 7 and 50 to 0, respectively. The County Government Reorganization Act of 1988 was signed into law by Governor Mabus. The compromise bill included the following major provisions:

(a) Voters in each county were to vote in November of 1988 to decide whether the county should have a district (beat) or a countywide (unit) approach to road administration.

(b) Central purchasing and inventory control systems were mandated for all counties.

(c) Countywide personnel systems were mandated for counties choosing to operate under the unit system.

(d) Counties choosing to operate under the unit system were required to establish central maintenance facilities (barns). In all counties, maintenance facilities (barns) were to be located on property owned by the county or leased on a long-term basis from another governmental entity.

(e) Counties choosing to operate under the unit system were required to appoint county administrators who could be the chancery clerks.

(f) The board of supervisors in each unit county was required to appoint a road manager to manage the county road department. Road managers remained optional in those counties choosing the beat system.

(g) In counties choosing the unit system, supervisors were directed to set countywide construction and maintenance priorities for roads and bridges and to establish a countywide road department to be responsible for carrying out these priorities.

As noted in chapter 9, the act included a provision that allowed supervisors to request that the state auditor provide an estimate of the costs to switch to the unit system. The Department of Audit gave briefings to county officials on the format, procedures, and forms to be used to describe costs of implementation.

The political action began to heat up as supporters of the two systems marshaled their resources to take their stories to the voters. In early September, a front-page article in the *Clarion-Ledger/Jackson Daily News* related the upcoming unit system vote directly to Pretense. It noted that the November referendum would show how people really felt about the FBI sting. Many in the state had been embarrassed that the federal government had to step in to help clean up county government and push the legislature to take action. The real and lasting clean-up work was now in the hands of county voters who could throw out the hopelessly flawed beat system in favor of the unit system.

Supervisors apparently saw estimated costs to implement the unit system as their best weapon. By mid-September, thirty-nine of the eighty-two counties had submitted estimated costs to the Department of Audit for certification. The estimates, which ranged from less than $500 to $1,487,200, were based on projected costs to build central barns ($69,500 to $750,000), establish central purchasing functions ($12,000 to $75,000), hire a county administrator ($12,000 to $104,000), and hire a road manager ($25,000 to $104,000). Deputy State Auditor Steve Duncan said that he planned to call many of the county officials for more explanation to justify their numbers. He indicated that many of the estimates would have to be adjusted to bring them in line with research done by the Department of Audit.

Governor Mabus held a press conference in late September on the steps of the MAS headquarters in Jackson to denounce "bogus and inflated" costs estimates of switching to the unit system. By then, State Auditor Pete Johnson had received estimates that ranged from $500 to $1.48 million from forty-seven of the eighty-two counties. None of the estimates included savings expected from administrative changes. Johnson had said that he intended to verify the figures. Mabus added, "This is an absolute sham, and I don't think the voters will be fooled. . . . I'm sure that he [Johnson] won't go along with this transparent flimflam." Mabus suggested that Johnson reject any estimate that didn't include cost savings.

Two days later, the MAS fired back at Mabus and charged him with using "scare tactics." "The unit system of county government is not going to cost supervisors money, but the public at large," the association said in a prepared statement. The statement also indicated that a vote for the unit system "has nothing to do with honesty or corruption in state or local government, but is a vote for increased costs, added bureaucracy and higher taxes." Eddie Washington, executive director of the MAS, said that he had considered holding a news conference on the steps of the governor's mansion.

On October 18, Pete Johnson released his final estimates; it would cost fifty-three counties then operating on the beat system $19.5 million to implement central road construction and maintenance. Johnson offered no estimate of savings once the changes took place because of the problem of documenting them. Sixty-one counties had submitted estimates, and Johnson said all of the estimates had been adjusted downward to remove projected costs for implementing central purchasing and inventory control. These were apparently the only adjustments, other than correcting an addition error made in the auditor's office. Mabus responded immediately, "At best the unit system cost estimates released today by the state auditor's office are inadequate. At worst, they contribute generously to a campaign of disinformation and distortion designed to discourage voters from supporting the unit system on November 8." Mabus indicated that Johnson's figures "don't pass the straight face test." Mabus stuck by his earlier claim that "the numbers provided by the counties were bogus and inflated." He also said that it was "sad" that the state auditor had "given his imprint to the figures."

Three CPAs who were members of the MEC studied the cost estimates and weighed in on the controversy. Mark Bullock, Paul Breazeale, and Roger Muns stated at a news conference that the cost estimates had distorted the facts and confused the taxpayers. They said fifty of the estimates were so exaggerated that they "test the intelligence" of taxpayers. Singled out was Lee County's estimate that included $950,000 to build a central maintenance barn and four satellite barns and $130,000 to purchase ten pickup trucks. They noted that these were not required by the unit system and that the law required little or no expenditures by the county. Lafayette County's numbers also invoked severe criticism. Breazeale said that the county's projections were grossly out of line and that they reflected "a worse case scenario." Bullock noted that the estimate included purchasing unnecessary vehicles and equipment.

As the November 8 referendum approached, the *Clarion-Ledger* published an "analysis" column that captured the phenomenon that was unfolding. The column was headlined "Expect county unit vote to test politics of defiance. The maverick impulse of supervisors springs from a deeply rooted Southern logic." It decried the supervisors' lame excuses for not supporting the unit system and concluded with the following paragraphs:

> Writing for *The Atlanta Constitution* earlier this year, Southern author Will D. Campbell traced the roots of that brand of "redneck" defiance and political Stoicism in the South that began with colonialism, continued through the Civil War and the civil rights era and beyond. . . .
>
> Campbell writes of the Southern redneck sentiment (of which he is proud): "The South stands today, I think—neither integrated nor segregated, neither bused or unbused, neither integral part of the nation nor a nation unto herself—because the redneck has never been party to any of the alliances formed or truces written." Aptly, he also cites a fine passage from Mississippi's own William Faulkner, who spelled out in the lines of his 1957 novel *The Town* the baser instincts that inform the defiance of the Southern community.
>
> "Ours (is) a town established and decreed by people, neither Catholics nor Protestants not even atheist but incorrigible nonconformist," Faulkner wrote. "Nonconformist, not just to everybody else, but to each other in mutual accord."

When the smoke cleared after the November referendum, forty-six of the eighty-two counties had opted for the unit system. While only 56 percent of the counties approved the unit system, the measure actually garnered 61 percent of the statewide vote. Although there was no clear pattern in the voting, some aspects of the results stood out. Voters in thirteen of the twenty-six counties touched by Pretense, including Pontotoc County, which saw all five of its supervisors plead guilty, rejected the unit system. Choctaw County, Governor Mabus's home county, likewise rejected the unit system. Every county that had a large urban population voted for the unit system, as did several rural counties. Alcorn County supervisors were in the process of implementing a unit system that voters had previously approved only to see voters reject the unit system in the referendum. Five other counties that were supposedly operating on some type of unit system also voted not to adopt the unit system.

The counties that opted for the unit system had until October 1, 1989, to make the switch. However, flexibility in the law gave supervisors much room to maneuver. Don Kilgore, former attorney for the Neshoba County Board of Supervisors and a unit proponent, warned, "You're going to see all sorts of innovative ways around it. Only a fool would think that all 46 counties would be on a pure unit system."

The 1988 legislation did, however, contain provisions that provided the state auditor an enforcement big stick. For both beat and unit counties, the auditor was to determine whether counties established, implemented and maintained central purchasing, inventory control, and relevant personnel systems. For unit counties, the auditor was to determine whether the counties adopted and put into operation countywide systems of construction and maintenance of roads and bridges and whether all equipment and facilities were controlled by county road managers. The auditor was required to give thirty days' notice to a county's board of supervisors of his or her intentions to issue a certificate of noncompliance to the State Tax Commission and to the attorney general. When a certificate of noncompliance was issued, the State Tax Commission was required to withhold all allocations and payments to the county until the certificate was canceled by the state auditor.

The central purchasing and inventory control parts of the 1988 law were applicable to all counties, and they included the following key provisions: (a) after the first Monday in 1989, purchasing was to be administered by a county department of purchasing run by a purchase clerk; (b) a physical inventory of all county property was to be completed by April 1, 1989, by an appointed inventory control clerk; (c) a receiving clerk was to be appointed in all counties; and (d) the Department of Audit was to provide continuing professional education programs for purchasing, receiving, and inventory control personnel. The major improvements were the features of the law that limited the supervisors' involvement in purchasing; professionalized the purchasing, receiving, and inventory functions; and required segregation of duties among purchasing, receiving, and inventory.

As the deadline for implementation of the unit system approached, rumors were flying that the supervisors in some of the counties that had voted for it were not going to implement it. As noted in chapter 9, State Auditor Pete Johnson's resolve was soon tested by Tallahatchie County. On November 29, Johnson said that Tallahatchie County supervisors faced criminal prosecution if they refused to abandon the beat system. In a letter to the Tallahatchie County Board of Supervisors, Johnson alleged: (1) There were still five road crews, one for each district, instead of a countywide crew. (2) Road maintenance was still conducted on a beat system, with each road foreman taking orders from a supervisor instead of a county administrator. (3) Invoices for items purchased for road maintenance were still billed to individual road districts. (4) Supervisors issue special orders each month to approve purchases that didn't comply with purchase laws. (5) Supervisors regularly circumvented purchase laws by purchasing items without proper documents from the purchase clerk. (6) The sheriff was allowed to purchase items from his office without going through the purchase clerk. (7) Requisitions and purchase orders were backdated and completed after the purchases were made.

Noting that some of the violations appeared to be deliberate, Johnson said that if the supervisors were found to have intentionally violated the law, "we intend to turn the findings over to the district attorney's office. All the evidence we have is that they are continuing to operate along beat lines with total disregard to maintaining the roads on a countywide basis." The county stood to loose $476,000 in state funds for failure to switch to the unit system. Johnson gave the county the 30 days required by law to correct the "very serious" violations. He also indicated that 19 other unnamed counties had been targeted for possible abuses.

Johnson lived up to his word and came down hard on Tallahatchie County on January 10, 1990. After concluding that the county had failed to implement the unit system, he stopped payment on $476,000 in state funds. Auditors had found that road crews were still run by individual supervisors instead of a countywide road manager, purchases were not made through a central office, and the sheriff's department was without an adequate personnel policy. While noting that the county had made some improvements, Johnson said, "We are committed to seeing that the unit system is implemented in the fashion that the people of this state voted on." Donald O'Cain, chief of the audit department's investigative division, added, "We're just going to break their backs to start with and let them know that we mean business."

The Tallahatchie board requested that Pete Johnson meet with them to discuss the matter, and a meeting was held in Jackson on January 17. Johnson agreed that his office would provide assistance to the board of supervisors, who still maintained that they were trying to comply with the law. After the meeting Johnson said, "There's not as much innocence in their conversions as many would like to think there is. But I think there is a commitment there to do the right thing now. I think part of that is because they've seen our commitment now."

Ray Mabus established the Governor's County Unit Task Force in January of 1991 to examine the operations of Mississippi county governments under the unit system and make recommendations for improvement. Approximately forty-five people, including county supervisors, chancery clerks, county administrators, county engineers, attorneys for boards of supervisors, legislators, MEC representatives, and private citizens, were appointed to the task force. Both beat and unit advocates were included. The Stennis Institute of Government at Mississippi State University was engaged to conduct research for the task force. Marty Wiseman directed the research project, which involved securing and analyzing information from three primary sources: financial and other numerical data available from the state and the counties, a written questionnaire, and public hearings. The financial and numerical data allowed comparisons by county of such things as road department employees and expenditures per hundred miles of road, road department expenditures per capita, property tax revenue per capita, and expenditures per capita. The questionnaires were administered to county officials and employees in a sample of ten of the forty-six unit counties.

There were several limiting factors associated with the research methodology. The fact that the counties had operated on the unit system for only a little more than a year limited the value of the numerical and financial analysis. Not all of the items on the questionnaires were completed by all of the sample counties, and there were some obvious biases in the responses of some officials. Finally, the public hearings, which did not draw well, were often dominated by county officials or task force members. Nevertheless, the Stennis Institute's report contained several excellent observations and some well-reasoned conclusions and recommendations. Some of the most important of these can be summarized as follows:

(a) There had been resistance to what was seen as increased "bureaucracy" and its associated costs. However, most of the complaints along these lines were associated with central purchasing that had been mandated for all counties.

(b) Lines of administrative authority inherent in the unit system had not always been followed. There had been many cases of supervisors giving direct orders regarding implementation of policy to professional appointees. This had limited the power of appointees to perform their duties with a countywide viewpoint and had caused high turnover among professional employees.

(c) Duties of the county administrator and road manager were not clearly established by law. These two appointees served at the "will and pleasure" of the board of supervisors. The officials' ability to carry out their duties as envisioned by the law was impaired by the threat of termination.

(d) While personnel policies were mandatory for the board of supervisors, they were not for other county officials such as the chancery clerk and sheriff, who could choose to adopt the board of supervisors policies if they so desired.

(e) There were some claims of inefficiencies and increased costs under the unit system caused by moving equipment greater distances and by employees working outside of their own beats.

(f) Prescribed purchasing procedures were considered too cumbersome for routine purchases.

By the time the Stennis Institute's report was completed, the political landscape in Mississippi had changed dramatically. Governor Mabus lost his 1991 bid for reelection, and the drive for reform in county government had cooled considerably. In fact, the Stennis Institute's report was never considered by the task force that Mabus had appointed because it, in effect, disbanded after his defeat. Opponents of the unit system continued to voice their views and to wield their political influence.

The 1988 law contained a provision that allowed citizens of a county to petition the board of supervisors to put the unit/beat issue to another vote. The law allowed citizens to petition to put the issue on the ballot in counties that had voted for the beat system as early as 1992, but citizens in counties that opted for the unit system were prohibited from doing so until 1995. The idea was to give the unit system time to prove its worth. Unit foes were determined to change this situation, and a bill to allow petitions for a vote in all counties as early as 1992 passed the legislature and was signed into law by new governor Kirk Fordice. Petition drives got under way in several unit counties to revisit the issue. Eventually, petitions put the issue on the ballot in twenty-two of the forty-six unit counties.

The MEC released the results of a study of spending patterns on roads before and after conversion to the unit system for ten of the counties that were to vote again on the issue. The study conducted by CPA Steve Duncan showed that eight of the ten had spent more on roads under the unit system than under the beat system. "Improvements were noted because the road manager is looking after the roads on a day-to-day basis. In counties where supervisors have not tried to undermine the unit system, improvements are very noticeable. If supervisors want it to work, it will work," Duncan said.

The November 1992 balloting found voters giving the unit system an overwhelming endorsement. Twenty of the twenty-two counties voted to stay with the unit system. Only Jones County (57 percent) and Tate County (50.28 percent) voted to go return to the beat system. In most of the counties, the vote was not close. Some of the most outspoken proponents of voting on a return to the beat system had been the supervisors of Panola County. They were sure that the citizens of Panola County did not understand what they were voting for when they had opted for the unit system in 1988. Given a second opportunity to get it right, Panola County again embraced the unit system by a 60 to 40 percent margin. The overall results of the 1992 voting temporarily cooled the fervor of beat supporters in counties under the unit system.

On the bright side, much improvement in county government in Mississippi has occurred since Pretense broke in 1987. All eighty-two counties now operate centralized purchasing systems that are more efficient, include some built-in controls, and are mostly operated by trained personnel. Most counties operate under the unit system with professional managers in charge of day-to-day administration, while the board of supervisors acts as a policy-making body. All counties have benefited from these developments, but unit counties have realized more benefits as countywide planning and centralized professional administration have paid off. Still, nearly half of the counties continue operating their road programs under the antiquated beat system. Five supervisors plan and control their own road operations and compete with each other for scarce resources.

The lack of mandatory central receiving for all purchases is a major flaw in the central purchasing systems as operated in beat counties. This makes it makes it fairly easy to engage in corrupt purchasing practices involving direct deliveries to the beats. Supervisors designate persons to act as receiving clerks for their beats, and those clerks do not have to be trained and certified by the Department of Audit as do receiving clerks in unit counties. While purchases (except those involving less than $100 and "emergency" purchases) must be made through central purchasing, beat county supervisors can initiate the purchasing process by requesting items for their road programs. They can then apply pressure to their designated receiving clerks to sign receiving reports whether all, part, or none of the ordered items have actually been delivered. These conditions leave open the door for kickbacks and busted invoices.

11. State Highway Commissioners

We Play Too

Until 1992, building and maintaining state highways were responsibilities of the State Highway Department. In 1992, the State Highway Department was renamed the Department of Transportation and given additional responsibilities. The state is divided into three districts, northern, central, and southern, each of which elects a transportation (prior to 1992, highway) commissioner. The commissioners supervise the work on state highways and divide up moneys that the legislature appropriates for highways. The three-district arrangement perpetuates at the state level a fragmented system that almost invites corruption. Thus, the state as a whole suffers from inadequate planning and control of the highway program. Mississippi is still the only state in the nation that elects transportation (highway) commissioners.

In the 1980s, the three highway commissioners were virtual barons in their districts, controlling highway programs like county supervisors controlled road programs in beat counties. The districts were like very large beats, with the highway commissioners managing much larger budgets than county supervisors. Thus, highway commissioners had leverage that allowed them to extort much larger sums of money from vendors. Given the system, it is not surprising that two of the three highway commissioners pleaded guilty in the 1980s to crimes uncovered by the state Department of Audit and the Operation Pretense team.

Testimony in the trials of Wayne County supervisors Alfred Grant Revette and Jimmie T. Duvall had ominous implications for another powerful political figure from Wayne County. The two supervisors testified that an FBI agent posing as a pipe salesman wanted to meet Robert Earl "Bob" Joiner, who was Southern District highway commissioner. The fifty-eight-year-old Joiner had been mayor of Waynesboro for three terms before he was elected highway commissioner in 1979, defeating incumbent Shag

Pyron. Coincidentally, Pyron pleaded guilty in August 1987 to federal charges that involved the sale of bogus oil and gas leases.

In December 1987, Joiner was indicted in federal court in Jackson on four counts of extortion, three counts of bribery, and four counts of tax evasion. He was accused of extorting more than $230,000 in kickbacks from four paving contractors during the 1980s. The indictment also charged that he owed some $122,000 in back taxes and penalties. He faced maximum penalties of 130 years in prison and fines of up to $1.9 million. Joiner, who was represented by Hattiesburg attorney Jim Dukes, pleaded innocent to all charges and was released on a $5,000 bond. A trial was scheduled for March 7, 1988, before U.S. District Judge Tom S. Lee in Jackson. Joiner had been elected to a third term in November and was scheduled to be sworn in on January 4, 1988.

The Joiner investigation was started by the Investigative Audit Division of the Department of Audit in 1984. After a substantial amount of information had been developed, the Department of Audit began conferring with the FBI in 1985 and later with the Internal Revenue Service (IRS) and the U.S. attorney's office according to Louisa Dixon, director of the Investigative Audit Division. The Department of Audit gave federal investigators information on purchases, contracts, and the results of interviews with contractors and Highway Department employees. According to Dixon, "There is a tremendous amount of money expended without bids—such as the purchase of asphalt." The department obtained price quotes from suppliers for a number of maintenance supplies such as asphalt, sand, and gravel. After a list of bids was compiled, suppliers were contacted directly for materials. Referring to the circumstances that resulted in the indictments, Dixon said, "We're talking about a contractor paying a commissioner a certain amount of money in return for business."

Assistant U.S. Attorney James Tucker said the contractors involved would not be charged because they had been the victims of extortion. While the charges against Joiner were unrelated to Operation Pretense, Tucker said, "The Pretense team teamed up with an IRS agent and completed the investigation." Tucker would not say whether the tax evasion charges were related to the $88,000 that Joiner allegedly kept in a Crown Royal whiskey bag in an office safe. A recent divorce revealed that Joiner claimed the money belonged to his mother and his political campaign.

Several Wayne County citizens were quoted December 19 in the *Clarion-Ledger* as strongly supporting Joiner, a former shoeshine boy and high school football hero. They stated that he had been a good mayor and a good highway commissioner and that he had many friends. The overall sentiment seemed to be that of feeling sorry for him and his family. The popular Joiner had easily won the August Democratic primary race for Southern District highway commissioner. When Hattiesburg television station WDAM ran an unscientific call-in poll shortly after the indictment, 70 percent of the 413 respondents thought that he should stay in office. In the Democratic primary, Joiner had defeated former Harrison County Supervisor Billy McDonald by a two to one margin, while carrying Wayne County with 82 percent of the vote.

Joiner was sworn in for a third term as Southern District highway commissioner as scheduled on January 4, 1988. He took the occasion to say, "There is a future in Mississippi, but it isn't in assassinating and hanging our public officials on a cross. The future is with the children." He said that he "takes the office with pride" and that "people don't see the sacrifices people make in public office." He claimed to have missed seeing his son receive a sports award while in Washington on business for the city of Waynesboro and to have left family reunions three times to speak to groups.

Joiner and his attorney made a plea bargain with federal prosecutors on February 11, 1988, and the agreement's contents were made public on March 11. Joiner agreed to plead guilty to the charge that he extorted money from a contractor from 1980 through 1986. He also agreed to plead guilty to a charge of evading federal income taxes for 1984. These two charges carried combined maximum penalties of twenty-five years' imprisonment and $350,000 in fines. The government agreed to recommend a seven-year prison term, a fine of $100,000, payment of all taxes owed, restitution of an unspecified amount, and five years' probation. Joiner also agreed to cooperate in ongoing investigations. Sentencing was delayed by Judge Lee to allow Joiner to testify in the upcoming trial of Marion County supervisor Sim Ed Moree of Columbia.

Joiner testified on March 10 in the federal trial of Sim Ed Moree that Moree had offered to fix federal charges against him in exchange for $160,000. Moree was on trial for obstruction of justice and conspiracy to obstruct justice. As chronicled in chapter 7, Joiner's testimony was instrumental in convicting Moree of all the charges against him.

In early April 1988, Joiner pleaded guilty to two counts of the eleven-count indictment in federal court in Jackson. He pleaded guilty to extorting $161,000 from James Williams of Southwest Paving, Inc. from 1980 to 1986 and to not reporting $83,000 on his 1984 federal income tax return. That underreporting of income meant that he owed income taxes of $42,000 to the federal government. The guilty pleas followed the February plea bargain in which Joiner was required to resign from his post by May 9. The plea agreement called for Joiner to cooperate with the broadening investigation of how Highway Department officials conducted business with contractors. No sentencing date was set in order to allow Joiner to continue cooperating in the investigation that soon snared another highway commissioner, Sam Waggoner of the central district.

Joiner made no statement in court; he simply answered "Yes, sir" or "No, sir" to Judge Lee's questions. Before the hearing, Joiner asked newspaper reporters, "Are the fish biting?" Then he answered his own question, "I plan to find out about 1 p.m." When a reporter asked if he had a favorite spot, Joiner replied: "No I haven't been fishing in 20 years—that's how long I've been in public service. You don't get to go fishing when you work 12 hours a day." No doubt Bob Joiner had found his twelve-hour daily public service very lucrative. He had received at least $238,000 in kickbacks from four contractors since 1980. Ironically, because it was illegal for contractors to make such payments, Joiner did not have to repay the contractors.

Two days after Joiner's guilty plea, the state Senate Rules Committee considered but failed to act on a resolution that had already passed the House asking for his resignation. Joiner's plea agreement called for him to resign by May 9, but legislators wanted payments to Joiner stopped immediately. In an interview aired by WDAM television in Hattiesburg, Joiner claimed that he planned to resign on May 9 as required by the plea agreement. He said to do so earlier might jeopardize funding for three major South Mississippi highway projects. Joiner maintained that two of the sponsors of the resolution calling for his immediate resignation, State Representatives Billy McCoy and John Pennebaker, would try to divert the funding to North Mississippi. Representative McCoy of Rienzi termed this charge "ridiculous."

The Senate Rules Committee appointed Pud Graham of New Albany to research Joiner's plea bargain. Graham said he was awaiting a response from Attorney General Mike Moore on whether state law could be used to force Joiner's resignation. Assistant Attorney General Jim Warren said that the attorney general could file for a public official's resignation only after a written judgment of guilt had been certified by a judge. Such judgment is usually entered at sentencing, but Joiner's sentencing date had not been set. Warren indicated that taking action to force Joiner's resignation sooner than required by his agreement with the federal government could jeopardize the plea agreement. Joiner informed Governor Ray Mabus that he would resign effective 5 p.m. May 9. Under the law, Mabus would then have fifteen days to call a special election, which had to be held within sixty days. Although he did not attend any of the twice-monthly Highway Commission meetings after his plans to plead guilty were made public in early March, Joiner remained in office until May 9. He continued to collect his $3,333 per month salary until the bitter end.

Bob Joiner's sentencing hearing was held before Judge Lee in Jackson on February 8, 1989. At the hearing, Joiner expressed regrets "for the sorrow, hurt, and embarrassment I have caused." He also said, "Your honor, I would like to apologize to you and this court and the fine men and women of the Mississippi Highway Department. Whatever time is allotted to me, I hope that I can spend that time to make up for the wrongs I have done." Jim Dukes pointed out that, after his indictment but prior to the plea bargain, his client had willingly and of his own accord reported to the FBI plots to obstruct justice in what could have been a life-threatening situation (the Sim Ed Moree affair). Dukes also claimed that Joiner and his family had already suffered much and that Joiner was the sole supporter of his mother who was in her eighties. Assistant U.S. Attorney Ruth Harris told the judge that Joiner's cooperation with the government had been significant in the successful prosecution of Sim Ed Moree and in the investigation of fellow highway commissioner Sam Waggoner. Because of Joiner's "substantial cooperation," Harris recommended a maximum sentence of six years although the plea agreement called for the government to recommend a seven-year prison sentence.

Judge Lee was not impressed with Joiner's contrition or his lawyer's plea for leniency. The judge commented:

> Mr. Joiner, according to the presentence report, you blatantly solicited kickbacks from contractors in an aggressive manner, which to this court demonstrates an insatiable greed and a perverted sense of the powers and privileges of the office you held. You had understandings with contractors that in order to successfully do business with the State in highway construction, they had to pay you substantial kickbacks. The contractors regularly made kickbacks to you of thousands and thousands and thousands of dollars. Payments were made to you by other contractors on demand. All of this is reflected in the presentence report. Your multiple breaches of the public trust over the years, as reflected by the report, are of a far greater magnitude than any case involving a violation of the public trust with which this court has been confronted. The only redeeming factor in your behalf is the fact that

you have cooperated extensively with the prosecution and have contributed to the prosecution of other significant cases. Your cooperation convinces the court to adhere and give effect to the plea agreement, into which you've previously entered with the Government, and the recommendation by the prosecutor this morning.

Judge Lee sentenced Joiner to six years in prison on the extortion charge and to a five-year suspended sentence on the tax evasion charge. The prison time was to be followed by five years' probation. Joiner was also fined $100,000 and ordered to pay all back taxes including fines and interest.

On Monday, March 6, 1989, Bob Joiner reported to the federal penitentiary at Eglin Air Force Base, Florida. He would become eligible for parole after serving eighteen months. Joiner's new lawyer, Alvin Binder, filed papers in June with the court asking Judge Lee to reduce Joiner's sentence "to reflect the value of this defendant's substantial assistance in the investigation and prosecution of other persons." Sam Waggoner had pleaded guilty to similar charges based on a plea bargain that called for a recommendation of only two years in prison. Waggoner was awaiting sentencing, and Binder asked that Judge Lee postpone a decision in Joiner's case until after Waggoner was sentenced. Binder claimed that "should the court accept the recommendation of the government and sentence Waggoner to two years' incarceration, this certainly would be a disproportionate sentence when considering the sentence of Joiner." Binder also claimed that Joiner's sentence was disproportionate to the six-year sentence of Bobby Little, who had recently been convicted of 241 counts involving payoffs to county supervisors.

Again, Judge Lee was not impressed. In an order made public on November 8, 1989, he refused to change Joiner's sentence. Judge Lee wrote, "The court is persuaded that because of the different circumstances that exist in the two cases, the sentence to be imposed on Waggoner has no relevance to the sentence imposed on this defendant." The judge also refused to grant Joiner a hearing on the case, noting that Joiner and his attorney had been given every opportunity to speak. Joiner had challenged the U.S. Probation Office's report, claiming that it had not detailed all his efforts in helping the government. Judge Lee noted that "indeed, based on Joiner's substantial cooperation, the government recommended a sentence of six years, rather than the seven-year recommendation contained in the defendant's plea agreement; the court did accept that recommendation and so sentenced the defendant."

Sam Waggoner began working on Mississippi roads in the 1930s for 12 cents an hour. Leaving his father's farm near Carthage, Waggoner earned a degree in civil engineering from the University of Mississippi, served in the navy during World War II, and returned home to take a job as a highway road worker in 1946. In 1948, he was appointed engineer for highway projects in Scott and Newton Counties. Waggoner left the Highway Department in 1961 and spent two years as assistant director in charge of construction of the Ross Barnett Reservoir. After failing in his first race for Central District highway commissioner, he was elected to the post in 1967. In announcing his intentions to seek a sixth four-year term in 1987, Waggoner cited the importance of the recently passed $1.6 billion highway construction legislation. "Highways in Mississippi are entering a new era, with the most comprehensive construction program in state history. The road to this milestone has been a long one. This historic legislation is the most progressive and comprehensive highway program ever enacted in Mississippi. It will not only link every area of the state with four-lane highways, but will also allow needs of other highways outside the four-lane network to be met much more quickly." Waggoner had been an ardent supporter of the bill, which promised construction of 1,077 miles of four-lane highways by the year 2001. He was easily elected to a sixth term with 73 percent of the vote.

Waggoner held the second-longest tenure as an elected official in state government; only Agriculture and Commerce Commissioner Jim Buck Ross had served longer. The tobacco-chewing Waggoner was recognized as a stern taskmaster who expressed his feelings with sharp language and a jab of a finger. He was well respected statewide for his contributions to the state highway system. Anse Dees, vice president of AHEAD, an organization of business leaders that lobbied for the four-lane highway legislation, called him a very fine and serious businessman who worked hard at improving Mississippi highways. Tone Garrate, head of the Mississippi Asphalt Pavement Association, said, "The man's tenacity and endurance was very beneficial to the highway program. He worked tirelessly for it."

It turned out that the esteemed commissioner, who had been called Mississippi's Mr. Highways, had also worked hard to line his own pockets at taxpayers' expense. On December 22, 1988, sixty-seven-year-old Sam Waggoner pleaded innocent to charges of extortion and filing false federal income tax returns over a three-year period. Waggoner, who resigned as of December 31 from his $48,000 a year position, made his plea based on an information charging one count of extortion, and three counts of filing false income tax returns. The extortion charge carried maximum penalties of 20 years in prison and a $250,000 fine, while each of the income tax charges could be punished by three years' imprisonment and a $100,000 fine. The information charged that: (a) in 1984, Waggoner's gross income was $181,896, rather than the $109,925 he reported; (b) in 1985, his gross income was $168,619 rather than the $96,648 he reported; and (c) in 1986, his gross income was $116,749 rather than the $70,168 he reported. It also charged that Waggoner extorted $127,000 from Freddy Rogers Construction Company, Inc. during the period 1981 through 1985. Assistant U.S. Attorney Tucker indicated that Waggoner would change his plea to guilty and that he would be sentenced at a later date.

In a written statement addressed to Highway Department employees, Waggoner expressed his regrets: "Unfortunately, in recent years I have used some very bad judgment in campaign financing and related circumstances. I am deeply sorry and I apologize. I am resigning because I have made a mistake, and I must now pay the price for that mistake." While Waggoner claimed that the charges were related to "campaign financing and circumstances evolving therefrom," federal and state officials had not even subpoenaed his campaign reports.

Waggoner's alleged criminal actions were very similar to those of Bob Joiner. The commissioner and contractor would make contact, and through an offer from one or a request from the other, a cash payment would be discussed. The contractor would then agree to give the commissioner cash to ensure obtaining business from the state Highway Department. Under the law, it did not matter who made the first approach, a violation occurred either way. The law made the public official responsible. It was the official's responsibility to avoid any illicit conduct. However, there was one major difference between the cases against Joiner and Waggoner. Joiner had been indicted for income tax evasion, which carried a maximum five-year prison sentence, while Waggoner had been charged with filing false income tax returns, which carried a maximum sentence of only three years in prison. Assistant U.S. Attorney James Tucker explained the difference, "Joiner made me indict him."

Former governor Bill Allain, who had feuded openly with Waggoner and Joiner in 1986, refused to claim vindication or gloat over Waggoner's predicament. He said, "Anything that I would say would sound like I told you so." In seeking to streamline the system, Allain had attempted to merge it with other transportation-related agencies into a department of transportation with a board appointed by the governor. Allain claimed the three commissioners were little more than county supervisors and that they divided up the highway funds almost equally rather than directing the money to needed areas. Allain's January 1986 announcement that he was seizing control of the Highway Department had prompted a tirade from the three highway commissioners. Bob Joiner said, "This is a egotistical, power-hungry play. It is a shame that we have allowed ourselves to elect a man like Bill Allain."

The people of Newton, Waggoner's home for forty years, rallied behind this favorite son who was a Sunday school class president. Attorney George Monroe said, "Most of the people in Newton are behind Sam Waggoner. He is just one of us, when he hurts, we hurt." Mayor Albert Carr commented, "It's just sad because he helped a lot of people." Likewise, officials of the Highway Department expressed their regrets. Director John Tabb said, "It's a sad day for the department. The man has done a tremendous job for the highways in Mississippi—we regret this but can't excuse it." Ronnie Shows who had been elected to replace Joiner as Southern District commissioner indicated that he had sought Waggoner's advice several times since joining the commission in August, and he said, "I hate to see the system go through this. . . . He's recognized, not just in the state, but nationally. Everybody in the highway business knows Sam Waggoner." Northern District highway commissioner Zack Stewart said, "I regret it's happened. It's been a bad day for me. Anytime anything happens like this, it reflects on the department. I feel that we have one of the finest highway departments in the country, and I'm proud to be a part of it." Even State Representative John Pennybaker, chair of the House Transportation Committee, noted that the state is "losing one of the most loyal highway department individuals I've ever dealt with."

The charges against Waggoner came in the wake of federal charges filed December 8 against a sitting and a former public service commissioner. Public Service Commissioner D. W. Snyder and former commissioner Lynn Havens had been indicted on bribery charges. The three public service commissioners, like highway commissioners, were elected on a district basis. The whole scenario gave impetus to an ongoing movement to make the district-level positions appointive. This was comparable to the movement toward the unit system of county government. Under an appointed highway commission, professional management would conduct day-to-day operations with overall policy being set by the commission with the best interest of the entire state in mind.

The *Clarion-Ledger/Jackson Daily News* ran an editorial in its December 23, 1988 edition that put state and county road programs in perspective:

Former Gov. Bill Allain was too polite to say it but we're not. He told you so. We told you so. Allain in 1986 battled unsuccessfully to restructure the state's highway department, arguing that the political agency had short-changed the people of this state in spending the state's giant highway budget. A series of stories in the *Jackson Daily News* in 1986 pointed to myriad high-way problems, and editorials urged that the three-member commission be abolished in favor of more accountable highway management. Those efforts failed. What has happened since should convince any doubter, however. The guilty plea by Central Highway Commissioner Sam Waggoner to extortion charges Thursday should be the last gasp for a political system that has en-couraged corruption and political wheeling and dealing for too long. Many legislators were reluctant in the past to tackle the politically-potent highway commissioners. Within the past few days, however, some have changed their minds. Back when the commissioners simply did a bad job in managing the state's highway funds, things were bad enough. Now we have Waggoner acknowledging some "bad judgment in campaign financing" then resigning and admitting extorting $127,000 from a construction company. Waggoner follows in the footsteps of Bob Joiner, who left the Southern District seat in May after pleading guilty to extorting $161,100. Joiner had trailed William H. "Shag" Pyron who pleaded guilty in August of 1987 to operating a bogus oil and gas royalties scheme. It is abundantly clear that electing three politicians to split up the state's giant highway budget three ways is not the way to run a highway program. It's time to establish a new system under which highway planning will fairly consider highway needs and make decisions equitable to the entire state. Hiring one top administrator would work. The commission could be expanded into an advisory body representing the entire state. The most important aspect of any workable plan is to have those running the highway program responsible to someone, preferably the governor. Missis-sippians are reluctant to give up direct election of public officials. Many be-lieve standing for election makes officials responsible to the voters. However, the state district system makes little sense as does the beat system for county supervisors, and for the same reasons. Commissioners are just like supervi-sors, except with giant districts and more millions of dollars. Their districts are bigger. Their temptations are larger. The state is the only one in the nation to elect highway commissioners. The reason should be increasingly obvious. Being responsible to everybody is pretty close to not having to an-swer to anyone.

Sam Waggoner pleaded guilty to the charges in the information on Feb-ruary 9, 1989. Assistant U.S. Attorney Ruth Harris indicated that he had provided "many investigative leads." In exchange for his cooperation, the government recommended that he be sentenced to two years in prison, fined $40,000, and put on probation for five years. He would also have to pay all back taxes. Waggoner, who had posted a $205,000 cash bond with the IRS, was allowed to stay free on bond, and a sentencing date was not set. He was continuing to help in the investigation of contractors involved in kickback schemes, and his agreement to plead guilty included a promise to testify before a federal grand jury. U.S. Attorney George Phillips and State Attorney General Mike Moore agreed that Waggoner's cooperation had been substantial.

Ruth Harris claimed that the case against Waggoner included evidence that Freddie Rogers agreed in 1979 to pay Waggoner 75 cents to $1 for each ton of asphalt laid under state road maintenance contracts. Rogers kept up with the payments made to Waggoner in a separate book that he kept "under lock and key," she said. Rogers delivered cash payments to Waggoner at various places, including highway rest stops, according to Harris. Rogers had secured the cash for the kickbacks by writing salary checks to himself. Harris also indicated that Bob Joiner had supplied information that led to the charges against Waggoner.

On April 19, 1990, Judge Lee sentenced Waggoner on the extortion charge to two years in prison and fined him $100,000. A suspended sentence on the tax charges was also imposed, and Waggoner was ordered to report to a federal prison by May 23. The $100,000 fine, which Waggoner had sixty days to pay, exceeded what the prosecutors had recommended by $60,000. According to the judge, Waggoner had kept records of kickbacks from three contractors in a notebook that he later burned. Explaining why the government waited fourteen months after his guilty plea to impose sentence, U.S. Attorney George Phillips praised Waggoner's assistance in the government's ongoing investigation of public corruption. Waggoner reported to the federal prison in Montgomery, Alabama, on May 21, 1990.

Prosecutors and friends praised Waggoner at his sentencing hearing, which was attended by more than fifty supporters including his pastor, members of his Sunday school class, politicians, friends, and staff at a recovery center where he had worked with alcoholics. Perhaps U.S. Attorney George Phillips's words were the most weighty for the man who had admitted accepting $434,000 in kickbacks from three contractors. "One of the major considerations in this sentencing recommendation was he saved us by his coming forward so early in this investigation . . . probably eighteen months to two years of investigative work, grand jury work . . . and literally thousands of dollars. I admit to you it is a light recommendation. But I think it is absolutely justified in this instance."

At his sentencing, Waggoner told the judge, "Not in any instance did a contractor ever get a bid that he was not the low bidder nor did he ever get any special favors." Judge Lee noted, "It appears that you did not take any aggressive role in soliciting the illegal kickbacks." Waggoner was barred from seeking public office in the future by the plea bargain. Nevertheless, Judge Lee indicated that Waggoner "will work with the State of Mississippi in the future in order to reorganize the Mississippi Highway Department and make a public statement on how it should be changed." Ironically, in the 1990 legislative session state lawmakers had actually legalized campaign contributions by contractors while not changing the structure of the highway commission. Attorney General Mike Moore commented that in his opinion the change was not reform.

In early October 1990, Judge Lee rejected Waggoner's request to reduce his prison sentence to a year and a day. In his petition, Waggoner claimed, "I came forward voluntarily at the very beginning of their investigations and thereby saved the federal government 18 months to two years of investigative and grand jury time and tens of thousands of dollars." Waggoner also claimed to have worked 2,800 hours with alcoholics. But Judge Lee wrote, "The court is of the opinion that the defendant's conduct while incarcerated, however laudable, does not provide a basis for a reduction of the sentence imposed. At the time of sentencing, the court was aware of and considered his community service and the cooperation and assistance he had provided the government."

12. Madison County

Who Pays for the Backhoe?

Named for the fourth president of the United States, Madison County, located just north of Jackson in the central part of the state, was ranked twelfth among Mississippi's eighty-two counties in population in 1990 with nearly 54,000 residents. Canton, the county seat, was the picturesque location for the filming of John Grisham's *A Time to Kill*. Madison, one of the state's fastest growing counties, contains some of Jackson's most affluent suburbs. In the late 1990s, Madison County was selected by Nissan Motors as the site of a large new manufacturing facility.

Unfortunately, for the past two decades Madison County government has been a virtual circus including a center-ring election of a district five supervisor that spawned several court challenges and four different ballots over a two-year period in the 1990s. This episode brought into question the county's ability to conduct fair elections. Further tarnishing the county's reputation was the board of supervisors' support of an ill-fated effort by a convicted felon to build a multimillion dollar theme park in the county and a costly feud between the board and the sheriff concerning overtime pay for sheriff's deputies. While Madison County voted in 1988 to convert to the unit system of county government, the battle over how to run the county was still being fought in the courts in the late 1990s.

Although some of those involved in the county's shenanigans did have Pretense connections, no Madison County supervisor was ever indicted as the result of Operation Pretense. However, a thirteen-year purchasing saga that involved a vendor who was convicted as a result of Pretense vividly reflect the problems in Madison County. Irregular equipment purchases made in 1984 by Madison County supervisors resulted in a legal battle that made its way to the Mississippi Supreme Court twice before all aspects were finally settled in 1997. The events surrounding the purchases vividly illustrate the lengths to which some supervisors went to subvert Mississippi's purchasing laws and the arrogance with which they handled county business. The case involved four Madison County supervisors and two equipment companies, Tubb-Williamson, Inc. and Canton Farm Equipment, Inc.

Early in 1984, two Madison County supervisors had Tubb-Williamson deliver backhoes to their beats. This equipment was operated as if it had already been purchased, but it was April 19 before the board of supervisors authorized advertisement for bids for the two backhoes. The bids were to be received on May 18. Canton Farm Equipment underbid Tubb-Williamson, but the board rejected these bids because of "improper specifications." A new request for bids was ordered, and these were received on June 15. Canton Farm Equipment again underbid Tubb-Williamson. Upon examination, it was discovered that the specifications for the two beats had been reversed, and these bids were rejected. A third advertisement was approved by the board with a return date of July 27. Only Canton Farm Equipment responded to this request for bids, and the supervisors took its bid under advisement. At an August 20 meeting, the board of supervisors rejected this bid, stating that they now wanted to go from a lease-purchase to a cash transaction. They directed a new advertisement noting the cash purchase method and changing the wording to read "two new or slightly used rubbertired backhoes." The new advertisement that called for a September 14 deadline was not written properly as it actually called for a lease-purchase rather than a cash transaction. Canton Farm Equipment again underbid Tubb-Williamson on the lease-purchase.

On September 24, four members of the board of supervisors rejected the Canton bid and accepted the Tubb-Williamson bid. While acknowledging that "dollar-wise Canton submitted the lowest bid for each backhoe," the board minutes gave five reasons for awarding the contract to Tubb-Williamson: lower maintenance costs, better quality equipment, operators familiar with equipment, equipment demonstrated and used on job site (by now they had been using it for about six months), and more durable equipment. The minutes gave no indication that Canton's bid failed to conform to specifications of the advertisement.

Canton Farm Equipment sued the four supervisors who voted to accept the other bid and Tubb-Williamson in the chancery court of Madison County. Canton Equipment alleged that the supervisors had engaged in a concerted course of conduct to acquire its competitor's backhoes in disregard of state purchasing laws. The complaint demanded that the supervisors reimburse the county for all sums illegally spent and that the court assess penal damages and attorney's fees. It also named Tubb-Williamson and demanded that the contracts for sale be held for naught. The case was transferred to the circuit court of Madison County, which dismissed it on an assortment of preliminary grounds. This decision was appealed to the State Supreme Court, which held that the circuit court had subject matter jurisdiction, the complaint stated a claim on which relief could be granted, and that Canton Farm Equipment as both an aggrieved bidder and taxpayer had standing to bring action. The circuit court, acting on Canton Equipment's motion, entered partial summary judgment against the supervisors and Tubb-Williamson because the lease-purchase bid advertisement was not authorized, only a cash purchase was. Therefore, the supervisors had no valid power to accept any bid that involved lease-purchase.

The court also noted "[T]he board advertised for the purchase of the backhoes four times . . . looking at the whole picture, it appears that the Board of Supervisors was determined that Tubb-Williamson, Inc. be awarded the sale." The court held the defendants jointly and severally libel to the county for compensatory damages for all expenses involving the backhoes, attorney's fees that the county paid to defend the suit, repairs, and insurance, totaling $111,372.21 plus interest and court costs. After noting that "the damages assessed as compensatory damages are considerable," it concluded that "a nominal amount of penal damages is sufficient." In response to Canton Equipment's demand for penal damages, it assessed only $10 to each of the four supervisors involved. The court ruled the sale of the backhoes void and that title to the backhoes should be assigned to the defendants in proportion to their payments toward the judgment. The court denied Canton Equipment's plea for their reasonable attorney's fees and legal expenses. The defendants appealed the decision to the state Supreme Court, and Canton Equipment cross-appealed denial of attorney's fees and legal expenses.

The second Supreme Court ruling dealing with this case was rendered in August 1992. In affirming in part, reversing in part and remanding, the court ruled that the purchase contracts were entered in violation of statutory law and were void; compensatory damages assessed against the supervisors should be the actual loss (not all expenses) the county sustained (the court directed how these should be computed); penal damages could be assessed against the board; the board was liable to repay the county one half of all attorney's fees and legal expenses (the supervisors could not have the county pay for their actions which were in bad faith, but they could have it pay for their defense against the excessive compensatory damages); and the trial court had the authority to consider awarding attorney's fees to the disappointed bidder.

The case went back to the circuit court where, after several delays and hearings, it was finally settled in 1997. Two sitting and one former Madison County supervisors personally paid more than $90,000 to the county for compensatory damages and to Canton Equipment's lawyer for attorney's fees. The county received $22,500 and the lawyer $69,000. Tubb paid $25,000 to the county to cover the cost of the backhoes minus wear. Through it all, the supervisors involved maintained that they had done nothing wrong and that a simple clerical error in the bid advertisement was to blame.

This was a civil case, and there was never any allegation that Tubb-Williamson had paid any supervisor a kickback on the backhoe deal. However, Stanley F. Stater III, the attorney who represented Canton Equipment, said that feedback from the Supreme Court on the first appeal encouraged him to determine whether the state wanted to investigate the case for possible criminal prosecution. He wrote letters to the state auditor, the attorney general, and the local district attorney informing them of the facts in the case and asking if they would like to follow up. All three declined to do so. Absent a sting and tape-recorded incriminating evidence, auditors and prosecutors probably would have been unsuccessful had they pursued the case.

Johnnie A. Williamson of Tubb-Williamson did get caught up in the Pretense investigation and actually pleaded guilty to paying bribes to several county supervisors. Williamson's legal difficulties began in March 1988 when he was charged in federal court with six counts involving kickbacks to county supervisors. A plea-bargain agreement with the U.S. Attorney entered into in June 1986 allowed Williamson to plead guilty to one of the six counts if he would cooperate with the Pretense investigation. On February 8, 1989, Williamson was given a suspended sentence and placed on probation for three years. He was ordered to make restitution in the total amount of $8,900 to three counties, fined $10,000, and ordered to pay a special assessment of $50. When the Madison County case was finally settled, Williamson was no longer associated with what had been Tubb-Williamson, which was by then just Tubb, Inc. In the November 1988 election held in the wake of Operation Pretense, Madison County citizens rejected the old beat system and voted in the unit system of county government.

Part III.

Plea Bargains

13. Action in North Mississippi

Panola, Pontotoc, and Monroe Counties

Panola County—The Vice President on the Take

Established in 1836, Panola County is located in northwestern Mississippi along the eastern edge of the Mississippi Delta. Panola is a Choctaw word for cotton. The county is one of the nine in Mississippi with two county seats, Batesville and Sardis. Having two county seats is an anachronism left over from the poor transportation systems of the 1800s and a reminder of how slowly political changes occur in Mississippi. The two towns are about ten miles apart and are connected by I-55. With a population of 29,996, the county ranked twenty-ninth in the 1990 census. Batesville, with fewer than 7,000 inhabitants, is the largest municipality. South Panola High School produced several dominant football teams during the 1980s and 1990s, including the 1998 5A state champion. Unfortunately, the county's most influential supervisor of the 1980s was corrupt.

Panola County district one supervisor Horace C. Mathews pleaded guilty to Pretense-related charges in October 1987. Mathews had been a supervisor for twenty years, and as first vice president of the Mississippi Association of Supervisors, he was next in line for the presidency. In an October 27 plea agreement with U.S. Attorney Robert Q. Whitwell, Mathews agreed to waive indictment and plead guilty to a one-count information. He was charged with aiding and abetting a scheme with L&M Equipment Company of Pearl to defraud Panola County and obtain money by false pretense and with using the U.S. mails to perpetrate the scheme.

Specifically, Mathews was charged with busting two L&M Equipment Company invoices. He signed both invoices and had the county pay them knowing that the county did not receive the equipment listed on either invoice. Mathews accepted $200 from a representative of L&M for his part in the fraud. He faced maximum penalties of five years' imprisonment and a $1,000 fine. The plea agreement required Mathews to resign from his position of supervisor no later than one day before actually pleading guilty, not to seek reelection to the office of supervisor in the future, and to pay Panola County restitution of $833.68. The agreement also required him to "give full and truthful statements to the Federal Bureau of Investigation as to all knowledge he may have of extortion, bribery, fraud, kickbacks, payoffs, 'busted' invoices and all other forms of corruption involving all vendors and suppliers of all types of goods and services who have sold to him as a county supervisor, and to testify fully and truthfully to said facts before all grand juries and trial juries which may subpoena him."

In late October, the fifty-seven-year-old Mathews resigned from his position as supervisor and pleaded guilty before Judge Neal B. Biggers Jr. in U.S. District Court in Oxford. Mathews was immediately released on a $5,000 unsecured bond, and sentencing was delayed to allow him to cooperate with the investigation. Mathews was represented in the plea agreement and at the pleading by William H. Liston, a Winona attorney. Mathews was the only Mississippi Association of Supervisors officer and the only supervisor from a northwest Mississippi county to be charged under Operation Pretense.

Mathews had been unopposed in his candidacy for reelection as district one supervisor in the November 1987 general election. He bowed out of the race the same day that he pleaded guilty, October 29. Thus, there was no candidate for the position. Mike Bartlett, a farmer and Como resident, was appointed by the board of supervisors to fill Mathews's unexpired term. A recent election reform had removed the power of calling a special election from the supervisors, so another appointment had to be made when the new board convened in January. The appointment would be for eleven months, or until the November 1988 general election.

On April 22, 1988, Judge Biggers sentenced Mathews to two years in prison and fined him $1,000. However, no probation was to be served after the prison sentence. Mathews reported to the Federal Prison Camp at Maxwell Air Force Base, Alabama, to begin his sentence on the date required. Attorney William Liston filed a Motion for Reduction of Sentence on June 26, 1988, asking that the sentence be reduced to probation. The motion claimed that Mathews had made restitution, had paid all fines imposed by his sentence, and had cooperated as agreed to and was willing to continue to do so. It noted that he had no previous record of criminal misconduct and that numerous citizens of Panola County had written to the court in his support. Judge Biggers denied the motion in an order dated September

28, 1988. Nevertheless, Mathews was released from federal prison on January 23, 1989.

In adjoining Tate County, citizens had voted to switch from the beat to the unit system in the November 1988 referendum. Under the unit system legislation, the county had to hire a road manager to administer all aspects of the county's 480 miles of roads and 146 bridges under the overall direction of the board of supervisors. In a surprising development, Horace C. Mathews surfaced in early 1989. In late spring, the Tate County Board of Supervisors voted three to two to appoint the former convict to the position of county road manager. The job was to begin July 1 if Mathews could obtain a performance bond of $75,000.

Although the vote to hire Mathews had been by secret ballot, supervisors Albert Freeman and Emmett Hale requested that the board minutes reflect their "no" votes. Board of supervisors president Hale expressed his displeasure, "I'm disappointed. I think we probably took the least qualified. As far as what I think individually, I think my vote reflects that. We did not go into detail about the guilty plea. The only thing we asked was if he had his citizenship and if he had the right to vote. He called back and said he did." Mathews had been chosen over two other applicants, Billy Wayne Maxwell and Sammy Ashe, both of whom were Mississippi Highway Department employees and residents of Tate County. Maxwell said, "I was upset, yes. I thought I was qualified. I don't feel like it's right for Tate County to go out of county to fill the job. As far as Horace Mathews, I don't really know anything about him."

When the appointment was first made public, all the three supervisors who voted for it, James Sowell, Tommy Dickinson, and John Thomas Moore, declined comment. Assistant U.S. Attorney John Hailman wasn't at all reluctant to comment. He said, "It will be interesting to see just how much the people will tolerate." Citizens soon registered their complaints to Governor Ray Mabus's office and to the local newspaper. Sally Bondurant, editor of the *Tate County Democrat*, reported negative reaction to the decision. Noting that the job is "next to being supervisor," she said, "a lot of people can not understand why the board would hire somebody convicted of doing something like that. I have not heard anybody who's happy over the situation."

The *Clarion-Ledger* ridiculed Tate County for hiring Mathews in a May 3, 1989 editorial. Under the headline "Tate County, Hiring Fox to Protect Chickens":

Poor Tate County. Its board of supervisors has made it the laughingstock of Mississippi. The federal government conducts a sting operation and catches Panola County Supervisor Horace C. Mathews taking kickbacks. A federal court sentences him to prison. The state adopts a law allowing the county unit system statewide to try to weed out corruption. And what does Tate County do? Its supervisors vote 3–2 to hire Mathews fresh out of prison. And what job do they give him under the unit system that is supposed to dampen corruption? They make him road manager. Get it? Funny, huh? Tate County hires a fox to guard the hen house. The unit system is supposed to keep supervisors from running their beats like little fiefdoms. And Tate County picks a convicted criminal to run its county road operations. It's not a question of lack of candidates. One was a maintenance supervisor for the state Highway Department for more than 12 years. We feel sorry for Tate County. The good people there don't deserve the ridicule three of their supervisors caused in choosing to be good ol' boys instead of leaders.

Soon those involved with the hiring were trying to explain their actions. Mathews said, "The Tate County Board of Supervisors approached me. I'm looking forward to working with the people of Tate County." Tommy Dickerson, district one supervisor, stated, "With the qualifications of Mr. Mathews and his experience in handling a road crew, I feel Mr. Mathews was the best qualified." James B. Sowell, district three supervisor, indicated that he thought Mathews was the best qualified for the job because he would come into the position without showing favoritism to any one of the county's five districts. Sowell said, "I hate all this controversy came up. I think Mr. Mathews paid his dues. Should we put him on welfare? I think we should give him the job he has been trained to do."

The *Tate County Democrat* published a letter to the editor on June 1, 1989, that reflects a remarkable ability of one citizen to forgive and forget and to rationalize away the implications of putting a convicted criminal in a tax-paid position similar to the one he had recently pleaded guilty to abusing. This letter exalts experience and forgiveness at the expense of common sense and the interest of the taxpayers.

Dear Editor:

I have observed the furor over the hiring of Mr. Horace Matthews [*sic*] by the Tate County Board of Supervisors. Whether or not the issue has calmed or been resolved by the time this letter is printed is of no consequence. For the record, I have not seen or spoken to Mr. Matthews [*sic*] in over 25 years. I have no ax to grind or windmill to tilt as do many residents of the county.

The people who would doubt the experience and capabilities of Mr. Matthews [*sic*] and his ability to fill this position have not driven many of his crew maintained roads while he was in office, or did not realize which supervisor district they were driving in at the time. Until his resignation, he kept some of the best county roads anywhere in the state—and he did it without signs of partonage [*sic*] to any one particular individual. This I have observed on a first hand and regular basis for the full time he was supervisor. For someone to say that he is not qualified to handle a work crew is ludicrous.

As for the image presented by the three supervisors who voted for Mr. Matthews [*sic*], I would say they presented a side of humanity rarely observed in todays [*sic*] society—the ability to realize when a debt has been paid. They have not shamed themselves by their vote. Their vote should be felt by the people who have let rampant human emotion and lack of forgiveness to become [*sic*] a common personality trait.

Finally, there seems to be no little amount of concern by the local residents as to what type of example this hiring would set for their children, possibly that crime pays. Children's minds are not permanently molded by strangers if there is the correct nurture and supervision as they are growing up. This is the perfect time to see how well your children have learned by parental teaching. If a parent is afraid their children can not separate right from wrong in a situation, then the parent either doubts their parental guidance or severely underestimates their child. Let us all remember that casting stones is a favorite sport of the narrow minded and that in itself sets a very poor parental standard.

Respectfully,
Bob White

The Pontotoc County Saga—A New Board of Supervisors

Pontotoc County, located in north Mississippi between Oxford and Tupelo, is very much a rural county; it had a 1990 population of 22,237. The county, which was established by an act of the legislature in 1936, probably got its name from the Treaty of Pontotoc which was signed October 20, 1832, near the ancient Indian village named Pontotoc. By the Treaty of Pontotoc, the Chickasaw ceded the last of their homelands in Mississippi, Alabama, and

Tennessee to the United States. With a population of fewer than 5,000, the city of Pontotoc is the county's largest urban area and the county seat. The city is the home of All-Pro tight end Wesley Walls of the Carolina Cougars and singer/songwriter Jim Weatherly, who wrote Gladys Knight and the Pips's smash hit "Midnight Train to Georgia." Both Walls and Weatherly were outstanding football players at nearby Ole Miss.

In the 1980s, Pontotoc County was the epitome of corruption in county government in Mississippi. All five county supervisors were defrauding taxpayers and obtaining kickbacks through bribery, conspiracy, and extortion. These duly elected officials conducted county business with audacity, arrogance, and sheer greed at a level that was simply shocking. The conditions and events surrounding the crimes of Pontotoc County supervisors as revealed by Operation Pretense illustrate just about every facet of the weaknesses and corruption in county government that the FBI investigation brought into such sharp focus. The fates experienced by the supervisors and the corrupt vendors with whom they did business illustrate how the justice system meted out punishment as a result of Pretense.

Operation Pretense was first revealed to the public in mid-February 1987, when nine county supervisors and a heavy equipment salesman were indicted on numerous corruption charges. Five county supervisors were indicted in Oxford by a Federal Grand Jury of the Northern District of Mississippi. The salesman and four county supervisors were indicted in Jackson by a Federal Grand Jury of the Southern District of Mississippi. The five supervisors indicted in Oxford included two from Pontotoc County. Grady O. Baker was indicted on five counts of mail fraud involving accepting kickbacks from a supplier, and Theron Baldwin was indicted on four counts of mail fraud involving accepting kickbacks from a supplier. Within nine months, Baker, Baldwin and the other three Pontotoc County supervisors, Bobby Dean Stegall, Talmage M. Nix, and O. L. Finley, would plead guilty to charges arising from Pretense.

The cases against the Pontotoc supervisors were based on their dealings with five vendors: Davis Chemical Company of Hattiesburg and its owner, Ray Davis; Holiman Equipment Company of Jackson and its salesman, Max Gilbert; the FBI front Mid-State Pipe Company of Carthage; Northeast Mississippi Supply Company of the Rienzi community in Alcorn County and its president and CEO, Bobby Little; and Bull Mountain Gravel Company of Amory and its operator, Lee Hollis Burt. Apparently, information provided by Ray Davis was the key that opened the door for the FBI in Pontotoc County.

In a plea bargain, Ray Davis agreed to cooperate with the FBI in the investigation. He fingered supervisors in a number of counties, including one or more in Pontotoc County. Another compromised vendor, Max Gilbert of Holiman Equipment, played a similar role. Knowing that Pontotoc County supervisors were predisposed to take kickbacks, the FBI, using its agents and the front company Mid-State Pipe, stung a couple of Pontotoc County supervisors by tape recording their involvement in kickback schemes. As conditions of plea bargains, compromised supervisors agreed to cooperate with the investigation, and their cooperation provided information that implicated other supervisors, Bobby Little and Lee Hollis Burt.

The schemes to which the supervisors pleaded guilty involved extorting payments and accepting bribes from vendors. Supervisors would agree to initiate purchases, and later the county chancery clerk would disburse the payments based on approvals by the board of supervisors. The vendor would then make cash kickbacks to the supervisors on those purchases. Under state law, such kickbacks are considered gratuities that must be returned to the county. Of course, the supervisors would keep the money. Usually, the county would get all of the materials described on the paperwork supporting the disbursements. Sometimes, however, invoices were busted, and the county would receive only part of what was invoiced or nothing at all. A kickback usually involved mail fraud because the supervisor would cause a check made payable to the vendor on the fraudulent transaction to be placed in an authorized mail depository for delivery by the U.S. Postal Service.

All five of the supervisors conspired with Bull Mountain Gravel Company and its operator Lee Hollis Burt to accept kickbacks of approximately $.25 per cubic yard, or approximately $200 to $300 per month per district, on purchases of gravel by Pontotoc County. This scheme ran from January 1982 to February 1987, during which time Bull Mountain paid cash kickbacks to four of the five supervisors without missing a month. Stegall's district purchased gravel from Bull Mountain for only a few months during the time period covered by the scheme. Because the county received assistance of more than $10,000 a year from the U.S. government, participation in the scheme involved supervisors in a conspiracy that violated federal law.

The manner in which the gravel scheme was arranged and the way it was carried out reflect the arrogance and audacity of the supervisors and vendor involved. The scheme was described in the one-count information to which Lee Hollis Burt pleaded guilty as a part of the Pretense investigation. Burt was approached by Nix and Finely, who suggested that he increase his bid amount by $.50 per cubic yard and pay each supervisor the increase for their district's purchases. Later Baldwin brought Baker to meet Burt and confirmed that Baker would receive the same deal. One of the five supervisors would pick up the cash kickbacks from Bull Mountain and distribute the money to the other four. White envelopes containing cash with only county district numbers written on the outside would be left on the hood or trunk of a car outside the Ready-Mix office in Amory. Nix, Finely, and Baldwin made pick ups one or more times over the life of the scheme. Baldwin told Burt that the supervisors had been getting only $.10 to $.15 a cubic yard kickbacks from the previous gravel supplier. At least the free market provided some discipline: because of the depressed gravel market, the kickbacks were reduced to $.25 per cubic yard in 1987.

Nix and Finley eventually pleaded guilty to charges involving purchases of gravel from Bull Mountain. Baker, Baldwin, and Stegall eventually pleaded guilty to accepting kickbacks from Mid-State. Baker and Baldwin also eventually pleaded guilty to taking kickbacks from Davis Chemical Company and Holiman Equipment Company. The chronology of the indictments, arrests, guilty pleas, and sentences associated with these five supervisors vividly illustrates how Pretense worked and its effects on county government.

Sixty-six-year-old Grady Baker, district one supervisor and president of the Pontotoc County Board of Supervisors, was indicted on five counts of mail fraud and arrested on February 12, 1987. The charges involved Baker's taking three kickbacks totaling $360. Baker was released on bond and appeared in court on February 19 to plead innocent to all five charges. In June he was reindicted on a total of thirty-one charges of mail fraud for allegedly accepting $2,973 for authorizing fraudulent purchases from Mid-State Pipe Company, Davis Chemical Company, and Holiman Equipment Company. Arraignment was set for June 25, 1987, in Oxford, but Baker's attorney, Will R. Ford, said that he was too ill to appear in court. Assistant U.S. Attorney Hailman asked Ford to provide the court documentation of Baker's illness. Hailman said that he wanted to make sure that Baker was not suffering from "supervisor's disease." A rash of ailments apparently had struck supervisors in the southern part of the state and forced postponements of scheduled trials. Ford provided the requested documentation in the form of a letter from a Tupelo doctor.

Based on a plea agreement with the U.S. attorney, Baker pleaded guilty to three counts on August 29, 1987. He admitted accepting $1,745 in kickbacks for authorizing fraudulent purchases from Mid-State Pipe Company,

Davis Chemical Company, and Holiman Equipment Company. Each count carried a maximum penalty of five years' imprisonment and a $1,000 fine. One count involved a $50 kickback on the purchase of transmission oil from Davis Chemical Company in January 1983. A second count involved a $600 kickback on the purchase of an $11,800 boom mower from Holiman Equipment company in August 1985. The third count involved a fictitious purchase (busted invoice) of a fifty-five-gallon drum of hydraulic fluid for $200 in June 1986 from Mid-State Pipe Company on which Baker received a $100 kickback. Baker also agreed to make full restitution to Pontotoc County in the amount of $1,745.

The three counts to which Baker pleaded guilty were representative of all thirty-one counts listed in the Indictment. Twenty-four counts involved dealings with Davis Chemical Company, two counts involved the mower purchase from Holiman Equipment company, and five counts involved purchases from Mid-State. The evidence that convinced Baker to plead guilty was provided by tape-recorded dealings with FBI agents working undercover as salesmen for Mid-State and information provided by two compromised vendors who were cooperating with the FBI, Ray Davis and Max Gilbert.

Apparently, Baker was a member of what federal prosecutors called the "drum-of-the-month club," which was built around an invoice-busting scheme. Supervisors who were members of this exclusive "club" were automatically mailed a phony invoice each month for a drum of a petroleum product. After the county paid for the nonexistent and never-delivered drum, the vendor mailed the corrupt supervisor half the price in cash with a note in the envelope thanking him for the short-term "loan," just in case someone else opened the envelope.

Baker attempted to plead "probably guilty," but that did not satisfy U.S. District Court Judge Biggers, who insisted on a clear plea of guilty. Judge Biggers explained that while a defendant could disagree with some prosecution evidence, a plea must be either guilty or not guilty. The judge asked Baker if he needed to have the charges explained more thoroughly. "If you think it is necessary, I've got plenty of time," replied Baker. During the description of evidence against him, the acceptance of kickbacks was described as a scheme. "There wasn't no scheme," Baker said, "He just put it out there and I took it." Sentencing was delayed to allow Baker to cooperate in the investigation as provided for by the plea bargain.

In Baker's plea agreement, dated July 24, 1987, the U.S. attorney agreed not to prosecute Baker for any other acts related to or similar to those charged in the indictment, not to seek enhanced fines as provided for by law, and to recommend to the appropriate state district attorney that Baker not be prosecuted in state court for acts charged in this federal indictment. Baker agreed to give full and truthful statements to the FBI as to all knowledge he had of extortion, bribery, fraud, kickbacks, payoffs, busted invoices, and all other forms of corruption involving all vendors and suppliers of all types of goods and services who had sold to him as a county supervisor, and to testify fully and truthfully to said facts before all grand juries and trial juries which might subpoena him. The U.S. attorney agreed to make known to the sentencing judge in writing via the presentence report the nature and extent of Baker's cooperation prior to sentencing.

Baker had qualified to run for reelection and was scheduled to be on the August Democratic primary ballot. But on July 30, 1987, he resigned his position and withdrew from the upcoming Democratic primary. The plea bargain did not require Baker to resign, and he cited his recent heart trouble as the reason for his resignation.

Seventy-six-year-old Theron Baldwin of district four was the other Pontotoc County supervisor who was among first nine supervisors indicted and arrested on February 12, 1987. He was indicted in Oxford on four counts of mail fraud for accepting $175 in cash for various transactions with Mid-State Pipe Company. Baldwin was freed on an unsecured $25,000 bond on the same day of his arrest. He appeared in court on February 20 and pleaded not guilty to all charges. March 31, 1987, was set as the date for a criminal trial before a jury. On March 3, Gregory D. Keenum, Baldwin's lawyer, requested an extension of the discovery deadline and made a motion for continuance. This request was granted, and on June 4 Baldwin was notified to appear in court for a trial by jury on July 20. On June 18, 1987, a Superseding Indictment charged Baldwin with a total of forty-seven counts of mail fraud. He pleaded not guilty to all charges June 25.

Under a plea bargain worked out with the federal prosecutor, Baldwin pleaded guilty on July 8 to three counts of mail fraud, each of which carried a maximum penalty of a $1,000 fine and five years in prison. One of the counts involved using the U.S. Postal Service in a fraudulent scheme to accept a cash kickback of $100 from Davis Chemical Company on a county purchase of two fifty-five-gallon drums of oil for $968.90 in 1982. Another count involved a cash kickback of $200 from Holiman Equipment Company on a $1,858.27 purchase of repairs to a mower cutter head in 1986. The final count involved a cash kickback of $80 on the alleged purchase of thirty grader blades for $495 from Mid-State Pipe Company in 1986. The invoice was busted and the county actually received only twenty of the thirty grader blades it paid for.

The three counts to which Baldwin pleaded guilty were representative of all forty-seven counts in the indictment. Counts one through forty-one involved kickbacks from Davis Chemical Company on purchases of oil, gear grease, degreaser, road signs, diesel oil, and transmission fluid from 1982 to 1987. Two counts involved kickbacks from Holiman Equipment Company for repair work done on mower cutter heads owned by the county. Four counts involved kickbacks from Mid-State Pipe Company for various transactions in 1985 and 1986. Evidence that led to these indictments was provided by the two compromised vendors, Ray Davis and Max Gilbert, and by an FBI agent who had posed as a salesmen for Mid-State.

Count forty-one of the indictment charged that in early February 1987, Baldwin agreed with Davis Chemical Company to accept cash in the amount of $60 on a $357.50 purchase of a drum of antifreeze for his district. The $60 in cash was handed to Baldwin personally on February 3, and the company's invoice was dated February 5. On February 12, 1987, Baldwin called Davis Chemical and said that he no longer needed the antifreeze because "the weather in Pontotoc County has changed." Earlier in the day it had become public knowledge that Mid-State Pipe Company, from which Baldwin had accepted kickbacks on busted invoices, had been cooperating with the FBI and that tapes had been made of all supervisors dealing with Mid-State.

Baldwin's plea agreement dated June 26, 1987, required him to plead guilty to three counts of the Superseding Indictment and to make restitution in the amount of $1,660 to Pontotoc County. Other provisions of the agreement were very similar to those included in Grady Baker's agreement. However, there were some interesting differences. Baker agreed to give full and truthful statements to the FBI about knowledge that he had of extortion, bribery, fraud, kickbacks, payoffs, busted invoices and all other forms of corruption involving all vendors and suppliers who had sold to him (Baldwin's agreement says to county supervisors) as a county supervisor, and to testify fully and truthfully to said facts before grand juries and trial juries that might subpoena him. This difference could have caused Baldwin to implicate his fellow supervisors in discussions with the FBI. Baldwin's agreement did not require him to resign, although he did resign the day before entering his plea. Finally, Baldwin's agreement did not prohibit him from running for public office in the future. He had already announced that he would not be a candidate for reelection in 1987. On July 8, 1987,

Judge Biggers accepted Baldwin's plea of guilty as outlined in the plea agreement. Sentencing was delayed while Baldwin cooperated with the FBI in the continuing investigation.

Baldwin's resignation statement was transparently false as to the reason for his resignation. He wrote, "This is to advise the Board of Supervisors of Pontotoc County, Mississippi that due to health problems and based upon the advice of my treating physician I must tender my resignation as a member of the Board of Supervisors of Pontotoc County, Mississippi effective midnight July 7, 1987."

The first supervisor to plead guilty as a result of Pretense was Bobby Dean Stegall, supervisor of Pontotoc's district five. The fifty-two-year-old Stegall was the tenth supervisor in the state to face publicly disclosed charges related to Pretense and the third from Pontotoc County. After reaching a plea agreement with federal prosecutors, on February 18, 1987, Stegall waived indictment and pleaded guilty to Count one of an information filed in federal court in Oxford. He was released on a $25,000 unsecured bond, and sentencing was delayed to allow him to cooperate with the FBI in the investigation.

The *Pontotoc Progress* reported that after his guilty plea, Stegall said, "I apologize first to my God, then to my family and then to the people of my district and county, in that order. I don't blame anybody but myself, I had the option to say no. You get caught at a weak moment sometimes. I am sorry for the embarrassment I've caused my family and the people who had confidence in me. Everybody who has talked to me [since the plea was made public] agrees that I did the right thing. My friends have indicated that they are still my friends."

The guilty plea involved mail fraud in securing four kickbacks for a total of $325 on county transactions with Mid-State Pipe Company during the period October 1985 to June 1986. Stegall admitted accepting $25 on the purchase of a $175 drum of antifreeze, $50 on a $390 purchase of grader blades, and $90 on a $840.60 busted invoice for forty grader blades, of which the county received only thirty. He also admitted that twice he accepted $80 on $495 busted invoices for purchases of a total of sixty grader blades, of which only forty were actually delivered. The maximum penalty for the count to which he pleaded guilty was a $1,000 fine, five years' imprisonment, or both.

While the provisions on the plea agreement were very similar to those of Baker and Baldwin, there were important differences. Stegall agreed to resign within ten days after the plea agreement was made public and not to run again for public office. Stegall also agreed to give full and truthful statements to the FBI about knowledge that he may have had of extortion, bribery, fraud, kickbacks, payoffs, busted invoices, and all other forms of corruption involving all vendors and suppliers of all types of goods and services who had sold to him as a county supervisor and to all other supervisors of which he had knowledge. No doubt, Stegall implicated at least one vendor and several of his fellow supervisors in discussions with the FBI.

Talmage Nix waived indictment on August 27, 1987, and pleaded guilty to one count of an information filed with the U.S. district court in Oxford. The sixty-four-year-old supervisor of district two was immediately released on a $5,000 bond. Two days earlier, Nix had coasted to victory in the Democratic runoff election in his quest for a fourth consecutive term as supervisor. After his guilty plea, he immediately resigned from office. Nix pleaded guilty to conspiring with other Pontotoc County supervisors and Bull Mountain Gravel Company and its agents and other persons to accept for himself and others cash in an aggregate amount exceeding $5,000 for county purchases of gravel and other supplies from Bull Mountain. Nix had conspired with Bull Mountain and other Pontotoc County supervisors to accept approximately $.25 per cubic yard, or approximately $200 to $300 per month per district, kickbacks on purchases of gravel by the county. Under the scheme, which ran from January 1982 until February 1987, Nix had accepted kickbacks approximately nine times per year and had agreed to continue to do so indefinitely. The maximum possible penalties for these violations were a $10,000 fine and five years in prison.

Nix's plea agreement dated August 26, 1987, was very similar to Baker's. It included a provision that he was not to seek reelection to public office in the future and that he make restitution to Pontotoc County in the amount of $490. The restitution was the result of kickbacks he had received on busted invoices from Mid-State. Sentencing was delayed while he cooperated in the continuing investigation.

O. L. Finley, the fifty-nine-year-old supervisor of district three, lost a close Democratic runoff election to Kent Anderson of Randolph on August 25, 1987. Two days later, Finley waived indictment and pleaded guilty to count one of an information filed with the U.S. district court in Oxford. Sentencing was delayed to allow Finley to cooperate in the ongoing investigation as agreed to in a plea bargain that led to the guilty plea. Finley was immediately released on a $5,000 unsecured bond, and he agreed to resign from his elected position.

Count one of the information alleged basically the same thing that Nix had been charged with. It charged that Finley had conspired with Bull Mountain and other Pontotoc County supervisors to accept approximately $.25 per cubic yard, or approximately $200 to $300 per month per district, in cash kickbacks on purchases of gravel by the county. He allegedly had accepted these kickbacks each month from January 1982 until February 1987 and had agreed to continue to do so indefinitely. The maximum possible penalties for these violations were a $10,000 fine and five years' imprisonment.

Finley's plea agreement required him to make restitution in the amount of $90 to Pontotoc County for accepting cash kickbacks from Mid-State Pipe Company on invoices submitted to the county and not to seek reelection to public office. Other provisions were similar to Baker's agreement, including his promise to cooperate with the FBI in the investigation and to testify truthfully and fully before any jury that might subpoena him.

Assistant U.S. Attorney Hailman indicated that the charges against Nix and Finley were the first to come as a result of information given to the federal prosecutors by other supervisors in Operation Pretense. "You can call this Pretense Plus," said Hailman. Obviously, Bobby Dean Stegall had been singing to the federal prosecutors since his plea bargain and guilty plea in February 1987, and Theron Baldwin had been doing the same since his plea bargain and guilty plea in July 1987.

Mississippi law allowed the county board of supervisors to appoint a replacement to serve out the remaining term of any member who vacated his or her position before completion of his or her term of office. When the Pontotoc County supervisors began to plead guilty to Pretense-related charges and resign, a very convoluted scenario started to unfold regarding their replacements. By September 1987, all five members of the board had been appointed by other board members who had either pleaded guilty to Pretense-related charges and resigned or who were appointees themselves. By the end of the year, one of the appointed supervisors had resigned under pressure from citizens for performing work that favored his father—who just happened to be Theron Baldwin, one of the disgraced supervisors who had pleaded guilty and was forced from office.

Bobby Dean Stegall's plea agreement required that he resign from office by February 28, 1987, and that he not run for public office again. William C. Mathews was appointed by the remaining members of the board of supervisors to serve out Stegall's term as district five supervisor. Mathews, a school bus driver, had previously served as a district five supervisor for three months in 1981 when the incumbent resigned. All of the four supervisors who voted on Stegall's replacement would plead guilty within a few months to Pretense-related charges. Mathews was defeated in the August 1987 Democratic primary when he ran for a full term.

District four supervisor Theron Baldwin's resignation from office was effective July 7, 1987, one day before his guilty plea. Gerald K. Baldwin, Theron's son, was appointed by the board of supervisors to serve out his father's term, which was to expire in January 1988. The three supervisors attending the board meeting—Talmage Nix, O. L. Finley, and the recently appointed William C. Mathews—voted unanimously to appoint the younger Baldwin. Grady Baker was ill and did not attend the meeting. At the same meeting, O. L. Finley was appointed to the position of vice president of the board to replace Theron Baldwin. Six men had qualified to run for the district four post in the August Democratic primary; Gerald K. Baldwin was not one of them.

On July 29, 1987, it was Grady O. Baker's turn to plead guilty to Pretense-related charges and resign his position. The president of the board of supervisors also withdrew from the August 1987 race for supervisor. On July 30, the board appointed Baker's neighbor, John W. Russell, to complete Baker's term, which was to expire in January 1988. Russell was unanimously approved by Gerald K. Baldwin, William C. Mathews, and O. L. Finley after having been nominated by Baldwin. Talmage Nix was not at the meeting. Russell was not a candidate in the upcoming August primary.

At the beginning of August 1987, three of the five members of the board of supervisors had been appointed to replace members who had pleaded guilty to Pretense-related charges. August 1987 brought the downfall of the remaining two elected supervisors. On August 27, Talmage Nix of district two and O. L. Finley of district three pleaded guilty to Pretense-related charges and resigned their positions. Nix had just won the Democratic run-off election for a fourth term, but Finley had lost in a runoff. Interestingly, on August 8, Nix had delivered a signed statement to the circuit clerk's office requesting that his name be removed from the August 25 second primary ballot. However, the very next day he delivered another statement asking that his request for withdrawal be disregarded, and it was. The plea agreements of Nix and Finley prohibited them from running for public office in the future. In his resignation message, Nix, who had recently undergone quadruple heart bypass surgery, cited health and other reasons. He said, "Due to health and other problems, I just had to do it. I got to where I just couldn't serve the people the way they ought to be served." The *Pontotoc Progress* quoted Nix as saying, "I went in there in '76 flat broke, no money in my district, and worked more than three years in the red. I never put any bonds on my people. . . . This is a bitter pill to swallow."

At the county level, winning the Democratic nomination was tantamount to election to office because there was usually no strong Republican or Independent opposition in the general elections. At Nix's request, the state Board of Election Commissioners in early September removed his name from the November ballot. Without Nix's plea agreement, there was nothing to bar him from seeking reelection. Mississippi law prohibited anyone who had been convicted of a Mississippi felony from holding public office. However, apparently as the result of a legislative oversight, persons convicted of felonies in other states' courts or in federal court were not barred from public office in Mississippi.

After the resignations of Nix and Finley, there were two vacancies on the board of supervisors, and all three remaining members had been appointed by the board to serve out the term of supervisors convicted of Pretense-related charges. All of the remaining supervisors had been appointed by a board that included one or more men who had now pleaded guilty to Pretense-related charges. O. L. Finley had supported all three appointments, Theron Baldwin and Grady Baker had supported Mathews's appointment, and Talmage Nix had supported the appointments of Mathews and Gerald Baldwin.

Henry "Hank" Hodges was appointed on August 29 by the board to serve out Nix's term of office. Hodges had tied for third in the first Democratic primary for the district two post. On August 31, the board of supervisors appointed Kent Anderson to complete the term of O. L. Finley. Anderson had defeated Finley in the August 25 Democratic runoff election. Thus, at the beginning of September 1987, Pontotoc County's five supervisors had all been appointed by the board to serve out the terms of elected officials who had pleaded guilty to Pretense-related charges.

The Pontotoc County Democratic Executive Committee in mid-September selected Leighton Benjamin to replace Nix on the November general election ballot. Since there was no Republican or Independent opposition, this selection was tantamount to election to office. Benjamin had been defeated by Nix in the Democratic runoff election. At the same meeting, the committee adopted a resolution recommending that all the appointed supervisors, with the exception of Kent Anderson who had won the Democratic nomination for the district three post and was unopposed in the general election, resign from office. The resolution also contained a recommendation that the unit system of county government be adopted. Apparently, the Democratic Executive Committee hoped that the supervisors who had not been candidates or had been defeated in the Democratic primary would resign and that Anderson would then appoint the men who, like himself, were on the November ballot as Democratic nominees and almost assured of election in the November general election. That's not the way events played out; only Gerald Baldwin ended up resigning, and he did so under pressure.

At an early December meeting of the board of supervisors, a group of about twenty-five district four residents appeared to complain that Gerald Baldwin had just paved a road leading to his father's home while their requests for road work had been ignored for years. Gerald Baldwin said that the road going by former district four supervisor Theron Baldwin's house had been paved at the request of a lot people who lived on that road. He denied that his father had any part in the decision to pave the stretch of road. The younger Baldwin said, "Theron Baldwin did not have the road paved; he didn't even know it was going to happen." He also asserted that the road was in poor condition because of repeated trips by heavy county equipment to his father's house where it had been stored. The beat barn was on Theron Baldwin's property.

On December 10, 1987, Gerald Baldwin resigned as district four supervisor, and James R. "Riley" Seale was appointed to the post the next day by the board of supervisors. Seale had won the recent election to the district four position, and he was scheduled to take office in January. Gerald Baldwin told the board of supervisors that he was leaving to accept a job offer in Fort Worth, Texas. Ironically, in October 1988, Theron Baldwin reported to the Federal Correctional Institution in Fort Worth, Texas.

The younger Baldwin's tenure as supervisor had been short but revealing. At the Mississippi Association of Supervisors annual convention in Natchez in late August, several supervisors had expressed their anger over Operation Pretense. The newly appointed Gerald Baldwin was quoted in the *Clarion-Ledger* on August 28 as saying, "It makes the whole state look bad. I think corruption should be gone after, but all of the publicity has done a lot of damage to the state. I think they (state and federal officials) could have handled it without all this much attention." Baldwin indicated that authorities had made the supervisors appear much more corrupt than they actually were. He said that supervisors often paid for minor expenses—such as replacing a tire on a county vehicle or repairing a broken piece of equipment—out of their own pockets because it was more convenient than having to abide "by the letter of the over-complicated and time-consuming purchasing laws." The replacement Baldwin said, "I can see how a supervisor could tell himself that little bonuses (from kickbacks) is just making up for money he's shelled out. I don't approve of it, but I see how it could happen."

After all the guilty pleas had been entered, more than a year passed before any sentences were imposed on the former Pontotoc County supervisors. In their plea bargains, all five supervisors had agreed to cooperate with the government in the investigation and to testify in court if subpoenaed. Judge Biggers delayed sentencing in each case to allow cooperation in the ongoing investigation. They did indeed cooperate. Information provided by Baker apparently implicated the vendors Lee Hollis Burt and Bobby Little. Information provided by the other supervisors apparently implicated not only the Burt and Little but their fellow supervisors as well. Sentencing was delayed until late 1988 after all five of the supervisors had testified for the government against Bobby Little in September 1988.

Stegall was sentenced September 30, 1988, to two years' imprisonment, all but six months of which was suspended, and to two years' probation. Stegall, who was facing maximum penalties of five years in prison and a $1,000 fine, was also fined $1,000. At sentencing, Stegall said, "I did wrong. I'm sorry for it, and I've admitted it. I've had my life threatened, and [people] threatened to have my house burned. I'm here at the mercy of the court." Stegall's sentence was the lightest imposed on any of the five supervisors, and it probably reflects his extensive cooperation in the investigation over an eighteen-month period. O. L. Finley, who was facing a possible $10,000 fine and five years' imprisonment, was sentenced on October 4, 1988, to eighteen months in prison and fined $1,000. Both Stegall and Finley were ordered to report to the Federal Prison Camp, Eglin Air Force Base, Florida, by noon on October 24, 1988.

Baldwin, Baker, and Nix were sentenced by Judge Biggers on October 4, 1988. Theron Baldwin, who faced maximum penalties of fifteen years in prison and $3,000 in fines, was sentenced to two years in prison and fined $1,000 on each of the three counts He was also ordered to pay $1,660 in restitution to Pontotoc County. Grady Baker was fined $1,000 on each of three counts and sentenced to two years in prison. Baker had faced maximum penalties of $3,000 in fines and fifteen years in prison. Talmage Nix, who was facing possible penalties of five years in prison and a $10,000 fine, was fined $500 and sentenced to two years in prison. Baker, Baldwin, and Nix were ordered to report to the Federal Correctional Institution in Fort Worth, Texas on October 24, 1988.

In December 1987, a petition had been submitted to the federal probation service in Oxford bearing 169 signatures of Pontotoc County district four residents requesting that Judge Biggers sentence the five convicted supervisors to maximum jail terms. The petition contained the following wording: "We, the undersigned citizens of Pontotoc County, want justice done. The history of crime of misappropriation of funds by Pontotoc County supervisors, especially District Four Supervisor Theron Baldwin, should be punished to the fullest extent of the law. These men must serve time for their criminal behavior . . . make restitution for neglect, restore to the public what they have stolen and be prevented from further damage to the county." Phyllis Gober, a district four resident who helped with the petition, said that she hoped the petition would wake up residents in other counties touched by corruption. She was quoted as saying, "These men have robbed not only the community, not only the county, but the state. These men have robbed the United States of a state. Mississippi is the laughing-stock of the nation because of the stupidity."

The transcript of Theron Baldwin's sentencing hearing before Judge Biggers includes the following exchange:

THE COURT: All right. Let Mr. Baldwin come up before the bench. All right. Mr. Baldwin, on a previous day of this court, you entered a plea of guilty to 3 counts of mail fraud, 3 counts of a 47 count indictment. You are before the court now to be sentenced. Is there anything that you wish to state to the Court before sentencing is imposed?

THE DEFENDANT: Well, Your Honor, I just would like to say that this thing has troubled me much. It has almost destroyed my wife and I, and I'm not here today to plead justification, but I'm here to beg for compassion and for mercy. I hope to spend the rest of my days in trying to make right the wrong that has been committed.

THE COURT: All right, sir. Mr. Keenum, either Mr. Greg or Thomas Keenum, do either of you have anything you want to say on his behalf?

MR. KEENUM: Just a few comments on behalf of Mr. Baldwin. I would like to point out that in this circumstance, Mr. Baldwin took office eleven and a half years prior to his resignation.

In my dealings with this man, I have never felt that he really considered the actions that he took to be criminal, to have a criminal intent, that he felt that he was trying to do the job as supervisor, and maybe he looked at it wrong and did look at it wrong as to the funds that were involved, but just two or three points I would like to make on the type of supervisor I think he made that is in his file.

He took office with about $12,000 in his road working fund. The day he resigned, he had $142,000, I believe, in the fund. I don't think it has ever been questioned the type supervisor he made there for his people. The actions that were committed that he has just pointed out to you that he feels remorse for, he made a mistake, but I do feel that in all the circumstances involving the county in this case, there was never indications that I saw anywhere where there was ever a busted invoice. The county got the product it purchased, they were always purchased at the State bid price or at the low bid price.

I would simply ask the court to consider all of these things and consider the fact of him being 77 years old, that he has resigned from office, that he has, based on his acts, been embarrassed in his community, he and his wife and his family, and he has suffered humiliation already, and I will ask for mercy of the Court.

T H E   C O U R T : Mr. Hailman, is there anything that you wish to state to the court in regard to this sentencing on behalf of the government?

M R .   H A I L M A N : . . . I would have to strongly disagree with what Mr. Keenum said, however, in his behalf, in that his actions were not criminal. They were criminal. He has pled guilty to criminal conduct, the various transactions that we are talking about are busted invoices done with the FBI undercover agents, whom he thought were vendors. The idea that somehow this system is a defense to us is absurd. The system is, of course, on trial and I hope the voters will adopt the unit system and reject this system that has to a degree brought all of these men in these criminal acts that they have contribution in.

Today he is sorry he did. As a matter of fact, he says he is not trying to justify. I disagree with Mr. Keenum. He is trying to justify and that is wrong.

Many citizens of Pontotoc County have filed petitions in all of these cases, which Your Honor is familiar with. There is even one letter that I thought was—a couple of letters that were particularly interesting.

One of them from a man who at first had written on Mr. Baldwin's behalf withdrew the letter when he found out all the facts. There is a letter in here from Mr. Vincent. As you will recall, he is one of the men who was involved in the scheme with Mr. Cockerham. He was falsifying invoices and involved with fraudulent deals with Monroe County, and here he is asking for mercy for Mr. Baldwin saying that he is a judge of what should be done, so we would simply ask the Court to consider the entirety of the case and what a serious matter this is in passing whatever Your Honor feels is a fair sentence.

T H E   C O U R T : All right, thank you.

Well, Mr. Baldwin, you certainly pose a unique Defendant standing before the Court, a man of your years, a man of your statute in the community. It is unique to my experience to come before the Court on this serious of a charge. You also, from the standpoint that you are the only person I have ever known to come before the Court for sentencing, and I have been in this business for a long time. I look out over the courtroom, and I see—I see some lawyers out there probably that have a little more experience in criminal law than I, I see one or two, but I have been at it since 1963 on a full-time basis, and I have never known anybody else to come before the Court and people present a petition asking to give them the maximum under the law. That is unique.

On the other side of the coin, you have got some good people speaking on your behalf. I have gotten letters from former U.S. Congressmen and ministers and other people, prominent people, who speak well of you.

You have pled guilty to these counts, three counts. I think you did the right thing in pleading guilty. The evidence was obviously overwhelming, and there is no question in my mind that had you chosen to go to trial on this 47 count indictment, you would probably have been convicted on all or at least the vast majority of those 47 counts and been in a much worse position than you are here today.

I'm taking into consideration that you did plead guilty, that you did testify at one other trial. I understand that it was somewhat ifie at times and uncertain at times about your testimony, but you did end up doing it.

I understand that what you did, even though it is illegal, it is something that has been winked at in this state for many, many years and accepted for the most part for many years. However, it is obviously illegal, and, as I recall, there was another supervisor from Pontotoc County who was up before the Court for approximately the same thing about five or six years ago. There is no—there is no question that you and the other supervisors from Pontotoc County knew accepting kickbacks and gifts was against the law.

In sentencing all five supervisors, Judge Biggers took into consideration the petition by citizens of Pontotoc County and letters of support; in the cases of Nix, Baldwin, and Baker, he also considered their age and health. Apparently, age and health factors influenced the assignment of Nix, Baldwin, and Baker to incarceration in the Federal Correctional Institution in Fort Worth, Texas. Bobby Dean Stegall served his six-month prison sentence at the Federal Prison Camp at Eglin Air Force Base, Florida.

The guilty pleas of all five Pontotoc County supervisors as a result of Pretense and the petition signed by many citizens demanding stiff sentences for the convicted supervisors made it appear that the county was ready for a change to the unit system of county government. When the votes were counted in November 1988, it become obvious that such was not the case. While forty-six of the state's eighty-two counties voted for the unit system, Pontotoc was one of the thirty-six that voted for the beat system. No doubt the referendum results reflect the rural nature of the county and the fear that central management of the roads would diminish service to those in remote locations, a theme that the supervisors hammered home before the election. Voters apparently believed that the problems with corruption lay with the individuals who had previously been elected and not the beat system or that the advantages of decentralized service to constituents outweighed the flaws of the beat system.

Monroe County—How About a Used Tractor?

Named after the fifth president of the United States, James Monroe, Monroe County was established in 1821. Located in northeast Mississippi along the Alabama border and boasting 36,582 residents, Monroe ranked nineteenth in population among the state's counties according to the 1990 census. Aberdeen, the county seat, and Amory are the county's two largest cities; each has more than 7,000 residents. The county has a rich high school football tradition—both Amory and Aberdeen regularly field outstanding teams. Monroe is known as a prosperous and progressive county, but two of its five supervisors pleaded guilty to Pretense-related felonies and were sent to prison in the late 1980s.

District one supervisor Leonard G. "Bud" Faulkner was one of the first county officials in Mississippi to feel the sting of Operation Pretense. On February 10, 1987, he was indicted by a federal grand jury in Oxford on five counts involving bribery, extortion, and mail fraud. The sixty-six-year-old Faulkner had been elected three times and was serving his twelfth year as supervisor. Count one of the indictment accused Faulkner of agreeing in November 1985 to bust a Mid-State Pipe Company invoice for $396 for twenty-four grader blades that were never delivered to Monroe County and to accept a $200 cash kickback for doing so. Count two accused him of scheming with Mid-State to substitute Mid-State invoice number 2026 (transmission and hydraulic fluids) for its invoice number 1190, which the Monroe County chancery clerk had refused to pay because the vendor was not authorized to sell grader blades to the county. Count three involved causing a Monroe County check to be placed in the U.S. mails to pay Mid-State for its invoice number 2026. Counts four and five involved conspiring with Mid-State to bust a $200 invoice for a fifty-five-gallon drum of hydraulic fluid and accepting a $100 kickback for effecting the scheme by use of the U.S. mails.

Faulkner; his attorney, William P. Mitchell; and Assistant U.S. Attorney Hailman signed a plea agreement on May 15, 1987. This document called for Faulkner to plead guilty to counts three and four that charged mail fraud, to cooperate in the ongoing investigation as to the involvement of vendors and suppliers, and to resign from office no later than July 10, 1987. Faulkner also pledged not to run for any public office after his resignation. The U.S. attorney agreed to make known to the sentencing judge via the presentence report the extent of the defendant's cooperation and not to make any recommendation concerning sentencing. The charges to which Faulkner agreed to plead guilty carried maximum penalties of $20,000 in fines and ten years in prison. Faulkner's plea bargain was somewhat unusual among Pretense-related cases. He did not agree to cooperate with the investigators concerning the involvement of other supervisors. He agreed not to run for any office in the future, whereas most Pretense-related agreements prohibited seeking or holding public office only during any probation time imposed by the court. Finally, the agreement stated that the U.S. attorney was not to make any recommendation as to sentencing; in most cases, the government made specific sentencing recommendations.

Judge Biggers accepted the plea bargain and sentenced Faulkner on September 30, 1988, in Oxford. He was sentenced on count three to eighteen months imprisonment and placed on probation for two years. Sentence was suspended on count four, but probation was imposed for a period of two years. Probation was to begin with completion of the prison sentence imposed on count three. Faulkner was also fined $1,000 and ordered to pay $623 in restitution. He was to report to prison on October 24, 1988. Judge Biggers requested that the advanced age and health of Faulkner be considered by the attorney general in determining the institution of confinement.

In the spring of 1989, Judge Biggers signed an order, which read as follows:

Came on to be considered this day the motion of the defendant in the above styled and numbered cause filed under Rule 35(b) of the Federal Rules of Criminal Procedure moving this court to reduce the sentence previously imposed upon this defendant on September 30, 1988, in which the defendant was sentenced to serve 18 months in the custody of the Attorney General of the United States, fined $1,000 and cost of court, and ordered to pay $623.00 in restitution; and after due consideration of the same, including the advanced age of the defendant, the illness of the defendant's wife who is dependent on the defendant, the previous payment of the fine and assessments in full, and the excellent cooperation and truthful testimony of the defendant before trial and grand juries as confirmed by the United States Attorney's office, it is the opinion of the court that the motion is well taken and should be granted.

In view of the above, it is the order of the court that the sentence previously imposed upon this defendant should be reduced to that of time served as of this date.

ORDERED AND ADJUDGED this, the 31st day of March, 1989.

As noted in chapter 8, Faulkner provided valuable testimony for the prosecution in the trial of Bobby Little, a vendor who was convicted on more than 200 counts of bribery and mail fraud.

Without question, one of the most brazen crimes related to the Pretense investigation was committed by district three supervisor John A. Cockerham. In mid-summer 1987, Cockerham and his attorney, Michael D. Jonas, entered into a plea bargain with Assistant U.S. Attorney Hailman. The plea agreement called for the sixty-four-year-old supervisor to plead guilty to a one-count information. In accordance with the plea bargain, Cockerham waived indictment, and pleaded guilty to the one-count Information before Judge Biggers on July 31, 1987. Judge Biggers accepted the plea, and Cockerham was released on a $5,000 unsecured bond. Cockerham was the 37th supervisor to be charged with a crime as a result of Operation Pretense.

The information read as follows:

The United States Attorney Charges that:

COUNT ONE

From on or about November, 1986, to on or about the date of this indictment, in Monroe County in the Northern District of Mississippi and elsewhere, JOHN ALLAN COCKERHAM, defendant herein, being the duly elected and acting Supervisor and agent for District 3 of Monroe county, a political subdivision and agency of the State of Mississippi which received federal assistance and benefits in excess of $10,000.00 in a one-year period, did knowingly, willfully, and corruptly solicit and accept and agree to accept things of value of more than $5,000.00 from another person intending to be influenced and rewarded thereby in connection with a business transaction of the Monroe County Board of Supervisors, to-wit:

Defendant JOHN ALLAN COCKERHAM did accept a secret payment of $17,500 in cash money from an employee of Columbus Ford Tractor in return for defendant COCKERHAM's agreement to have his district accept bids on and purchase a used Warner & Swasey Model G660 Gradall for $24,500.00, well knowing that COCKERHAM already personally owned the equipment, having recently purchased it for only $2,400, and procured a falsified, backdated appraisal of the said equipment; in violation of Section 666 of title 18 of the United States Code.

In addition to pleading guilty to this one count, the agreement required Cockerham to make full restitution to Monroe County of all costs and property related to all criminal acts charged in the information in the amount of $15,100 and to resign from office no later than July 31, 1987. Cockerham also agreed to give full and truthful statements to agents of the FBI as to all knowledge he might have of extortion, bribery, fraud, kickbacks, payoffs, busted invoices, and all other forms of corruption involving all vendors who had sold to him as a county supervisor. He further agreed to testify fully and truthfully to said facts before all grand juries and trial juries that might subpoena him. The U.S. attorney agreed not to prosecute Cockerham for any other acts related to or similar to those charged in the information, not to ask for enhanced fines as provided for by the U.S. Code, and not to make any recommendation concerning sentencing. The prosecuting attorney also agreed to inform the sentencing judge of the nature and extent of Cockerham's cooperation prior to sentencing.

Newspaper accounts of Cockerham's guilty plea gave additional details about the former supervisor's escapades. The Warner & Swasey Model G660 Gradall equipment mentioned in the information was similar to a backhoe; it was a 1953-model ditch-digging machine. It had originally been owned by Clay County, which had sold it for $1,600 at a public auction to an unnamed private buyer. Cockerham bought the equipment from that buyer for $2,400. He persuaded Columbus Ford Tractor to conceal his ownership and offer it to the county for $24,750. Monroe County paid that amount, and John Partridge, owner of the company, paid Cockerham $17,500 in $100 bills, with the company keeping the difference. Neal Benson, sales manager for Allied Equipment of North Mississippi, Inc. in Amory, gave Cockerham a fictitious and backdated appraisal on the equipment.

The charge against Cockerham was not actually a direct result of Operation Pretense. Discrepancies had been discovered after Cockerham had accepted cash kickbacks from an undercover FBI agent, and his activities were closely scrutinized. This scheme was uncovered by state auditors, who turned the case over to the FBI. Both Partridge and Benson denied any wrongdoing in connection with the case, and Assistant U.S. Attorney Hailman confirmed that no charges had been filed against either of them. Partridge said, "I was the middleman, but I didn't know where it [the equipment] was coming from." Benson denied the appraisal was false, but he admitted backdating it. Documents introduced in court by the government showed that "the transaction was handled in such a manner as to conceal from Monroe County the fact that Mr. Cockerham personally owned the Gradall as well as the dramatic difference in price between what he had paid for it and what he charged his district." Prosecutors also had evidence that Cockerham had accepted two kickbacks from an undercover FBI agent posing as culvert salesman for Mid-State Pipe Company. Because of the plea bargain, Cockerham was not charged regarding his dealings with Mid-State. Assistant U.S. Attorney John Hailman said that in conversations taped by the FBI, Cockerham admitted taking cash kickbacks for several years from other companies.

Cockerham cooperated in the ongoing investigation for ten months before Judge Biggers imposed sentence. At sentencing, the former supervisor said, "I made a mistake, and I'm very sorry. I made the mistake, and I am sorry for my church, family and friends. I'm truly sorry for them." Cockerham was a deacon in his church. Assistant U.S. Attorney Hailman credited Cockerham with being the most cooperative among those indicted as a result of Pretense. He told the court that Cockerham had appeared before several grand juries and had aided in other investigations of county-level corruption. The sentence was two years in prison and a fine of $10,000. Cockerham was also required to make restitution to the county in the amount of $15,100. He was to report to the institution designated for confinement on May 23, 1988, and he was to stand committed until the fine was paid in full. This was the first sentence imposed as a result of Operation Pretense in the U.S. District Court of the Northern District of Mississippi.

When he was a district attorney, Judge Biggers himself had secured convictions of two Monroe County Board of Supervisors presidents. He believed that Cockerham's behavior was outrageous, and he said that the defendant's actions were "more culpable and criminal than a supervisor taking a kickback." The judge's comment probably reflected the fact the sale of very old equipment that Cockerham owned personally to the county at a greatly inflated price was nothing short of brazen. Co-opting private businessmen to help accomplish the scheme only added to its outrageousness. Nevertheless, the judge was impressed with the number of letters he had received from Monroe County supporting the disgraced supervisor. The judge had received letters from the sheriff, circuit clerk, chancery clerk, superintendent of education, attorneys, state legislators, and "an awful lot of preachers." "It would appear that everyone in Monroe County is behind you," Biggers said. "But you know as well as I that is not true in all respects. Anyone can get friends and relatives to write letters of support." The district three supervisor's post from which Cockerham had resigned had been held at different times by Cockerham's father, mother, and brother.

14. The Vortex of the Maelstrom

Attala, Leake, and Neshoba Counties

Attala County—A Famous Dirt Road

Established in 1833, north-central Mississippi's Attala County is said to be named after a Native American heroine. That the name was derived from the Cherokee word *"otale,"* meaning mountain, is also a possibility. Since there are no mountains anywhere in the state, the first possibility seems more likely. The county had a 1990 population of 18,481, and Kosciusko, the county seat, had a population of 7,415.

Attala County is the birthplace and early childhood home of Oprah Winfrey, the celebrated talk show host and Oscar-nominee for her performance in Steven Spielberg's *The Color Purple.* Winfrey was born and spent her first six years in the Buffalo community just east of Kosciusko. Winfrey's grandmother, Hattie Mae Lee, raised her until she reached the age of six and moved to Milwaukee with her mother. In November 1986, Winfrey visited Jackson and reminisced about her early life in Mississippi: "Growing up in Mississippi with my grandmother is what enabled me to be where I am today. I know that." She recalled taking the cow out to pasture, drawing water from the well, selecting her own switch for whippings, and churning butter on the back porch. She continued, "Had I not had that kind of upbringing, I might be somewhere else doing something entirely different."

The county held a "Welcome Home Oprah" day on June 5, 1988. Funds raised at the event benefited the Buffalo Youth Center and the Kosciusko Cultural Center. Winfrey brought a film crew from WLS-TV in Chicago to begin a television special about celebrities going home. Following her appearance at the festivities, the thirty-four-year-old Winfrey remarked, "It's a deeply humbling experience to come back to the place where it all started, where you all started and think about how far you have come. I believe none of us progresses in life unless we remember where we have come from. This day will forever be a part of my memory and a part of who I am, to consistently—physically as well as emotionally—remind me of where I have come from."

Old Ethel Road, the dirt road "where she was born," according to her mother, Vernita Lee, was renamed Oprah Winfrey Road in honor of the county's most famous native. Winfrey's cousin, Jackson veterinarian Oscar Glen Presley, added that the road is "real muddy when it's wet and real dusty when it's dry. Nevertheless, it's the main artery of this community. It passes by this church where Oprah made her first speeches." Had Attala County been governed by honest supervisors over the years, it is quite possible that not only Oprah Winfrey Road but many other dirt and gravel roads in the county could have been paved. Unfortunately, however, in the 1980s, the county was burdened with four corrupt supervisors.

On February 12, 1987, in Oxford, Robert Ellard, a forty-eight-year-old Kosciusko resident and Attala County district three supervisor, was one of the first nine supervisors indicted in Operation Pretense. Ellard was arrested and released on a $25,000 unsecured bond the same day. He was charged with one count of extortion and eight counts of mail fraud for accepting $865 for authorizing payments totaling $3,921.69 on fraudulent county purchases. Ellard was also charged with using bogus invoices to bill Attala County for part of the cost of a tractor that he bought for his personal use. Arraigned before U.S. Magistrate Norman L. Gillespie on February 20, he entered not guilty pleas to all of the charges. Ellard was represented by J. P. Coleman, former governor of Mississippi and former judge of the U.S. Fifth District Court of Appeals. Trial was set for April 6, 1987, in federal court in Aberdeen.

Ellard's dealings with the FBI front, Mid-State Pipe Company, involved purchases and purported purchases of culverts, grader blades, shop towels, a drum of hydraulic fluid, Perma-Bond paving material, and pothole sealant. Count six included the following statement:

> It was also a part of the scheme that on or about March 6, 1986, defendant ROBERT C. ELLARD would and did agree with Mid-State Pipe Company ("Mid-State") to bill Attala County for part of the $3,000 purchase price of a used Case model 1030 tractor for the personal use of defendant ELLARD. To conceal the transaction, ELLARD agreed to sign as approved by him "busted" Mid-State invoices to Attala County for other items that were to be billed but not delivered to the county by Mid-State. ELLARD told Mid-State to split the invoices so that the dates and amounts would appear smaller and

less suspicious. Thereafter defendant ELLARD paid $2,000 by check for the tractor, which he received personally, and approved payment by Attala County District #3 on Mid-State invoices numbers 2029, 2030, and 2031, dated March 10 and 14, 1986, in the amounts of $396.00, $382.00, and $293.00, which purported to be grader blades, perma-bond, pot-hole sealant, and hydraulic fluid and grease, which defendant ELLARD well knew were not for these items at all, but to pay Mid-State for part of the purchase price of the Case tractor for ELLARD's personal use. The supplies listed on the three invoices were paid for by Attala County check/warrant #2603, dated April 7, 1986, but never received by the county.

The defendant requested a continuation of his trial, which had been scheduled for April 6. On March 16, U.S. District Court Judge Neal Biggers Jr. signed an order that granted the request.

In early May, Ellard withdrew as a candidate for a sixth term as supervisor. Ellard; his attorney, J. P. Coleman; U.S. Attorney Robert Q. Whitwell; and Assistant U.S. Attorney John R. Hailman signed a plea agreement on May 15, 1987. Ellard, who agreed to plead guilty to two counts of mail fraud, faced maximum penalties of ten years in prison and $2,000 in fines. He also agreed to make full restitution to Attala County, to cooperate with the government in the ongoing investigation, and to resign from office by July 10. The prosecution agreed not to recommend any particular sentence, to inform the court via a presentencing written report of the nature and extent of Ellard's cooperation with the investigation, and to ask that the remaining seven counts be dropped. Ellard tendered his resignation as district three supervisor to the board of supervisors in June and made it effective July 3, 1987.

More than a year and two months after his indictment, Ellard pleaded guilty before Judge Biggers according to the terms of the plea agreement. Judge Biggers accepted those terms, dismissed seven counts, sentenced Ellard to eighteen months in prison, imposed a $1,000 fine on one mail fraud count, and suspended sentence on the other mail fraud count, while imposing a fine of $1,000 and three years' probation. The fines were to be paid prior to the expiration of probation. Ellard was to report to prison on May 23, 1988. The two counts to which Ellard pleaded guilty were egregious crimes. Count six, as outlined above, involved Ellard having the county pay part of the costs of a tractor that he bought for his personal use. Count eight involved busting two Mid-State invoices for a total of $611 and accepting a $305 kickback on the purported purchase of twenty-four grader blades and a fifty-five-gallon drum of hydraulic fluid that were never delivered to the county. The time that elapsed between the date of the plea bargain and sentencing and the relatively light sentence imposed for such serious crimes no doubt reflect the value and extent of information that Ellard gave the government.

Ellard was also linked to an alleged kickback paid by Johnnie A. Williamson of Tubb-Williamson, Inc. to an Attala County supervisor. According to count one of the March 9, 1988, six-count indictment of Williamson: "On or about September 7, 1984, Williamson prepared a false and fraudulent invoice which he submitted to Attala County for payment in the amount of $36,000 and paid a supervisor a kickback on said sale of approximately $2,000." The *Star-Herald* of Kosciusko reported in its March 24, 1988, edition that Attala County's district three purchased a $36,000 extendahoe from Tubb-Williamson, Inc. in September 1984. The request for bids on the equipment contained many detailed specifications. Tubb-Williamson had been the only bidder, and Ellard was district three supervisor at the time. Ellard was incarcerated in the Federal Correctional Institution in Montgomery, Alabama. The warden of that institution was directed in an Order for Writ of Habeas Corpus Ad Testificandum dated May 31, 1988, to deliver Ellard to Jackson to testify against Williamson in a trial scheduled for June 13, 1988. Williamson entered into a plea agreement with the federal government on June 6, 1988, and Ellard never testified.

Ellard was also implicated in Pretense-related charges against Dowell Smith, owner of Smith Diesel Sales and Service in Carthage. Although Ellard was not named in Smith's October 1988 indictment, it contained charges that linked Ellard to a $2,000 kickback that Smith made to a supervisor in Attala County on the sale of a used $41,500 Caterpillar motorgrader to district three in April 1984 when Ellard was supervisor. Ellard served as district three supervisor for nineteen years.

On July 29, 1988, David Fancher, president of the Attala County Board of Supervisors, and his attorney, Thomas A. Coleman (J. P.'s son), promised in a now fairly standard plea agreement executed with Assistant U.S. Attorney Hailman to waive indictment and plead guilty to a one-count information charging Fancher with mail fraud. The fifty-one-year-old third-term district two supervisor and McCool resident agreed to plead guilty to accepting a total of $170 in the form of two cash kickbacks on county purchases from Mid-State and using the U.S. mails to carry out the underlying scheme. The charges carried maximum penalties of five years in prison and a $1,000 fine. Fancher also agreed to pay $370 in restitution to the county for kickbacks he received from Mid-State and Tubb-Williamson, Inc., to resign from office and not seek reelection, and to cooperate in the ongoing investigation. Fancher resigned his post in early August. At a July 29 hearing, Judge Biggers questioned Fancher about his involvement in the kickbacks. Biggers asked, "Why did you do it?" "That's a good question," Fancher answered. "I really don't know why I did it. I knew it was wrong. It's wrong to take anything that doesn't belong to you." The judge indicated that Fancher could expect to be sentenced in 20 to 30 days, to which the defendant replied, "The sooner the better."

On September 30, 1988, Fancher stood before Judge Biggers for sentencing. He told the judge, "I'm sorry for what I've done. . . . I apologize to the people." His attorney noted that Fancher had two sons in college and that he had pleaded guilty without having been indicted. However, prosecutor Hailman noted that Fancher had voted with all other members of the board of supervisors against the unit system in 1987. He also pointed out that Fancher had condoned letters submitted on his behalf by several people who stated that Operation Pretense was "a waste of time." Fancher maintained that he had known nothing about the letters. Judge Biggers saw the letters, which appeared to be photocopies of one original, in a different light. He told Fancher that he had not considered the letters in passing sentence and added, "It's almost like someone was trying to hurt you." However, Judge Biggers chided Fancher, saying, "You gave in to the temptation of the system to commit fraud, one of many supervisors who could not withstand the temptation to get money in addition to your salary." Judge Biggers sentenced Fancher to eighteen months in prison, fined him $500, and ordered him to pay $370 in restitution to Attala County. The defendant was to remain in custody until the fine was paid in full. Fancher reported to the federal prison at Eglin Air Force Base in Florida on October 24, 1988.

Although he was not named in the indictment, Fancher was implicated in Pretense-related charges against Dowell Smith. Smith's October 1988 indictment included charges that he paid a $1,000 kickback to a supervisor in Attala County on the sale of a $43,500 Caterpillar motorgrader to district two in April 1984. He was also charged with paying a $200 kickback on repairs billed at $10,763.21 to district two in April 1984. Fancher was district two supervisor at the time.

Fancher mailed U.S. Attorney Whitwell a Motion to Correct Sentence Pursuant to Federal Rule of Criminal Procedure Rule 35(a) in early April 1989. In this motion, he claimed that his sentence was grossly disproportionate to sentences imposed in equivalent cases. The motion was strange. Fancher began by comparing his case with the cases of other Mississippi supervisors. He then went on to include cases of a woman in Kentucky who had been running a vehicle theft ring with the help of her imprisoned husband and of former Beech Nut Nutrition Company executives involved in fraud in selling apple juice for babies. Nevertheless, on June 29, Judge Biggers, citing Fancher's motion signed an Order Reducing Sentence to Time Served as of July 3, 1989.

After his release from prison, Fancher made a political comeback. Mississippi law, which prohibited a person convicted of a state felony from holding political office but was silent concerning a person convicted of a federal felony, allowed him back in the political arena. Fancher ran for supervisor in Attala's second district in 1995 and won. He was said to be planning to complete this term and retire in the year 2000. A bill that prohibits federal felons from holding state office passed the legislature in the 1990s and was signed into law by Governor Kirk Fordice.

Colon Belk, Ethel resident and former three-term supervisor of Attala County's fifth district, entered into a plea agreement with federal authorities on August 2, 1988. Belk agreed to waive indictment and plead guilty to a one-count information that charged him with mail fraud in connection with his acceptance of kickbacks. His plea bargain was similar to the one Fancher had struck. Belk also agreed to make restitution to the county in the amount of $400 for taking cash kickbacks from Mid-State and Tubb-Williamson, Inc. The seventy-five-year-old Belk had not sought reelection in 1987, although he was serving as president of the board of supervisors at the time.

Belk pleaded guilty to accepting a $100 kickback from Mid-State on county purchases of culvert pipes, grader blades, and shop towels and to using the U.S. mails as a part of the scheme. He faced maximum penalties of five years in prison and a $1,000 fine. Judge Biggers accepted the terms of the Plea Agreement and sentenced Belk to eighteen months in prison and fined him $1,000. He was also ordered to pay $400 in restitution to Attala County and $50 in court costs. Belk was ordered to report to prison on October 24, 1988. Assistant U.S. Attorney Hailman stated at sentencing that Belk had testified before a federal grand jury and that information he provided authorities could lead to charges against others. Judge Biggers noted that he was aware of the help that Belk had given the prosecutors and of his excellent reputation. The judge added, "This is the first time you have been before the court on any illegal charge." Judge Biggers indicated that he viewed the prison sentence as a warning to others in similar circumstances.

On March 31, 1989, Judge Biggers signed an Order Reducing Sentence to Time Served. In this order, the judge cited Belk's motion for reduction of sentence, his advanced age and poor health, his payment of the fine, and his cooperation in the investigation.

In early September 1988, Jesse Fleming, who was serving a second term as district four supervisor and was president of the board of supervisors, appeared voluntarily before Judge Biggers at the federal district court in Oxford to plead guilty to a one-count information charging him with mail fraud. The information charged that during October 1985 and March 1986, Fleming agreed to make purchases of grader blades, nuts, bolts, and grease from Mid-State Pipe Company and received a total of $160 in kickbacks on the transactions and that he committed mail fraud by causing checks to be mailed by the county to pay for the purchases. Fleming had previously signed an agreement with federal prosecutors to resign from office, to plead guilty to mail fraud, to pay $160 in restitution to the county, and to cooperate fully in the investigation. U.S. Attorney Whitwell had agreed to make Fleming's cooperation known to the sentencing judge and to make no recommendation concerning sentencing. The mail fraud charge carried maximum penalties of five years in prison and a $1,000 fine.

Subsequently, Judge Biggers refused to accept Fleming's guilty plea. When the judge was giving instructions regarding the defendant's rights and questioning him as to the extent of guilt, Fleming claimed that he did not recall any discussions of kickbacks prior to placing an order for equipment and supplies from a salesman who turned out to be an FBI agent. Biggers told him that if the case went to trial the government would have to prove that he "knowing and willfully" devised a scheme to defraud Attala County by using the mails to make payments for goods with prior knowledge that he was to receive kickbacks on the purchases. Fleming told the judge, "To say that I knowing and willfully did is not what actually took place, but since the act took place, I'm guilty."

The judge asked for details, and Fleming said that on the first transaction with the agent he had placed what he felt was a legitimate order for goods needed in road maintenance operations. According to Fleming's account, as the salesman/agent was writing up the order, he said that he was going to give the supervisor money in appreciation for the business. He recalled telling the salesman, "That's not necessary." Then the salesman dropped an envelope on Fleming's desk and walked out of the office. Fleming said that after he made a second purchase from Mid-State the salesman dropped an envelope that contained money in the yard of his home. He also maintained that on another occasion the salesman walked up to him in the courthouse and put money in his pocket. Judge Biggers asked, "What was the intent?" Fleming replied, "The whole scheme of things was me simply making purchases of supplies that I needed and the salesman, who turned out to be an agent, induced it."

Assistant U.S. Attorney Hailman immediately contested that version of events, saying, "I think Mr. Fleming has a lapse of memory. He has heard the tapes where they discussed percentages prior to and continuate with the sale." The judge then questioned Fleming as to whether he recalled such discussions of percentages of the sales price of goods that were to be rebated to him as kickbacks. "I remember him offering a certain percentage after the sale. I don't remember any discussion before the sale," Fleming responded. Judge Biggers continued, "If that is your recollection, I don't want you to plead to something that you did not do. This case will have to be carried out in another manner." Hailman then told the judge, "We'll present it to the next grand jury."

When Fleming appeared before Judge Biggers, he had not conformed to one of the conditions of the plea agreement that he had struck with the government. He had agreed to "resign from office no later than the day before his plea of guilty is entered." He had not done so. In fact, Fleming returned to Attala County and presided over the next board of supervisors meeting as president. Fleming was never indicted by a federal grand jury. Federal prosecutors decided they did not have enough credible tape-recorded evidence to continue the case.

After his seemingly miraculous escape from a Pretense-related federal indictment, Fleming was indicted on state charges in September 1991. He was charged with fraud by a public officer for allegedly feloniously defrauding Attala County of $156.93 by having the county pay for repair of a twenty-four-volt John Deere starter that belonged to him. By the time his trial began in March 1992, Fleming was serving his third term as supervisor. Department of Audit investigative auditor Waltine Drane testified at the trial that a complaint had been filed against Fleming alleging that he had caused a personal starter to be repaired with county funds. Drane indicated that after he questioned Fleming about the starter, he and Fleming went to Fleming's home where the supervisor removed the starter from his tractor and gave it to the auditor. Based on the auditor's work, Fleming paid the county the $153.93 repair cost and the state $76.56 to cover the costs associated with the investigation. Fleming testified that the starter belonged to the county and that it had been repaired to serve as a spare part. He also testified that it was installed on his tractor simply to test it to see whether it was working properly. In fact, the county did not own a single tractor that the starter would fit.

On March 25, 1992, Fleming was convicted by a jury, and on the next day he was sentenced to five years in prison with four years suspended. Fleming immediately filed a Motion for Judgment Notwithstanding the Verdict or for a new trial, which the court denied. He subsequently filed a notice of appeal. The appeal was based on the fact that one of the jurors, Clarence T. Foster, was a convicted felon who had not revealed his conviction when asked whether he had ever been charged with or convicted of a crime. On January 9, 1997, the Mississippi State Supreme Court reversed the verdict and remanded the case to the lower court. The case was tried again, and Fleming was found guilty by another jury on September 17, 1997.

This verdict was also appealed, and the case went to the Mississippi State Supreme Court a second time. The state's highest court affirmed the lower court's decision on January 28, 1999, and on April 12, 1999, issued a mandate to the Attala County circuit clerk to proceed with carrying out the sentence. As of July 1999, Jesse Fleming was serving his jail time. Part of his duties as a prisoner included helping to maintain the grounds around the Attala County courthouse.

In a 1988 referendum, the citizens of Attala County rejected the unit system and voted to remain on the beat system. The vote was 3,362 for the unit system and 3,873 against. This vote is puzzling in light of the fact that between May 1987 and the November 1988 referendum, three Attala County supervisors had been convicted of taking kickbacks and a fourth had been implicated in kickbacks as a result of Pretense. The unit system held out the promise of more efficient and less corrupt county government. The results of the 1988 unit system referendum, along with the 1991 reelection of the indicted Jessie Fleming and the 1995 election of convicted felon David Fancher, make it likely that Oprah Winfrey Road will remain a dirt strip for a long time in the future.

Leake County—At the Center of the Storm

Leake County, named for Virginia native Walter Leake, was created by a legislative act of 1833 incorporating territory that was part of the Choctaw

Cession of 1830. Thomas Jefferson had appointed Leake as chief judge of the Mississippi Territory, and he later was a member of Mississippi's 1817 constitutional convention. Leake became one of the state's first two U.S. senators, a judge of the Mississippi State Supreme Court, and the state's first two-term elected governor. He died in 1825 while serving his second term as governor. Leake County had a 1990 population of 18,463, and Carthage, the county seat, had a population of 3,453.

Leake County is located almost in the geographical center of the state, and Carthage is almost in the exact center of the square-shaped county. Leake County and the city of Carthage were also at the very center of Operation Pretense. As related in chapter 1, the Reverend John Burgess, a Pentecostal minister from Carthage, was probably the key figure in Operation Pretense. The FBI front, Mid-State Pipe Company, was established in and operated out of Carthage, and three of Leake County's five supervisors pleaded guilty to Pretense-related charges.

The U.S. District Court in Jackson issued a warrant for the arrest of Leake County district three supervisor Deward Dean Myers on March 10, 1987. A federal grand jury had handed down a nine-count indictment against Myers on March 9. Myers was charged with bribery, mail fraud, and extortion. On March 11, Myers was arraigned before U.S. Magistrate John R. Countiss III in Jackson. He pleaded not guilty to all charges and was released on a $5,000 personal recognizance bond. All the charges against Myers involved his dealings with Mid-State Pipe Company. Myers was charged with approving ten false Mid-State invoices for a total of $6,808.66 and accepting kickbacks totaling $817. The charges also included bid rigging, busting invoices, and assisting in making arrangements for Mid-State to make fraudulent deals with other county supervisors. Trial was set for June 1, 1987.

On May 30, 1987, Myers and his attorneys, James E. Smith and J. P. Coleman, entered into a Memorandum of Understanding with Assistant U.S. Attorney Nicholas B. Phillips. Under the agreement, Myers was to plead guilty to counts one, two, three, and four of the indictment and to cooperate in the ongoing investigation. Maximum penalties for these four counts were twenty-five years in prison and fines totaling $1 million. The government was to inform the court about the extent of Myers's cooperation at the time of sentencing, to make no recommendation concerning the sentence on count two, and to recommend suspended sentences and concurrent terms of five years' probation for counts one, three, and four, with probation to begin after release from any incarceration. In addition, the government was to recommend that a special condition of probation be that Myers neither seek nor hold public office during the probationary period. The government also agreed to recommend that the charges in the other five counts of the indictment be dropped.

U.S. District Court Judge Tom S. Lee passed sentence on Myers on December 21, 1987. The former supervisor was sentenced to three years in prison on count two, while sentence was suspended on Counts one, three, and four. A five-year probation was to begin after completion of the prison time imposed on count two. Myers was also fined $5,000, assessed $200 in court costs, and prohibited from seeking or holding public office during the term of probation. Myers reported to the Federal Prison Camp at Maxwell Air Force Base, Alabama, on January 19, 1988.

James L. Freeny was the second Leake County supervisor charged as a result of Pretense. The district one supervisor was indicted on nine counts by a federal grand jury in Jackson on May 4, 1987. The charges against Freeny included bribery, mail fraud, and extortion. According to the indictment, Freeny had engaged in bid rigging, busting invoices, and assisting in making arrangements for other supervisors in the county to engage in fraudulent activities. All of the charges involved the supervisor's dealings with Mid-State Pipe Company. He was accused of approving ten false Mid-State invoices totaling $5,373 and accepting $583 in kickbacks during the period May 1985 through April 1986. An order for Freeny's arrest was issued by the U.S. District Court on May 5, 1987, and it was executed the same day. Freeny appeared before U.S. Magistrate Countiss on May 11 and pleaded not guilty to all of the charges. He was released on a $5,000 personal recognizance bond, and trial was set for August 3, 1987.

A Memorandum of Understanding constituting a plea bargain was signed by Freeny; his attorney, J. P. Coleman; and Assistant U.S. Attorney Phillips on August 13, 1987. In this rather standard agreement for a Pretense-related case, Freeny agreed to plead guilty to counts two (mail fraud) and nine (extortion) of the nine-count indictment and to cooperate in the ongoing investigation. The prosecutor agreed to inform the court of the extent and effect of Freeny's cooperation, to make no recommendation as to sentencing on count two, and to recommend a suspended sentence and five years' probation on count nine. The U.S. attorney was to recommend that any probation imposed should begin after release from any incarceration required and that Freeny be prohibited from seeking or holding public office during probation. The government agreed to seek dismissal of the remaining seven counts, and it reserved the right to recommend restitution of funds. The maximum penalties that could be imposed on counts two and nine were twenty-five years in prison and fines of $750,000.

U.S. District Court Judge William H. Barbour Jr. passed sentence on November 23, 1987, in Jackson. Freeny was sentenced to five years in prison on count two and to five years' probation on count nine. He was also fined $10,000, ordered to pay restitution of $30 to Leake County and $553 to the FBI, and assessed $100 in court costs. Probation was to begin after release from prison, and a special condition of probation was that Freeny neither seek nor hold public office. The remaining seven counts were dismissed. Freeny reported to the Federal Prison Camp at Maxwell Air Force Base, Alabama, on January 4, 1988.

Based on a seven-count indictment by a federal grand jury, a warrant for the arrest of Thomas Jack Jones was issued by the district court in Jackson on June 9, 1987. On June 10, the district five supervisor was arrested, entered a not guilty plea before U.S. Magistrate Countiss, and was released on a $1,000 personal recognizance bond. Trial was set for September 8, 1987. The charges against the fifty-eight-year-old Walnut Grove resident included bribery, mail fraud, extortion, and aiding and abetting mail fraud and extortion. The charges were related to transactions that the county entered into with Mid-State Pipe Company and Shine's Supply between February 1984 and June 1986. Jones was alleged to have accepted a total of $1,849.48 in kickbacks from two vendors for approving ten false invoices totaling $18,579.51.

On August 17, 1987, Thomas Jack Jones; his attorney, Percy Stanfield Jr.; and Assistant U.S. Attorney Ruth R. Harris signed a Memorandum of Understanding that constituted a plea bargain. Jones agreed to plead guilty to count two (mail fraud and aiding and abetting mail fraud) and count seven (extortion and aiding and abetting extortion) and to cooperate with the ongoing investigation. The prosecutor agreed to recommend that the court accept the guilty pleas, to inform the court of the extent and effect of Jones's cooperation at the time of sentencing, to make no recommendation as to the sentence on count two, to recommend that the court suspend imposition of sentence on count seven, and to recommend that Jones be placed on five years' probation to begin upon release from confinement, if such was imposed. A further special condition of probation was to be that Jones neither seek nor hold public office during the probationary period. The government was to make no recommendation for or against fines and reserved the right to recommend restitution as appropriate. Finally, the government was to recommend at the time of sentencing that the other five counts be dismissed. The maximum penalties that could be imposed for the crimes to which Jones agreed to plead guilty totaled twenty years' imprisonment and $500,000 in fines.

Jones had withdrawn from the Democratic primary runoff for the district five supervisor post, which had been held in early August. Jones later pleaded guilty in accordance with the plea bargain before Judge Lee in Jackson on August 28, 1987. Judge Lee accepted the guilty plea and deferred sentencing so that Jones could cooperate in the investigation.

At the sentencing hearing, Jones told the judge, "Your Honor, I'm sorry for the grief I've caused my church, my family, and my county. I've asked the Lord to lead and guide you in your decision." Jones's attorney, Percy Stanfield Jr., asked that his client not be sent to prison saying, "What went wrong, I don't know. Maybe it was the power of politics." The attorney noted that Jones had cooperated with the investigation and had admitted to two other crimes not in the indictment. Stanfield also said, "He served and did a good job. Never did he bill the county for anything it did not receive." Claiming that Jones suffered from severe heart problems, the attorney said, "Incarceration is not the best thing for Mr. Jones." Assistant U.S. Attorney Richard Starrett said that the government believed that Jones has cooperated, but "he has not gone overboard in his zeal." Starrett noted that Jones had agreed to take a polygraph test but that it could not be administered before sentencing. He said, "My understanding is that there was insufficient time during the holidays."

On December 29, 1987, Judge Lee sentenced Thomas Jack Jones to three years in prison on count two and five years' probation on count seven. Jones was required to pay a $5,000 fine within the first six months of probation and to pay $1,499.98 in restitution to Leake County and $340 to the FBI within the first sixty days of probation. He was also prohibited from seeking or holding public office during probation. In passing the relatively light sentence, Judge Lee cited Jones's agreement to take a polygraph test and said, "I've imposed five years in some similar cases, but here I conclude you have provided cooperation." Jones was the eighteenth former supervisor sentenced to prison as a result of Operation Pretense. He reported to the Federal Prison Camp at Maxwell Air Force Base, Alabama, on January 25, 1988. Jones's court file contains a Satisfaction of Judgment dated April 19, 1988, indicating payment of the fine, assessment, and restitution.

According to the 1990 census, Neshoba County's population of 24,800 ranked thirty-third of the eighty-two Mississippi counties. Neshoba County is located in the east-central part of the state, and Philadelphia is the county seat. Home to a Choctaw Indian reservation, Neshoba is said to come from a Choctaw word meaning "wolf." Philadelphia, one of thirteen cities of brotherly love in the United States, is the only city of any size in the county. For many, however, this bustling county and the lovely city of Philadelphia are known only for the murders of civil rights workers James Earl Chaney, Andrew Goodman, and Michael H. Schwerner in the summer of 1964.

The county is home to the annual Neshoba County Fair, a unique midsummer spectacle and celebration. Many fair participants come for a week of socializing and fun in the outdoor heat and stay in "fair cabins" that range in quality from crude shacks to well-furnished condos. Each year, the fair features outstanding entertainment, all the usual fair activities, and horse and harness racing on the state's only licensed racetrack. During election years, the fair features political stumping, which often has great flair. Ronald Reagan spoke during his 1984 campaign for the presidency and pronounced the fair a unique American happening. The county also hosts the annual Choctaw Indian Fair, which is another major attraction. In the 1990s, casino gambling came to the Choctaw reservation and brought with it a great increase in tourism and economic development for the whole county.

Many sports fans identify Philadelphia with the exploits of Marcus Dupree, a great high school football player of the 1970s. Dupree was one of the most highly recruited high school players in the history of college football. His recruitment is the subject of *The Courting of Marcus Dupree* by famed Mississippi writer Willie Morris. Dupree had a stormy but outstanding one-year stint as a running back under coach Barry Switzer at the University of Oklahoma and a brief professional career that was brought to an abrupt end by an injury.

The story of Neshoba County government in the 1980s and 1990s is an admixture of bold progressive actions and corruption. On a positive note, the county's board of supervisors voluntarily switched from the beat system to the unit system in the mid-1980s. However, while the change was successful in terms of cost efficiency and service to citizens, three of the five supervisors who initiated the improvements were later charged and pleaded guilty under Operation Pretense. Unfortunately, newly elected supervisors disparaged the unit system and attempted to reinstate the old beat system.

In August 1987, Mississippi State University published a report entitled *Converting to the Unit System: The Neshoba County Experience*. The report is a case study of the county's conversion from the beat to the unit system, and it details the cost savings and other benefits related to the change. The author, William "Marty" Wiseman, directed a project that provided assistance in the conversion process. The report was cited many times in discussions of the two systems and in newspaper articles and editorials during the 1987–1988 controversy over unit system legislation.

The Neshoba County Board of Supervisors voted unanimously on July 2, 1984, to adopt the county unit system citing the following rationale: (a) it lends itself to hiring the best in professional and supervisory personnel, (b) it encourages and promotes the best purchasing practices, (c) it creates a sense of unity in the board of supervisors that carries over into every area of responsibility they bear, and (d) it enables a county to own and operate a minimum of equipment while being assured that special types of construction equipment can be obtained and used for the benefit of the entire county.

When Mark Nixon became the first Neshoba County administrator on September 1, 1986, the county had essentially finished the transition to the unit system. Nixon was given broad authority and sufficient freedom to develop the proper relationships with the board of supervisors and other county officials. The success of the transition is documented in *Converting to the Unit System*. This report used actual data for fiscal year 1985–1986 and annualized three months' data for 1986–1987 to make the comparisons shown in Table 1.

The report attributes the steep drop in the costs of utilities and contractual services to the unit system's "in-house" capabilities for equipment repair. Under the beat system, much of the equipment repair had been contracted, but a new unit facility provided new and better tools, a more comfortable work environment, and more skilled mechanics. These factors combined to provide increased and more efficient repair capabilities. An astounding drop in expenditures for materials of $323,357, or 53.8 percent, is attributed to the effects of centralized purchasing and implementation of inventory control procedures. Centralization of road and bridge maintenance under a road manager led to attention being given to roads and areas of the county that had been lacking repairs. In addition, centralization

Table 1. Comparison of Beat System and Unit System Modes of County Operations

	Personnel	Utilities & Contractual Services	Materials	Total
Beat	$352,072.46	$113,405.37	$600,808.52	$1,066,286.35
Unit	327,730.48	55,045.80	277,451.28	660,227.56
Difference	24,341.98	58,539.57	323,357.24	406,458.84
% Savings Unit over Beat	14.5%	51.5%	53.8%	38.1%

Per Mile Comparison of Beat Versus Unit System

	Miles	Expenditures	Cost per Mile
Beat	762	$1,066,286.40	$1,399
Unit	762	660,227.56	866
Savings	762	406,058.84	533

highlighted the unnecessary duplication of road equipment and led to the identification of $151,800 of surplus equipment.

The report concluded that the unit system had brought greater efficiency in existing operations, monetary savings, capable professional administration, economic development, increased policy-making capabilities, and overall expansion of county government capacity. As a result, for fiscal year 1986–1987 the county was able to implement a tax cut of about 15 percent. All of this was powerful ammunition in the hands of unit system supporters. Meanwhile, Wiseman became and remains a major player in the beat versus unit system controversy.

John Holley, district five supervisor, was arrested on federal charges on March 11, 1987. Holly pleaded innocent to all charges that same day before U.S. Magistrate Countiss in Jackson. He had been indicted by a federal grand jury on one count each of extortion and bribery and nine counts of mail fraud. The charges involved scheming to rig bids on culvert pipe, busting invoices on grader blades and petroleum products, and assisting in accomplishing arrangements for other Neshoba County supervisors to enter into similar agreements. All of the charges involved the supervisor's dealings with Mid-State Pipe Company. Holley stood accused of accepting a total of $1,609 from Mid-State related to fourteen county transactions that were consummated during the period August 1985 to July 1986 and using the U.S. mails to accomplish the underlying schemes. The sixty-five-year old third-term supervisor was released on a $5,000 personal recognizance bond.

On June 5, 1987, Holley pleaded guilty before Judge Lee to one count of extortion and one count of bribery as the result of a plea bargain worked out with the U.S. attorney's office. He admitted taking cash kickbacks from a representative of Mid-State in the amount of $1,609. The plea bargain called for the government to drop the nine mail fraud counts, make no recommendation concerning sentencing on the bribery charge, and to recommend a suspended sentence and five years' probation on the extortion charge, with the probation to begin after any prison time imposed on the bribery charge. Other conditions of the plea agreement were that Holley resign from office within two weeks of his plea being accepted and that he not seek or hold public office during the time of probation. Judge Lee deferred sentencing for at least forty-five days because of the probation department's heavy workload.

Sentence was imposed by Judge Lee on November 20, 1987. Holley was sentenced to five years in prison, ordered to pay a fine of $5,000 and $1,609 in restitution, placed on probation for five years after imprisonment, and prohibited from seeking or holding public office during the time of probation. He was to report to federal prison on January 4, 1988. Holley had faced a maximum of thirty years in prison and $500,000 in fines on the charges to which he pleaded guilty. On the nine mail fraud counts that were dropped in accordance with the plea bargain, Holley had faced possible maximum sentences of forty-fie years in prison and fines totaling $2.25 million.

At sentencing, Thomas E. Royals, Holley's attorney, asked the judge for leniency because of the poor health of Holley's wife. Holley said, "I'd just like to say, your honor, that I'm guilty, and I just pray that you will have mercy on me, and I won't ever do it again, your honor." Sentencing Holley to prison with no special terms, Judge Lee chided him by saying, "Mr. Holley, over an eleven-month period you defrauded the taxpayers through accepting kickbacks, 'busting' invoices and rigging bids, and were involved in 17 such fraudulent transactions which constitutes a violation of the public trust of an elected official of Neshoba county."

Assistant U.S. Attorney Starrett noted that Holley had turned down an invitation to cooperate with the government in the investigation and that he had given no information about other wrongdoings. Judge Lee indicated that Holley had threatened an FBI agent. According to the judge, "Holley advised him [the agent] that he was concerned that he might be from the state auditor's office, and if the agent messed him up, he'd kill him." Royals claimed that his client did not mean the statement as a threat. However, the transcript of an August 13, 1985, taped conversation between Holley and FBI Agent Cliff Chatham, working undercover as Mid-State salesman Cliff Winters, revealed that the supervisor actually threatened to kill the agent three times. The transcript reflects Holley using extremely vulgar language in what were without question serious threats to kill the agent. No doubt, Holley's desire to keep a jury from hearing that conversation influenced his decision to make a plea agreement.

Fifty-nine-year-old Arlo Winstead, a resident of Union and district three supervisor, was indicted by a federal grand jury in Jackson on August 7, 1987. Winstead had lost his bid for reelection in the August 4, 1987 Democratic primary. The seven-count indictment charged Winstead with one count each of bribery and extortion and five counts of mail fraud. On August 10, he was arrested and arraigned before U.S. Magistrate Countiss. Winstead pleaded innocent to all charges and was released on a $5,000 personal recognizance bond. The charges against Winstead involved scheming with Mid-State Pipe Company to rig bids on culvert pipe, to accept kickbacks on county purchases, and to bust invoices on purported sales to Neshoba County of materials and supplies that were either not delivered or not delivered in the proper quantities. The charges also included using the U.S. mails to accomplish the schemes. It was alleged that Winstead extorted bribes totaling $421 from Mid-State on five separate transactions carried out between June 21, 1985, and June 4, 1986, and that the U.S. mails were used to effect payment of the bribes. An FBI audiotape made at the time Winstead took a $100 cash kickback from an FBI agent posing as a Mid-State salesman making a $672 sale to the county caught the supervisor saying, "You might be a federal man." He then went on to say, "All of this money stays in the county anyway."

A Memorandum of Understanding was signed by Arlo Winstead and Assistant U.S. Attorney Phillips on November 3, 1987. Winstead agreed to plead guilty to the extortion count and one count of mail fraud and to cooperate in the investigation. The government agreed to seek dismissal of the other five counts, ask for delay in sentencing, inform the court of the extent of Winstead's cooperation at sentencing, make no recommendation on the mail fraud charge, and recommend five years' probation on the extortion charge. Winstead also agreed to resign his elected position within two weeks of the plea being accepted by the court and neither to seek nor hold public office during the time of any probation imposed. Total maximum penalties on the two charges to which Winstead agreed to plead guilty were twenty-five years in prison and $500,000 in fines.

On February 12, 1988, Judge Barbour sentenced Winstead to five years' imprisonment on the mail fraud count, with all but six months suspended, and five years' probation on the extortion charge. The probation was to begin after release from incarceration. Winstead was fined $10,000 on the extortion count and ordered to pay restitution of $421 to the county and a special assessment of $100 to the U.S. government. He was also prohibited from seeking or holding public office during the time of probation. Winstead was released on the existing bond and ordered to report to federal prison on March 7, 1988. The court recommended that the former supervisor be assigned to Federal Prison Camp at Maxwell Air Force Base, Alabama.

Judge Barbour sentenced Winstead at the same time he sentenced former Clarke County supervisor Lige Becton. At the sentencing hearing, Judge Barbour said, "It is indeed a shame to be caught in the middle of a situation where you have clearly violated the public trust. If not for the fact that you are public officials, probation might be an alternative. But you were public officials who happened to get greedy for relatively small amounts of money. As much sympathy as I have for you and your families, I can not justify not giving you a jail term." In a courtroom where his family and friends filled three rows of seats, Winstead told the judge, "I made a terrible mistake. I'm guilty, and I'm sorry."

Willard Posey, district one supervisor, was charged with two counts of extortion and seven counts of mail fraud by a federal grand jury in Jackson on September 11, 1987. He was arrested on September 14 and arraigned before U.S. Magistrate Countiss. Posey pleaded not guilty to all charges and was released on a $5,000 personal recognizance bond. He was the 43rd supervisor to be charged as a result of Operation Pretense. Posey was completing his second term as supervisor, and he had not stood for reelection. The charges against the forty-year-old Posey involved a $1,500 kickback extorted from Holiman Equipment Company of Jackson, extorted kickbacks from Mid-State Pipe Company totaling $250 on six county purchases from November 1985 to May 1986, and use of the U.S. mails to accomplish the schemes involved. The charges carried total combined maximum penalties of seventy-five years' imprisonment or $1.7 million in fines or both.

In an Order of Dismissal dated October 16, 1987, Judge Lee dismissed the

September 11 indictment without prejudice. The original indictment was simply not worded properly, and Posey was reindicted on the same charges. Trial was set on the second indictment for December 2, 1987. In early December, Posey made an agreement with the government and pleaded guilty to one count of mail fraud and one count of extortion. He faced maximum penalties of twenty-five years in prison and $500,000 in fines on the two counts. Willard Posey was sentenced by Judge Barbour on March 29, 1988, to two years in prison. He was also ordered to serve five years' probation and ordered to pay a fine of $5,000.

In late 1987 and early 1988, events related to Neshoba County's conversion to the unit system took a turn for the worse. Three of the five supervisors who had voted to implement the unit system were indicted and subsequently pleaded guilty to Pretense-related charges. In 1988, the county had three new supervisors, A. J. Chaney of district one, Dudley Warren of district three, and George Baxter of district five. They joined two holdovers, Dale Reynolds of district four and Wallace Cox of district two. Neshoba's new board of supervisors began dismantling the unit system soon after taking office in January 1988. Among the first acts of the new board was purchasing new pickup trucks for themselves. They also voted to relieve the road foreman of his duties and return those responsibilities to the individual supervisors. Marty Wiseman was quoted as saying, "It boils down to where four men have essentially taken control of the government, like in a banana republic. They want to return to the beat system because that's the way it has always been done. And the people are the ones who will pay for it."

The board of supervisors and its newly appointed attorney, Terry Jordan, who was also a state senator, strongly denied the charges. Jordan claimed that the supervisors had decided that the acting road foreman, who had taken over after the old one had resigned, was unable to handle the responsibilities of both shop and road foreman. Jordan indicated that the supervisors were aware that some kind of unit system might be mandated by the legislature, and they were waiting for the outcome of the session before hiring a foreman. "In the meantime, they took over the responsibilities of road foreman in each of their districts," Jordan said. Nevertheless, two of the supervisors, Baxter and Warren, disputed Wiseman's 1987 report, claiming that the cost savings estimates were exaggerated.

In a May 24 editorial, the *Meridian Star* called for a grand jury investigation of possible wrongdoings in Neshoba County.

When the Neshoba County Board of Supervisors made the switch in 1984 to the unit system of government, the plan was held as a model for others to follow.

The phased changeover was completed in early 1987 with the opening of a centralized "Unit Facility," which replaced the county's five beat-level road work "barns."

A centralized purchasing plan was established.

Mississippi State University Professor Marty Wiseman, who had participated, was so impressed with the changeover that he wrote a book entitled *Converting to the Unit System: The Neshoba County Experience.* He wrote that the county's 24,000 residents would realize an annual 38% savings in taxes under the unit system.

Well, folks, serious problems have developed.

Troubles began last year when three of the county's supervisors were arrested in the Federal Bureau of Investigation (FBI)'s Operation Pretense probe. They were accused of having engaged in corrupt buying practices prior to the changeover to centralized purchasing.

Election of three new supervisors last November was followed by charges from Mr. Wiseman and others that the replacement board was determined to change back to the beat system of government.

Supervisors, although naming themselves as road foremen in their respective beats, denied the charges.

Now County Administrator Mark Nixon, who had guided the changeover to the unit system, has resigned. He, too, contends that the "Neshoba County Experience" has turned sour.

Neshoba County taxpayers have cause for concern. Where there is so much smoke, there must also be a fire of some sort.

Perhaps a grand jury investigation would be in order.

In the November 1988 referendum on the beat versus the unit system, the voters of Neshoba County overwhelmingly (5,983 to 1,643) endorsed the unit system. Since then, the state auditor has been able to enforce a real unit system of government for Neshoba County.

15. The I-20 East Corridor

Scott, Newton, and Lauderdale Counties

Scott County—Little Cooperation and a Light Sentence

Located between Jackson and Meridian and bisected by I-20, Scott County is in the very midsection of Mississippi. Established in 1833, the county was named for Abram M. Scott, Mississippi's seventh governor (1831–1833) and the last governor elected under the constitution of 1817. Scott, a South Carolina native, moved to the Natchez District and served as a captain of militia during the 1813–1814 Creek Wars. He represented Wilkerson County at the 1817 constitutional convention, and he served as lieutenant governor from 1828 to 1830. With 24,137 residents, the county had the thirty-fourth largest population of the state's eighty-two counties according to the 1990 census. Forest, with a population that exceeds 5,000, is the county's largest metropolitan area and the county seat. It is not clear whether the city was named for the pine forest that once covered the site or for the Confederate general Nathan Bedford Forrest. Both spellings are included in legislation concerning the city.

In a federal indictment dated June 9, 1987, Scott County district five supervisor Isaac Weems Jr. was charged with three counts of mail fraud. A warrant for the second-term supervisor's arrest was issued the day of the indictment, and he was arrested the next day. The sixty-one-year-old Forest resident was arraigned before U.S. Magistrate John R. Countiss III on June 12. He entered a not guilty plea and was released on a $1,000 personal recognizance bond. Trial was set for August 3, 1987. Weems, the thirty-third supervisor charged under Pretense, faced maximum penalties of fifteen years in prison and $750,000 in fines.

All of the charges against "Junior" Weems involved his dealings with Mid-State Pipe Company, and its salesman, undercover FBI special agent Jerry King. The charges involved bid rigging, busting invoices, and accepting bribes in the form of kickbacks on county purchases. Count one of the indictment charged that the defendant approved three false and fraudulent Mid-State invoices for a total of $1379.18 and received a total of $230 in cash kickbacks from Mid-State for doing so.

On February 12, 1987, the date Operation Pretense was made public, the State Department of Audit seized Mid-State invoices that had been approved by three Scott County supervisors, Weems, Monzell Stowers of district one and Powell Jones of district two. The *Scott County Times* asked the three supervisors at a public meeting of the board of supervisors about these Mid-State invoices. All three denied any wrongdoing in connection with the seized invoices. On March 4, the newspaper quoted Weems that he was offered "a 10 percent kickback on purchases on one occasion and a 'busted invoice' deal on another" by Mid-State representatives, but he said he refused their offers. "I just kept walking," he said.

Neither Stowers nor Jones was ever charged as a result of Operation Pretense. FBI and Justice Department sources had noted when the investigation was first made public that some of Mid-State's transactions with supervisors were legal. Apparently, Stowers and Jones had only engaged in legal transactions with the FBI front. In fact, Rev. John Burgess, who had worked undercover for the FBI at the beginning of Operation Pretense told the author that Powell Jones was an honest supervisor who would not engage in illegal activities.

U.S. District Court Judge Tom S. Lee issued a Recusal Order June 16, 1987. In this Order, Judge Lee disqualified himself from the case. Lee had served as attorney for the Scott County Board of Supervisors prior to beginning his service as a federal judge, and Weems had been a member of the board during the last five years of Lee's service as board attorney.

Weems and his attorney, Thomas E. Royals, entered into a Memorandum of Understanding with U.S. Attorney Richard T. Starrett on July 16, 1987. In this standard plea agreement, the defendant agreed to plead guilty to two counts of mail fraud and to cooperate with the ongoing investigation. Weems was to resign from his post within two weeks of his guilty plea. The U.S. attorney agreed to make no sentencing recommendation on one count and to recommend that a suspended sentence and five years' probation be imposed on the other count. The government was to also recommend that any probation should commence after any incarceration that was imposed and that a special condition of probation be that Weems not seek or hold public office. The prosecution was to inform the court the extent and effect of Weems' cooperation at sentencing and to request strongly that such cooperation be considered in determining his sentence. Weems faced a maximum of five years in prison and a $500,000 fine in conjunction with the plea bargain.

In the August 4, 1987, Democratic primary election, Weems garnered nearly 41 percent of the vote in his quest for a third term as district five supervisor. He was scheduled to face Joe Risner, who received about 43 percent of the vote, in a run-off in late August. In mid-August 1987, the sixty-one-year-old Weems pleaded guilty before Judge William H. Barbour Jr. in accordance with the plea bargain. Weems resigned as district five supervisor and withdrew from the scheduled August 25 second primary. Despite Weems's guilty plea, the board of supervisors appointed his wife, Nelia Weems, to serve out his term.

Judge Barbour sentenced Weems on November 23, 1987 to a year and a day in prison on one count and five years' probation to begin after release from prison the other count. Weems was also required to pay $130 in restitution to the FBI and $100 to Scott County. He was also fined $5,000, which had to be paid by November 24, 1987. Finally, Weems was prohibited from seeking or holding public office during the time of probation. The other charge was dismissed.

At sentencing, U.S. Attorney Starrett told Judge Barbour that Weems had not cooperated with the investigation as required by his plea agreement. Weems's attorney claimed that the former supervisor had told the FBI "all that he knew" about the case. Despite Weems's lack of cooperation in the investigation, Judge Barbour imposed the lightest Pretense-related sentence that had yet been imposed. The judge indicated that in passing sentence he considered the amount of money involved in the crimes, the defendant's health, and the fact that Weems had come forward without forcing the government to go to trial. Weems was under treatment for prostate cancer and a subsequent colostomy procedure, and Royals argued that a prison sentence could result in a "death situation" for the former public official. Barbour countered that a number of federal prison facilities could successfully treat Weems's ailments. Weems surrendered to the warden at the Federal Medical Camp in Rochester, Minnesota, on January 11, 1988.

Newton County—Four of Five

Newton County, located in east-central Mississippi, is named after Sir Isaac Newton, the great English scientist and mathematician. With 20,291 residents, Newton was the forty-third most populous county according to the 1990 census. Decatur is the county seat and the birthplace of the 1960s civil rights activist, Medgar Evers. Interstate 20 runs through the county linking it to Jackson on the west and Meridian on the east and making two of Mississippi's largest cities easily accessible. The city of Newton, with a 1990 population of fewer than 4,000, is the county's largest municipality. In the late 1980s, four of the county's five supervisors were charged with Pretense-related offenses.

Newton County district three supervisor Henry Mack Smith was indicted on February 11, 1987, on one count of conspiracy to defraud, one count of bribery, one count of extortion, and nine counts of mail fraud. He was accused of accepting $2,928 from Mid-State Pipe Company from about August 1984 until about June 1986. The charges included conspiring with Mid-State to rig bids on culvert pipe and grader blades submitted to the Newton County Board of Supervisors, conspiring to bust invoices for purported sales of grader blades, nuts/bolts and culvert pipe, and using the U.S. mails to further the schemes. Smith was also charged with using the U.S. mails to facilitate the transactions as outlined and with obstructing, delaying, and affecting commerce and the movement of articles in interstate commerce by extortion. He was immediately freed on a $5,000 personal recognizance bond. Smith pleaded innocent on February 17, 1987, and remained free on bond. Trial was set for May 11 before Judge Barbour in Jackson.

Specifically, Smith was accused of approving 11 false and fraudulent invoices to the county for more than $12,000 and receiving cash kickbacks amounting to $2,928 on these county purchases. Smith was also charged with agreeing to assist Mid-State in selling culvert pipe to other supervisors in Newton County and with receiving $70 for introducing Mid-State to other Newton County supervisors.

Thomas Royals, Smith's attorney, filed a motion in early May for dismissal of eleven of the twelve charges including the bribery charge and all ten of the mail fraud charges. The motion did not challenge the extortion charge. The motion asserted that the bribery statute under which Smith had been charged, which prohibits any public official from accepting a bribe or stealing government money, did not apply to the allegations made by the prosecution. Royals claimed that the statute applies to the misuse of federal revenue-sharing money and that the transactions cited by the prosecution in the indictment involved money collected through local taxes. U.S.

Attorney Starrett maintained that the source of the money did not matter. Judge Barbour said he would rule on the motion before Smith went to trial.

In a Memorandum Opinion and Order dated May 6, 1987, Judge Barbour wrote:

> Section 666 (of the U.S.C.) was designed to fill a gap which the difficulty of tracing federal monies caused. Not every petty bribery is included in the section, however, congress has put a floor on certain amounts to avoid offenses that would otherwise be state offenses. It is enough on the face of the statute that federal funds are provided to a county in the amount of $10,000 and that there is bribery of a supervisor or other local government agent involving a transaction or a series of transactions of at least $5,000 concerning the affairs of the government or organization. The language in section 666 is clear that it is not an essential element of this crime that the government trace the $5,000 to specific federal government funds.
>
> The acts as alleged in the indictment are sufficient to fall within the provisions of 18 U.S.C. Section 666. The motion of Defendant Henry Mack Smith to Dismiss Counts I through XI of the indictment is denied.

On May 13, 1987, Smith made a plea agreement with the government and pleaded guilty to two counts of the indictment. Under the agreement, Smith was to plead guilty to accepting $2,928 in the form of a bribe and kickbacks from Mid-State and to extortion. The government was to seek dismissal of the other ten charges. Smith was to cooperate in the ongoing investigation, and the U.S. attorney was to inform the court of the extent and effect of that cooperation and to recommend that the court suspend imposition of a sentence on the extortion count and impose five years' probation. The government was to make no recommendation as to a sentence on the bribery charge. The total maximum penalties for the bribery and extortion charges were $500,000 in fines and twenty-five years in prison. The U.S. attorney was to make every effort to have sentencing postponed until Smith had completed the cooperation required by the agreement.

The plea bargain did not require Smith to resign from office immediately or not to seek public office while on probation, if probation was imposed. Judge Barbour pointed out the omission of a requirement to resign immediately when he accepted the plea, and U.S. Attorney George Phillips made it clear that he intended to include such a provision in future plea agreements. Smith could remain in office until sentencing, which Barbour delayed. Smith's lawyer said that Smith would not run for reelection. Nevertheless, Smith did resign as supervisor in May 1987, and the board of supervisors appointed Martin Milling to serve out his term.

Henry Mack Smith was sentenced on April 3, 1989, to three years in prison and placed on probation for five years to begin with release from imprisonment. He was also ordered to pay a fine of $1,000 to be paid by monthly installments during in the first year of probation. Smith was ordered to pay restitution in the amount of $95 to the U.S. government and $2,928 to Newton County within thirty days of the sentence. The former supervisor was also prohibited from seeking or holding public office during the term of his probation. The two-year delay between Smith's guilty plea and his sentencing and the relatively harsh sentence give different impressions of the extent and usefulness of his cooperation with the ongoing investigation. The length of the delay indicates continuing useful participation, while the harshness of the sentence indicates a lack of useful cooperation. However, the relative harshness of the sentence may simply be a reflection of the seriousness of Smith's crimes. Included in the FBI evidence against Smith was a tape-recorded exchange between a Mid-State representative and the supervisor discussing whether or not Smith would mind payoffs in $20 bills. "All I can tote," Smith replied to the representative.

Newton County district five supervisor William E. Edwards was indicted on eight counts May 4, 1987, by a federal grand jury in Biloxi. The two counts of extortion, one count of bribery, and five counts of mail fraud carried maximum penalties of seventy-five years in prison and $2 million in fines. The charges against Edwards included scheming with Mid-State to rig bids on culvert pipe and to bust invoices on grader blades and petroleum products and using the U.S. mails to carry out the schemes. The seventy-four-year-old Hickory resident, who had served as supervisor since 1976, was arrested and charged on May 5.

Edwards negotiated a plea bargain, and on July 27, 1987, pleaded guilty to an extortion charge and a mail fraud charge while admitting to taking $1,180 in illegal kickbacks. He admitted that from June 1985 until April 1986 he took $570 in kickbacks from FBI special agent Jerry King, who was posing as a salesman for Mid-State Pipe Company. He also admitted taking $1,060 in payoffs from Davis Chemicals of Hattiesburg between September 1983 and December 1985. Edwards was the nineteenth supervisor to plead guilty to Pretense-related charges. Edwards stood before U.S. District Court Judge Lee on December 21, 1987, for sentencing. He was sentenced to three years in prison and ordered to pay $1,060 to Newton County and $570 to the FBI. About thirty family members and friends attended the sentencing hearing, and as Judge Lee read the sentence, some of them wept.

Newton County district two supervisor Durwood "Doc" Pinson, a resident of the Little Rock community, was indicted by a federal grand jury on November 8, 1987. He was arrested November 10 and arraigned before U.S. Magistrate Countiss on four counts that involved mail fraud, aiding and abetting, and extortion. Pinson was accused of scheming with Mid-State Pipe Company to purchase various items for the county in return for cash kickbacks. He was also accused of scheming with Mid-State to bust invoices by submitting false and fraudulent invoices to the county that either overstated quantities of supplies and materials delivered or included quantities of materials and supplies never delivered. The charges involved payments ($60, $50, $58) to Pinson by Mid-State related to his approval of three invoices from Mid-State ($379.20, $473.60, $624.58) from February 1985 to June 1986. The sixty-six-year-old Pinson pleaded innocent, and trial was set for February 16, 1988. He was released on a $5,000 personal recognizance bond.

In a February 8, 1988, Memorandum of Understanding negotiated by attorney Marcus Gordon with Assistant U.S. Attorney Nicholas B. Phillips, Pinson agreed to plead guilty to two counts, extortion and mail fraud, and to cooperate with the government in the ongoing investigation. The government agreed to seek dismissal of the other two charges and at the time of sentencing to inform the court of the extent of Pinson's cooperation and to ask that such cooperation be considered in sentencing. The government also agreed to make no recommendation concerning sentencing on one of the counts and to recommend five years' probation on the other one. Judge Barbour accepted Pinson's guilty plea on February 17, 1988, and delayed sentencing so Pinson could cooperate with the investigation.

On March 31, 1989, more than a year after his guilty plea, Pinson stood before Judge Barbour for sentencing. On the mail fraud charge, he was sentenced to five years with four and a half years suspended, leaving six months of actual prison time. He was to serve five years' probation after being released. Pinson was also sentenced to five years' concurrent probation on the extortion charge. In addition, he was fined $5,000, ordered to pay restitution of $168 to Newton County, and prohibited from seeking or holding public office during the period of probation. He was to report to the Federal Prison Camp at Maxwell Air Force Base, Alabama, by May 1, 1989. The long delay between conviction and sentencing and the relatively light penalties imposed by Judge Barbour no doubt reflect Pinson's extensive and fruitful cooperation in the FBI's investigation.

Harold Hollingsworth, district one supervisor, was indicted on April 7, 1987, on nine counts. The indictment charged the first-term supervisor with bribery, extortion, and mail fraud for his dealings with Mid-State from about September 1984 until about May 1986. He was charged with receiving a total of $1,945 from Mid-State for scheming to rig bids on culvert pipe, accepting kickbacks, and busting invoices; he was also charged with using the U.S. mails to carry out the schemes. Hollingsworth was arrested April 8 and arraigned before U.S. Magistrate Countiss that same day. He pleaded not guilty to all charges and was released on a $5,000 personal recognizance bond.

The forty-four-year-old Hollingsworth, who had previously undergone heart surgery, suffered a heart attack at his home April 26, 1987. He was pronounced dead at 10:15 P.M. that night at the Laird Hospital in Union. Judge Barbour signed an Order of Dismissal on July 29, 1987, at the request of U.S. Attorney George Phillips. The order dismissed all of the charges against the deceased Harold Hollingsworth.

Lauderdale County—Let's Transition to the Unit System

Located in east-central Mississippi along the Alabama border and part of the Choctaw Cession of 1830, Lauderdale County was the third of sixteen counties created by a legislative act of 1833. The county was named for Colonel James Lauderdale of Tennessee, who was killed by the British in the December 1814 Battle of New Orleans. Lauderdale County boasts a population in excess of 75,000, which ranks it fifth in the state. Meridian is the county seat; its population of approximately 42,000 makes it one of the state's largest cities. Because the city was a rail hub, Yankee general William T. Sherman burned Meridian to the ground in the War between the States. Among the general's many boasts was "A Meridian no longer exists." The city was home to the Father of Country Music, the Ole Blue Yodeler, Jimmy Rodgers. There is a Jimmy Rodgers museum in the city, and annually it hosts the Jimmy Rodgers Festival.

Among the first people arrested in Operation Pretense was first-term Lauderdale County district four supervisor Billy Joe Harris. Harris was arrested by FBI agents at his Meehan home and taken to Jackson in handcuffs, where he was arraigned before U.S. Magistrate Countiss. Harris was charged with bribery, extortion, and mail fraud in a four-count indictment. The charges included: (a) conspiring with Mid-State Pipe Company to falsify invoices and fraudulently charge Lauderdale County for materials and supplies not delivered, (b) conspiring to obtain preferential treatment for Mid-State in regard to bids and quotes submitted to the county for materials and supplies, (c) conspiring to determine the bids from other competitive vendors so that Mid-State could use the information in making its bid, and (d) receiving monetary kickbacks from Mid-State. Harris was alleged to have accepted a total of $3,860 in kickbacks from Mid-State from April through June 1985. The indictment also alleged that Harris had agreed to approach other county supervisors about accepting kickbacks and busting invoices. Harris was released on a $5,000 personal recognizance bond, and trial was set for May 11.

The day after Harris's arrest, his attorney, Joe Clay Hamilton, indicated that Harris had no intention of resigning from his position as district four supervisor. The following Monday, Harris read a prepared statement just prior to a board of supervisors meeting in which he said his family had been "embarrassed," "hurt," and "shocked" over his indictment. He asked that judgment against him be withheld until the case had been concluded. He also told fellow board members that he had "done no wrong and that he would be exonerated after the matter is concluded." Harris could not have been shocked over the indictment. The U.S. Attorney had offered him a plea bargain in September 1986, but that offer had been refused.

After Harris's arrest, the *Meridian Star* approached William Brown, district two supervisor, and asked if he had done business with Mid-State. Brown replied that he had but that the purchases amounted to no more than about $300. On February 20, the newspaper reported that county records told a different story. Brown had purchased pipe, grader blades, and road repair materials from Mid-State for more than $3,600 during 1985. Some of these purchases were not supported by purchase orders or receiving reports, and Brown had approved one December payment by phone according to a note on an unsigned delivery ticket. Ironically, Brown had seconded and voted for a motion passed by the board of supervisors in September of 1985 to require purchase orders for purchases exceeding $100.

Joe Mosby, a former two-term district three supervisor and strong advocate of the unit system, surmised at the end of February 1987 that, even with the current developing scandal, things had improved over the past fourteen years. Mosby said that shortly after taking office he had received a phone call from a constituent advising him to "put me down for so many hours." It seems that individuals, who did a little maintenance work on county property at their own initiative, were paid by supervisors after simply reporting that they had done so. Mosby reported that in his eight years of service he was able to convince only one other Lauderdale County supervisor of the need to go to the unit system with its much better purchasing and inventory controls. This was true even in light of the 1973 culvert purchasing scandal and grand jury report discussed in chapter 10. In 1984, the board of supervisors finally adopted a resolution to adopt the unit system. However, when Pretense was made public, a committee was still ironing out the details of how a unit system would work in Lauderdale County.

Information about the roles played by Mid-State and its representatives in the Pretense investigation began to surface in early 1987. Citing staff and wire reports, the *Meridian Star* speculated that Mid-State might have been an FBI front used as part of a scam that uncovered alleged kickback schemes, bid riggings, and other improprieties. The role of Mid-State had been revealed by federal authorities on February 12, when indictments of nine supervisors were made public. A Carthage businessman, the sudden disappearance of two of the company's salesmen, and the owner provided some clues concerning Mid-State's part in Pretense.

Buddy Myers, a Carthage businessman who operated Pearl River Pipe Company and did business with Mid-State, said he became suspicious when Mid-State closed down in 1996 and its two salesmen "evaporated into thin air." He indicated that he thought the two salesmen, whom he knew as Jerry Jacobs and Cliff Winters, were shady, but they were actually part of an FBI sting operation. Myers said, "I thought they were crooks, but I guess they were just FBI agents undercover." He indicated that Rev. John E. Burgess, the owner of Mid-State, seemed like an honest man, but the salesmen were the subject of unpleasant rumors. Myers had become even more suspicious of the salesmen when Pontotoc County supervisors Grady Baker and Theron Baldwin came to his business looking for them. "I thought they were hiding from the law," said Myers.

Burgess, who at the time the Pontotoc County supervisors were looking for the salesmen said that he did not know where they had gone, was quoted as saying, "I am not at liberty to discuss it at this point." Federal authorities confirmed that Mid-State was a legitimate private company that had cooperated with the two-year probe. Nevertheless, the authorities would not comment on any specifics concerning Mid-State or its employees. Al Waits, a special agent in the Jackson FBI office, would not even say whether Jacobs and Winters were federal agents.

The *Meridian Star* editorialized on February 24 as follows:

Unit system plan could be reality in election year

Could it be that members of the Lauderdale County Board of Supervisors are about to follow through on a promise they made to the people of this county nearly three years ago? It's about time they did. Perhaps it takes an election year to make the supervisors move. They were preparing for an election when, on March 5, 1984, they voted to adopt the unit system for county road construction and maintenance. Since that time they have hemmed and hawed and generally dragged their feet on moving to a unit system, slowly accepting some small parts. Now the supervisors are again talking about the county unit system. Why? Perhaps because it is an election year. But whatever the motivation, it would be good news for the people of Lauderdale County were the supervisors to fully implement the unit system. On Monday, they accepted some recommendations offered by a study committee that would bring the county several steps closer to the goal of a full unit system. Among the proposals was the establishment of a central garage at what is now the District 1 barn and the opening of satellite garages in place of the District 2, District 3, and District 5 barns. The supervisors will look for a site for the District 4 satellite because District 4 Supervisor Billy Joe Harris's current facility is located in his back yard. The committee must still draft a purchasing system for items to be used in the areas other than the central garage and provide a plan for allocation of the funds, personnel and equipment to the central and satellite facilities. The people of this county have waited long enough for our supervisors to keep the promise they made. If it takes an election for them to do so, then so be it. It is long overdue.

In April 1987, Rev. William C. Brown, district two supervisor, faced Pretense-related charges. He was indicted on five counts by a federal grand jury on April 7 and arrested at the district two barn the next day. The day he was arrested he was transported to Jackson where he pleaded not guilty before U.S. Magistrate Countiss. He was released on a $5,000 personal recognizance bond, and trial was set for July 20. The charges against Brown included one count of extortion and four counts of mail fraud. He was alleged to have schemed with Mid-State to bust invoices submitted to Lauderdale County for overstated quantities and for supplies and equipment billed to the county but never delivered. He was also charged with using the mails to accomplish the scheme. Specifically, Brown was charged with using the U.S. mails to accomplish schemes that involved approving false and fraudulent invoices to the county for more than $4,000 and accepting cash kickbacks in the amount of $920 from Mid-State in return. The supervisor was also charged with interfering with interstate commerce by extorting the $920 in kickbacks.

Billy Joe Harris was reindicted on April 9, 1987. This indictment, which superseded the one dated February 11, included all four counts of the original indictment and added a fifth. The new charge was that in 1986 Harris accepted a $600 kickback on the county's purchase of an $11,854 Terrain King boon mower from Holiman Equipment Company of Jackson. On April 24, 1987, Judge Barbour signed an Order dismissing all four counts of the February 11 Indictment.

In a plea agreement dated June 8 and signed June 12, 1987, Rev. William Brown agreed to plead guilty to one count of mail fraud and one count of extortion and to cooperate in the ongoing investigation. In return, the government agreed to drop the other three charges, to inform the court concerning Brown's cooperation with the investigation at the time of sentencing, to make no recommendation concerning the sentence to be imposed on the mail fraud charge, and to recommend a suspended sentence and five years' probation on the extortion count. If probation were imposed, it was to begin after completion of any prison sentence imposed for the mail fraud count. Another provision of the agreement was that Brown would neither seek nor hold public office during the probation time. He was also to resign from his position as supervisor within thirty days of the date of plea acceptance by the court. Brown pleaded guilty before Judge H. Barbour in Jackson on June 18.

A somewhat confusing article concerning Brown's decision not to seek reelection appeared in the *Meridian Star* June 15. The article noted that Brown had announced that he would not run so "we could concentrate on our case." Brown was quoted as saying he did not plan to change his plea of innocent to the April 7 five-count indictment and that he was "going to fight it out." The article indicated that the newspaper had learned that Brown was to appear in federal court in Jackson on June 12, the date he signed the plea agreement, to change his plea. The article also stated that Brown's attorney, Larry Primeaux, said that he had "no input to the order," did not know who entered it or its purpose, and could not say how it came about. The attorney was also quoted as saying that, on the twelfth, it was "clearly understood" with the U.S. attorney's office that, "we were not going over there [to Jackson] today." Primeaux actually signed the agreement that is dated June 12, 1987.

Elected in 1984, Baptist minister William Brown was the first African American to serve on the Lauderdale County board of supervisors since Reconstruction. Brown's election came about after the county had been redistricted for the purpose of creating a majority black district. Brown said that he was now endorsing Meridian Police Detective Jimmie Smith, the only African American in the five-way race to succeed him, "because I think he would represent our district, which is majority black."

Billy Joe Harris pleaded guilty in federal court in Biloxi on July 9, 1987, to bribery and extortion charges based on a plea bargain with the U.S. attorney. The agreement almost fell apart at the last minute when Harris disagreed with a summary of the extortion charge. He was accused of extorting $600 from Holiman Equipment Company on the county's purchase of a bushhog. While admitting taking the cash, Harris said, "He put a brown envelope into my pocket. We bought the bushhog at low bid and the kickback had nothing to do with the bushhog." Several times Harris retired to a hallway outside the courtroom with his attorney, David H. Linder. Harris returned to the courtroom after one such conference to state, "Basically, I agree with what they have charged me with." Upon further questioning, Harris continued to maintain that he took the money but that it had nothing to do with the mower in question.

Judge Lee informed Harris that he could not accept the guilty plea if he were to continue to maintain his innocence to the one charge. Judge Lee said, "We've been at this hearing one hour. I've never had anything like this." Assistant U.S. Attorney Ruth Harris told the court that if Billy Joe Harris would not admit to the charge, the government would take it to trial. After additional meetings with his attorney, Harris finally agreed that he had taken the money as a condition of doing business with Holiman. In return for the guilty plea, the U.S. Attorney agreed to recommend a twenty-year suspended prison sentence and five years' probation on the extortion charge, make no recommendation on the bribery charge, and recommend that the remaining four charges be dropped. Under the bargain struck with the prosecutor, Harris was to resign from office within two weeks, and he was prohibited from seeking or holding public office during the time of any probation imposed at sentencing. Harris had filed qualifying papers in early June to run for reelection as an independent. The plea bargain did not require Harris to cooperate with the government in the ongoing investigation. Sentencing was set for August 5 before Judge Lee in Meridian.

The behavior of Billy Joe Harris at his pleading seems to capture the thinking that allowed some supervisors to rationalize accepting kickbacks. He seems to have convinced himself that the $600 payment he took from Holiman and the other $3,860 he took from Mid-State were simply gifts and that they were unrelated to the county's purchases from the two vendors. Even if that had been true, he had violated Mississippi law by not turning the "gratuities" over to the county.

Harris's resignation produced a dilemma for the county because he had located the district four barn in his own backyard. As the county moved toward the unit system, it needed a satellite maintenance facility in the district. In early August 1987, the board of supervisors voted unanimously to approve an agreement that would allow the county to continue to use the barn until another site could be found. Under the agreement, the county would pay no rent, and it would not hold Harris, his heirs, and others responsible in case of legal action resulting from any injury that might occur while the county was using his property.

William Brown finally submitted his resignation as district two supervisor making it effective July 17, one day before the thirty-day time limit agreed to in his plea bargain. At a July 21 board meeting, board president Billy Melton circulated a document containing Brown's written resignation. In the document, Brown stated, "I would like to express that I have enjoyed working with this board of supervisors, individually as well as collectively. We've had humorous times, sad times, good times, bad times, sunshine and storms; but overall, I believe our board ranks as one of the best. However, my greatest enjoyment has been serving the people of District 2. I shall forever cherish the relationship we've established and will work in whatever capacity I can to help the people of District 2."

At this July 21 meeting, the board of supervisors appointed James Bishop, the owner of a Meridian funeral home, to complete Brown's unexpired term. Four Democrats had qualified for the upcoming August primary election for the district two post. The winner of the primary would face the lone Republican candidate in the November general election. Bishop was not a candidate for election to the post, and under the terms of his appointment he was to resign after the November 3 general election to allow the individual elected to take office early.

Billy Joe Harris finally submitted his resignation effective July 23, the last day allowed under his plea agreement. Cattleman Jeff Williams was appointed by the board to complete Harris's term. Williams was appointed by the three remaining members of the board of supervisors and sworn in on July 28. Brown's replacement, James Bishop, was formally sworn in at the same time. The motion concerning Williams's appointment was made by Ikie Ethridge; it did not contain a requirement that he resign after the general election in favor of the person elected to the post. Ethridge indicated that Williams's intent was to do so, and he chided the news media because reports of Bishop's appointment had emphasized the requirement to resign after the November election. A reporter asked Williams whether he intended to resign after the general election. Williams responded, "I don't see any reason to comment on this sort of thing. . . . If I may suggest, let's just cut off right here where we are, 'cause you're just creating animosity is all you're doing." Williams was already a seasoned politician; he had served one term in the Mississippi legislature during the 1950s.

On December 18, 1987, Judge Lee sentenced fifty-one-year-old Billy Joe Harris to six years in prison to be followed by five years of probation. The judge also fined Harris $5,000 and ordered him to pay the county $4,400 in restitution. Harris, who requested that any prison time be served at the Federal Prison Camp at Maxwell Air Force Base, Alabama, was to report to federal prison by January 4, 1988. At sentencing, the former supervisor claimed that God had forgiven him saying, "The Lord has forgiven me for my part. . . . I plead with you for mercy." The judge countered, "You have clearly breached the trust the voters of Lauderdale County have placed in you."

Harris was the fifth former supervisor to receive a prison sentence as a result of Operation Pretense, and his six-year prison sentence turned out to be the longest imposed on a supervisor who made a plea bargain with the government.

As noted above, the plea agreement did not require Harris to cooperate with the investigation. Assistant U.S. Attorney Ruth Harris told the judge that the former supervisor had not cooperated in the investigation. Attorney Joe Clay Hamilton claimed that the former supervisor had done his part and maintained that his client didn't know of other corruption because he had only been a supervisor for a year. Hamilton said, "The presumption is that he knew something else. He should not be presumed non-cooperating because he had not met with them and cooperated." Ruth Harris countered that the argument that Billy Joe Harris had cooperated with the investigation "simply makes no sense." She said, "He was given the opportunity to cooperate several months before he was indicted. He flatly refused to cooperate with the government. What's more aggravating than non-cooperation is that after Harris knew the government had a case . . . he goes out and commits another crime."

The judge believed the prosecutor. He concluded that the former supervisor had not cooperated and that, if he had, it could have been "a factor" in his favor. Judge Lee said, "You refused to cooperate, claiming your innocence. Then around November 1986 you were paid a $600 kickback from Holiman Equipment Company. You clearly have compounded the wrongs you have committed."

The indictment of Billy Joe Harris contained the following statement that was somewhat common in Pretense-related indictments: "The defendant would and did propose to Mid-State that other supervisors within the County were willing to enter into similar false and fraudulent arrangements as described in subparagraphs (a) [rig bids on culvert pipe] (b) [submit to the county "busted" invoices for materials and supplies], and (c) [accept kickbacks on "busted" invoices]." A newspaper reporter questioned the board of supervisors about this statement at its mid-July meeting. At the time of this meeting, William Brown and Billy Joe Harris had already pleaded guilty to Pretense-related charges and had agreed to resign. However, the time frames imposed for their resignations had not expired, and neither had done so. Brown attended the meeting, but Harris did not. Ikie Ethridge, district three supervisor, claimed that he had never been approached by Harris with any such scheme, and the other supervisors, including Brown, concurred. Ethridge objected to additional questioning about Operation Pretense saying that the board meeting was neither the time nor the place "for such an interrogation."

Brown and Harris were the only Lauderdale County supervisors ever indicted as a result of Operation Pretense. However, Ikie Ethridge soon found himself in the middle of the unit system controversy, in a dispute over his attempt to purchase surplus state equipment for the county, and in serious trouble with the state auditor for misspending county funds. Ethridge was opposed the unit system, and he obstructed its adoption by the county.

During April 1987, after Brown and Harris had been charged under Pretense, the Lauderdale County Board of Supervisors started to move toward implementation of what it described as a unit system of county government. The *Meridian Star* noted in an April 15 editorial: "Members of the Board of Supervisors voted prior to the 1984 election to adopt the unit system—giving voters the message that the beat system, under which each supervisor has his own little spoils-rich roads fiefdom would be immediately abandoned. With the election safely past, however, the board re-neged."

Even as supervisors met to plan transition to the unit system of road management, Ethridge challenged a statement by Ernest West, the county's appointed road and bridge manager, that the system could save money. Ethridge rejoined that he could not "buy" that idea. He said, "It's left to be proved. . . . Government is to provide services, not to save money." He did, however, agree with other board members that the system would provide for more efficiency.

In May 1987, Ethridge set out to subvert the central purchasing requirement of the unit system. He said that he did not believe allowing supervisors to sign requisitions and receiving reports was a step backward from the county unit system or central purchasing. At a May 19 board meeting, Ethridge noted that a list of county employees authorized to requisition and receive materials did not include supervisors or their road foremen. He said, "Supervisors are still in charge of this county, no matter what," and added, "going into the unit system has nothing to do with completely changing basics of county government. If I'm elected and I'm not authorized to sign, buy, or receive anything, we better take another look." The supervisor's comments were completely contrary to the very idea of the unit system of county government. Under the unit system, the board of supervisors was to establish policies, while professional managers were to carry out those policies in conducting the county's business. The board did not act on the matter at this meeting.

The *Meridian Star* editorialized two days later:

> Mr. Ethridge should note that the FBI is already taking a look. The results thus far have been the indictments of 31 Mississippi supervisors, including two from Lauderdale County—William C. Brown and Billy Joe Harris. The sting operation into corrupt county purchasing continues. More indictments are expected. The indictments clearly show the need for a trained professional to handle purchasing and leave the county supervisors to limit themselves to the assignment of setting policy. Mr. Ethridge's suggestion and the board's failure to reject it are contradictory to the need to clean up purchasing practices in county government.

Ethridge, a two-term supervisor, was first vice president of the Mississippi Association of Supervisors (MAS) when Pretense began to unfold. On August 29, 1987, he became president of the MAS. Ethridge won a third term as supervisor in the 1987 general election, running as an independent against Meridian bakery owner Lloyd King. In early 1988, Ethridge maintained that he had thought of quitting his supervisor post because of Operation Pretense. The *Clarion Ledger* quoted him in February 1988 as follows: "A lot of supervisors have been defeated under this cloud. I don't mind telling you, I got to one point where I didn't want to tell anyone I was a supervisor." He claimed that he saw the presidency of the MAS as a chance to improve the image of supervisors statewide. Ethridge said, "That's the only reason I ran for supervisor again. I feel like it [MAS] was at the lowest level it has been in years. I couldn't desert them."

March 1988 found Ethridge admitting that he had not repaid $1,308.96 in misspent county funds. The Department of Audit had made an informal request that he repay the county for a 1986 purchase of sweat suits from the state. He had distributed the sweat suits to four Lauderdale County schools and to one private school. He just happened to be running an unsuccessful campaign for superintendent of schools at the time he distributed the sweat suits. Ethridge claimed the questioning of the legality of his purchase was politically motivated. He noted that the Department of Audit's preliminary demand for repayment had been hand delivered to him just four days before the November 1986 election. Ethridge claimed that a formal demand had not yet been delivered and said that, in the event a formal demand was delivered, "I'll do what the law says for me to do."

Despite the county's supposed move toward the unit system, in March 1988, Ethridge was still operating in the beat age. He signed an invoice to buy a surplus state two-and-a-half ton truck for the county without going through central purchasing. Supervisors were not authorized to requisition or receive items under the county's central purchasing operation. This incident came to light when Jessie Newell, the county purchase clerk, voided a previously issued purchase order for the truck after discovering that the invoice was dated the day before she had been informed by County Administrator Rex Haitt and board of supervisors president Raymond Fountain that the board had unofficially approved the purchase. Upon voiding the purchase order Newell said, "I can't put a purchase order on something that has already been purchased." At its next regularly scheduled meeting, the board approved the $1,000 truck purchase. Board president Fountain indicated that at a Friday work session the board had agreed to purchase the truck and added, "Then we would have to come back in an official meeting and okay to do that. Then I found out this morning (Monday) that it was invoiced out the 24th."

The board of supervisors' foot dragging over the unit issue was vividly illustrated by a mid-May incident between Ethridge and a fellow supervisor. The *Meridian Star* editorialized:

The political squabble between District 3 Supervisor Ikie Ethridge and District 5's Ray Boswell has revealed to the public something it isn't supposed to know. The "secret," not very well kept, is that Lauderdale County, officially a unit-system government, still operates under the antiquated and discredited beat system. The argument between Mr. Boswell and Mr. Ethridge during Monday's board meeting was over which has the rights to a county-owned front end loader. The piece of equipment, controlled by Mr. Ethridge, had been given to Mr. Boswell with the understanding that the latter would pay $2,000 in needed repairs. The repairs were made. Then, Mr. Ethridge, angered, he said, because Mr. Boswell has twice threatened to "whup" him, changed his mind. He wanted to take back the loader and transfer it to the county's central garage. After a heated argument between the two supervisors, the full board voted to repay Mr. Boswell and transfer the piece of equipment to the central garage. Under the unit system of county government, all road manpower and equipment would be placed under the control of County Engineer Neal Carson. He would make all decisions on day-to-day work under broad policies set by the Board of Supervisors. In Lauderdale County, day-to-day decisions on roadwork in the five beats are still being made by individual supervisors. They control the work forces too. Each has his own equipment. The time is long overdue for Lauderdale County to end the games and make the changeover to the county unit system of government. All manpower and equipment should be turned over to Mr. Carson and individual supervisors should get out of his way.

In a letter dated November 2, 1988, State Auditor Pete Johnson requested that the Mississippi Attorney General's Office proceed against Ikie Ethridge for failure to reimburse the county for the funds he used to purchase the sweat suits in 1986. Johnson noted that his office had made a formal demand on Ethridge and his bonding company on September 20 for $1,098 plus interest of $274.50 and $392.96 in recovery costs.

Lauderdale County citizens voted nearly three to one (13,267 to 4,642) in the November 1988 referendum in favor of the unit system. The unit system won a majority of votes in seventy-seven of the county's eighty-eight boxes, including sixteen of twenty boxes in Ethridge's district. Ethridge, now past-president of the MAS, expressed his displeasure by criticizing the flood of publicity put out by unit advocates such as the Mississippi Economic Council and Governor Ray Mabus. He said, "It's not a surprise to me. But I'll tell you this, it won't be as hard for me to vote to levy taxes in the future as it has in the past. That's the way I feel if that's what the people want. I think time will tell on who's right about this."

16. Rankin County

Three Boards of Supervisors in One Year

Rankin County is home to about 90,000 people, placing it fourth in population among Mississippi counties. Located in the central part of the state, Rankin County is separated from Hinds County and the capitol city of Jackson by the Pearl River. Brandon, the county seat, was the childhood home of Mississippi's first (1958) Miss America, Mary Ann Mobley. Over the past three decades, the county, which usually boasts a low unemployment rate, has been one of the state's most prosperous. Nevertheless, Rankin County has a long history of corruption. For example, in the days of Prohibition, Rankin County was a haven for bootleggers, as its corrupt sheriffs took payoffs to allow fairly open illicit liquor sales. It was common knowledge in Jackson that the only thing you had to do to buy whiskey was "go across the (Pearl) river." Unfortunately for its citizens, developments in the 1980s and early 1990s revealed Rankin County government as a virtual cesspool of corruption.

Rankin County politics in the 1980s and early 1990s was dominated by brazen characters who often mixed county and personal business and conducted both with impunity. During 1988, the board of supervisors was completely reconstituted twice; as a result, fifteen different people served on the five-member board during the year. All five men who began the year as supervisors resigned and pleaded guilty to various corruption charges, including purchase law violations and accepting kickbacks. One of the supervisors accepted kickbacks in the form of Christmas turkeys, and one had an illegal payment deposited to his son's bank account. Another supervisor was charged with obstruction of justice for attempting to influence potential jurors in the scheduled trial of a former chancery clerk. In May 1988, the governor appointed four men and one woman to serve as supervisors until a special election could be held in November. The special election produced five new, supposedly reform-minded supervisors who took office in November. One of the new supervisors was convicted in 1992 of extorting a bribe from the county attorney.

County supervisors were closely linked to the two chancery clerks who served between 1984 and 1992. One of the chancery clerks, Irl Dean Rhodes, truly led a cat-of-nine-lives existence. He was convicted of income tax evasion and failure to properly report his earnings to the secretary of state. Rhodes also had to pay the county more than $20,000 in interest and penalties on county funds that had been deposited in his own bank account. In 1987, Rhodes was defeated in his bid for a seventh four-year term. He was indicted on criminal charges of embezzlement involving hundreds of thousands of dollars, only to have the charges thrown out on a technicality after a change of venue and many court hearings.

Joe Barlow defeated Rhodes in 1987 and followed him as chancery clerk in 1988. Barlow lasted only four years, and it is easy to understand why. He was constantly at odds with the state auditor, the county administrator, the board of supervisors (all three boards), and the district attorney. Barlow admitted to violating purchasing laws and returned or paid for the unlawfully purchased items. He was later indicted for conspiracy to defraud the county, violating state bidding and purchasing laws, and embezzlement. All of these charges were eventually dropped because the state determined that he had sought proper counsel concerning each action and believed that he was following the legal requirements in each incident. Later, in response to a suit by the board of supervisors, Barlow paid the county more than $6,000 for interest that had been lost on checks that he had failed to deposit or turn over to the county in a timely manner. He took many county records with him when he left office and had to be sued before he would return them. While involved in all of this, Barlow's actions were often confrontational, abrasive, vindictive, and childish.

State Auditor Pete Johnson released an audit report on April 11, 1988, and demanded that the Rankin County board of supervisors repay $115,060 used to make purchases over a sixteen-month period. A letter attached to the report said that the supervisors had thirty days to repay the money and that the report was being turned over to the district attorney. Johnson said the demand for repayment was informal and that it was designed to give the officials an opportunity to return the money before any possible civil proceedings. "We feel that every elected official should have the opportunity to repay the taxpayers. We are giving them that opportunity. Once we move into the formal request and begin the civil litigation process it becomes a much more detailed process."

The alleged violations involved eleven invoices paid by the board between November 1986 and February 1988 for the purchase of various items, including automobiles and a contract for a paving project. Johnson said, "In these eleven instances the laws were not followed to the letter, and it is our job to report our findings in every investigative matter. That's what we've done. Now it's up to the normal legal process to take our place and move forward with the recovery of dollars and any other action that might be taken." According to Johnson, all five supervisors were deemed guilty of the violations because none voted against them. Although none of the supervisors were found to have benefited personally, according to the report, under state law, any supervisor who voted to pay for an unlawful purchase was personally liable. District Attorney David Clark planned to present the findings of the investigation to the grand jury in late April.

In a prepared statement, board attorney John McLaurin said, "This is a rather strict interpretation of the bidding and purchasing statutes. I can truthfully say that it is now dangerous for any persons to serve on any board or commission which makes public purchases." County Administrator Joe McCraney said the supervisors had violated the letter of the law but not its spirit, and he indicated that the supervisors had considered resigning to avoid any further liability. McCraney also said the supervisors would not challenge the Department of Audit's demand for restitution. He explained, "You're not going to beat the state auditor's office. They're the undefeated state champs."

When the details of the Department of Audit's demand against Rankin County supervisors hit the newspapers, the Department of Audit and the governor's Office of General Services were flooded with calls from across the state. Many asked about the legality of specific transactions that had already been consummated, and some proposed amnesty, promising full compliance in the future. State Auditor Pete Johnson said, "It's got people from one end of this state to another moving to make sure they're in compliance with the purchasing laws." Johnson said he didn't understand the confusion since the current purchase laws had been in effect since 1981. The biggest problem seemed to be in drafting bid specifications so tightly as to prevent competitive bidding. Johnson said vendors had called because they felt shut out by the bidding process. The Department of Audit was investigating one instance where the bid specification actually included the serial number of the item being sought.

In mid-April 1988, district one supervisor Herbert D. Smith was linked to Operation Pretense through charges against a former salesman for Mississippi Pipe and Oil Company. Charges released by U.S. Attorney George Phillips accused William L. Polk III with conspiring with Smith to bust a December 1982 invoice for $537 worth of goods never delivered to Rankin County. Polk waived indictment and pleaded innocent to an information, but his attorney, Barry Gilmer, said that he intended to change his plea to guilty later. Polk, the thirteenth salesman to be charged as a result of Pretense, was cooperating in the investigation, but he had not yet been called to testify before a federal grand jury. The U.S. Attorney's Office would not comment as to why the fifty-six-year old Smith had not been charged. Gilmer said that he understood that Polk used the money to buy Christmas turkeys for Smith. "He [Polk] simply did what he was asked to do," said Gilmer. "He did it and made a mistake." Gilmer claimed that Smith approached Polk about splitting the money as a condition of doing business for a particular job.

District Attorney Clark said that the grand jury, scheduled to reconvene April 25, would be asked to hand down the first local rather than federal Pretense-related indictment. The grand jury was to hear charges against Herbert Smith and the alleged conspiracy to bust an invoice with William Polk. Clark said that the federal authorities were cooperating with his office to see that he had the facts to present to the grand jury.

Fifty-six-year-old Kenneth Bridges, who had been district three supervisor since 1972, began negotiating a deal with the district attorney on April 21. Bridges had already been indicted on charges of attempting to influence a potential juror in the embezzlement case against former chancery clerk Irl Dean Rhodes and now faced possible indictment based on the Department of Audit's charges. Through his attorney, John McLaurin, Bridges offered to resign to keep from going through any other investigation or indictment. Bridges indicated that a plea bargain would save him and his family "all the embarrassment that I've had to go through. I don't think that I can continue to be investigated without something eventually coming up."

The next day, District Attorney Clark revealed that two unnamed Rankin County supervisors had offered to resign in exchange for halting future criminal proceedings against them. Clark said, "It is my official position that no offers made by public officials to resign without prosecution will be accepted by this district attorney. Statements in the media attributed to potential defendants have been inaccurate, self serving, and without remorse."

Both Herbert Smith and Kenneth Bridges were indicted on April 28 on

Pretense-related felony charges involving three kickback schemes. Smith and Bridges were each charged with one count of embezzlement, and Bridges was charged with one count of conspiracy to defraud the county and state. The embezzlement charges carried a maximum prison sentence of ten years and a $5,000 fine, while the conspiracy charges could result in five years' imprisonment and a $5,000 fine.

Smith was charged with accepting eighteen turkeys valued at $300 as his share of an invoice that had been busted in 1982 with William Polk and Mississippi Pipe and Oil Company. The indictment stated that Polk actually delivered the turkeys to Smith. Bridges was charged with approving in October 1982 a $1,480 payment to Mississippi Pipe and Oil Company and accepting from Billy Ray Harrison, an employee of the company, a $750 cash kickback for goods that were never delivered. The second charge against Bridges involved a scheme to defraud the county of $2,000 on the purchase of a tractor. The indictment stated that the tractor was purchased by district three road foreman Clarence A. Hall for $11,110 using Bridges's money. Equipment valued at $3,076 was installed on the tractor by Holiman Equipment Company, with the county paying for it. Then the county advertised for bids on tractors. Under that bid, the county purchased the tractor for $13,110. The funds were deposited into an account of Kenneth Bridges's son, Russell J. Bridges. Clarence Hall and Jury B. Jones, the salesman who had sold the tractor, were also indicted. These were the first Pretense-related indictments in a state court.

All five supervisors were indicted and arrested on April 28 on multiple counts each of violating state purchasing laws. They were charged with buying from Roger-Dingus Chevrolet, in November 1986, two 1987 Chevrolet Caprices for $21,119 which exceeded the state contract price by $569; from Van-Trow Oldsmobile, in October 1987, one Oldsmobile Delta 88 for $13,693 which exceeded the state contract price by $2,884; from Boyce Ford, in January 1988, two 1988 Ford Crown Victorias for $22,220, which exceeded the state contract price by $521.

Because of his close association with all of the defendants, Circuit Court Judge Alfred Nicols disqualified himself from the case on April 29. Each of the supervisors waived arraignment and pleaded not guilty on May 2, the same day that District Attorney Clark filed a motion to recuse Judge Robert Goza from the case. Clark's request was based on the judge's public association with the defendants, which might cause an apparent conflict of interest, and the fact that Goza had dismissed an indictment against the former clerk of the court (Irl Dean Rhodes) and stated in the order an opinion on the merits of the cause. Clark maintained that the judge had a personal and present relationship with the defendants. Judge Goza was not removed from the case, because within a week the defendants had worked out plea bargain agreements with the district attorney.

On May 10, 1988, Ralph Moore, Hilton Richardson, and Mike Ponder withdrew their pleas of innocent and pleaded guilty to the charge involving the purchase of the two Ford Crown Victorias. The state dropped the other charges against these defendants, which involved failing to advertise properly for the purchase of vehicles and equipment, wording advertisements in such a way as to prevent competitive bidding, accepting bids on items not included in an advertisement, and purchasing items at prices above those approved by the state Office of General Services.

The sentence imposed by Judge Goza on these three supervisors was as follows:

> IT IS FURTHER ORDERED AND ADJUDGED that the sentence recommended by the District Attorney be accepted and that in accordance therewith the Defendants be and they are each hereby sentenced to serve a term of six months in the Rankin County Jail; provided, however, that this sentence be stayed and suspended conditioned on the following:
>
> (A) That they maintain good behavior and conduct for a period of one year; and,
>
> (B) That they resign as members of the Board of Supervisors of Rankin County effective immediately; and,
>
> (C) That they not participate in the appointment of successors to any vacancy in office created by such resignation; and,
>
> (D) That they not seek election to the office vacated by them for one (1) year.

On the same day, the other two Rankin County supervisors, Kenneth Bridges and Herbert Smith, pleaded nolo contendre to the same charges, and the government dropped other charges related to purchase law violations. Smith and Bridges pleaded guilty to the Pretense-related charges. District Attorney Clark agreed to drop four other charges of purchasing violations against these two supervisors and the jury tampering charge against Bridges. Clark also agreed that the supervisors would be barred from returning to the board for only one year. Bridges's and Smith's sentences were similar to those listed above, and both were required to cooperate in the FBI's investigation and to submit to polygraph tests to prove their cooperation.

District Attorney Clark soon tired of hearing ongoing criticisms that three of the five former supervisors, Moore, Ponder, and Richardson, had been unjustly forced from office because of technical violations of purchasing laws. In mid-August, he responded by releasing a letter written by federal officials who had played a part in the plea bargain agreements. The body of the May 9 letter from James B. Tucker of the U.S. Attorney's Criminal Division to attorney John McLaurin reads as follows: "Pursuant to our meeting earlier today, this is to advise that, in the event your subject clients enter pleas of guilty to current indictments by the Rankin County Grand Jury and resign from the office of Supervisor, this office will not pursue federal charges based on the subject matter of the County indictments nor the Metro Equipment invoice. No other representations have been made."

Clark said, "I'm releasing this letter because of constant insinuations that these three supervisors were forced out of office on mere technicalities of the purchasing laws. I feel that the public has the right to know the contents of this letter, which was part of the plea bargain agreement and is to be part of the public file." No information was given about the Metro invoice. The upshot of this was a strong implication that supervisors Ralph Moore, Hilton Richardson, and Mike Ponder could have been prosecuted on Pretense-related charges.

The supervisors' resignations left Rankin County without any elected government. Because the county operated under the recently installed modified unit system, County Administrator Joe McCraney could continue to administer day-to-day activities, but there was no one with approval authority to pay bills and employees. Board attorney McLaurin said that the supervisors had resigned to stop a wave of negative publicity about the county and to take pressure off their families and themselves. McLaurin promised to resign as soon as a new board took power. Attorney General Mike Moore said that Governor Mabus would appoint new supervisors to serve out the unexpired terms.

Rankin County legislators said on May 11 that Governor Mabus was soliciting resumes from people interested in serving as interim supervisors. The full county delegation had met with the governor to offer support, with one member, Robert Smith, saying, "We weren't in any manner going to let this situation destroy Rankin County." County legislators had already received about thirty calls from people interested in being appointed. A special election to fill the remaining three years of the resigned supervisors' terms would take place at the time of the November general election in accordance with state law.

The Department of Audit in late April began issuing formal demand letters to the former supervisors for repayment of the $115,000 spent in violation of purchasing laws. The former supervisors had thirty working days to respond before the case would be turned over to the attorney general for prosecution. Claiming that the violations were mainly clerical errors, the former officials indicated that the insurance companies for the board of supervisors should pay the claim under the county's errors and omissions policy. Insurance consultant Shappley Harris said that if the state sought restitution from the bonding agent, the bulk would come from United States Fidelity Guarantee Company (USF&G), which bonded the supervisors when most of the offenses took place. Because of the supervisors' inability to get insurance, their performance had been backed by pledged property since January 1988. According to Harris, approximately $22,000 in restitution could eventually be sought through the property. Harris also indicated that one company involved, Dominion Insurance, would probably challenge the claim in court.

On April 27, Governor Mabus appointed five interim supervisors: Wade Lee Overby, Bennie O. Hilton, Gladys Gallop Jackson, Eddie Dwaine Dear, and Jimmy L. Carr. All appointees were experienced leaders in civic, business, or political circles. Overby and Jackson indicated that they planned to run for the offices in the November special election, while the other three said that they were unsure whether they would run. Mabus insisted that all five appointees support a move to a "pure" unit system for the county. In July, the Rankin County Grand Jury recommended the continuation of a mandatory pure unit system of government.

None of the interim supervisors appointed by Governor Mabus were elected in the November 1988 election. Late November 1988 saw the newly elected board vote unanimously to give themselves pay raises of nearly $5,000 per year. In doing so, they took advantage of legislation passed earlier in the year that allowed for 20 percent increases that raised their salaries to $29,520 from $24,600. Also included in the budget amendment was $47,000 for pickup trucks for each supervisor and $60,000 to fund the county Economic Development Authority for half a year. The interim board had cut off funding of the Authority following a consultant's report recommending that it be merged with the Chamber of Commerce. The interim board had not been pleased that the authority had hired, and refused to fire, former chancery clerk Irl Dean Rhodes. The board had asked authority chair Albert Moore to fire Rhodes, arguing that it hurt the county's image to have Rhodes in a position to attract industry. Moore had refused.

Another Pretense-type sting took place in Rankin County during 1992. Mike Younger had been appointed attorney for the board of supervisors and had served at the board's pleasure. He had been nominated for the job by District Three Supervisor Pete Patrick, who had been elected to the board as a reform candidate in 1988 and reelected without opposition in 1991. Patrick attempted to extort money from Younger in 1992 in return for Patrick's vote to reappoint him as the board's attorney. Younger reported the matter to the FBI and cooperated in an FBI investigation by tape recording conversations with Patrick about $1,000 in payoffs.

Forty-eight-year-old Pete Patrick, who also farmed and ran a newspaper route in Rankin County, was indicted on federal bribery charges for accepting two $500 payments from Younger. He went to trial in Jackson on July 10, 1992. Patrick had also been indicted in Rankin County for accepting money in exchange for his vote to reappoint Younger as board attorney. Patrick faced maximum penalties of ten years' imprisonment without parole and a $250,000 fine on the federal charges.

Testimony in the jury trial before U.S. District Court Judge David C. Bramlett III in Jackson had an all too familiar ring. Younger testified that Patrick had begun pressuring him for money as early as 1990 and that he had demanded $900 for "spending money" for a trip to Colorado. According to Younger, after a brief series of demands, Patrick had stopped asking until the question of Younger's reappointment arose in September 1991. Younger testified that Patrick solicited and accepted $1,000 in two $500 payments and that Patrick told him that $500 would be given to board of supervisors president Charles Sheppard. Younger's five hours of testimony focused on Patrick's claims that several people retained on county contracts were making payments to supervisors and not complaining. He also testified that Patrick had suggested that he inflate his legal bills to the county to cover the payoffs. Sheppard, who was not charged, claimed that the $500 had been represented to him strictly as a campaign contribution and that was how he had accepted it.

Tape-recorded conversations between Younger and Patrick about the payments were played to the jury. One tape revealed that when Younger told Patrick that he had $500 for him, Patrick said, "Do a little something for [supervisors] Larry [Swales] and Lynn [Weathersby] too." Patrick was also caught on tape saying, "Over a run of twelve months, each supervisor, if you helped him out $700 or $800, it would mean the world to him." But no testimony linked either District One Supervisor Weathersby or District Two Supervisor Swales directly to the bribes. In fact, Weathersby testified that Patrick had talked to him about changing attorneys and hiring Hal Ross because "[Ross] would make sure if you wanted to take a trip it wouldn't cost you anything. And he'd make sure you had campaign funds." Weathersby also said that Patrick disliked the board attorney because Younger had refused to take supervisors and their guests out for lunch. Weathersby said that he had gone to lunch "a couple of times" with the other supervisors but had quit because they loaded charges on the man who treated.

Patrick's attorney, Anselm McLaurin, claimed that Weathersby's testimony was tainted because he was in a dispute with Patrick and another supervisor over some engineering fees. He also maintained that Younger feared losing his job because Patrick had become dissatisfied with his work and wanted someone more concerned with the county.

Patrick testified that he had lied in the conversations taped in October 1991 because he thought Younger was taping them. This seems a strange defense, especially since he had been caught on tape saying such things as: "All we need is just a little support, and like I said, just once a month. I mean it ain't against no damn law for you to take a $100 bill and feed us." Patrick claimed he had been playing a charade. He testified, "That still does not say 'You give me $500 or I'm not going to vote for you.'" He said, "I was dogging Mr. Younger too. You forget who is dogging who. I knew Mike and I was going head to head." Later, he explained that he had expected the board attorney to protect him. "I had no idea my own legal counsel was going to get me arrested and murdered," he said. The jury took just two hours and five minutes to return a guilty verdict on July 11, 1992. Judge Bramlett set sentencing for September 10.

Patrick resigned his post on July 14. That same day Brandon police increased security around Mike Younger's home. Police Chief Walter Tucker said, "As a precautionary reason against somebody doing something, we are patrolling the area and (Younger's) house pretty heavy." The chief said that this was being done because someone had uttered remarks "that could be considered threats" in the presence of people viewing Patrick's trial.

The Clarion-Ledger reported on July 14 that Younger was receiving much support for his actions. He was quoted as saying, "(Response was) nothing but overwhelming . . . really. I was very much surprised. I've had lots of phone calls, and I've had nothing but positive comments made."

The *Clarion-Ledger* captured the whole sorry episode in a July 15 editorial.

CORRUPTION
A moral lesson in Rankin County

We sympathize with the anguish of Rankin County Board of Supervisors Attorney Mike Younger. He worried over the predicament that Supervisor Pete Patrick placed him (in): Either play along and pay bribes to keep his job or risk losing it and exposing the corruption. Younger did the right thing. Had he "played along," he would have sacrificed his principles and also put himself in a vulnerable position for blackmail for having done it. But that's how corruption goes. Though it may start off small, a meal here, a forged bill there, it quickly grows—like the adage, you can't be a little pregnant. Saturday's conviction of Patrick for extorting a bribe reminds of the Operation Pretense probe. That federal investigation into corrupt county purchasing practices resulted in charges against 57 county supervisors in 26 counties. That included two Rankin County supervisors who resigned in 1988, with three others who faced various other charges. The scandal, ironically, led to the November 1988 election of Patrick—supposedly to clean up the board. But it was one man, as well, who got Pretense going. Rev. John Burgess of Carthage, a Pentecostal minister, bought into a construction business and was shocked to find that it was customary to pay a 10 percent kickback to supervisors in order to do business with them. It hurt his conscience and he told the FBI. Nine years later, after 13 percent of the state's supervisors were charged with corruption charges, he accepted the FBI's prestigious national Lewis E. Peters Award for his courage. He said at the time: "I didn't know the FBI had to have help. I didn't intend to (help). When I saw the job had to be done (to expose the corruption) and I had to do it, I did it." That's all it takes: a person with a conscience who refuses to sully himself, however much pressure is brought. Younger should be treated with the respect he deserves. He refused the good ol' boy credo that you have to go along to get along. He wouldn't compromise his principles. In Rankin County, as well as the rest of the state, Younger should be saluted and emulated by others. Corruption can not exist where citizens stand up to it.

Judge Bramlett on September 10,1992, sentenced Pete Patrick to a twenty-eight month prison term with no chance of parole and fined him $6,000. He could have been sentenced to thirty-three months and fined

$60,000. At the sentencing hearing, Patrick said, "Your honor, I accept my responsibility. I'm a grown man. I'm only concerned about the welfare of my wife and family." The judge retorted, "You are very fortunate to have a supportive family. I can assure you that they will be here when you return home."

17. Three Southern Counties with Five Crooked Supervisors

Smith, Jasper, and Clarke Counties

Smith County—FBI Agents Beware

Established in 1833 in south-central Mississippi, Smith County was named for David Smith of Hinds County. When Smith County was established in December 1833, David Smith's daughter was married to Mississippi's governor, Hiram Runnels. Smith, a North Carolina native, moved to the Natchez District after serving in the North Carolina militia during the American Revolution. The county had a 1990 population of 14,798, and Raleigh, with a 1990 population of only 998, is the county seat. The city was named for England's Sir Walter Raleigh or for the city of Raleigh, North Carolina, which was named for the renowned sailor. Taylorsville is the county's largest metropolitan area; its 1990 population was 1,387.

Smith County district two supervisor Charles "Hop" Blakeney was indicted on eight counts by a federal grand jury in Jackson on March 9, 1987. The Taylorsville resident was arrested March 10 and entered a not guilty plea to all of the charges before U.S. Magistrate John R. Countiss III the next day. At the arraignment, prosecutors noted that Blakeney verbally abused and struck the FBI agent who arrested him. Countiss asked the defendant, "Was there an altercation?" Blakeney replied, "Yes. Sir, my wife is in the hospital." The third-term supervisor was freed on a $5,000 personal recognizance bond, and trial was set for June 1, 1987. Countiss indicated that he did not require a larger bond because he knew that the Blakeney family had lived in Smith county for years and "it would probably take a truck of dynamite to get him out of there."

The indictment, which charged bribery, mail fraud, and extortion, involved Blakeney's dealings with Mid-State Pipe and Supply Company, the FBI front, and with Davis Chemicals and its owner, Ray Davis. The transactions described in the indictment took place from 1984 to early 1987 and involved busted invoices on county purchases of grader blades. Maximum penalties that could be imposed upon conviction on all counts were seventy-five years in prison and fines totaling $2 million.

Counts Two, Seven, and Eight provided the details. Count Two charged that Blakeney approved approximately thirteen Davis Chemicals invoices to Smith County for which he received cash payments from a representative of Davis Chemicals. It also charged that the defendant indicated that Mid-State Pipe and Supply Company would be able to do business with supervisors in Smith County if Mid-State would do favors for the supervisors. The count outlined three instances in which the defendant approved false invoices totaling $581.04 and received cash kickbacks totaling $300. Count Seven charged that Blakeney obstructed, delayed, and affected interstate commerce by knowingly and willfully obtaining property, specifically cash in the sum of $2,380, from Davis Chemicals, wrongfully under the color of official right. Count Eight charged that the defendant obstructed, delayed, and affected interstate commerce by knowingly and willfully obtaining property, specifically cash in the sum of $300 from Mid-State Pipe and Supply Company, wrongfully under the color of official right.

Count two of the indictment charged that Blakeney proposed with Mid-State that other Smith County supervisors were willing to enter into similar false and fraudulent arrangements (busting invoices and mail fraud). Blakeney is reported to have said at a supervisors' meeting on February 19, 1987, "If I go, I'm not going alone, I'm taking everybody else with me." However, no other Smith County supervisors were ever charged as a result of Operation Pretense.

Blakeney was one of the first supervisors charged under Pretense. Court documents indicate that his attorney, Thomas E. Royals, wanted to defend his client by employing the entrapment defense and by claiming his client had not committed a federal crime because the alleged bribery did not involve funds exclusively provided by the federal government.

In preparation for the scheduled trial, the defendant submitted a discovery request that included the following wording:

> 4. In order to prepare any possible defense of entrapment defendant needs to have the Government produce all documents, tapes, memoranda, notes, videos, letters, diagrams, orders, rules, regulations, or any other thing, written, recorded, or otherwise, which go to the planning, implementation, conception, origination, description, and operation or execution of an undercover project known as "Operation Pretense."

5. The defendant is entitled to copies and discovery of all notes between and among FBI agents, other law enforcement agencies of the United States Government, state law enforcement agencies, state and local prosecutorial officials, and any and all other law enforcement officials or state officials who had and have anything to do with Operation Pretense. . . .

6. All documents and memoranda dealing with the funding of Operation Pretense.

In response, U.S. Magistrate Countiss ruled:

4. The Court is reviewing the FBI guidelines as to sting operations. If the Court discovers anything that the Court considers exculpatory to the defendant because of a possible entrapment defense, or otherwise, the Government will be ordered to turn this material over to the defendant. All requests set out in paragraph four are denied.

5. Denied.

6. Denied.

The defendant then submitted to the Court a Petition to Review Magistrate's Order. The petition included the following wording:

Defendant's attorney argued to the Magistrate that the material having to do with the conception and execution of the project pretense would be material to his defense of entrapment. Defendant further argued that he needed to see the material in order to be aware of the game plan involved in project pretense and the way it was executed. It would be particularly important for the defendant to know what instructions were given to the operatives, both agents and cooperating individuals, as to their conduct toward prospective defendants. For example, were they warned to stop their efforts to get the defendants to commit illegal acts if the defendant refused one time, two times, three times or some number of times. To what lengths were they instructed to go? These are things that the defendant cannot know unless he has the discovery requested materials.

Assistant U.S. Attorney James Tucker gave the prosecution's position in a document entitled "Government's Response to Defendant's Petition to Review Magistrate's Order, and Incorporated Brief." Basically, this document noted that the defendant had not asserted or shown any evidence that he was not predisposed to commit the crimes he was charged with, and lack of predisposition was essential to the entrapment defense. The document also cited several case decisions supporting the prosecution's position. The court sustained the magistrate's ruling. Essentially, the disclosure request was a fishing expedition on the part of the defense.

The case did not go to trial. Blakeney and his attorney entered into a Memorandum of Understanding with, Assistant U.S. Attorney Nicholas Phillips on May 30, 1987. In the plea bargain, Blakeney agreed to plead guilty to one count of mail fraud and one count of extortion and to cooperate in the ongoing investigation. He also agreed to resign from the position of supervisor effective July 6, 1987. Total maximum penalties for the two counts were twenty-five years' imprisonment and fines of $500,000.

The government agreed to request that the court accept Blakeney's guilty plea, make no recommendation as to sentence on the mail fraud count, recommend a suspended sentence and five years' probation on the extortion count, recommend that a special condition of probation be that Blakeney neither seek nor hold public office, and to recommend that the other six charges be dismissed. The prosecutors also agreed to inform the court of the extent and effect of Blakeney's cooperation at sentencing and to request that such cooperation be considered in determining his sentence.

Blakeney's plea bargain was struck while the trial of Perry County supervisor Trudie Westmoreland was under way in federal court in Hattiesburg. That trial ran from May 27 through June 2, and it ended with the conviction of the Perry County district four supervisor. Westmoreland had also been charged with taking kickbacks from Ray Davis of Davis Chemicals and from Mid-State Pipe Company, and her defense was basically that she had been entrapped. Westmoreland's trial featured some revealing FBI tape recordings, testimony from an FBI agent who had worked undercover for Mid-State, and testimony from Ray Davis. Apparently, the prosecution had the same types of evidence against Blakeney, and the supervisor and his attorney probably concluded that a court fight would be futile.

Blakeney resigned his position as agreed to in the plea bargain, and the board of supervisors appointed Benjie K. Ford of Taylorsville to serve out his term. At the time of his appointment, Ford was an active candidate for the district two supervisor's post.

At his December 11, 1987, sentencing, the forty-nine-year-old Blakeney said to U.S. District Court Judge Tom S. Lee, "I put my family through a lot of trouble. My people in my district, I put them to a lot of trouble, the people in my county. Have mercy on me." Assistant U.S. Attorney Tucker indicated that the defendant had cooperated in the investigation. "Mr. Blakeney did reveal to the agents the extent of his complicity and describe to the agents various other situations they were looking at. The agents have advised me that they are satisfied with his cooperation," Tucker said. Judge Lee sentenced Blakeney to three years in prison and five years' probation to begin upon release from incarceration. The former supervisor was also fined $5,000 and ordered to pay restitution of $300 to the FBI and $2,040 to Smith County. The other six counts in the indictment were dismissed, and Blakeney was ordered to report to federal prison on January 11, 1988.

Jasper County—Two County Seats, Two Convicted Supervisors

Jasper County was established in 1833 and named for Revolutionary War soldier Sergeant William Jasper. Although the county had a 1990 population of only 17,114, it has two county seats, Bay Springs and Paulding. The south-central Mississippi county is one of nine Mississippi counties that cling to this two-seat anachronism that reflects poor nineteenth-century transportation systems. Located in the western part of the county, Bay Springs had a 1990 population of 1,884. Paulding, located in the eastern part of the county near the large, private Masonite Corporation Game Refuge, is not incorporated. Two Jasper County supervisors were convicted of crimes in the late 1980s as a result of Operation Pretense.

On March 9, 1987, L. Rex Graham, district four supervisor and resident of the Moss community, was indicted by a federal grand jury on seven counts that included charges of bribery, mail fraud, and extortion. Because he was in ill health, Graham's arrest and arraignment were delayed until March 16, 1987. Graham was represented by attorney William R. Ruffin at his arraignment before U.S. Magistrate Countiss in Jackson, where he pleaded not guilty to all charges. Graham was immediately released on a $5,000 personal recognizance bond, and trial was set for June 1, 1987.

Graham was charged with scheming to procure and accepting a total of $1,506 in kickbacks on a series of Jasper County purchases from Mid-State Pipe Company and Davis Chemicals during the period January 1985 through July 1986. He was charged with scheming with Mid-State to rig bids on culvert pipe and to "bust" invoices for materials not delivered to the county. Graham was also charged with proposing to Mid-State that other county supervisors were willing to enter into similar arrangements and assisting in accomplishing such arrangements. The charges involving

Davis Chemicals included scheming to accept kickbacks on county purchases of Perma-Bond, pressurematic oil, and hornet spray. The supervisor was also charged with use of the U.S. mails to effect the schemes and with obstructing interstate commerce by extorting the kickbacks from the vendors. The charges carried maximum penalties of fifty-five years in prison and $1.75 million in fines. Count two of the indictment detailed the $1,506 alleged to have been accepted by Graham by listing thirteen separate kickbacks that the supervisor supposedly took from the two vendors. He was alleged to have accepted $360 in the form of six kickbacks of $60 each from Davis Chemicals and $1,146 in the form of seven kickbacks ($156, $180, $200, $100, $170, $170, and $170) from Mid-State.

Graham's trial, which had been scheduled for June, was delayed after the defendant's new attorney, Thomas Royals, told the court that Graham was not mentally competent to stand trial. Royals said that Graham was taking medication for Parkinson's disease and that the medicine and a recent stroke caused him to have problems with his mental abilities. Royals indicated that his client could not control his muscular movement and that the drugs made him dull, confused, addled, nauseous, and unable to think. On June 11, 1987, Judge Lee signed an order directing Graham to undergo a psychiatric examination to be used by the court in determining the defendant's mental competency to stand trial. The examination was to be conducted in Jackson by Dr. Donald Guild on June 30, 1987. Counsel for the defense was to make arrangements for needed transportation, and all costs for the examination were to be paid by the defendant.

Graham was determined to be mentally competent to stand trial. He and Royals entered into a Memorandum of Understanding with Assistant U.S. Attorney Richard T. Starrett on July 15, 1987. This plea bargain called for Graham to plead guilty to counts two and seven (mail fraud and extortion) and for the other five charges to be dropped. Graham was to resign from his post within ten days of the court's acceptance of his pleas of guilty and to cooperate in the ongoing investigation. The government was to recommend that the court accept the guilty pleas, make no recommendation as to sentence on count two, and recommend a suspended sentence on count seven, with the imposition of five years' probation to commence upon release from any confinement that might be imposed for count two. At sentencing, the government was to inform the court of the results of Graham's cooperation with the investigation and to request strongly that such cooperation be considered in determining the defendant's sentence. The maximum penalties for the crimes outlined in the two counts were twenty-five years in prison and fines of $500,000.

The Memorandum of Understanding addresses possible fines and restitution as follows:

> It is specifically understood that the United States Attorney will make no recommendation for or against the imposition of fines, such to be left to the sole discretion of the Court at the time of sentencing. However, if the investigation substantiates that Graham should be required to pay restitution to any individual or agency as a result of his conduct which constitutes any offense which could have been charged, whether the subject of the charges in the indictment or not, then the United States Attorney will recommend to the Court that it order Graham to pay such restitution, and impose such payment as a special condition of his probation, and Graham hereby agrees that such restitution should be ordered.

On November 13, 1987, Graham's attorney filed a Motion in Opposition to Government's Theory of Restitution. The motion indicated that the presentence investigator had said that the U.S. Attorney's Office would take the position at sentencing that Graham should be liable under Mississippi law for restitution in the full amounts of all invoices where kickbacks were involved. The motion stated the position that any restitution imposed should be governed by federal law and that the state statute was not applicable to the case.

Judge Lee passed sentence on Graham on November 20, 1987. The mail fraud count brought a five year prison sentence, while the extortion count resulted in a suspended sentence and five years' probation to begin with release from confinement. Special conditions of the probation included a $5,000 fine, a prohibition against seeking or holding public office, and the payment of $1,506 in restitution. Graham was to report to prison on January 4, 1988, and the judge recommended that he be allowed to serve his sentence at Eglin Air Force Base, Florida. Apparently, the judge accepted the defendant's argument about restitution because Graham was ordered to pay only the amounts he pleaded guilty to taking as kickbacks. He was ordered to pay $1,146 to the U.S. government, which was the amount he accepted in kickbacks from the FBI front Mid-State, and he was also ordered to pay Jasper County $360, which was the amount he accepted in kickbacks from Davis Chemicals.

Soon after his indictment, the fifty-nine-year-old Graham resigned as district four supervisor for "health reasons." In mid-March 1987, the board of supervisors appointed his wife, Celeste Graham, to serve as the district's supervisor until the upcoming general election. State law allowed Celeste Graham to serve as district four supervisor until January 1988. In September, Phil Carter, of the Secretary of State's Office, indicated that in an election year an appointee may serve until the elected candidate takes office. If 1987 had not been an election year, a special election would have been held to fill the post, and the elected candidate would have taken office immediately after the election.

A federal grand jury indicted John Robert Ulmer on April 7, 1987, on eight counts of bribery, mail fraud, and extortion. He was arrested and arraigned the next day. Ulmer pleaded not guilty and was immediately released on bond. All of the charges against the sixty-one-year-old district three supervisor involved his dealings on the county's behalf with Mid-State Pipe Company and Davis Chemicals. He was charged with conspiring to take and actually taking cash kickbacks amounting to $892 on Jasper County purchases from the two vendors during the period May 1985 through June 1986. The charges included bid rigging, busting invoices, using the U.S. mails to effect the schemes, extortion, and assisting in arranging for other supervisors in the county to engage in similar activities. Maximum penalties for the charges were seventy-five years in prison and $2 million in fines.

Count two of the indictment gave details of nine specific kickbacks that Ulmer was alleged to have taken from Mid-State and Davis Chemicals. He was charged with taking a total of $737 in the form of six kickbacks ($120, $160, $315, $12, $40, and $90) from Mid-State and with taking $155 in the form of three kickbacks ($60, $35, and $60) from Davis Chemicals. The alleged $12 kickback represented approximately 12 percent on the purchase of nuts and bolts reflected on two separate Mid-State invoices. The alleged $315 kickback is especially interesting because of the method used to compute the dollar amount. The total of $315 was derived by adding the value of 12 grader blades not delivered on a busted Mid-State invoice to 12 percent of the value of grader blades actually delivered on that invoice and 12 percent of the value of culvert pipe delivered on another Mid-State invoice. Extraordinary accounting was required to make sure that Ulmer got his correct share of the graft.

In a Memorandum of Understanding dated July 14, 1987, John Robert Ulmer and his attorney entered into an agreement with Assistant U.S. Attorney Richard T. Starrett that called for Ulmer to plead guilty to two (mail fraud and extortion) of the eight counts included in the indictment. Ulmer was to resign his post within thirty days of the court's acceptance of his

pleas and to cooperate in the ongoing investigation. The government was to make no sentencing recommendation on the mail fraud charge and to recommend a suspended sentence and five years' probation on the extortion charge. The government was also to recommend that any probation imposed begin after completion of any prison time imposed on the mail fraud charge and that a special condition of probation be that Ulmer neither seek nor hold public office. At sentencing, the U.S. Attorney's Office was to inform the court of the extent and effect of the defendant's cooperation in the investigation. The maximum penalties that Ulmer faced for the crimes for which he agreed to plead guilty were twenty-five years in prison and $500,000 in fines.

Soon after pleading guilty, Ulmer resigned from office as required by his plea bargain agreement. In mid-August, the board of supervisors unanimously appointed forty-five-year-old Andrew Lee Evans, who had worked for district two for twelve years, to the remainder of Ulmer's term. Evans thus became the first African American to serve as supervisor in Jasper County. Board of supervisors chair Weldon McCellan indicated that Ulmer had recommended Evans for the post in a move to protect the district's workers at least until the end of his term. Evans indicated that he did not plan any personnel changes.

Nearly ten months passed before Ulmer was sentenced. On March 29, 1988, Judge William H. Barbour Jr. imposed an extremely light sentence. On the mail fraud count, Ulmer was sentenced to custody of the attorney general for a term of two years, but execution of the sentence was suspended, and a five-year probation term was imposed. Ulmer was required to perform 400 hours of community service during the first year of probation, and he was not to seek or hold public office during probation. He was also fined $5,000 and ordered to pay restitution to Jasper County in the amount of $892. Both payments had to be made by April 4, 1988. On the other charge, Ulmer was given five years' probation that was to run concurrently with that imposed on the mail fraud charge. Ulmer was the first supervisor who pleaded guilty or was convicted by a jury not sentenced to serve time in prison.

One factor in Ulmer's light sentence was months of valuable cooperation with the Pretense investigation. Assistant U.S. Attorney Richard Starrett told Judge Barbour that Ulmer's cooperation had been extensive and that he had testified at least once before a grand jury regarding vendors. Starrett said, "The defendant has cooperated more than any other supervisor. He has substantially cooperated. That's more than the government can say for any other defendant." In addition, Starrett said, "The government has found this defendant to be remorseful from the beginning." Defense attorney Thomas Royals said that the former supervisor deserved probation. "This man's got some real mitigating factors," Royals said. "He's cooperated more than any other supervisor." Ulmer's family situation was another factor. His seven-year-old son, who had recently received a liver transplant, was taking drugs to prevent a second organ rejection, and his mother was in critical condition in a Meridian hospital. Ulmer indicated that he took his son to Meridian twice a week for blood work and that his mother was on life support machines.

Judge Barbour said that in determining Ulmer's sentence he had to be fair with supervisors already sentenced and that this caused a dilemma. He said, "If the court were imposing a sentence in comparison with those equally culpable, it would be a sentence of approximately two years." The judge asked defense attorney Royals, who had defended several other supervisors, how the others would view a more lenient sentence because of family members' poor health. Royals replied, "I think no supervisor would stand up and ask the court to do anything other than be lenient." In passing sentence, Judge Barbour said, "I have a great deal of personal sympathy for you. I hope the situation with regard to your two family members works out as well as possible."

The resignations of Graham and Ulmer and the elections of 1987 gave Jasper County an entirely new board of supervisors in 1988—the voters obviously thought it was time for a house cleaning. In the August 4 primary, the supervisors in all but district one were voted out, and district one supervisor Herman Sims received only 36 percent of the votes in the late August runoff against Grady James. The newly elected supervisors included Wendall Harvey of district two, the first African American ever elected supervisor in Jasper County.

Clarke County—Two Guilty Supervisors

Located in the east-central part of the state on the Alabama border, Clarke County had a 1990 population of 17,313. The county was established in 1883 and named for Judge Joshua Clarke, Mississippi's first chancellor. Quitman, with a population of fewer than 3,000, is the county's largest city and the county seat. Quitman is the hometown of Antonio McDyess, the great basketball player for the NBA's Denver Nuggets, former University of Alabama star, and member of the 2000 U.S. Olympic Team. Two of Clarke County's five supervisors were convicted of felonies in the late 1980s as a result of Operation Pretense.

As the Pretense maelstrom swirled and the related unit-versus-beat controversy boiled in the summer of 1987, the *Meridian Star* printed a letter to the editor from a member of the state legislature and a unit system proponent from Clarke County that depicted the statewide problem very well.

> The recent action by the Clarke County Board of Supervisors in again turning down the county unit system of road management compels me to write this letter.
>
> During the last 50 years more than 20 studies have been made on the operation of county road departments. The studies all have one thing in common. They recommend doing away with the beat system and replacing it with the unit system. In fact, the Mississippi Legislature has been notified on more than 20 occasions by various study agencies that the county road administration in the state is criminally wasteful and an open invitation to fraud.
>
> The continued use of the beat system by a great majority of our counties results in Mississippi being one of the most expensive states in maintaining roads. On a per capita basis we are first in the nation and in total dollars expended, we have never been lower than ninth.
>
> In comparing Coahoma County, where the unit system has been in operation more than 55 years, with the average beat county on five different expenditures, we find that for fuel Coahoma spend $66,000 against $247,000, for in-house repairs $92,000 against $117,000, for outside repairs $15,000 against $253,000, for equipment $240,000 against $425,000 and for tires $21,000 against $69,000.
>
> Mississippi needs the county unit system in all of our counties, not to keep people from stealing, but because it is more efficient. The fact that the unit system makes stealing more difficult is an added advantage.
>
> Some members of the Clarke County Board of Supervisors visited Coahoma County a few years back. The main concern raised upon their return was that the waitress in the restaurant where they had breakfast did not know who her supervisor was. If notoriety is what they were seeking, I think they have succeeded far beyond their own expectations.
>
> James D. Price
> Quitman
> July 15, 1987

Clarke County district five supervisor Lige Becton was indicted on five counts by a federal grand jury April 7, 1987. He was charged with one count each of bribery, mail fraud, aiding and abetting mail fraud, extortion, and aiding and abetting extortion. Becton pleaded innocent to all charges before U.S. Magistrate Countiss on April 8 and was released on a $5,000 personal recognizance bond. Becton was charged with conspiring with Mid-State Pipe Company to rig bids on culvert pipe and to bust invoices on materials billed to Clarke County but never delivered. He was also charged with using the U.S. mails to accomplish the schemes. Becton was accused of accepting $690 in the form of three kickbacks ($60, $230, and $400) from a Mid-State representative. All of the charged offenses were said to have taken place between October 1985 and February 1987. The seventy-one-year-old Becton had served as supervisor since 1979.

In a Memorandum of Understanding dated May 22, 1987, negotiated by attorney William E. Ready and Assistant U.S. Attorney Ruth R. Harris, Becton agreed to plead guilty to one count each of mail fraud and extortion and to cooperate with the government in the ongoing Pretense investigation. In exchange for Becton's guilty plea and cooperation, at the time of sentencing the prosecutors were to inform the court of the extent and effect of his cooperation, request that the other three counts be dropped, make no recommendation as to sentence on the mail fraud count, and recommend five years' probation on the extortion charge. The U.S. attorney was to recommend that, if probation were imposed, it begin immediately after release from any prison time served for the mail fraud charge and that Becton be prohibited from seeking or holding public office during the time of probation. The total maximum penalties for the two counts to which Becton agreed to plead guilty were twenty-five years in prison and fines of $500,000.

Based on the terms of the plea bargain, Lige Becton pleaded guilty on June 12, 1987, before U.S. District Court Judge Barbour in Jackson. Sentencing was delayed to allow for a presentencing investigation and for Becton to cooperate in the ongoing investigation. Becton was the tenth supervisor to plead guilty to Pretense-related charges.

Becton stood before Judge Barbour for sentencing February 12, 1988. He was sentenced to five years in prison on the mail fraud charge with all but six months suspended, placed on five years' probation on the extortion charge, and fined $10,000. Becton was also ordered to pay $690 in restitution to Clarke County. The other three counts were dismissed. The fine had to be paid by February 16, 1988. A special condition of probation was that

Becton neither seek nor hold public office. Becton's cooperation had obviously been helpful to the ongoing investigation. The former supervisor reported to the Federal Prison Camp at Maxwell Air Force Base, Alabama, on March 7, 1988.

Francis M. Spivey, district one supervisor, was indicted by a federal grand jury on July 8, 1987, on charges of bribery, mail fraud, and aiding and abetting mail fraud. The supervisor was arrested July 9 by FBI agents and arraigned before U.S. Magistrate Countiss. He pleaded not guilty to all four counts in the indictment and was released on a $5,000 personal recognizance bond. The indictment charged that Spivey conspired with Mid-State Pipe Company and Shine's Supply Company of Jackson to defraud Clarke County and its citizens. Spivey had allegedly arranged for the county to purchase items from the two firms and had allegedly accepted cash kickbacks for such purchases. All the alleged transactions took place between November 1983 and November 1985. Spivey was accused of accepting a total of $765 on six county purchases and with using the U.S. mails to accomplish the schemes. The three counts of mail fraud and one count of bribery that the Stonewall resident faced carried maximum penalties of twenty-five years' imprisonment and $1 million in fines. At the time of his arrest, Spivey was serving his twelfth year as supervisor.

After the court denied several defense motions to dismiss the charges and to keep out certain evidence, the defendant agreed, in what was by this time a rather standard plea bargain, to plead guilty to three of the four counts and to cooperate with the investigation. In this August 1987 agreement, the prosecutors agreed to recommend five years' probation to run concurrently on two of the counts and to make no recommendation as to sentence on the other count. The government agreed to recommend that the fourth count be dropped. The U.S. attorney was also to inform the court as to the extent and effect of Spivey's cooperation at sentencing. The maximum penalties that could be imposed for the three counts to which Spivey agreed to plead guilty were fifteen years in prison and fines of $750,000.

Despite his indictment, Spivey was a candidate for a fourth term in the August 4 Democratic primary. He had to face Henry Van Chancellor in a late August runoff election because no candidate won a majority of the votes in the primary. Spivey lost the runoff; he received only 353 votes.

On December 21, 1987, Judge Lee accepted the plea bargain terms and sentenced Spivey to three years in prison and five years' probation to begin after release from incarceration. Spivey was also fined $3,000 and ordered to pay Clarke County and the FBI restitution in the amounts of $485 and $280, respectively. Judge Lee recommended that Spivey be assigned to the Federal Correctional Institution at Eglin Air Force Base, Florida. He was ordered to report to prison on January 19, 1988. Spivey's court records contain a Satisfaction of Judgment dated May 24, 1988, indicating that he had paid or otherwise settled through compromise all fines, restitutions, and assessments by that day.

18. Big-Time Corruption in South Mississippi

Copiah, Lincoln, Covington, and Greene Counties

Copiah County—Unbounded Corruption

Copiah County, with a 1990 population of 27,592, is located in southwest Mississippi, and Hazlehurst is the county seat. Beth Henley, an award-winning playwright and a Jackson native, set her Pulitzer Prize–winning play, *Crimes of the Heart*, in the fictitious MaGraft family kitchen in Hazlehurst. The MaGraft family kitchen was modeled after the kitchen of Henley's grandmother, who lived in Hazlehurst during Henley's formative years. *Crimes of the Heart* won the Pulitzer Prize and the New York Drama Critics Circle award in 1981. It was the first drama to win the Pulitzer Prize before going on Broadway. Henley also received an Academy Award nomination in 1986 for the best adapted screenplay for *Crimes of the Heart*. The award-winning drama derives its title from a complex plot that involves three desperate sisters in a dysfunctional family.

During the 1980s, Copiah County government was as dysfunctional as the fictitious family of the sisters MaGraft. Four of the county's five supervisors pleaded guilty to felony charges. It is disconcerting to realize that men of such low character were elected and put in charge of the county's business. Moreover, one of those felons was reelected after he had been indicted on very serious offenses and remained in office for more than eighteen months after being indicted.

The environment of political corruption in Copiah County that Operation Pretense brought to light so vividly was evident even in the early 1980s when a thirty-year supervisor was convicted of vote fraud and removed from office. District four supervisor W. E. "Ed" Hood; his sons, Edwin Earl Hood and Frank Hood; district four employee Rickey Smith; and former district four constable Arnold Carraway were convicted of using absentee ballots to rig the December 23, 1983, runoff election between Ed Hood and

Manuel Welch for the district four post. Hood had been declared winner of the special election with 877 votes against Welch's 858.

Welch filed suit in federal court alleging discrimination under the Voting Rights Act of 1965. In August 1984, U.S. District Court Judge William H. Barbour Jr. ruled that Welch's rights had not been violated and that he should have filed his complaint in state court. In his ruling, Judge Barbour said, "The actions of the supporters of W. E. (Ed) Hood and Mr. Hood himself were no more than a concentrated effort to reelect the incumbent at all costs, including fraud." A Copiah County grand jury indicted the supervisor and his four supporters on February 25, 1985, on state charges of conspiracy to commit vote fraud. All five men were convicted by a state jury in Hazlehurst May 22, 1985. Ed Hood was sentenced to a five-year jail term. After his felony conviction, Hood was removed from office on May 24, 1985. Welch was elected district four supervisor later that year, thus becoming the county's first black supervisor since Reconstruction.

In June 1985, Circuit Court Judge Joe. N. Pickett reduced Hood's five-year prison term to probation and a $5,000 fine. Hood and his four supporters appealed their convictions. The Mississippi State Supreme Court threw out all the convictions in March 1988 and sent the cases back to Copiah County for future consideration by a grand jury.

District Attorney Dunn Lampton promised expeditious action in the upcoming April 1988 meeting of the grand jury, and all five men involved were reindicted the next month. The new indictments set the stage for guilty pleas. Lampton agreed to accept guilty pleas from all five in part because Hood agreed to accept a sentence that was almost the same as the original sentence. Another problem, which had originally prevented the district attorney from accepting a guilty plea to a misdemeanor charge before the case went to trial, was Hood's refusal to step down as supervisor. However, Hood had been removed from office after his conviction, and two elections had been held since then. Arnold Carraway had also been removed from office because of his earlier conviction.

All five men pleaded guilty in early April to the charges contained in the new indictments. Hood was fined $5, 000 and sentenced to a one-year suspended jail term. The other four defendants, who had originally been fined $3,000, were fined $500 each and sentenced to six-month suspended jail terms.

On February 12, 1987, Thomas M. Heard, supervisor of Copiah County's first district, was arrested and indicted on eleven counts in the first round of Pretense-related indictments. The forty-two-year-old Heard, a Gallman resident, was charged with one count each of bribery and extortion and nine counts of mail fraud. He was charged with proposing with Mid-State Pipe Company to rig bids on culvert pipe and grader blades and to bust invoices on Mid-State's purported sales to the county of several other products. The indictment alleged that from April 1985 through August 1986, Heard accepted $3,185 in kickbacks from Mid-State and that he repeatedly used the U.S. mails to carry out the schemes. Heard pleaded innocent to all charges, and trial was set for May 11.

Despite the indictment, Heard qualified as a candidate for reelection in the Democratic primary scheduled for August 1987. However, in mid-July, Heard asked the county Democratic Executive Committee to remove his name from the ballot. About the same time, his wife, Carl Nell Heard, threw her hat in the ring by qualifying to run in the Democratic primary for the post that her husband held. Reporting on the unofficial results of the race, the August 5, 1987, *Copiah County Courier* indicated that a runoff was assured in the district one supervisor's race between Carl Nell Heard and either Reeves Beasley or Ervin Kelly Jr. Ten candidates had sought the Democratic nomination, and initial results showed Carl Nell Heard leading with 295 votes, followed by Beasley with 288, and Kelly with 287. However, a county Democratic Executive Committee check of the results during the two days following the election showed that a vote total of 13 for Heard from the Georgetown North box had originally been recorded in error as 73. The resulting 60-vote correction reduced Heard's total to 235, leaving Beasley and Kelly to face each other in the runoff election.

Heard's scheduled May 11 trial was postponed because he was in the hospital for kidney stone surgery. The trial had been rescheduled for July 20, but it was delayed again because Heard had been under the care of psychiatrist Dr. Robert Ritter in the psychiatric unit of a Jackson hospital. He had been hospitalized for abusing painkillers and sleeping pills that were prescribed after the May operation. Judge Barbour ordered Ritter to provide periodic updates of Heard's condition. Based on information provided by Dr. Ritter, Judge Barbour ruled July 30 that Heard was competent to stand trial, and he rescheduled the trial for October 19.

The judge's order establishing the October 19 trial date, among other things, required: (1) that the defendant remain under the care of Dr. Ritter and undergo therapy on a weekly basis, on a schedule to be set by Dr. Ritter, until one week prior to trial, at which time the defendant will submit to hospitalization as directed by Dr. Ritter and remain hospitalized during the trial except as needed to attend sessions of court; (2) that the defendant refrain from excessive use of drugs and alcohol pending trial and, to that end, submit to weekly urinalysis testing for drug and alcohol abuse; (3) that should defendant either miss a weekly session with Dr. Ritter, or not submit to a weekly urinalysis test, or should any weekly urinalysis test indicate that the defendant is excessively using drugs or alcohol, then Dr. Ritter should immediately report such to both defense counsel and the U.S. Attorney's Office.

In an interview with the author, former FBI special agent Jerry King noted that during court appearances he observed Tommy Heard laying on hall benches disheveled and unkempt. King thought it was all part of Heard's act to show that he was having mental and other problems. King explained, "He was in dire straits with the Pretense case, and he knew it and was playing a role, as he often did in dealing with this undercover agent and other salesmen."

In an order dated October 9, 1987, Judge Barbour rescinded the portion of the July 30 order that required Heard to submit to hospitalization one week prior to the trial scheduled for October 19. This order followed the defendant's decision to change his plea from not guilty to guilty based on a plea agreement that had been worked out with U.S. Attorney George Phillips.

In an October 9 plea bargain, Heard agreed to plead guilty to two counts of the eleven-count indictment and to cooperate with the government in the Pretense investigation. The agreement also called for Heard to resign as supervisor and not to seek public office during a five-year probationary period to begin after release from any confinement that would be imposed. The government was to ask the court to drop the other nine charges. On October 14, Heard pleaded guilty in the U.S. District Court in Vicksburg to one count of extortion and one count of mail fraud. The charges carried maximum penalties of twenty-five years' imprisonment and fines of $500,000. Sentencing was delayed so that Heard could cooperate in the investigation.

According to Assistant U.S. Attorney James Tucker, Heard's guilty plea was significant because "this particular case would have been a very long and complicated trial. It has far reaching implications and complicity." Tucker described Heard's dealings with undercover FBI agent Jerry King, who was posing as a salesman for Mid-State Pipe Company. He said that King would prepare invoices for products, such as road-surfacing materials and road signs, that would never be delivered and Heard would authorize payment by the county and receive about half of the invoice price in cash from King. After Heard became comfortable with the operation, Tucker said, "he became bolder, even to setting his own figure."

Heard resigned from office on November 9, 1987. On December 12, 1987, Judge Barbour sentenced him to ten years' imprisonment and five years' probation. In accordance with the plea agreement, nine of the eleven counts in the indictment were dismissed. Heard was ordered to report to federal prison on January 4, 1988. No restitution was imposed because of Heard's dire financial condition. The judge recommended that Heard be assigned to a facility where he could get treatment and counseling.

In accordance with the plea agreement, the U.S. attorney originally suggested that Heard be sentenced to five years' probation on the extortion charge and made no recommendation on the mail fraud charge. At sentencing, prosecutors withdrew that recommendation and recommended the ten-year prison sentence. Assistant U.S. Attorney Tucker maintained, "The government's obligation was breached by the defendant's misconduct." In November, Heard had taken Copiah County equipment and used it as his own while preparing to resign because of his guilty pleas in federal court. The ten-year prison sentence turned out to be the longest imposed on a supervisor for Pretense-related crimes.

Defense attorney Lisa Binder Milner told Judge Barbour that debts, including a number of garnishments, had caused Heard to suffer depression and had contributed to his wrongdoings. She said, "He's strapped financially. It wasn't the right way to go about it. He had $113,000 he owed, which contributed to reasons for his committing the wrong." She added, "He realizes he's breached the agreement with the government," and noted that as a result of his depression that he had been undergoing psychiatric and shock therapy.

Jerry King, in an interview with the author, indicated that Heard was probably the most brazen and colorful character that he encountered in Pretense. King noted that Heard would talk incessantly before a deal was consummated and that he was often afraid his two-hour tape would run out before the payoff was made. Transcripts of FBI tapes obtained by the author under the Freedom of Information Act support King's recollections.

Heard was biased against African Americans and Jews, and his bigotry is depicted in taped conversations. According to King, Heard said, "Hitler had the right idea about those Jews. He gave them five dollars and a bicycle and told them to get out of Germany." King noted that Heard's historical review was, of course, not quite as severe as the actual Holocaust. In an ironic twist, Heard engaged the very capable Jewish lawyer Al Binder and his daughter, Lisa Binder Milner, as defense attorneys. No doubt, in discovery, the attorneys heard the tapes that so vividly depicted their client's biases.

King noted that Heard liked to give the impression that he was the "big dog" in his county. According to King, once when he was with Heard at his beat barn, the supervisor received a telephone call informing him that an FBI car was down the road at a particular house. He told King, "Jump in the car, we've got the FBI in the neighborhood, and we're going to do a surveillance." King said he started sweating en route, hoping it wasn't the FBI. When the two approached the plain, four-door car with blackwall tires, Heard told King to write down the tag number. They proceeded to the sheriff's office where Heard had the sheriff "run the tag." It turned out to be a social worker's car. At about the same time, King said Heard told him that they had to be careful about the FBI, and King started sweating again, thinking that Heard might be on to him. Heard then told King about his conversation with an FBI agent who supposedly told him how the FBI conducted an investigation. King related that Heard said, "They would go to your neighbors, pull out their notebook, and ask questions about the your finances, sex life, etc." Heard finished this conversation with King by saying, "Don't worry about me, the fish that don't bite stays in the pond."

Heard's comments about how the FBI conducted an investigation made King wonder whether some agent had talked to Heard. This information was forwarded to the Pretense case agent, Keith Morgan. It was later learned that there had been an agent from South Mississippi who had been released from FBI Academy Training School and had returned to Mississippi. King surmised that Heard had talked with the released agent. Nothing ever came out of this incident, and Heard continued to do business with the FBI front, Mid-State Pipe Company.

In early November, Thomas Heard was indicted on state charges unrelated to Pretense. A Copiah County grand jury indicted the district one supervisor on two counts of embezzlement and one count of fraud, charges that could result in a prison sentence of fifty years. The indictment alleged that Heard converted Copiah County road equipment, some of which had been written off as junk, to his own personal use. A road grader, bulldozer, roller, trailer, and dragline owned by Copiah County were located in Madison, Warren, and Hinds Counties by sheriff's deputies who cooperated with the state highway patrol on the investigation. Some county-owned barrels of motor oil and hydraulic fluid were found in or near a gravel pit in Copiah County, and some county-owned treated bridge timbers were found buried in a gravel pit with gravel and sand piled on top. In addition, a bulldozer was found in the woods in Copiah County. Finally, Heard was charged with giving certain county property to county resident Thomas Lee.

Heard pleaded guilty on November 30 in circuit court to two counts of embezzlement. One of the counts charged him with converting to his own use a lowboy trailer, a Rex steel wheel roller, a dragline, a motor grader, and an AC dozer with ripper, all of which were owned by Copiah County. The other count charged him with giving away county-owned property to Thomas Lee. The property transferred to Lee included two Chevrolet engines; two twelve-volt batteries; two truck transmissions and drive shafts; one hydraulic cylinder; one truck radiator; one two-and-a-half-ton truck rear end complete with four wheels, tires, and springs; one dash from a two-and-a-half-ton truck; one dash from a half-ton pickup truck; one bucket from a dragline; and one pile driver attachment for a dragline complete with hammer. Some of the items listed in the second count apparently had been stripped from county-owned equipment shortly before Heard resigned as supervisor.

Heard was sentenced to sixteen years in prison on December 10, 1987, on the state charges. Circuit Court Judge Joe Pigott asked Heard if he had anything to say prior to sentencing, and Heard replied, "No, sir. I just made a little mistake." The judge did not buy this explanation. Pigott told Heard, "You were the youngest person ever elected supervisor in Copiah County, and you were reelected four times. You made more than a little mistake." The judge then ask Heard if he gave Lee the county property after entering his plea in federal court. Heard indicated that most of it was given before the plea, but that he could not remember what was done before or after the plea. At this point, District Attorney Dunn Lampton stated that the evidence showed that the transfers were made after the guilty plea in federal court. The judge also asked Heard if he had anything to say about the second count, and he replied, "No, sir." Piggott asked if this conversion of county property to his own use was done before or after the plea in federal court, and Heard said that he could not remember.

The judge then proceeded to chastise the defendant and to engage in an interesting exchange with his attorney:

> "It would be nice just to forget all our mistakes. The people of Copiah County have to pay more taxes to replace the equipment you damaged and stole. They will remember a long time what you did. I hope they never forget

as long as there is a person living in this county. I hope they remember how you betrayed their trust. Now whoever comes in to replace you will have to increase taxes to replace what you took off and tore up. Do you have any excuses, any reason for it? Any justification?"

Defense attorney Lisa Binder Milner replied that Heard was under severe financial strain, that he knew what he did was not right and that he owed $113,000 in judgments. She said, "He has a family to support and has been under psychiatric care for quite some time." The judge said that Heard's financial problems were of his own making and that the county had never missed paying him since he took office. "If he accumulated $100,000 in expenses, it was his own doing," Judge Pigott said, noting that he did not think for one moment that Heard had stolen from the county to feed his family. "The checks from the county were sufficient to feed his family. It just doesn't ring true."

The sentence imposed by Judge Pigott was to run concurrently with Heard's federal sentence on the Pretense-related charges. Any time that remained on the sixteen-year state sentence after release from federal confinement was to be served at the state penitentiary at Parchman. Judge Pigott ordered that Heard be held in custody if he was released from the hospital before he was scheduled to report to federal prison on January 4, 1988. District Attorney Lampton said, "He won't be spending Christmas at home. As much as he has taken from the county, I think that's fair." Judge Pigott told Heard, "You're not going to be home until January 4."

District five supervisor Barry B. "Ted" Berry was indicted in May 1997 in federal court in Jackson on seven counts that involved bribery, extortion, and mail fraud. The fifty-four-year-old supervisor was accused of accepting $1,720 in kickbacks and $400 from a private citizen on purchases made by Copiah County during the period January 1986 through June 1986. Berry was arrested, arraigned, and freed on a $5,000 personal recognizance bond. The charges against Berry involved busting invoices with Mid-State Pipe Company, bid rigging, splitting invoices with Mid-State to avoid legal requirements to advertise for bids, having Mid-State deliver culverts to a private citizen and then billing the county, accepting $400 from the private citizen for the pipe delivered by Mid-State, and using the U.S. mails to accomplish parts of these schemes.

Berry pleaded guilty on August 13, 1987, to one count of extortion and one count of mail fraud based on an August 11 plea bargain with U.S. Attorney George Phillips. He pleaded guilty to scheming with Mid-State to use his position as supervisor of the fifth district of Copiah County to cause and arrange for various items to be purchased by the county from Mid-State in return for cash kickbacks on some purchases, accepting $400 from a private citizen for items purchased by the county but delivered to the private citizen, and using the U.S. mails to carry out the scheme. The agreement required Berry's resignation from office by October 1 and prohibited him from seeking public office during any probationary period that might be imposed by the court. In addition, Berry agreed to cooperate with the federal authorities in the Pretense investigation. Berry faced maximum penalties of 25 years in prison and $500,000 in fines.

Even though he was under indictment, Berry was a candidate for reelection in the August 5 Democratic primary election. With 405 votes, Berry finished second to Winfred "Wimp" Hammack's 581 votes. The two were to face each other in a runoff scheduled for August 25 to determine the Democratic nominee in the upcoming general election for the fifth district supervisor post. After pleading guilty, Berry asked that his name be removed from the ballot, and the county Democratic Executive Committee replaced his name with that of Leon Canoy, who had finished third in the primary election. Berry resigned his post on August 31, 1987.

Judge Barbour passed sentence in federal court in Jackson on June 14, 1988. Berry was sentenced to three years in prison on mail fraud and aiding and abetting mail fraud; sentence was suspended on the extortion charge, and he was ordered to serve five years' probation that was to commence upon release from prison. He was also ordered to pay Copiah County $2,753 in restitution and to pay a fine of $5,000. The restitution and fine were to be paid within the first four and a half years of the probation on a schedule to be determined by the probation office. Judge Barbour recommended that Berry be incarcerated in the Federal Correctional Institution at Eglin Air Force Base, Florida. He was ordered to report to prison on July 15, 1988.

Copiah County district three supervisor Sidney Thompson was indicted by a federal grand jury in Jackson on October 7, 1987. In the five-count indictment, he was charged with conspiracy to defraud, extortion, and mail fraud. Thompson pleaded innocent to all counts on October 8. The charges involved actions taken by Thompson in his official capacity as supervisor during the period December 1984 through March 1987, including taking kickbacks, busting invoices, having the county pay for equipment delivered to him, and using the U.S. mails to facilitate these actions.

On May 10, 1989, Thompson pleaded guilty in the last Pretense case to be prosecuted. The sixty-six-year-old Hazlehurst resident pleaded guilty to charges of mail fraud and extortion. Thompson admitted taking $300 in kickbacks from undercover FBI agent Jerry King. He also admitted that he and J. H. Holiman Sr., president of Holiman Equipment Company, agreed that Holiman Equipment would bill Copiah County for a mower that would actually be delivered to Thompson for his personal use. Thompson faced maximum penalties of twenty-five years in prison and fines of $500,000.

In November 1987, Thompson had been reelected to a third term despite his October 1987 indictment. Thompson delayed his resignation until July 5, 1989, one day before he was to be sentenced, despite the fact that he had pleaded guilty in May. Assistant U.S. Attorney Ruth Harris indicated that Thompson had remained in office because of his county medical insurance coverage. He suffered from cancer of the mouth and from heart problems.

The Memorandum of Understanding of May 10, 1989, did not require Thompson to resign from office; it included the following wording: "Further, if the pre-sentence investigation substantiates the extent of defendant's illnesses as represented by his counsel, the government will not oppose his request for an alternative sentence." Despite the fact that the plea agreement did not mention resignation, Judge Barbour told Thompson during the May pleading that he should resign from office. On July 6, 1989, Judge Barbour fined Thompson $2,000 and sentenced him to five years in prison with all but eighteen months suspended. Thompson was also ordered to serve five years' probation and to pay restitution to Copiah County in the amount of $1,474.65. The fine and the restitution were to be paid within the first four and a half years of probation, and Thompson was prohibited from seeking or holding public office, either elected or appointed, during probation. Thompson was ordered to report to prison August 7, 1989, and the judge recommended that he be assigned to the Federal Correctional Institution at Maxwell Air Force Base, Alabama.

At sentencing, Judge Barbour commented about the defendant's claimed medical problem, "I however note you have continued to serve as a supervisor and draw a salary until yesterday. . . . In spite of your medical problem, I think if you can serve as supervisor, you can serve the time period." Defense attorney Bill Waller said that Thompson stayed on as supervisor because he needed his county-paid health insurance. Judge Barbour also said, "I'm not totally convinced that you are contrite about this matter. You wanted in the interviews with probation (officers) to blame it on the system and somebody trapped you. Nobody trapped you on this mower deal."

J. H. Holiman Sr. died during the investigation, and no charges were ever filed against him. Holiman Equipment did bill the price of the mower that had been delivered to Thompson to Copiah County on eight phony invoices. When Operation Pretense was made public, Thompson paid six of the invoices himself, but Copiah County paid the other two.

Lincoln County—The Eleventh Guilty Plea

Carved out of Lawrence, Copiah, Pike, Franklin, and Amite Counties in southwestern Mississippi, Lincoln County was formed in 1870 under the state's third constitution. The county had a 1990 population of 30,278. Brookhaven, the county seat, with a 1990 population of 10,243, is the largest town in the county. The county was named for Abraham Lincoln, but in the 1980s one of its supervisors proved not to be as honest as Abe.

On June 12, 1987, Lincoln County fifth district supervisor F. H. Britt Jr. waived indictment and pleaded guilty to a criminal information that charged him with one count of bribery and one count of mail fraud. Under a plea bargain worked out with federal prosecutors, Britt also agreed to resign from office within two weeks. Britt pleaded guilty to mail fraud for receiving kickbacks on county purchases from L&M Equipment Company of Pearl during the period December 1984 through February 1987. The mail fraud count involved mailing a busted invoice for $415.25 for grader blades and parts the county never received. The bribery charged involved receipt of $600 in kickbacks from L&M representative Pete Dacus in May of 1985 on the county's purchase of two used tractors for $32,000.

While making no recommendation concerning fines, Assistant U.S. Attorney Richard T. Starrett recommended a maximum three-year sentence on the mail fraud charge and five years' probation on the bribery charge. Sentencing was delayed, and Britt was released on a $5,000 personal recognizance bond. Britt faced maximum penalties of fifteen years in prison and $500,000 in fines. The sixty-year-old Britt was the eleventh supervisor to plead guilty to Pretense-related charges.

Attorney Jerome Steen indicated that his client was cooperating with the investigation. Steen said, "From day one, whenever the Federal Bureau of Investigation investigators mentioned these matters to Mr. Britt, himself personally and myself have undertaken to do everything properly and right." Steen also indicated that Britt planned to make full restitution to the county.

U. S. Attorney George Phillips indicated that Britt was among "a few" supervisors who, after learning of the investigation, stepped forward to work with the government. Phillips added, "Those who have dealt with an undercover agent must know that, and if they are smart they will get an attorney" and come forward before they are indicted. In fact, the U.S. attorneys generally sent letters to supervisors on whom they had evidence and asked them to come forward and cooperate with the investigation.

Judge Tom S. Lee subsequently sentenced Britt to five years in prison, with all but six months suspended, and fined him $3,000. Britt's court file includes a Satisfaction of Judgment dated October 13, 1992, that shows the fine had been paid.

Covington County—First Termer Learns Fast

Covington County is strategically located in south-central Mississippi about halfway between the cities of Magee to the north and Hattiesburg to the south. Heavily traveled U.S. Highway 49 intersects U.S. Highway 82 at Collins, which is the county seat. According to the 1990 census, the county had a population of 16,527 residents, and Collins, with 2,131 residents, was the only incorporated area with more than 1,000 residents. There are several small manufacturing plants located around Collins, and a state-supported veterans' home was built there in the 1990s. People commute from outlying areas to work in Collins, and it has been said that there are more jobs in Collins than residents. Mt. Olive, with a population of fewer than 1,000, is the second largest town in the county.

In February 1819, Covington County was formed out of the western part of Wayne County and the eastern part of Lawrence County. It was the first county established after Mississippi's admission to the Union. From January 1823 until January 1824, the county was wholly removed from its geographic territory during the one-year existence of Brainbridge County. During that year, Covington County consisted of only two tracks of townships in what is now Jones County. The county was named for General Leonard Covington of Maryland, who was killed during the War of 1812 as American troops invaded Canada. General Covington once lived in Washington, Mississippi, and several family members including his wife, continued to live in Adams County after his death.

The Okatoma River, with its beautiful canoe route, traverses the county. Each year Collins hosts the Okatoma Festival, which draws large crowds for arts and crafts, games, and a 5K run. Gerald McRaney, television star and Covington County native, was a featured attraction at the festival in the mid-1990s. Another native son, Randolph Keys, led the University of Southern Mississippi basketball team to the 1987 National Invitation Tournament championship and later played in the NBA. Steve McNair, Mt. Olive native and record-setting quarterback at Alcorn State University, led the Tennessee Titans to the January 2000 Super Bowl.

Unfortunately for Covington County, in the 1980s a first-term supervisor learned all too quickly how to manipulate the system to line his own pockets at taxpayers' expense. Forty-nine-year-old Wiley Tom Wade, district five supervisor, was caught up in Operation Pretense. In a September 4, 1987, Memorandum of Understanding signed by Wade; his attorney, Samuel H. Wilkins; and Assistant U.S. Attorney Starrett, Wade agreed to plead guilty to an information filed against him and to cooperate with the ongoing Pretense investigation.

The agreement called for the U.S. attorney to make no specific recommendations regarding sentencing, to inform the court of the extent and effect of Wade's cooperation, and to request strongly that such cooperation be considered in determining the sentence. In addition, the U.S. attorney was to make no recommendation for or against the imposition of fines. The maximum penalties that could be imposed under the relevant federal statute for the offenses charged in the information were five years in prison and a $250,000 fine. However, the agreement noted that "should the investigation substantiate that Wade should be required to pay restitution as a result of his conduct which constitutes an offense which could have been charged, whether the subject of the charges in the Information or not," the U.S. attorney would recommend that the court order Wade to pay restitution. The agreement contained a specific statement that Wade, by signing the agreement, agreed that such restitution should be ordered.

Wade pleaded guilty to an information that vividly depicts the many corrupt practices of the first-term supervisor:

> The defendant would and did propose with L&M Equipment Company (hereinafter "LMEC") to use his position as supervisor of the Fifth District of Covington County (hereinafter, "the County") to cause and arrange for various items to be purchased by Covington County from LMEC in return for the defendant being paid a kickback in cash or goods for such purchases.

The defendant would and did propose with LMEC to submit fraudulent bills for materials and goods to be furnished by LMEC to the County and did actively assist in accomplishing such activities.

The defendant would and did propose with LMEC to submit "busted" invoices to the Board and Chancery Clerk by mail or otherwise for purported sales by LMEC to Covington County for materials and goods; busted invoices being false and fraudulent invoices reflecting either overstated quantities of materials and supplies delivered to the County or reflecting quantities of materials and supplies never delivered to the County.

The defendant would and did propose with LMEC to falsely and fraudulently charge the County for materials and supplies not delivered to the county and receive a percentage of the warrant/check to be issued and mailed by the State of Mississippi, Covington County, to LMEC in payment for the materials and supplies not delivered.

It was further a part of the scheme and artifice to defraud and to obtain money and property by means of false and fraudulent pretenses, representations and promises that:

On several occasions between December 1985 and January 1987, defendant discussed with a representative of LMEC and with others, numerous fraudulent activities including, the defendant's agreement to accepting a 40% to 50% kickback on materials purchased from LMEC, to "splitting" or "shorting" materials purchased from LMEC, and to accepting kickbacks in the form of liquor from LMEC on "busted" invoices to the County.

On or about December 19,1986, the defendant approved LMEC invoice 123 dated December 19, 1986 in the amount of $415.72 for a rebuilt cylinder billed to the county.

On or about December 19, 1986, defendant obtained a "kickback" of approximately $200.00 worth of liquor from a representative of LMEC representing the defendant's approximately 50% split on the invoice billed to the County but for which no rebuilt cylinder was provided by LMEC, on the order referenced (above).

That on or about January 12, 1987, the defendant, for the purpose of executing the above-described scheme, and attempting to do so, did knowingly cause to be placed in an authorized mail depository for delivery by the Postal Service, an envelope containing a County warrant/check in the amount of $415.72 from the Board of Supervisors of Covington County to LMEC, representing payment on invoice 123 referenced (above) in violation of Section 1341 and Section 2, Title 18, United States Code.

Wade pleaded guilty on February 11, 1988, in U.S. district court in Jackson to the single count of mail fraud that involved his accepting $200 worth of liquor in exchange for approving and sending payment for equipment that was never delivered to Covington County. Judge Barbour accepted his plea and set sentencing for March 22, 1988.

In a Judgment in a Criminal Case actually rendered by Judge Barbour on April 5, 1988, Wiley Tom Wade was sentenced to five years' imprisonment, with all except three months suspended. Five years' probation, which was to begin after release from incarceration, was also imposed. In addition, Wade was fined $5,000 and ordered to pay restitution to Covington County in the amount of $2,115.72. The sentence contained a provision that prohibited Wade from seeking or holding public office during the term of probation. No doubt, this relatively light sentence was the result of Wade's cooperation with the government. His pleading guilty to an information allowed the prosecutors to avoid both an indictment and a trial. Wade's cooperation with the ongoing investigation must have been especially helpful. The former supervisor was to report to prison on April 25, 1988, and the judge recommended that he be assigned to the Federal Correctional Institution at Eglin Air Force Base, Florida. Wade had not sought reelection in 1987.

Although he had admitted to the FBI accepting a $1,700 kickback from Buffington Ford Tractor Company of Collins on the county's purchase of a tractor and mower, Wade was not charged with that offense. Nevertheless, despite attorney Samuel Wilkins's objection, but in accordance with the plea bargain, the restitution that Wade was ordered to pay the county included the $1,700. The $2,115.72 in restitution was calculated by adding the $1,700 kickback to the $415.72 paid by the county on the transaction with L&M Equipment Company that involved the liquor payoff.

During the sentencing hearing, Wade said, "I want to apologize to Covington County for my wrongdoings and for violating my oath." About eighty residents of Collins, Hot Coffee and other communities in Covington County showed up at the hearing in Jackson to show their support for Wade. The *Jackson Daily News* quoted three of Wade's supporters as making the following comments after the hearing. "He's one of the finest supervisors we ever had in Covington County." The guilty plea "doesn't shake my faith in him in any way. A lot of people crucify a person for a minor offense, and a lot of them go free and are never caught." "He'll go down in the annals of history as one of the greatest supervisors Beat 5 ever had." Wade's friends "just got together ourselves and said we was coming to give our support. We never had a supervisor that did as much with as little." After the hearing, Wade said, "They are friends from Covington County. The people of Covington County have been good to me. I've done wrong and I admit it."

One wonders whether Wade would have had so many supporters had they known the whole story of how this first-term supervisor had systematically gone about using his position to steal from the taxpayers of Covington County. If they had seen or heard the evidence that the FBI had secured about his dealings with both L&M Equipment Company and Buffington Ford Tractor Company, it is doubtful. As shown above, that evidence allowed the government to charge in the information that "on several occasions between December 1985 and January 1987, defendant discussed with a representative of LMEC and with others, *numerous* fraudulent activities including, the defendant's agreement to accepting a 40% to 50% kickback on materials purchased from LMEC, to 'splitting' or 'shorting' materials purchased from LMEC, and to accepting kickbacks in the form of liquor from LMEC on "busted" invoices to the County."

If the contents of Wade's actual conversations with the vendors had been available to the citizens of Covington County, it's doubtful that eighty supporters would have showed up at his sentencing. More than likely, such revelations would have resulted in something similar to what happened in the Pontotoc County case involving Theron Baldwin chronicled in chapter 13. In that case, when the extent of the supervisor's chicanery became public, there was a public outcry that he be given the maximum sentence, and one person who had written the judge a letter of support for Baldwin actually withdrew the letter.

This case shows how effective the FBI could be in using vendors who had been involved in paying bribes to secure evidence against supervisors. Wade pleaded guilty to an information that did not mention an undercover FBI agent or an FBI front company. The government must have convinced the two vendors mentioned in the information to testify against Wade, and the vendors must have made tape recordings while conducting business with Wade.

Greene County—The Poor Get Poorer

Greene County was named for a hero of the American Revolution, Nathanael Greene, who served as General Washington's second-in-command and led the American forces in the South in the late stages of the war. Located in the southeastern part of the state and bordering Alabama, the county was carved out of Wayne County by a legislative act of 1811 when Mississippi was still a territory. The county is part of the Piney Woods area that was acquired by the United States through a series of treaties with the Choctaw Indian Nation. The county had a 1990 population of only 10,220. In January 1987, the month before Operation Pretense became public, Green County had an unemployment rate of 22 percent and was one of the state's poorest counties. The financial condition of Greene County was so poor in the mid-1980s that Department of Audit personnel thought the county might have to declare bankruptcy, for which there was no precedent.

Leakesville, with a population of fewer than 1,500, is the county seat and the largest town in Greene County. McLain and State Line are the only other towns in the county, and even State Line's northern part is in Wayne County. Aubrey Lucas, the distinguished president emeritus of the University of Southern Mississippi, hails from State Line. In discussing complicated money matters involving the university, President Lucas was fond of alluding to his State Line "arithmetic." Using State Line arithmetic or otherwise, three-fifths of the Green County's Board Supervisors pleaded guilty to felonies in as a result Operation Pretense.

John M. "Buddy" Crocker Jr., the fifty-three-year-old supervisor of district four, was one of the first supervisors charged under Pretense. He was arrested on February 12, 1987, based on a federal indictment that charged him with one count of bribery, one count of extortion, and seven counts of mail fraud. Crocker appeared before U.S. Magistrate John R. Countiss III in Jackson and pleaded not guilty the day of his arrest. He was released on a $5,000 personal recognizance bond. Maximum penalties for all nine counts in the indictment were sixty-five years in prison and fines of $2.25 million. The charges against Crocker included conspiring with Mid-State Pipe Company and another vendor to defraud the county with fraudulent purchases involving kickbacks (ten from Mid-State totaling $2,600 and one from another unnamed vendor for $50) and busted invoices, using the mails to accomplish the schemes, assisting Mid-State in making fraudulent arrangements with other supervisors in Greene and other counties, bid rigging, and obstructing interstate commerce by entering into and carrying out the schemes described in the indictment. Trial was set for May 11.

One of the charges illustrates just how brazen supervisors could be: "On December 3, 1984, the defendant instructed Mid-State to charge the County for materials not delivered, and received on that date a kickback of $1,053 in cash from Mid-State, and on December 14, 1984, the defendant received an additional kickback of $100 from Mid-State." This transaction involved a partial bust; that is, Crocker received the $1,053 as his share (half) of the invoice price of materials not delivered on a partially busted invoice and then demanded his normal $100 kickback on the purchase of those materials that were delivered. According to former FBI special agent Jerry King, such demands and payments were common.

In a March 25, 1987, Memorandum of Understanding signed on April 1, 1987, by the supervisor; his attorney, Thomas E. Royals; and Assistant U.S. Attorney Harris, Crocker agreed to plead guilty to counts two (mail fraud) and nine (extortion) of the indictment and to cooperate with the ongoing investigation. In return, the U.S. attorney was to inform the court of the extent of Crocker's cooperation and request that such cooperation be considered in determining Crocker's sentence. Further, the government was to make no recommendation as to sentence on count two and was to recommend suspension of sentence and five years' probation on count nine. The government was to recommend that Crocker be prohibited from seeking or holding public office during any imposed probation. Finally, the government was to recommend restitution as appropriate and dismissal of the remaining seven counts of the indictment.

Judge Barbour accepted the guilty plea under the terms of the plea bargain on April 1, 1987. Sentencing was deferred so that Crocker could cooperate with the investigation. Crocker resigned as supervisor effective August 1, 1987. Judge Barbour sentenced Crocker on November 23, 1987, to three years in prison on count two and five years' probation on count nine, fined him $5,000, and required him to pay restitution of $2,178 to Greene County and $522 to the FBI. He was also prohibited from seeking or holding public office during the time of probation. At sentencing, Crocker asked for leniency saying, "I ask for forgiveness. I'm asking for mercy from the court." Assistant U.S. Attorney Harris told the court that Crocker had not cooperated with the government and that he had refused to testify in the trial of former Wayne County supervisors Alfred Revette and Jimmie Duvall. Crocker reported to the Federal Prison Camp at Eglin Air Force Base, Florida, on January 4, 1988.

Lauvon Pierce, Greene County district five supervisor and Leakesville resident, waived indictment and pleaded innocent to federal mail fraud charges on March 10, 1987. He was charged in an information with authorizing $2,511 in fraudulent county purchases during the period February through November 1985, accepting kickbacks, and using the U.S. mails to accomplish the schemes. The charges involved $730 in kickbacks paid to the supervisor by Mid-State Pipe Company. Maximum potential penalties were five years in prison and fines of $250,000. Pierce pleaded innocent before U.S. Magistrate Countiss in Jackson and was released on a $1,000 recognizance bond. At the time of this pleading, Pierce told Judge Countiss that he planned to change his plea to guilty at a later date, though no date was set for the change. Pierce, who also waived his right to legal representation, was already cooperating with the Pretense investigation. Pierce was the eleventh supervisor charged as a result of Operation Pretense.

Pierce resigned as supervisor on April 1, and Murdoc Walley, a district five grader operator, was appointed by the board of supervisors to serve Pierce's remaining term. Pierce was quoted as saying, "I wasn't going to run anymore. I resigned for more or less personal reasons." He also indicated that Walley had been appointed to the post "probably because he's familiar with the roads and all that." Walley told the board of supervisors that he would not be a candidate for the office in the upcoming election.

Pierce and Assistant U.S. Attorney Harris signed a Memorandum of Understanding on April 9, 1987. Paragraph one of the plea agreement outlined the expectations that Pierce would cooperate with the government "concerning all information and knowledge that he has regarding the subject matter of an ongoing investigation presently being conducted by agents of the United States regarding the receipt of monies by public officials from vendors and the submission of false and inflated invoices to local county or state government for payment."

The U.S. attorney pledged that upon Pierce's guilty plea the government would recommend that the court accept his plea and that, at the time of sentencing, the government would inform the court of the effects of Pierce's cooperation and request that such cooperation be considered in determining his sentence. If Pierce's cooperation was deemed satisfactory, the government was to recommend a maximum sentence of three years, make no recommendation concerning possible fines, and recommend that Pierce be allowed to pay any restitution ordered in installments. On May 17, 1987, Pierce, now a forty-eight-year-old unemployed construction worker, pleaded guilty to mail fraud before Judge Lee in Jackson. Sentencing was delayed to allow the former supervisor to continue cooperating with the investigation.

Undercover FBI agents Jerry King and Cliff Chatham first met both Pierce and Crocker when the two supervisors came to Carthage to collect kickbacks that John Burgess owed them. King noted that the supervisors seemed unconcerned that Burgess was lying in bed heavily medicated with one eye patched up completely as the result of a recent accident—they walked right in and asked for their money. Both Assistant U.S. Attorney James Tucker and Jerry King indicated that Pierce was quite a character and that he proved very helpful in the investigation. Pierce was the first supervisor "flipped" into working undercover for the FBI; that is, when confronted with the evidence against him, Pierce readily agreed to cooperate. King said that the affable Pierce was a typical "good ole boy" and that he grew to genuinely like the supervisor as they did their "dirty deeds" together. King indicated that Pierce had a penchant for relating funny stories in his Mississippi drawl.

Pierce's cooperation with the government in the ongoing investigation was instrumental in the indictment of Billy Ray Harrison of Morton, a salesman for Mississippi Pipe and Oil Company of Pearl. The fifty-two-year-old Harrison was indicted in May 1987 on one count of bribery and two counts of mail fraud for paying approximately $2,418 in cash to Pierce and fellow supervisor John Crocker to influence them in connection with purchases of materials and supplies for Greene County. However, the specific counts listed only Pierce in connection with the alleged transactions that involved busting invoices. As noted above, after first agreeing to cooperate in the investigation, Crocker apparently balked. Pierce's cooperation was also instrumental in the government's convincing Jessie Smith, owner of Consolidated Culvert and Supply Company of Petal, to plead guilty to three counts of mail fraud. Because the FBI had taped evidence about busted invoices that Pierce had secured, Smith pleaded guilty to federal charges in August 1987. Jarvis Dearman, a Leakesville businessman, was indicted in November 1987 also as the result of Pierce's cooperation. Dearman was charged with agreeing to pay Pierce cash on three separate occasions in connection with purchases of fuel and supplies by Greene County.

On September 1, 1988, nearly eighteen months after Pierce was charged, Judge Lee suspended sentence and placed him on probation for five years. Pierce was ordered to pay $730 in restitution to Greene County immediately and a $5,000 fine on a schedule to be determined by the Probation Office. Pierce was also prohibited from seeking or holding public office during the term of probation. This light sentence reflected the "flipped" supervisor's valuable participation in the undercover investigation. Pierce's court records contain a Satisfaction of Judgment dated August 6, 1991, indicating that the fine had been paid or otherwise settled by compromise.

On April 7, 1987, a federal grand jury handed down an eight-count indictment against fifty-five-year-old district three supervisor George Ivan Smith. That same day the U.S. district court in Jackson issued a warrant for his arrest. Smith was promptly arrested, and he made an initial appearance before a federal judge on April 9. Arraignment was set for April 15, at which time he pleaded innocent to all charges. Smith had announced in March that he would seek reelection. The charges against Smith, which included mail fraud, aiding and abetting, and extortion, involved his dealings with Mid-State Pipe Company and Davis Chemicals during the period June 1984 through June 1986. He was charged with accepting a total of $666 in the form of six kickbacks on county purchases.

Smith and his attorney, Thomas Royals, entered into a July 20, 1987, Memorandum of Understanding with U.S. Attorney George Phillips and Assistant U.S. Attorney Peter H. Barrett. The agreement called for Smith to plead guilty to counts one (mail fraud) and seven (extortion) of the eight-count indictment and to cooperate with the ongoing investigation. Maximum penalties that could be imposed on the two counts were twenty-five years' imprisonment and $500,000 in fines. In exchange for the guilty pleas, the government agreed to make no recommendation concerning sentencing on count one and to recommend five years' probation and suspension of sentence on count seven. The government was to recommend that if probation were imposed, it begin after release from any prison time imposed. The government was also to recommend that as a special condition of probation Smith be prohibited from seeking or holding public office. Finally, the government was to make no recommendation concerning imposition of fines, but it reserved the right to make recommendations concerning restitution. Smith pleaded guilty, as agreed to in the plea agreement, before Judge Barbour on July 20. His plea was accepted, and sentencing was deferred so that he could cooperate in the ongoing investigation. Smith resigned as supervisor of district three effective August 1, 1987.

Judge Barbour passed sentence on Smith on November 23, 1987, at the U.S. district court in Jackson. Smith was sentenced to two years in prison on the mail fraud charge. On the extortion charge, he was given five years' probation to begin after his release from confinement. Smith was also fined $5,000, prohibited from seeking or holding public office while on probation, and ordered to make restitution in the amount of $666 to Greene County. The former supervisor reported to the Federal Prison Camp at Eglin Air Force Base, Florida, on January 4, 1988. Smith paid the $5,000 fine on March 22, 1988, by a cashier's check drawn on Richton Bank and Trust Company.

John Crocker was also sentenced on November 23, 1987, by Judge Barbour. At the sentencing hearing, the two former Greene county supervisors were represented by attorney Thomas Royals. Comments made by Royals at the sentencing hearing greatly irritated Judge Barbour. The attorney criticized the federal probe into corrupt county spending. He maintained that while the government's acts might not legally be entrapment, "It was a kind of entrapment that went on out there. The opportunity would not have been there. They [agents] were handing out money everywhere. The more money the better it looked to their superiors." He also claimed that the FBI had exaggerated the amount of corruption around the state. He said, "I think the agents have blown up what went on with the supervisors. Kickbacks made to supervisors from undercover agents far exceeded those offered by salesmen. While salesmen may buy supervisors Christmas turkeys, they don't go into these kind of amounts." Judge Barbour responded, "I've heard enough of this. These poor ol' supervisors have been stealing from the counties. You're not making a speech for the jury. It offends me. It's obvious to the court that there is widespread practice [of corruption]." Telling Royals that he was absolutely wrong, the judge continued, "It's clear . . . that the practice is widespread. The FBI has every reason to believe that there is widespread corruption."

After the trial, Royals said that Crocker had recently declared bankruptcy and that he did not have enough money to pay the fine. However, Crocker paid the $5,000 fine on May 31, 1988, with a cashier's check drawn on the First National Bank of Lucedale.

19. Crime on the Coast

Hancock, Harrison, and Jackson Counties

Hancock County—Tires as a Payoff

In 1812, while it was still a territory, Mississippi named a Gulf Coast county after John Hancock, who had made a big impression with his bold signature on the Declaration of Independence in 1776. The Pearl River separates Hancock County from Louisiana's St. Tammany Parish on the west, and Harrison County borders it on the east. According to the 1990 census, the county had a population of 31,760. The beautiful little city of Bay St. Louis is the county seat. Director emeritus of the Eisenhower Center and retired professor of history at the University of New Orleans, Stephen E. Ambrose, the famous author of many books, including *Eisenhower: Soldier and President, D-Day, Undaunted Courage,* and *Citizen Soldier,* makes his home in Bay St. Louis. Brett Favre, Green Bay Packer quarterback and three-time National Football League Most Valuable Player, who played his college football at the University of Southern Mississippi, hails from the small town of Kiln in Hancock County.

Hancock county government was corrupt to the core in the 1980s. Operation Pretense brought down four of the county's five supervisors. In early March 1987, soon after Fred Robinson Jr. of Jackson County became the first Gulf Coast supervisor arrested as a result of Operation Pretense, things became very uncomfortable for Hancock County supervisors. County controller Ken Walker said that about two weeks previously an assistant state auditor came and asked for all invoices from four companies, Holiman Equipment Company, Davis Chemicals, and two others that the county had not used and he couldn't name. District two supervisor A. A. "Dolph" Keller, Sam J. Perniciaro Jr. of district four, and James Travirca of district five said they had dealt with the companies but had never been offered a kickback.

Hancock County district four supervisor Sam J. Perniciaro Sr. was indicted by a federal grand jury in Jackson on nine pretense-related charges in early July 1987. He was arrested at his Bay St. Louis home on July 9, 1987. Perniciaro became the second Gulf Coast supervisor to be charged as a result of Operation Pretense. Maximum penalties for all nine counts of the indictment were 65 years in prison and $2.25 million in fines.

The charges against Perniciaro involved his conduct of county business during the period 1984 through early 1987. He was charged with devising a scheme to defraud the citizens of Mississippi and Hancock County, the board of supervisors, chancery clerk, state auditor, and all persons desiring to engage in legitimate business dealings with the county. The scheme was alleged to have been accomplished by means of false and fraudulent pretense, representations and promises and by use of the U.S. mails. The scheme to defraud involved a proposal to Holiman Equipment to use the mails to bust an invoice on cylinders; proposals to Holiman Equipment and Davis Chemicals to charge the county for equipment, materials, and supplies delivered to the county and receive as a kickback a percentage of the county check to be issued and mailed in payment; and a proposal to Mid-State Pipe Company that he was willing to enter into similar false and fraudulent arrangements.

The indictment further stated that Perniciaro approved a false and fraudulent invoice for $382.25 and received a $50 cash kickback and that he entered into an agreement with a representative of Holiman Equipment whereby he would receive tires for his personal automobile, and the county would be invoiced for parts, which were never to be delivered, in payment for the tires. It further charged that Perniciaro approved a false and fraudulent invoice to the county for $276.12 and received the tires for his personal use.

Additional charges included: (a) approving false invoices from Davis for $495 and $412.50 and accepting $100 as a cash kickback, (b) approving a $37,500 bid from Holiman Equipment for a pothole patcher and a holding tank in anticipation of a $500 kickback and accepting $500 cash, (c) receiving $50 in cash from Davis in anticipation of a false invoice of $382.25 for a fifty-five-gallon drum of Perma-Bond, (d) indicating to a representative of Holiman Equipment that he could devise a scheme and subterfuge in the future to thwart the unit purchasing system, (e) using the U.S. mails to accomplished the scheme outlined in the indictment, and (f) obstructing interstate commerce by extortion.

The third-term supervisor was arraigned before U.S. Magistrate John R. Roper on July 9, 1987; he pleaded innocent to all of the charges. After entering his plea, Perniciaro said, "I've always tried to do a damn good job for the county." He was released on a $126,000 unsecured bond, and trial was set for August 31, 1987. Perniciaro claimed that he never bought anything from Mid-State and that his dealings with Davis Chemicals and Holiman Equipment were honorable and legal. Concerning his dealings with Davis Chemicals, Perniciaro said, "I liked Ray Davis, I did a lot of business with him. He was a small businessman, so I always made a point of buying from him."

The sixty-two-year-old Perniciaro, owner of Sam's Auto and Wrecker Service in Bay St. Louis, was running for a fourth term as district four supervisor and indicated that he would not withdraw from the race. He was opposed in the upcoming August Democratic primary by Kelvin J. Schulz. Perniciaro said the indictment "won't help the election. It'll be rough. I hope [voters] will be broad-minded. Nothing's been proven."

Other Hancock supervisors were shocked, simply shocked, at their fellow public servant's indictment. Roger Dale Ladner, district three supervisor, was quoted as saying, "I hope that the people of the county will allow Sammy the opportunity to have his day in court." Burt Courrege, district one supervisor, agreed saying, "This is an indictment, not a conviction, so I'm not making any judgments" District two supervisor A. A. "Dolph" Keller said, "This is a sad day for all Hancock County. I don't know if this will change the board's operations. I don't think it could since we are under the unit system."

Perniciaro's was the first Pretense-related indictment to mention other co-conspirators. The indictment indicated that Perniciaro told FBI special agent Jerry King, who was working undercover, a salesman for Mid-State, that "other supervisors in Hancock County were willing to enter into" bribery and kickback schemes. The other supervisors denied any wrongdoing or knowledge of illegal acts. According to the charges, Perniciaro and others accepted kickbacks totaling $2,000 from Holiman Equipment on the purchase of a pothole patcher for which the county paid $37,750. Perniciaro supposedly received $1,000, with the remaining $1,000 going to the other co-conspirators. District five supervisor James Travirca said, "I doubt very seriously that Sammy got any money from Holiman, but I know I didn't get a penny." Both Bert Courrege and Roger Dale Ladner denied receiving any money from Holiman Equipment in connection with the purchase.

Perniciaro's indictment also accused him of scheming to thwart the unit system of purchasing. It charged that he told a representative of Holiman

Equipment in January 1987 that he could devise a scheme to thwart the unit system of purchasing. In a May 1986 referendum, the county had approved going to the unit system. Perniciaro had opposed the change, but after the election he had assured his constituents that he would do all he could to make it work. U.S. Attorney Don Burkhalter said that Perniciaro had been unable to thwart the unit system.

Perniciaro continued his race for reelection and won the August 4 Democratic primary; he faced no opposition in the November general election. A federal prosecutor was quick to address that victory and six other primary victories by indicted supervisors. Assistant U.S. Attorney James Tucker said, "We are taking the position that if they are convicted, we are going to seek to have them out of office. We will do so vigorously, probably even more vigorously because we will assume that they have sought office again knowing that they were guilty of violating the public trust."

Perniciaro's trial, scheduled to begin August 31 in Jackson, was postponed until October 5. The recent jury convictions of four other supervisors resulting from Operation Pretense apparently weighed heavily on the thinking of Perniciaro and his attorneys as the trial approached. Former Perry County supervisor Trudie Westmoreland had been convicted in June, Wayne County supervisors Alfred Revete and Jimmie Duvall had been convicted in July, and Lamar County supervisor Kermit Rayborn had been convicted in late August.

In early October, Albert Necaise, one of Perniciaro's attorneys, asked that the trial be delayed again because of a conflict in his schedule. This request was granted by U.S. Attorney Burkhalter, and the trial was rescheduled for November 16. Mid-November found Perniciaro's attorneys working out a plea bargain with Assistant U.S. Attorney Peter H. Barrett. Attorney Joe Sam Owen said that the defendant's age, the publicity surrounding the case, the unpredictability of a jury, and the convictions in the four Pretense-related cases that had been tried all influenced the decision to plea bargain. The by now rather standard Pretense-related plea bargain was documented in a Memorandum of Understanding between the federal government and Sam Perniciaro Sr. dated November 16, 1987.

Prior to the plea bargain, several motions had been made to the court in this case. Among those was a motion to delete and edit certain taped conversations that contained comments by the defendant that were prejudicial and highly inflammatory. These taped conversations contained racial slurs and offensive language. The motion claimed these could be removed without destroying the essential evidence. Another motion requested that the claim made by Perniciaro to a representative of Holiman that he could devise a scheme to thwart the unit system be deleted because it had no relevance to the actual charge in the count in which it appeared. WLOX Television filed a motion that asked access to the audiotape of the defendant's conversation with FBI agent Jerry King and a copy of any transcript of the conversation if the tape was introduced into evidence in the trial. No doubt, Perniciaro did not want to see the particulars of this conversation reported in the media.

In accordance with the plea bargain, Perniciaro pleaded guilty to the two counts on November 16, and seven charges were dropped. Specifically, he pleaded guilty to accepting from Ray Davis $100 in cash in July 1986 for signing sales orders showing receipt of drums of weed killer valued at $412.50 and $495 and using the U.S. mails to further the deal. Davis had tape-recorded this transaction. He also pleaded guilty to accepting a $500 cash kickback from Holiman in November 1984 and tires worth $276 in exchange for approving a purchase. A government prosecutor said that on a separate recording the supervisor had complained about the quality of the tires. Sentencing was delayed by U.S. District Court Judge Tom S. Lee until Perniciaro completed cooperating in the investigation as the plea agreement required.

Perniciaro had agreed to "answer truthfully all questions asked him concerning Hancock County government" and to resign from office by January 4, 1988. Of the five board members, only he and Roger Dale Ladner had been reelected in 1987. Keller had resigned the day after his defeat at the polls, and the board of supervisors had appointed his opponent, Ronald Cuevas, to complete the balance of Keller's term. Perniciaro was allowed to continue until January, when the new supervisors were to take office. Attorney Joe Sam Owen said, "Generally a person who pleads guilty is asked by the court to resign immediately. We asked that he be allowed to serve out the term through December, and the court agreed that it would not be fair to the new board to have a member appointed by the outgoing board."

No doubt, Perniciaro's agreement to "answer truthfully all questions asked him concerning Hancock County government" sent a chill through all supervisors who had served on the board of supervisors with him. His indictment charged that Holiman paid a total of $2,000 in kickbacks to him and other "unidentified co-conspirators" for approving the purchase of a pothole patcher for which Hancock County paid $37,750. The board's minute book showed that all five supervisors had voted to approve the purchase in September 1984. A. A. "Dolph" Keller, Bert Courrege, James N. Travirca, and Roger Dale Ladner had all denied getting kickbacks from Holiman.

Judge Lee sentenced Perniciaro in his Jackson courtroom on January 18, 1989. On count four (mail fraud), Perniciaro was sentenced to three years in prison, with all but two months suspended, fined $5,000, and ordered to pay $946.12 in restitution to Hancock County. He was placed on probation for five years and prohibited from seeking or holding public office while on probation. On count eight (extortion), he was sentenced to five years' probation that was to run concurrently with the probation imposed on the other charge. Perniciaro was to report to prison on February 14, 1989, and Judge Lee recommended that he be incarcerated at Eglin Air Force Base, Florida.

The particulars of the Perniciaro case have been reported in much detail here and in chapters 7 and 11. They vividly show that extensive cooperation with the federal investigators resulted in very light penalties (two months in prison, a $5,000 fine, and five years' probation) being imposed on a man who was originally charged with nine counts that carried maximum penalties of 65 years in prison and $2.5 million in fines. The government had much evidence that put Perniciaro in a very bad light. Jurors would probably not have been very sympathetic after hearing tape recordings that included vulgarities, racial slurs, schemes to circumvent the unit system, and complaints about the quality of automobile tires that the defendant had taken as a bribe.

Perniciaro's light penalties and the fact that he was not sentenced until a year and a half after his arrest reflect his extensive cooperation in the Pretense investigation. The government obviously considered Perniciaro's cooperation quite valuable. Some of that value is reflected in chapters 7 and 11, which deal with the convictions of Marion County Supervisor Sim Ed Moree, Southern District Highway Commissioner Bob Joiner, and two men, Larkey Wilborn Broome and Donald Frank Gowan, who attempted to extort money from Joiner and Perniciaro by claiming that they could "fix" the charges against them. The extent and value of Perciniaro's cooperation are also, no doubt, reflected in the guilty pleas of three of his fellow Hancock County supervisors.

A second hammer blow fell on the Hancock County Board of Supervisors when Roger Dale Ladner was arrested and arraigned on December 4, 1987. Ladner had been indicted by a federal grand jury in Jackson on December 3. The forty-year-old district three supervisor and Bay St. Louis resident pleaded innocent before U.S. Magistrate Roper to seven counts involving extortion, bribery, conspiracy, and mail fraud. A March 7, 1988, trial was set before Judge Lee. Ladner was immediately released on a $25,000 personal recognizance bond. Albert Necaise of Gulfport served as his attorney. Ladner, who faced no opposition in the general election, had won a third term as district three supervisor by a single vote in the August Democratic primary. Ladner was the fortieth Mississippi county supervisor indicted as a result of Pretense.

Ladner was charged with proposing to Holiman Equipment and Davis Chemicals to receive kickbacks in return for buying a pothole patcher, a holding tank, and wasp and hornet spray. According to the charges, prior to September 1984, Ladner agreed with a Holiman representative to vote in favor of Holiman's bid on the pothole patcher in exchange for a kickback. On November 7, 1984, he and other unnamed co-conspirators accepted a total of $2,000 in kickbacks, and Ladner, who had voted a month earlier to accept Holiman's bid, received $500. Between August 1984 and September 1986, he received $1,597 in kickbacks according to the charges. The charges alleged that he extorted $1,500 from Holiman Equipment from November 1984 to January 1985 and a $97 kickback from Davis Chemicals in August 1986.

Shortly before the scheduled March trial, Ladner claimed that he could not afford counsel and secured a court appointed attorney. He also asked for a continuance so that the appointed lawyer could prepare for trial. In a March 4 order, Judge Lee granted the continuance and set a June 13, 1988, trial date. In a Memorandum of Understanding dated May 25, signed by Ladner and his attorney, Lucien Gex, and Assistant U.S. Attorney Barrett, the defendant agreed to plead guilty to one count of mail fraud and one count of extortion and to cooperate in the ongoing investigation.

In late July 1988, Ladner resigned as supervisor. After accepting Ladner's resignation, the remaining four county supervisors, at their own expense, hosted a luncheon honoring their fallen comrade. About thirty public officials attended. They applauded when a resolution was read that expressed gratitude to Ladner for his work on the board of supervisors. Sheriff Ronnie Peterson said, "We're not honoring him for the things he did wrong. We are honoring him for the things he did right."

On January 9, 1989, Judge Lee sentenced Ladner to one year and one day in prison on the mail fraud charge and ordered him to serve five years' probation and pay a $2,000 fine on the extortion charge. The probation was to commence after completion of the prison sentence. Ladner was also ordered to pay Hancock County $1,598.25 in restitution with the unusual provision that, if Sam Perniciaro and/or Burt Courrege were ordered to pay restitution to the county, the Probation Office should proportionately reduce Ladner's restitution amount accordingly. Ladner was ordered to report to Eglin Air Force Base, Florida, on February 21, 1989, to begin serving his sentence.

James N. "Jimmy" Travirca, former district five supervisor, was indicted on February 10, 1988, on five counts of conspiracy, mail fraud, bribery, and extortion by a federal grand jury in Jackson. All of the charges involved his dealings with Holiman Equipment on the purchase a pothole patcher and holding tanks and using the U.S. mails to accomplish the scheme. He was alleged to have accepted $1,200 in kickbacks from 1984 to 1986. Travirca was released on a $10,000 personal recognizance bond after his February 12 arrest. The sixty-one-year-old Kiln resident had served as supervisor for sixteen years. He had been defeated in his 1987 bid for reelection. Travirca claimed he was unable to finance his defense, and the court appointed Herman Cox of Gulfport to represent him. Travirca pleaded innocent, and trial was set for May 9.

Under a May 20, 1988, plea agreement, Travirca pleaded guilty to two counts of mail fraud in connection with receiving a total of $1,200 in kickbacks from Holiman Equipment. The other three charges were dropped at the request of the U.S. Attorney. He faced a maximum of ten years in prison and $500,000 in fines on the charges to which he pleaded guilty. Assuming Travirca's cooperation in the ongoing investigation, the government agreed that at the time of sentencing it would inform the court of the extent and effect of that cooperation. The agreement also called for the government to make no sentencing recommendation on one count but suggest to the court that if it believed that incarceration was warranted, the prison time not exceed three years. The prosecution was to recommend a suspended sentence and five years' probation on the other count, with the probation to begin after completion of any prison time imposed. Sentencing was delayed indefinitely to allow Travirca to cooperate in the investigation.

A document introduced by Assistant U.S. Attorney Barrett at Travirca's pleading revealed much about the whole pothole patcher caper and Travirca's dealings with Holiman. The document indicated that Hancock County supervisors Travirca, Keller, Ladner, and Perniciaro were present at a meeting in June or July 1984 where Holiman Equipment Company vice resident Max Gilbert demonstrated the operation of the pothole patching machine. According to the document, Gilbert and the supervisors were discussing the machine when Ladner mentioned that he and the other three supervisors would possibly vote to buy it depending on the size of the kickback each supervisor would receive. About two weeks later, Gilbert told Ladner that he would pay $500 to each of the four supervisors if the board of supervisors approved the purchase. The board actually approved the purchase in September 1984. Gilbert paid Ladner $1,500 in January 1985 for distribution to the other supervisors. While attending a Mississippi Association of Supervisors meeting in Jackson in mid-January, Travirca asked Gilbert for his $500. The document also indicated that Travirca received $600 in July 1986 related to the county's purchase of a boom ax from Holiman. It stated that Travirca got the kickback after he asked Gilbert, "Where's my money? You're trying to short me."

At the pleading, Travirca told U.S. District Court Judge William Barbour Jr. he didn't think that he attended the pothole patcher demonstration, and that he was not included in the negotiations for the kickback. The judge asked, "You took the kickback?" "Yes sir," Travirca said. "[But] I didn't go ask no Max Gilbert for no $500." Gilbert, who was awaiting sentencing on Pretense-related charges, was cooperating with the government.

Travirca's sentencing came nearly a year after his guilty plea. On March 31, 1989, Judge Barbour sentenced him to five years in prison with all but six months suspended and five years' probation after incarceration on count one of the indictment and five years' probation on count two to run concurrently with the probation on count one. He was also ordered to pay a fine of $1,000 and to make restitution to Hancock County in the amount of $1,100. He was prohibited from seeking or holding public office during the time of probation. The relatively light penalties and the time between the pleading and sentencing, no doubt, reflect Travirca's extensive cooperation in the investigation.

The U.S. attorney's office filed an information in Hattiesburg against Bert Courrege, former district one supervisor, August 8, 1988. He was the fourth and last Hancock County supervisor charged as a result of Operation Pretense. The forty-six-year-old Lakeshore resident was charged with one count of mail fraud in connection with accepting a $40 kickback on the county's purchase of weed killer from Davis Chemicals. Courrege, who had served three terms as supervisor but had been defeated in his 1987 bid for reelection, faced a possible five-year prison sentence and a $250,000 fine.

Courrege was arraigned before U.S. Magistrate Roper in Biloxi on August 30. He pleaded innocent and was released on a $1,000 personal recognizance bond. No trial date was set. The fact that an information had been filed in this case in lieu of a grand jury indictment and that no trial date was set at the arraignment signaled that Courrege was cooperating with the government in the ongoing investigation. Nothing else was heard of this case until Courrege pleaded guilty before Judge Barbour in Jackson on March 10, 1989.

On April 12, 1989, Judge Barbour sentenced Courrege to one year in jail but suspended the jail time and placed him on five years' probation. Courrege was also fined $1,000 and ordered to pay Hancock County $60 in restitution. The restitution included the $40 kickback that he had pleaded guilty to accepting and an additional $20 that he had accepted from a salesman for Davis Chemicals. Courrege was only the second supervisor convicted under Pretense whose sentence did not include incarceration.

At sentencing, Courrege told the judge, "I'm very sorry, I have caused my family suffering and a good deal of grief because of the publicity." Carey Varnado, Courrege's attorney, indicated that his client might lose his job on an offshore oil rig if he served jail time and asked for leniency. The attorney also claimed that Courrege shopped for the best price for weed killer and did not buy it from Davis Chemicals expecting a kickback.

Commenting on the sentence, Judge Barbour said, "On too many occasions before, I have been faced with supervisors in the same position you are in. There is no way to justify the taking of any illegal payments in the form of kickbacks. But the court in this case is faced with the smallest amount of (money) that the court has been confronted with. The two offenses are relatively minor in amount." The judge indicated that he was impressed with the letters he had received from the former supervisor's friends, his community involvement, and his corporation with the Pretense investigation. After hearing the sentence passed, Courrege, who was accompanied by tearful family members, refused to comment other than to say that he "appreciated the judge's consideration."

Harrison County—Mississippi Mud

Located between the other two Gulf Coast counties, Hancock and Jackson, Harrison County had a 1990 population of 165,365, which trailed only Hinds County in the 1990 census. Two of Mississippi's largest cities, Gulfport and Biloxi, adjoin each other along the county's beaches. Gulfport is the county seat, and the county is home to several large industrial plants, the Port of Gulfport, and Keesler Air Force Base. Beginning with the legalization of dockside gambling in the early 1990s, the county has experienced explosive growth. Several casinos and luxury hotels now dot its beaches, which until the 1990s were the province of lackluster motels and family vacationers.

Biloxi is a city known nationally because so many airmen have trained at Keesler Air Force Base. Some of the airmen's experiences provided the inspiration for Neil Simon's play *Biloxi Blues*, which was later made into a movie with the same name. Unfortunately, the city has also long been known for its corruption. The author vividly remembers seeing open casino gambling in Biloxi in the mid-1960s, long before it was legal. Biloxi gained additional notoriety in the 1980s and 1990s because of a famous murder case. On September 14, 1987, Circuit Court Judge Vincent Sherry and his politically active wife, Margaret, were murdered in their Biloxi home. Several sensational trials followed involving alleged members of the Dixie Mafia and Sherry's law firm partner. The case ultimately resulted in convictions of a hired hit man, a notorious Louisiana prison inmate who was running a scam of homosexuals, and Sherry's law partner and former Biloxi mayor, Pete Halat.

Pulitzer Prize–winner Edward Hume chronicled the Sherry murder case in a chilling book entitled *Mississippi Mud*. Humes explained the title as follows: "Mississippi Mud is the purest form of poker, a game in which the cards become irrelevant and the ability to bluff and betray fellow players reaps the greatest reward. The name is synonymous with a certain brand of corruption in the Magnolia State, undisguised and unashamed. By either definition, lying is an art form in Mississippi Mud, morality a fool's distraction." This description rings all too true about the state of Harrison County government as revealed by Operation Pretense.

Eddie Moffat was first elected Harrison County district two supervisor in November 1985 in a special election that was necessitated when former supervisor Leroy Urie resigned following his election as mayor of Gulfport. When he was sworn in for his first full term as supervisor in January 1988, the forty-three-year-old Moffat was under pressure to resign or face indictment for taking $250 in 1984 from an equipment salesman while he was a county employee. Later, Moffat also admitted taking $700 on January 30, 1987, from the same salesman. After having second thoughts about the $700, Moffat claimed that in the presence of his superintendent, Kenneth Sumrall, he placed the money in a sealed envelope and turned it over to his attorney, Gerald Emil, for safekeeping.

The terms of a plea bargain offered Moffat by the government included three years in prison, five years' probation, and a fine. The proposed agreement would have required Moffat to plead guilty to an Information and to waive formal indictment on bribery and mail fraud charges that carried maximum combined penalties of five years' imprisonment and fines of $500,000. He would also have been required to resign from office. Moffat considered signing a Bill of Information but resisted having to resign. "They have only one charge against me [the $250] and that was as a superintendent, not an elected official," Moffat said. He claimed that officials in other counties accused of worse things had been allowed to keep their jobs. Concerning the $250, Moffat said he "knew it was wrong, but I was in a financial bind. I stuck it in my pocket."

Moffat had claimed a week earlier that he had been cooperating with the Pretense investigation since early 1987, shortly after Jackson County's Fred Robinson Jr. had been indicted. "I went to the FBI in Gulfport and they put me in touch with Pretense agents in Jackson," Moffat said. He said the FBI had asked him to wear a listening device to gather evidence against former district two supervisor Leroy Urie and former district three supervisor Billy McDonald but that he never wore the wire.

The $250 payoff had supposedly been made in early 1984 by Holiman Equipment Company salesman Pete Dacus after the company made modifications to a mower it sold the county. Dacus, who had pleaded guilty to Pretense-related charges and was cooperating with the government, had already testified against another supervisor. Moffat claimed that he had avoided Dacus after this 1984 payoff until he showed up unexpectedly in the district two county barn in January 1987. Dacus gave him the $700 that he had turned over to his attorney, who still had it in January 1988. Moffat claimed that he didn't know exactly what the $700 was for but that Dacus had talked about repairing a pothole patcher that had been purchased while Urie was supervisor. Urie denied receiving kickbacks from Holiman on the pothole patcher or any other purchase.

Moffat said the $700 could have been a kickback on the purchase of six tractors and six mowing machines the county bought from Holiman months after the company was declared the low bidder by the board of supervisors after a lower bid from Loftus Equipment failed to meet specifications. Moffat said that McDonald "had the specifications written, I think and presume Holiman Equipment wrote them." McDonald said the county purchasing agent wrote the specifications and that the board of supervisors bought equipment based on the agent's recommendation. Since October 1985, the county had spent $134,226 with Holiman, including the $124,800 for the tractors and mowers.

Moffat's position was, "I have done everything I can do to cooperate with the government. Once they get their fangs in you, they try to get you to help them get somebody else—in my case, Billy and Leroy." He also claimed that FBI special agent Jerry King had asked him to "wear a wire" to gather information on Urie and McDonald, but that he and attorney Gerald Emil had explained to King that he had not been on the board of supervisors long enough to have much influence. Moffat maintained there was a leak shortly after he was asked to cooperate and subsequently Mc-Donald and Urie would have nothing to do with him. McDonald said that "is totally untrue" and that he did not have a problem or know of anybody who did.

According to Emil, Moffat reached an agreement with federal prosecutors on January 6, 1998. The agreement required the supervisor to cooperate in the ongoing investigation, but it allowed him to remain in his post for the time being. At the same time, Emil said that the $700 that Moffat had taken from Dacus in January 1987 had been offered to the U.S. attorney's office but that officials had refused to take it. The attorney noted that "the next three or four months will be critical." He also said that Moffat "plans to continue in his job. Eddie feels he can function effectively on the board more so today than yesterday." However, Moffat had not signed an agreement.

When negotiations for Moffat's cooperation foundered, he was arrested in Saucier on March 11, 1988. Assistant U.S. Attorney Don Burkhalter remarked, "He failed to cooperate. Negotiations with Mr. Moffat broke down and as a result of that we felt it was prudent to file an indictment and have him arrested." Just a month earlier he had waived indictment on charges of one count of bribery and one count of mail fraud. Federal prosecutors had presented the same set of allegations to a grand jury and sought stiffer charges. A four-count indictment, one each of bribery and extortion and two of mail fraud, had been handed up on March 9. The charges carried a maximum sentence of forty years and fines of $1 million. Moffat pleaded innocent before U.S. Magistrate Roper in Biloxi and was released on a $25,000 unsecured personal recognizance bond. Trial was set for June 13 before Judge Lee in Jackson.

The indictment charged that in February 1986 Moffat accepted a $250 kickback from Holiman Equipment Company on the conversion and repair of a "Tiger" mower; allegedly the transaction was part of a scheme to defraud that involved bribery and extortion. He was also charged with accepting approximately $950 from persons or organizations other than his employer for his conduct related to a series of county transactions during the period January 1986 until January 1987. The charges also accused Moffat of using the U.S. mails to accomplish the schemes. The money that he admitted accepting in 1984 while he was a county employee was not mentioned in the indictment. Apparently, the $950 charge did include the $700 that he reportedly accepted from Pete Dacus and gave to his attorney in January 1987.

In early September 1988, Moffat pleaded guilty before Judge Barbour to one count each of mail fraud and bribery; the other charges were dropped in accordance with a plea bargain. At his hearing Moffat stated, "I hate to give up my position because I think I have done a real good job. I love my district and the other people in it. I'd love to continue to serve if I could." He pleaded guilty to accepting $950 from Holiman ($250 and $700) but he told the judge that he accepted the $250 in 1984, not in 1986. The indictment read 1986, and Judge Barbour at first wouldn't accept the guilty plea because of the conflicting dates. The judge later reversed himself, accepted the guilty plea, and delayed sentencing so that Moffat could cooperate with the investigation. The plea bargain required him to resign as supervisor no later than September 6, 1988.

Court papers filed in the Moffat case indicate that Billy McDonald, who was president of the Harrison County Board of Supervisors at the time, accepted $4,200 in September 1986 from Holiman for the six tractors and the mowers purchased by the county. The money, $700 for each set of six tractors and mowers, was supposed to be divided among the supervisors. Each of the five supervisors was to get $700,for a total of $3,500; there was no mention of what was to be done with the remaining $700. A document filed with the court detailed how McDonald and Holiman salesman Max Gilbert met in August 1986 at the Patio Club in Jackson to discuss buying the tractors and mowers for Harrison County for $124,000. The board of supervisors approved the purchase on August 26, 1986, based on a motion from McDonald and a second from Moffat. At least one other company had submitted a bid that was lower than Holiman's, but according to County Purchasing Agent Bill Emerson, the lower bid(s) did not meet specifications. According to the court document, Gilbert paid McDonald the $4,200 in September at the Coliseum Ramada Inn in Jackson.

As noted above, Pete Dacus met with Moffat at the district two county barn in January 1987. The purchase of the six tractors was discussed at that meeting. Dacus, who was by then cooperating with the investigation and was wired, asked if Moffat had been taken care of on the tractor purchase deal. Moffat replied, "I ain't got nothing," and Dacus removed seven $100 bills from his pocket. Moffat accepted the money and placed it in his pocket according to the court papers. This was the $700 that was said to have been turned over to Moffat's attorney.

In an Omnibus Motion filed with the court in the summer of 1988, Moffat requested that a tape recording of a conversation between him and a government agent be suppressed. The brief accompanying the motion alleged that the tape was of such poor quality that significant portions of the conversation were unintelligible and that the tape did not fairly and accurately depict the conversation that it purported to represent. The government challenged this statement, and in its reply argued: "It is the government's position that any complaints of inaudibility or unintelligibility are without merit and the tapes are clearly audible and furthermore are accurate, authentic, trustworthy and relevant. It is further the government's position that the matter of admissibility of the tape is a matter that should be addressed by this court at the time of introduction." The motion to suppress the tape that Dacus had made was denied. This decision no doubt contributed heavily to Moffat's decision finally to agree to a plea bargain.

Another factor contributed to Moffat's changing his plea to guilty. He remembered initialing a rough draft of a story that appeared in the January 5, 1988, edition of the *Biloxi Sun Herald* in which he admitted taking kickbacks. The reporter had been careful to get Moffat's signature on a copy of the story before it ran making it virtually indistinguishable from a confession. Both defense attorneys and federal attorneys had only recently learned of the initialed story. Defense attorney Chet Nicholson said, "I think that ultimately, while we did not feel (Moffat) had a particularly guilty mind, it was clear the government had facts to convict him."

With tears in his eyes, Moffat said minutes before submitting his resignation letter to the board of supervisors, "I don't want to leave. I've enjoyed serving the people. I've done a good job." In his letter to the board, Moffat stated clearly that he had been forced to resign. He recommended a long-time friend, Richard S. Miller, as his replacement. In his resignation letter, Moffat also said that Billy McDonald was not acting for him and the other three supervisors when he allegedly accepted the $4,200 from Holiman. Moffat wrote, "there wasn't any deal between Holiman Equipment Company and four of the previous board members including myself. By the grace of GOD and my families' [sic] LOVE, I will survive."

In a Memorandum of Understanding, Assistant U.S. Attorney Barrett had agreed that if Moffat cooperated, the government would recommend that the court not impose a prison sentence exceeding three years on the mail fraud count and that it suspend sentence on the bribery count and impose probation for five years. Moffat was not sentenced until March 21, 1989. Judge Barbour sentenced him to a year and a day in jail on the mail fraud charge. He was given a suspended sentence and placed on five years' probation on the bribery charge, and he was ordered to pay a fine of $2,000 and restitution of $950. The probation was to begin after release from confinement, and during the time of probation Moffat was prohibited from running for or holding public office. Moffat was ordered to report to the Federal Prison Camp, Eglin Air Force Base, Florida, by April 17, 1989. He reported on time.

As noted above, Moffat's case involved accusations that former board of supervisors president Billy McDonald had taken $4,200 from Holiman Equipment as a kickback to be distributed among all the county's supervisors. McDonald denied receiving any kickbacks for equipment purchases while he was president of the board of supervisors. The other four supervisors at the time of the alleged payoff were Moffat, Bobby Eleuterius, Hue Snowden, and C. T. Switzer. In a prepared statement, McDonald asserted, "I received no money. Therefore it was impossible to give any money to Mr. Switzer, to Mr. Snowden, to Mr. Eleuterius or to Mr. Moffat. Anyone who received any money must have acted on his own behalf."

When these accusations came to light, C. T. Switzer Jr. was district two supervisor, a post his deceased father had held in September 1986 when the alleged kickback was paid. Switzer expressed anger about the allegations. "I definitely feel it's a bum rap," he said. "I know for a fact my daddy was never involved. This has really affected my family, even more than his death." Former district four supervisor Snowden denied taking any kickback and criticized the U.S. Attorney's Office for listing a deceased supervisor as a possible recipient of kickback money. Eleuterius, who at the time of the revelations was serving as president of the board of supervisors, also denied any involvement with the alleged kickbacks.

No charges were ever filed against McDonald, Snowden, or Eleuterius. Apparently, the federal prosecutors doubted that they had strong enough evidence to convict them. It appears that the government did not have any tape-recorded evidence of Dacus's alleged dealings with McDonald on the alleged $4,200 kickback. In court, it would have simply been the supervisors' words against the word of Holiman's representative Pete Dacus, who had already pleaded guilty to Pretense-related charges and was cooperating with the investigation. Mississippi Mud.

Bordering Alabama on the east, Jackson County is one of three counties located along the Mississippi Gulf Coast. The county's 1990 population exceeded 115,000, ranking it third among the state's eighty-two counties. Pascagoula, the county seat, is the home of the state's largest industrial employer, Litton Industries' Ingalls Shipbuilding. The county has a number of other fairly large industries and a well-paid workforce. Many who work in the county commute from other Mississippi counties and Alabama. The county is generally viewed as prosperous and progressive. However, in the 1980s and 1990s, Jackson County was burdened with a corrupt and obstinate county government.

A federal grand jury in Jackson indicted Jackson County district two supervisor Fred Robinson Jr. on March 10, 1987, on seven counts—one of bribery, two of extortion, and four of mail fraud. Robinson was alleged to have accepted $4,368 related to county purchases of materials and supplies from Mid-State Pipe Company and Davis Chemicals. Robinson was accused of extorting $2,205 from Mid-State and Davis Chemicals in connection with the companies doing business with the county. He was also charged with accepting $3,163 in kickbacks from the vendors and using the U.S. mails to accomplish the schemes. The indictment charged that Robinson intimated that other supervisors would be willing to make similar arrangements and that he assisted in accomplishing such arrangements. If convicted on all seven counts, the second-term supervisor faced maximum penalties of seventy years' imprisonment and $1.75 million in fines.

The fifty-nine-year-old Robinson was the eighteenth supervisor to face Pretense-related charges and the first from a Gulf Coast county. Robinson, who owned and operated Robinson's Friendly Funeral Home in Moss Point, was Jackson County's first elected black supervisor. Running as a reform candidate, he had first been elected supervisor in 1982 to complete the unexpired term of Edward A. Khayat, who had been forced out of office on a misdemeanor charge. Robinson was a veteran politician, having served nearly eight years as judge of the district two justice court.

After his arrest, Robinson appeared before U.S. Magistrate Roper in Biloxi on March 1, but arraignment was postponed a week so he could engage an attorney. He was immediately released on a $1.5 million unsecured bond. Robinson told reporters that he was innocent and that "it looks like a mistake to me." On March 18, Robinson and his attorney, Wynn Clark, appeared before Judge Roper and the supervisor entered an innocent plea.

Trial was set for May 4. Robinson remained in office, and two weeks after his indictment he indicated that he had no plans to take a leave of absence during the pretrial period. "Why should I?" he asked, noting, "It's my own personal decision."

Meanwhile, one of Robinson's key employees was in trouble. In early April, Maury G. Thompson, Jackson County district two road foreman, was charged with mail fraud in connection with Operation Pretense. The fifteen-year county employee and Escatawpa resident waived indictment and pleaded innocent before U.S. Magistrate Roper in Biloxi on April 7. He faced possible penalties of five years' imprisonment and fines of up to $250,000. At the time of arraignment, Thompson told Judge Roper that he planned to change his plea to guilty later. Thompson had decided to waive his rights to an attorney. This decision, along with the promised guilty plea, signaled that he was working a deal with the U.S. attorney that would involve providing information about other Pretense-related matters. Thompson was released on a $250,000 personal recognizance bond, and Assistant U.S. Attorney Barrett indicated that Thompson had agreed to cooperate in the ongoing investigation.

Appearing before U.S. District Court Judge Walter Gex III in Biloxi June 15, 1987, Thompson pleaded guilty to one count of mail fraud contained in an information. The mail fraud involved inducing the county to pay a fraudulent invoice from Davis Chemicals for $461.25 for materials never delivered to the county and accepting $230 in cash from Ray Davis in return. Sentencing was delayed so that Thompson could cooperate with the ongoing investigation. Thompson said that he was still employed as district two road manager and that he did not know what effect his guilty plea would have on his job. He was quoted as saying, "So far, no one has asked me to leave. But I don't know what's going to happen after today."

Robinson's trial, originally set for May 4, was postponed until late June. On June 15, Robinson entered into a plea bargain with Assistant U.S. Attorney Barrett that called for him to plead guilty to one count of extortion and one count of mail fraud and to cooperate with the government in the continuing investigation. Senior U.S. District Court Judge Dan M. Russell signed an Order continuing the case for a plea and sentencing. Judge Gex was to set a date for Robinson to enter his plea. Robinson's guilty plea was accepted June 19 by Judge Gex in Biloxi. The plea agreement required Robinson to resign his supervisor's post within ten days of the plea being accepted. The agreement also prohibited him from seeking or holding public office during any probation time imposed at sentencing. Sentencing was to be delayed until September 21 so that Robinson could cooperate with the investigation and a presentencing investigation could be completed.

The two counts to which Robinson pleaded guilty carried combined maximum penalties of twenty-five years in prison and fines of $500,000. The plea bargain agreed to by U.S. Attorney Barrett called for the government to recommend a suspended sentence and five years' probation on the extortion charge and to make no recommendation on the mail fraud charge, which carried a maximum prison sentence of five years. Probation was to commence after completion of any prison sentence imposed. The government was not to make any recommendation as to fines on either charge. Robinson was the 14th supervisor to plead guilty on Pretense-related charges.

Had he gone to trial, Robinson would have been the second supervisor to be tried on Pretense-related charges. The decision to plead guilty rather than challenge the charges in court was probably triggered by the results of the first trial of a supervisor accused under Pretense. On June 2, a federal jury in Hattiesburg had convicted Perry County supervisor Trudie Westmoreland on six charges that were very similar to those Robinson faced. Jerry King, the FBI agent who worked undercover as a salesman for Mid-State, and Ray Davis, owner of Davis Chemicals, had testified against Westmoreland. They were scheduled to testify against Robinson along with former district two road foreman Maury Thompson. Robinson and his attorney, Wynn Clark, very likely read the tea leaves correctly.

The FBI first learned of Robinson's involvement in bid rigging and invoice busting schemes in February 1985 when Jerry King met with Ray Davis. Not knowing that King was an FBI agent, Davis told him that Robinson "would do business and take kickbacks." The following November, Davis told King that he had given Robinson a $300 kickback at the Mississippi Association of Supervisors convention and that Thompson, the road foreman, was "OK" and in on the deals. King entered into a series of transactions with Robinson in April 1986. Robinson told King that Thompson knew all about the deals and that it would be all right to deal directly with Thompson, who would act on Robinson's behalf.

Robinson admitted guilt to a mail fraud charge on a transaction that Davis had taped that involved an agreement with Thompson to bust an invoice for $461.25 for gear oil and hornet spray that would not be delivered to the county. Davis gave Thompson $230 in payment, and Thompson split the money with Robinson. The county mailed Davis a check for $858.50 that included $461.25 for the fraudulent transaction. The extortion charge to which Robinson pleaded guilty involved the purchase from Mid-State of twelve pieces of culvert pipe and a kickback of $130. This transaction arose from a meeting with Jerry King at Robinson's funeral home that agent Jerry King taped. During the meeting, Robinson also agreed to bust a $1,317.20 invoice for seven pieces of culvert pipe that were not to be delivered. The supervisor's take from the two transactions was $800.

Robinson was not sentenced until July 17, 1988. At the sentencing hearing, Robinson told Judge Gex, "First I apologize for doing wrong. I also want to apologize to my family for having to go through all of this. I want to apologize to the voters of district two for the mistakes I've made." Eleven businessmen, politicians, civic leaders, and clergy from Jackson County had written the Judge asking for mercy on Robinson's behalf. Probation officials had given the judge a petition in support of the former supervisor signed by 576 district two voters. Prior to imposing a relatively light sentence on the penitent former supervisor, Judge Gex indicated that he was about to give the defendant a break. He said, "Mr. Robinson, I'm going to give you a chance. I truly believe that you made a mistake. I believe you recognize that. I believe after you pay your dues, you will continue to lead an exemplary life." Then, Judge Gex sentenced the defendant to three years in prison on the mail fraud charge with all but a year and a day suspended. He also fined Robinson $10,000 and sentenced him to five years' probation on the extortion charge. No doubt, the long delay between Robinson's guilty plea and his sentencing and the relatively light penalties imposed reflect Robinson's extensive cooperation with the investigation.

Maury Thompson was not sentenced until July 6, 1989, when Judge Gex sentenced him to five years' probation on the mail fraud charge and imposed fines and restitution totaling $880. At the sentencing hearing, Thompson said, "I spent 15 years of my adult life honoring the trust of the taxpayers of Jackson County, and I let them down. I'm real sorry about that." After imposing sentence, Judge Gex warned, "Mr. Thompson, I truly believe that you have rehabilitated yourself. You are a good person. You have a good family. Don't get in trouble anymore." Without question, the length of time between Thompson's guilty plea and sentencing and the very light penalties imposed reflect extensive cooperation with the FBI in its investigation.

Fred Robinson Jr. was the only Jackson County supervisor ever indicted as a result of Operation Pretense. His indictment indicated that Robinson gave information that other supervisors were willing to make similar arrangements to defraud the county and that he assisted in accomplishing such arrangements. At the time of his arraignment, the four other Jackson County supervisors denied that Robinson had contacted them about taking kickbacks. The U.S. attorney had refused to comment about whether indictments against other supervisors were pending. When Robinson announced his intention to plead guilty in June 1997, James Tucker, chief of the criminal division of the U.S. Attorney's Office, would not comment on whether other Jackson County supervisors would be indicted. However, at about that time, District Attorney Mike Moore, who was a candidate for attorney general, told newspaper reporters that there would be no more Pretense-related indictments of Jackson County officials. Perhaps Robinson's cooperation with the government was limited to providing information about supervisors in other Gulf Coast counties.

The 1980s proved to be only a prelude to bigger troubles with county officials that surfaced in the 1990s. In the late 1990s, problems with Jackson County elected officials performing their duties became apparent. Chancery Clerk Lynn Presley was removed from office after he pleaded guilty to eight counts of embezzlement. His appointed replacement, Virginia Kirk, who ran for a full term and was defeated, attempted to collect a full year's salary from the county for the four months she served. Supervisor Tommy Broadnax was arrested on assault and disorderly conduct charges, thereby provoking a major brouhaha between the supervisor and the sheriff. Broadnax's operation of county equipment in his district brought a state auditor's investigation into whether the county was in compliance with the unit system law. The shenanigans in Jackson County contributed to reform recommendations that both the state auditor and attorney general submitted to the 1999 legislature.

20. The Vendors

It Takes Two to Tango

Chapter 8 outlines the charges leveled against a prominent vendor, Bobby Little, and chronicles the legal developments in the only Pretense-related case against a vendor that actually went to trial. There were, however, twelve other vendors charged with Pretense-related offences. This chapter summarizes their cases, including the many contributions that cooperating vendors made to the success of Operation Pretense.

In mid-February 1988, CBS's Mike Wallace and his *60 Minutes* crew arrived in Mississippi to tape a segment on Operation Pretense. Wallace interviewed some of the people involved in the now well-known FBI sting, including three of the main participants in the undercover operation: Reverend John Burgess, who facilitated the sting and was the nominal owner of the FBI front Mid-State Pipe Company; FBI special agent Jerry King, who worked undercover as a salesman for Mid-State; and Ray Davis, president of Davis Chemicals. The *60 Minutes* segment, "The Preacher and the Sting Man," which aired in May 1987, explained how Ray Davis became a key player in the investigation.

Ray Davis first met Jerry King when he and the undercover agent were attempting to secure purchases from the same supervisor. When the two talked, they realized that they were not competitors because they were not selling the same products. King was selling pipe, and Davis was selling chemicals and related products. They determined to help each other by sharing information. One bit of information they shared was that they had to pay kickbacks to do business with some supervisors. The two later met at Davis's place of business, took a list of county supervisors produced by the Mississippi Association of Supervisors, and went through the names to identify supervisors who would take bribes. Davis said in the *60 Minutes* interview that he had made kickbacks to twenty-five to thirty-five county supervisors all over the state.

In July 1986, federal authorities struck a deal with Ray Davis that made him a major player in Operation Pretense. The plea agreement, dated July 7, 1986, called for Davis to plead guilty to informations filed in the Northern and Southern Districts of Mississippi and to cooperate in the investigation. In exchange, the U.S. attorneys agreed that prior to his sentencing they would inform the judge in writing about the nature and extent of Davis's cooperation.

Davis admitted to scheming with supervisors in seventeen counties and provided information that was very useful to the FBI in establishing that some supervisors were predisposed to take bribes. He also taped under-the-table deals with supervisors and testified against several supervisors before grand juries and trial juries. Many of the indictments that flowed from Pretense mentioned Davis as a source of kickbacks to supervisors. His work was invaluable to the FBI and federal prosecutors. For example, Davis testified in the trial of Wayne County supervisors Alfred Revette and Jimmie Duvall that he paid kickbacks and busted invoices with both supervisors. During the trial, Davis said, "I felt I would get very little business, if any, if I did not pay the kickbacks." The value of Davis's cooperation is reflected in the ultimate disposition of the charges against him.

Davis pleaded guilty March 12, 1987, in Oxford to mail fraud charges for mailing a bogus invoice to cover a kickback he paid to a former Pontotoc County supervisor (Bobby Dean Stegall). The information indicated that from about January 1984 to about June 1986, Davis schemed to defraud the state of Mississippi and numerous counties by rigging bids on chemical products, paying numerous supervisors illegal gratuities or kickbacks, and busting invoices to counties for overstated quantities of supplies delivered to the counties or supplies never delivered at all. Davis waived indictment and pleaded guilty before U.S. District Court Judge Neal B. Biggers Jr. to an information. At the time of the plea, Davis was out of jail on bond from a similar pleading in the Southern District of Mississippi. No additional bond was required.

In May of 1989, U.S. District Court Judge Tom S. Lee accepted Davis's guilty plea on the Southern District Court information and rendered a finding of guilty to the charges of mail fraud contained in the information. He sentenced Davis to five years' probation. In October 1989, more than three years after the plea agreement was negotiated, the charges in the Northern District were transferred to the Southern District in accordance with the plea bargain. Judge Lee accepted the sixty-two-year-old Davis's guilty plea and rendered a finding of guilty to the charge of mail fraud on November 3, 1989. He sentenced Davis to probation, which was to run concurrently with that imposed on the Southern District Court charge, and thus was to run through May 17, 1994. Davis was prohibited from dealing with county supervisors during the time of probation.

Fifty-two-year-old Billy Ray Harrison of Morton was indicted on May 4, 1987, by a federal grand jury in Jackson on three counts of bribery, mail fraud, and aiding and abetting mail fraud. He was arrested and entered a not guilty plea before U.S. Magistrate John R. Countiss III on May 5. Harrison; his court-appointed attorney, John M. Colette; and Assistant U.S. Attorney Ruth R. Harris signed a Memorandum of Understanding on May 14, 1987. This plea bargain called for Harrison to plead guilty to counts one (bribery) and two (mail fraud) of the indictment and to cooperate with the investigation. At sentencing, the government was to inform the court as to the extent and effect of Harrison's cooperation, make no recommendation concerning count two, and to recommend a suspended sentence on count one with five years' probation that would begin after any prison time imposed. U.S. District Court Judge William H. Barbour Jr. accepted the guilty plea under the terms of the plea agreement and, at the request of the U.S. attorney, deferred sentencing so that Harrison could cooperate with the investigation.

Harrison, a former salesman for Mississippi Pipe and Oil Company in Pearl, was not sentenced until July 8, 1988, more than a year after the plea agreement. Harrison had admitted bribing two Greene County supervisors, John M. Crocker and Lauvon Pierce, by paying them a total of $2,418 for fictitious or altered invoices for county equipment. Assistant U.S. Attorney Harris said that Harrison had committed mail fraud and bribery from 1984 to 1987. One mail fraud charged was dropped, but Harrison faced a maximum penalty of fifteen years in jail and a $500,000 fine. Harris said, "He has admitted to similar acts with various supervisors around the state."

Judge Barbour gave Harrison a three-year suspended prison term, fined him $5,000, and ordered him to pay Greene County restitution in the amount of $2,358. Harrison was also placed on probation for three years with the stipulation that he join an alcoholic treatment program. Judge Barbour told the defendant, "There is a firm indication that you are an alcoholic. The list of DUI offenses against you is long. The list of marriages and divorces is long. By all indications you are in fact an alcoholic." The judge went on to warn Harrison that he could face a revocation hearing if he fell off the wagon. "I will not hesitate to impose a jail sentence," Judge Barbour said. Harrison apologized for his actions saying, "I'm sorry all this come up." Harrison's attorney, John Collette, said, "He's now running a wholesale truck and sells vegetables. If Mr. Harrison is shown mercy he will not be back in this court or any other court."

The long delay between Harrison's guilty plea and the imposition of his relatively light sentence are explained by his extensive cooperation with the Pretense investigation. At sentencing, Judge Barbour said Harrison was "a key player in Operation Pretense." Obviously, the system of corruption for county purchasing cannot be carried out without vendors willing to participate with crooked supervisors. The judge went on to say, "Because your cooperation is more than any other witness or vendor, the court feels you should be given credit for your cooperation." Assistant U.S. Attorney Harris described the former salesman's cooperation as extensive saying, "He gave us information against other defendants, and the information has resulted in numerous convictions. He's working with agents on a number of other cases. He has told us of numerous supervisors who extorted money from him and sought bribes."

Hattiesburg heavy equipment salesman Billy Rex Lott was indicted on February 11, 1987 on one count of giving a bribe to Greene County supervisor Lauvon Pierce. He was charged with offering in the fall of 1986 to pay the supervisor $5,000 to purchase a motor grader. The fifty-three-year-old Lott was arrested and arraigned on February 12; he entered a not guilty plea and was released on a $5,000 personal recognizance bond. Lott was employed by Puckett Machinery of Hattiesburg.

Billy Rex Lott was sentenced on June 14, 1987, by Judge Barbour to a six-year term in prison, fined $5,000, and ordered to pay restitution in the amount of $10,800. This was the first prison sentence imposed as a result of Pretense. Lott was to report to prison on July 15. The former salesman pleaded guilty to paying Pierce $5,000 between October 1986 and December 1986 to ensure that the county would buy a $38,800 road grader from Lott. Although Lott worked for Puckett Machinery Company, the bid for the equipment sale was not submitted under the company's name, and Puckett Machinery was not implicated in the scheme.

At sentencing, Judge Barbour told Lott, "If the system in this state allows an unscrupulous salesman to offer such bribes and kickbacks to supervisors then there is no way for a county to get a fair break for its tax dollars for the people. There is no justification for it and no way to excuse it." Lott's attorney, Jim Dukes of Hattiesburg, asked for a lenient sentence because Lott had pleaded guilty and because this was his first criminal offense. Dukes asked the judge not to use Lott as an example to others charged in the investigation. Assistant U.S. Attorney Harris said the government made no recommendation on the sentence. She did, however, tell the judge that Lott had refused to cooperate with the investigators.

Based on a plea bargain with prosecutors, in late August 1987 Petal resident Jessie M. Smith, pleaded guilty in federal court to an information outlining three counts of mail fraud. The fifty-five-year-old salesman for Consolidated Culvert and Supply Company was charged with paying kickbacks totaling $600 to Pierce to do business with Greene County. Prosecutors made no sentencing recommendations on two of the counts, each of which carried maximum penalties of five years in prison and $250,000 in fines. Prosecutors recommended five years' probation on the other count.

In a hearing before Judge Lee, Smith testified that he paid Pierce $200 on three occasions between October 1986 and January 1987 to purchase overstated or nonexistent road materials (busted invoices). Pierce had already pleaded guilty and was cooperating with the investigation. Earlier, Assistant U.S. Attorney James Tucker had said that Pierce wore a concealed tape recorder during three meetings with Smith, who admitted paying the supervisor $200 on October 23 and November 20, 1986, and on January 6, 1987. On November 20, 1987, Judge Lee sentenced Smith to five years in prison, fined him $10,000, and ordered him to serve five years' probation after release from confinement. He was to report to federal prison on January 4, 1988. Smith had faced maximum penalties of fifteen years in prison and $750,000 in fines. Smith was the second salesman charged as a result of Pretense who was sentenced to prison.

Although Smith had agreed to cooperate in the investigation, prosecutors claimed that he had not done so. His attorney, James Dukes, argued that he had nothing to cooperate about since he knew of no other kickbacks. Dukes said, "If ever a person was entitled to some consideration in a request for leniency or probation, he is. The stigma of what he pleaded guilty to is severe punishment." Assistant U.S. Attorney Harris responded that Smith not only knew of other kickbacks, he had given them. Harris said, "He's not truthful when he said the only time he did it was when the FBI caught him." She went on to say that when Smith found out that Ray Davis was cooperating with the investigation, he warned two Perry County supervisors, Junie Mixon and Trudie Westmoreland, to be wary of Davis. Harris also challenged Smith's claim that he paid Pierce because the supervisor "needed money for his child's medicine." She noted that Pierce's youngest child was nineteen and "that has been clearly shown a falsehood."

Gaston Barrett, president of Central Culvert and Supply Company of Philadelphia, pleaded innocent to 11 counts of mail fraud before U.S. Magistrate Countiss on January 12, 1988. He was accused of preparing fraudulent invoices totaling $10,426.30 between 1983 and 1986 for an unnamed Newton County supervisor. The supervisor allegedly received about ten percent of that in kickbacks. Trial was set for March 7 before Judge Lee in Jackson. The forty-one-year-old Barrett was released on a $5,000 personal recognizance bond.

In late February 1988, Barrett was reindicted on eleven counts of mail fraud and two counts of conspiracy. He was charged with conspiring with supervisors between September 1985 and May 1986 to submit false bids to defraud residents of Clarke, Copiah, Greene, Jasper, Kemper, Leake, Neshoba, Newton, Perry, and other unnamed counties. He was alleged to have agreed with Neshoba County supervisors to submit false bids for equipment or supplies so that the county would be induced to buy from him and that he later submitted such bids. The indictment also alleged that on September 6, 1985, Barrett proposed with Mid-State Pipe Company to join forces to submit false bids to counties across the state. If convicted on all thirteen charges, Barrett faced maximum penalties of sixty-five years in prison and $3.25 million in fines.

In early September 1988, Barrett pleaded guilty in Jackson to a two-count information charging mail fraud and aiding and abetting mail fraud. Federal officials dropped the other eleven counts against him. He pleaded guilty of paying two kickbacks, one of $7 and one of $10, to former Newton County supervisor Henry Mack Smith. In a plea bargain, Barrett had agreed to cooperate in the ongoing Pretense investigation. Assistant U.S. Attorney Nick Phillips recommended a cap of one year and a day on any sentence Barrett might receive and a $7,500 fine. Phillips also recommended that sentencing be delayed to allow Barrett to cooperate in the investigation. Frank Trapp, Barrett's attorney, said that Barrett didn't bill for any undelivered goods in the Pretense cases; that is, that he had not busted any invoices.

Judge Barbour sentenced Barrett on June 23, 1988. On count one, the sentence was three years in prison with all but six months suspended. The prison time was to be served at the Bannum House in Jackson. Imposition of sentence was suspended on count two, but three years active reporting probation was imposed. Barrett was also fined $7,500 to be paid by June 30, 1989. Court records contain a receipt indicating that the fine was paid on June 28, 1989. The fact that eleven counts were dropped and a very light sentence was imposed indicate that Barrett had been cooperating with the investigation since he was first charged a year and a half earlier. That he was allowed to plead guilty to a two-count information rather than face a thirteen-count indictment probably reflects the belief of the prosecutors that he was, in effect, a victim of extortion.

Ray Dowell Smith of Smith's Diesel Sales and Services in Carthage was indicted in early October 1988 on Pretense-related charges. Smith was charged with making payoffs to Newton and Attala County supervisors during the period October 1983 through May 1984. The FBI front, Mid-State Pipe Company, was located on Mississippi Highway 35 north of Carthage, not far from Smith Diesel Sales and Service. Smith was the fourteenth vendor arrested as a result of Operation Pretense. According to the indictment, Smith: (a) submitted a false invoice for $44,500 to Newton County on October 20, 1983 and paid a supervisor a $4,000 kickback; (b) submitted two false invoices to Attala County on April 3, 1984, one for $43,500 and another for $41,500, and paid related kickbacks of $1,000 and $2,000 to county supervisors; and (c) submitted a false invoice for $10,763 to Attala County in April 1984 and paid a county supervisor a related $200 kickback.

Based on a Memorandum of Understanding dated March 1, 1989, Smith pleaded guilty to one count of mail fraud in U.S. district court in Jackson. The charge involved Smith's paying a $4,000 kickback to Newton County supervisor Henry Mack Smith on the county's purchase of a $44,500 motor grader. Judge Barbour imposed sentence on April 10, 1989. Smith was sentenced to five years' imprisonment, with all but four months suspended. He was to serve four years and eight months probation after release from incarceration and to pay a fine of $10,000 by May 10, 1989. The judge ordered that the other three counts in the indictment be dismissed in accordance with the plea agreement. Smith was ordered to report to Bannum Place in Jackson to begin his incarceration on May 10, 1989. Court records contain a Satisfaction of Judgment dated May 12, 1989, indicating that Smith had paid the $10,000 fine.

Max Gilbert of Pearl, part owner of Holiman Equipment in Jackson and sole owner of L&M Equipment of Pearl, and Holiman salesman Pete Dacus waived indictment to Pretense-related charges on October 2, 1987, and pleaded innocent to informations dated September 29, 1987. Both men entered their pleas before U.S. Magistrate Countiss and indicated that they planned to change their pleas at a later date. Both were cooperating with the investigation. Gilbert and Dacus were released on $5,000 personal recognizance bonds.

Gilbert, who had been arrested in March and charged with lying to a grand jury investigating allegations of corrupt buying practices of a supervisor, was charged with mail fraud and accused of scheming with Sam Perniciaro, a Hancock County supervisor, to obtain money and property from Hancock County under false pretenses. He was accused of paying kickbacks to the supervisor on items the county purchased from Holiman and with busting invoices on items not delivered to the county. Specifically, Gilbert was charged with mail fraud in connection with Holiman invoice 6074 in the amount of $37, 750 to Hancock County.

Dacus was charged with paying kickbacks to Lauderdale County fourth district supervisor Billy Joe Harris for county purchases from Holiman. He was charged with mail fraud in connection with Holiman invoice 14505 to Lauderdale County. Neither the amount of the invoice nor the amount of the related kickback was mentioned in the information. However, as noted in chapter 15, Billy Joe Harris pleaded guilty to extorting $600 from Holiman Equipment Company on Lauderdale County's purchase of a bushhog.

Max Gilbert had actually entered into a Memorandum of Understanding with federal authorities on April 17, 1987. This plea bargain called for Gilbert to plead guilty to a one-count information to be filed in the Southern District of Mississippi and to a one-count information filed in the Northern District of Mississippi and to cooperate with the government in the ongoing investigation. The government agreed to recommend that if the court deemed a prison sentence appropriate for the charge in one information, the sentence should not exceed three years and that probation for five years should be imposed on the charge contained in the other information. Also, the government was to recommend that a special condition of probation would prohibit Gilbert from doing business with any county supervisor in Mississippi. The government also agreed to inform the court at the time of sentencing of the extent and effect of Gilbert's cooperation. The defendant faced possible maximum penalties under the plea bargain of fifteen years in prison and fines of $500,000.

Judge Lee sentenced Gilbert on July 18, 1989, to three years in prison with a provision that, after four months of incarceration, the remainder of the sentence would be suspended. The defendant was also fined $5,000 and ordered to serve five years' probation after release from incarceration. He was also prohibited from doing business with any county supervisor while on probation. Gilbert's light sentence and the time between his plea bargain and sentencing no doubt reflected his extensive cooperation in the investigation.

In the Pete Dacus case, U.S. Magistrate Countiss issued an Order Continuing Cause for Plea and Sentence on October 2, 1987. The order noted that

Dacus had previously appeared for arraignment and had expressed a desire to plead guilty. The order then continued the case until such time as a presentencing investigation was completed, a presentencing report was provided to the district court, and the court had scheduled the matter for plea and sentencing.

In June 1989, after more than a year and a half had elapsed, Assistant U.S. Attorney Harris and Pete Dacus submitted to the court a Request to Defer Prosecution under 18 U.S.C. Section 3161(h)(2). The request was as follows:

> Comes the United States Attorney, through his Assistant, and the defendant, PETE DACUS, individually, and request this Court to exclude, all period of delay as provided under Section 3161(h)(2), Title 18, United States Code (the Speedy Trial Act). And in support thereof, the Government and the defendant do hereby agree that prosecution should be deferred for a period of twelve (12) months for the purpose of allowing the defendant to demonstrate his good conduct, and do further agree to promptly report to this Court when and if sufficient demonstration has been accomplished to proceed herein, and do further agree that all periods of time within which trial herein should commence are hereby waived.

Judge Lee approved this request on June 23, 1989.

Another year passed before Assistant U.S. Attorney Harris, acting for U.S. Attorney George Phillips, issued an Order of Dismissal in September 1990. The order stated: "Pursuant to Rule 48(a) of the Federal Rules of Criminal Procedure, and by leave of Court endorsed hereon, the United States Attorney for the Southern District of Mississippi hereby dismisses the indictment against the defendant, PETE DACUS, without prejudice." On September 15, 1990, Judge Lee granted Leave of the Court for the dismissal.

Johnnie H. Williamson, former vice president and co-owner of Tubb-Williamson, Inc. of Jackson, was indicted by a federal grand jury on March 9, 1988, on six counts. He was arrested on the Pretense-related charges on March 18 and charged with five counts of mail fraud and one count of bribery. Williamson pleaded innocent in an arraignment before U.S. Magistrate Countiss, and he was released on a $1,000 personal recognizance bond. Trial was set for June 13 before Judge Lee.

The fifty-four-year-old Williamson was charged with paying kickbacks to supervisors in Attala, Claiborne, and Jasper Counties. Williamson was accused of paying John Robert Ulmer, former Jasper County supervisor, $3,100 to influence the county's purchase of a motor grader between December 1986 and February 1987. He was also charged with paying an unnamed Jasper County supervisor $1,500 to influence a $65,000 purchase made by the county in March 1984. Supervisors involved in the Attala and Claiborne transactions were not named in the indictment. The indictment also charged that Williamson had paid a $300 kickback to another unnamed Claiborne County supervisor to influence a $14,600 purchase in November 1984. He was further charged with paying an unnamed Attala County supervisor $2,000 to influence a $36,000 purchase in September 1984.

In 1987, Eddie Burrell, former Claiborne County supervisor, had pleaded guilty to two mail fraud charges and admitted taking at least $10,500 in kickbacks from July 1984 to August 1986. Burrell also admitted taking at least $3,500 in kickbacks from Williamson to approve Williamson's bid on a piece of heavy equipment. An FBI agent acknowledged that Burrell was the supervisor who accepted the $3,000 kickback.

On June 10, 1988, Williamson pleaded guilty to one count of the six-count indictment based on a plea bargain that required him to cooperate with the investigation. Williamson's guilty plea was for paying former Jasper County supervisor John Robert Ulmer $3,100 on the county's purchase of a $35,000 motor grader in January 1987. Judge Lee set sentencing for August 12. Williamson faced maximum penalties of ten years in prison and $250,000 in fines. The other five charges were dropped in accordance with the plea bargain.

Johnnie Williamson was not sentenced until February 9, 1989. Judge Lee imposed a suspended prison sentence, ordered Williamson to live in a halfway house for three months, fined him $10,000, and ordered him to pay restitution of $3,000 to Claiborne County, $4,100 to Jasper County, and $1,800 to Attala County. The restitution involved false invoices that resulted in kickbacks on county purchases to Robert Ellard of Attala County, Eddie Burrell of Claiborne County, and John Robert Ulmer of Jasper County.

In April 1988, federal prosecutors charged forty-year-old William L. Polk III with conspiring with Rankin County supervisor Herbert D. Smith to bust invoices for products never delivered to the county. According to the charges, Polk and Smith agreed to invoice Rankin County for $537.60 worth of goods that were never delivered, and Smith was paid half the amount of the invoice after the county mailed a check in payment of the invoice. Polk originally pleaded innocent, but his attorney, Barry Gilmer, of Jackson, indicated that his client planned to plead guilty at a later date. Polk made his plea before U.S. Magistrate Countiss on April 14, 1988, and was released on a $1,000 bond. The former employee of Mississippi Pipe and Oil Company was the thirteenth salesman charged as a result of Pretense, and he was cooperating with the investigation at the time he was charged.

Gilmer indicated that Polk had used the money to buy Christmas turkeys for Smith. Gilmer said, "He simply did what he was asked to do. He did it and made a mistake." Gilmer also said that Smith approached Polk about splitting the money as a condition of doing business for that particular job. At the time Polk was charged, Smith had not been charged with any crime. Assistant U.S. Attorney Don Burkhalter would not comment on why Smith was not also charged. As reported in chapter 16, Smith was later charged and convicted under state law.

U.S. Magistrate Countiss issued an Order Continuing Cause for Plea and Sentence on April 14, 1988. This order indicated that Polk had been arraigned, had expressed a desire to plead guilty, and had consented to the preparation of a presentence report. The order postponed the actual pleading until a presentence investigation could be completed and its findings reported to the court.

An Order of Dismissal initiated by Assistant U.S. Attorney Harris for U.S. Attorney George Phillips was granted by Judge Lee on November 10, 1988. This order dismissed the criminal charges in the information to which Polk had agreed to plead guilty. No doubt the presentence report contained several factors that led the government to recommend that the charges against Polk be dropped. He had obviously cooperated extensively and effectively with the ongoing investigation, and no doubt the prosecutors thought that he had been a victim of extortion.

Lee Hollis Burt, operator of Bull Mountain Gravel Company, pleaded guilty to one count contained in an information filed in federal court in Oxford on September 21, 1987. He also agreed to cooperate with the ongoing investigation of corrupt county purchasing practices. Burt was charged with paying Pontotoc County supervisors $.25 to $.50 per yard, or $200 to $300 per month per district, on gravel purchases for a five-year period until interrupted by Operation Pretense in February 1987. During that period, he had paid monthly kickbacks to district one's Grady O. Baker, district two's Talmage M. Nix, district three's O. L. Finley, and district four's Theron Baldwin. District five had purchased gravel for only a few months during that period, and when it did, its supervisor, Bobby Dean Stegall, also received kickbacks from Burt. Cash kickbacks to Pontotoc County supervisors over the life of the scheme totaled about $87,000. While dealing with

Pontotoc County in this manner, Bull Mountain was selling gravel to other counties at substantially lower prices. Stegall, Baker, and Baldwin had apparently implicated Burt as they cooperated with the government as agreed to in their plea bargains.

Court records outline Burt's involvement with the supervisors of Pontotoc County.

The United States would show by extensive documentary evidence and oral eye witness testimony of persons involved and by tape recordings as well as by admissions of Mr. Burt as follows:

After leasing a gravel pit just off Hwy. 25 in Itawamba County during December 1981, Mr. Burt began trying to sell gravel to various counties in Northeast Mississippi via the bid system. He named his company Bull Mountain Gravel. Just after he went into business, Mr. Burt was approached by Pontotoc County supervisors Talmage Nix and O. L. Finley at his ready mix plant at Amory and asked if he planned to sell gravel to Pontotoc County. When Mr. Burt said yes, they asked the price, and he told them $3.15 per yard for washed rock.

Nix and Finley said that they were paying at that time $3.65 per yard to North Mississippi Gravel Company at Amory. They suggested that Burt submit a bid 50 cents higher than he had planned and simply give the Pontotoc supervisors personally the difference, or 50 cents a yard, in cash. Mr. Burt stated that he had agreed to do this because he needed the work, thinking at first that he would stop the practice after one year when his business was established, that in fact he never stopped it until 1987 when the FBI's Operation Pretense became public with the indictment of two other Pontotoc county supervisors.

The United States would further show that Mr. Burt submitted bids to nine other northeast Mississippi counties and won the bid in one district in Itawamba County and three districts in Lee County, but that his bid to Pontotoc County was always substantially higher than his bids in all other counties.

Mr. Burt sold gravel to all five districts of Pontotoc County from January 1982 to February 1987, with the exception of former Pontotoc County supervisor Bobby Dean Stegall's district, which only purchased gravel from Mr. Burt for a few months and then transferred its business to another company.

Shortly after the visit of supervisors Nix and Finley, Pontotoc County supervisor Theron Baldwin also brought Pontotoc supervisor Grady Baker to meet Mr. Burt and confirmed that Mr. Baker would receive the same 50-cent per yard cash kickback all four others were receiving. Mr. Baldwin later told Mr. Burt that the supervisors had been getting only 10-cent or 15-cent kickbacks from their previous gravel supplier.

From January 1982 through February 1987 Bull Mountain paid cash kickbacks to the four Pontotoc County supervisors named above without ever missing a month. . . .

. . . About two months after supervisors Baker and Baldwin were indicted, supervisor O. L. Finley came to Bull Mountain one more time and asked for the payoff envelops but was told there would not be anymore and left.

In April 1988, Burt was sentenced by Judge Biggers to serve six months of a three-year prison term and three years' probation based on his plea of guilty to one count of fraud. After his sentencing, Burt said, "I'd just like to say that I'm glad that it's over with. It's been a burden and a hardship." Assistant U.S. Attorney John Hailman noted that Burt had been cooperating with the investigation and said that his case was "a commentary on the system more than it is on Mr. Burt." Hailman claimed, "The whole system is totally rotten. It's a systemic problem. The county government system is thoroughly and totally corrupt. It cannot be cured without a change in the system." No doubt Hailman's comments reflected the fact that Burt had himself been a victim of extortion by Pontotoc County supervisors. In fact, at sentencing, Judge Biggers said, "It's almost like the supervisors extorted you."

Fifty-three-year-old Jarvis Dearman, owner of Dearman Gulf Oil Products in Leaksville, was indicted on bribery charges on November 6, 1987, in Jackson. The three-count indictment alleged that Dearman paid Greene County supervisor Lauvon Pierce $800 in kickbacks on county purchases between November 1986 and January 1987. As noted in chapter 18, Pierce had been indicted in March 1987 on Pretense-related charges, and he pleaded guilty based on a plea bargain in May 1987. Dearman's indictment was the result of Pierce's cooperation with the Pretense investigation.

Dearman entered a plea agreement with the prosecution in which he agreed to plead guilty to one count of bribery, pay restitution, and cooperate in the ongoing investigation. The government agreed to recommend a sentence not exceeding three years and to make no recommendation as to fines. In late April 1988, Dearman pleaded guilty to one count of bribery, admitting that he paid Pierce a $300 kickback on November 5, 1986. Judge Barbour scheduled sentencing for June 14, at which time Dearman was sentenced to serve three months in prison and fined $5,000.

Epilogue

Will the Beat Return?

Claiborne County supervisors were in trouble again in early 1998, long after Pretense had been shut down. Two supervisors and a county employee pleaded guilty in April 1998 to bilking Claiborne County of nearly $25,000. District two supervisor Edward Carter, district five supervisor Charles Johnson, and secretary Charlene Moore pleaded guilty in Claiborne County circuit court to one count each of embezzlement. The charges resulted from of a year-long investigation by the state attorney general and the Department of Audit. At least one other supervisor was a target of the continuing investigation. Attorney General Mike Moore, who termed the setup a "Mickey Mouse" scheme, explained how it had worked from 1995 to 1997. "Basically the scheme was that these supervisors would submit invoices for work done by ghost employees, people who did not work for the county. A check would be written for these ghost employees, and the supervisors themselves and others for them would go to the bank—believe it or not—and the stores and cash these checks ranging anywhere from about $200 to $950, and get the cash money and take it home." At a news conference on April 13, 1998, State Auditor Phil Bryant said that he had issued demand letters to the two supervisors for more than $76,000. This amount included money misspent for advertisements and donations as well as the sum tied to the embezzlement charges. Claiborne is a poor county, and, Bryant said, "To embezzle tax money from among the poorest is the worst of the cases we have to deal with, and we are just not going to let that happen."

Johnson, who had been in office since before Pretense, pleaded guilty to embezzling $11,780. Carter, who had been in office seven years, pleaded guilty to embezzling $8,834. Charlene Moore, who had been employed by the county fifteen years, pleaded guilty to embezzling $4,165. Attorney General Mike Moore recommended full restitution and a sentence of at least one year in jail. He claimed that this recommendation was not the incentive for the defendants to plead guilty and not go to trial, it was the amount of evidence against them. The attorney general said, "These supervisors ought to go to prison. They stole from the public and they violated the public trust, and I think the judge ought to send them to prison." Moore also said that the supervisors had been removed from office by court action after they pleaded guilty.

Claiborne County operated under the unit system in 1998. This made it more difficult to defraud the county because collusion between county employees was required to circumvent internal accounting controls. It seems that this is what made it necessary for Charlene Moore, the county administrator's secretary, three clerks, and others to cooperate with the supervisors in the scheme outlined above. The clerks had agreed to cooperate in the investigation to avoid charges against them.

Albert Butler, who was the only supervisor tried and found innocent of Pretense-related charges, was now president of the Claiborne County Board of Supervisors. Butler revealed that a citizen's complaint had triggered the investigation by the Department of Audit and the attorney general. State Auditor Phil Bryant said that the system now in place to detect theft and the misuse of tax money had improved chances of catching those who cheat the taxpayer. Bryant also indicated that the corrupt practices in 1998 didn't compare to the blatant bribes and kickbacks that supervisors had accepted in the 1980s when supervisors purchased "invisible pipe" and shorted their counties on purchases of pipe, grader blades, and chemicals.

Another big improvement since the Pretense investigation was the amount of cooperation between the Department of Audit and the Office of the Attorney General in rooting out corruption. A lawyer from the attorney general's office worked with the Department of Audit to give advice up front and to work to collect repayment demands. Phil Bryant, the Republican state auditor, and Attorney General Mike Moore, a Democrat, had greatly enhanced coordination between their offices. Moore said, "It used to be that the state Department of Audit would work cases, and we would have very little involvement. They would just turn them over to our office, and then we would have to completely investigate and start from the beginning again and decide whether there was a prosecutable case." Bryant said the partnership had resulted in better investigations and clockworklike collections. Thirty days after a demand letter for repayment of misspent or misappropriated funds is issued, the case goes to the attorney general's office for legal action if the demand hasn't been paid

On May 19, 1998, Circuit Judge Lamar Pickard sentenced Edward Carter and Charles Johnson to a year in prison, imposed a four-year suspended sentence, and ordered them to repay Claiborne County the funds that they had embezzled. He also fined each man $2,000. The judge ordered both men jailed immediately, and they were taken from the courtroom in handcuffs. Charlene Moore was sentenced to five years, all of which were suspended, and five years' probation. She was also ordered to pay $4,165 in restitution.

This incident revived memories of Operation Pretense and the ensuing but unfinished struggle to move county government from the beat to the unit system. On April 20, 1998, a front-page story in the *Clarion-Ledger* headlined "Supervisors Guilt Eerily Reminiscent" related the Claiborne County convictions to Operation Pretense. It indicated that the whole scenario was similar to the conditions that caused the Reverend John Burgess to go to the FBI with a story that ultimately resulted in Operation Pretense. It noted, however, that Attorney General Mike Moore said the problem that he saw did not approach the level exposed by Pretense. Moore said, "We have a few cases under investigation right now with some inflated bills and kickbacks. After Operation Pretense, a few years went by and a lot of people were up to the same games. The good thing we've done is change the way county government operates. The unit system has helped a lot."

Probably the most significant thing about the 1998 prosecution of the Claiborne County officials and employees is that only state agencies were involved. Things had improved so much that there was no need for an FBI sting or for prosecution by the U.S. attorney. This was indeed different, and it showed that laws and institutions had changed for the better in the eleven years since Operation Pretense was revealed to the public.

Nevertheless, many of the state's counties were still operating under the beat system eleven years after Pretense became public. The *Clarion-Ledger* editorialized about this in its April 26, 1998, issue:

Counties—The Beat Goes On, Unfortunately

The move to the unit system of county government was a significant improvement for Mississippi taxpayers. The old "beat" system is inefficient and wasteful of taxpayers' dollars. Under that system, supervisors basically have five little fiefdoms, and each serves as a county road board of supervisors for a district. The unit system brought some sensibility to county government administration. Supervisors set policy, but a single road manager oversees the needs of the entire county, better utilizing personnel and equipment. It also brings more accountability for finances and forces supervisors to spend their time on matters of policy. There is only one problem in this county reform. Only 44 of the state's 82 counties operate under a unit system. Thirty-eight counties still use the old beat system, with all the political cronyism and inefficiency it brings. The Mississippi Economic Council (MEC) has been a longtime advocate of this very important county reform effort. It continues to urge citizens in beat system counties to tell supervisors to go to the unit system and quit wasting taxpayers' money. The MEC is right. As we move into the 21st century, county government should be moving to further refine government operations. Unfortunately, 38 counties are still stuck in the 19th century with the beat system. As Mississippi approaches county elections next year, the unit system should be a priority for voters in those 38 counties.

At least one Madison County supervisor was still resisting full implementation of a major feature of the unit system in the summer of 1998. David Richardson of district three, one of the supervisors who forced the purchase of the backhoes from Tubb-Williamson, Inc. in 1984, decided to become a heavy equipment operator on roads in his district in 1998. This led to a confrontation with fellow supervisor J. L. McCullough and to a series of events that would be comical if it were not for their implications concerning the quality of county government.

In the summer of 1998, McCullough charged fellow supervisor and one-time ally David Richardson with assault. McCullough had confronted Richardson on August 19, 1998, as Richardson operated a road grader while assisting a crew that was resurfacing Lake Castle Road in his district. From atop the road grader, Richardson kicked McCullough as he approached. McCullough said his presence at the site was motivated by his concern that Richardson was intimidating a road crew and interfering with their work, which was not appropriate under the unit system of county government. McCullough later charged Richardson with assault in Justice Court. Justice Court Judge Tommy Faulkner presided over the October 1998 case and found Richardson guilty of simple assault, sentenced him to a ninety-day suspended jail term and a year's probation, and fined him $250. Ironically, the judge in the case, Tommy Faulkner, had served as Madison County road manager for about two months in 1992. Both Richardson and McCullough had voted to fire him from that position.

The *Clarion-Ledger* ran the following editorial on October 19, 1998:

Madison Supes—McCullough, Richardson Both to Blame

The Aug. 19 foolishness between Madison County Supervisors J. L. McCullough and David Richardson has been settled by one court but it's a hollow victory. The tiff between them came about when McCullough discovered Richardson operating a road grader on Lake Castle Road. Madison county is under the unit system and supervisors are supposed to be independent of daily operations. McCullough blocked the grader and approached Richardson, McCullough admits thinking of attacking Richardson. Richardson kicked McCullough and now Justice Court Judge Tommy Faulkner has found Richardson guilty of simple assault. Richardson has been fined $250 plus court cost and one year probation. That's not enough. Since both supervisors are to blame (McCullough for rushing Richardson; Richardson for kicking McCullough; and both for behaving like children), they both should be punished. Both should be forced to apologize to the people of Madison County, pay all cost due taxpayers for their time wasted on this mess, and both be put on probation for jail time if they don't cease and desist in their childish displays. The People's Court will rule at the next election.

The board of supervisors, by a three to two vote on November 2, 1998, removed county equipment from David Richardson's district three. The board's action was designed to ensure that the county was actually operating the unit system as required by law. Richardson screamed foul but to no avail.

State Auditor Phil Bryant got into the fracas over the operation of road equipment as a result of the Madison County incident and a similar one in Jackson County. After Hurricane Georges passed through Jackson County in early October 1998, supervisor Tommy Brodnax operated county equipment for several days during the cleanup of his district. The Department of Audit discovered that the unit system law did not explicitly prohibit supervisors from operating road equipment. Consequently, Bryant requested an attorney general's opinion on whether supervisors in unit counties could operate road equipment. Bryant stated, "It is the position of the state auditor's office that the state law forbids supervisors under normal circumstances, in a unit system of government, from operating county equipment. The law is broad in nature and not well defined." Bryant said that he would probably ask the legislature to amend the law to explicitly prohibit such activity and to make violations misdemeanors punishable by fines and imprisonment. Bryant indicated that an attorney general's opinion could possibly give his office interim authority to prohibit supervisors from operating county equipment until the legislature had time to amend the statute.

In late September 1998, Brodnax was being investigated by the Department of Audit based on a complaint that he was violating regulations that govern the unit system of county government. The complaint had been filed in June, and the Department of Audit would not reveal who filed it. Brodnax denied the charges. The county stood to lose up to $750,000 in state road funds if the state auditor found that the supervisor had violated the unit system law. Brodnax was accused of maintaining a satellite office at the county's west roads district office in Ocean Springs and directing road crews. If Brodnax were found by the auditors to be in violation of the law, state funds designated for the county could be placed in escrow until the violation was corrected. If the violations were not corrected within ninety days of the funds being placed in escrow, the county would lose all of the money.

The auditors' investigation determined that Brodnax had violated the unit system law by giving road crews direct orders and that county officials had violated the law by holding state road taxes collected from cities in special accounts. A September 21 letter from Bryant to the board of supervisors outlined the violations and gave county officials thirty days to correct the problem. The deadline was extended after Hurricane Georges hit the county later that month. Brodnax admitted that he operated county equipment for several days after the passage of Hurricane Georges. Phil Bryant said, "The state auditor's office normally does not take exception to any supervisor working for the cleanup effort as long as the work is being done for the general health and welfare of the public at large." Bryant also said, "I have asked the attorney general's office to review the law on this matter to help this office better enforce compliance in the county's unit system." The resulting opinion said an elected supervisor, "may not physically operate county road equipment or personally perform any other work on road construction or maintenance."

In mid-November, State Auditor Phil Bryant announced that he would ask the 1999 legislature to pass a law that would impose a fine on individual county officials who break the unit system law. Langston Moore, a spokesperson for the state auditor, explained the problem, "Right now, if we go into a county and find it in non-compliance, we have to write a letter to the State Tax Commission and the attorney general. This starts the process of taking away state aid road funds. This is bad because we are making the citizens suffer because of the actions of one supervisor, who is not penalized for his actions. Instead, the citizens are."

In an early January 1999 letter to the Jackson County Board of Supervisors, State Auditor Bryant told the supervisors that a review of the steps taken in October had shown that the board had put the county in compliance with state law. Bryant indicated that, while his office would continue to monitor the situation, he recognized "the efforts made by all the officers and employees of Jackson County to correct your problems in order to substantially comply with the mandated systems." The county did not lose the $750,000 in state road funds.

The 1999 legislature strengthened the unit system law by making supervisors liable for violations that they personally commit. Each personal violation could cost a supervisor $5,000 under the new legislation. Brodnax said, "Some people are calling that the Tommy Brodnax law because of what I did during the hurricane, but I'm not ashamed of what I did. But I won't be doing it again. I can't afford $5,000 every time I put my hand on a piece of county equipment."

As inconceivable as it seems, Lincoln County voted to revert to the beat system in early 2000, and the Mississippi legislature considered forcing all unit system counties to vote on whether to switch to the beat system.

The *Clarion Ledger* ran the following editorial on March 5, 2000, after the bill was defeated.

UNIT SYSTEM
County Corruption Demands Change

Despite its legacy of corruption and inefficiency, it took years for Mississippi to start getting rid of the old "beat system" of county government.

But good ol' boy politicians keep fighting to bring it back.

Thankfully, their last attempts were thwarted.

On Tuesday the House killed a bill that would have allowed the 47 unit system counties to vote on reverting to the old system in 2003.

Backers complained that the unit system, which employs a central purchasing system, was not as cost-efficient.

That's a bogus argument.

In a beat system, supervisors control all aspects of county upkeep in their respective districts, or beats, including roads. A unit system requires a road manager to oversee the whole county and forces supervisors to do what they are supposed to do: operate in a policy-making role.

Some supervisors don't like the unit system one bit. They chafe under the restraints of being publicly accountable, rather than having a free hand to run their districts, or beats like fiefdoms.

The unit system was mandated for a vote by counties in 1988 for a very good reason: widespread public corruption uprooted by the massive FBI Operation Pretense sting.

About one-quarter of Mississippi's supervisors were found to be taking kickbacks and other bribes from equipment and material suppliers in the sting operation. Indeed, it was considered standard operating procedure for county business.

More than half the counties switched. Since then some counties have tried to maneuver a return to the old beat system. Their usual "pretense" is that the unit system is less cost-efficient. Less cost-efficient than what? Corruption?

As long ago as 1932 a Brookings Institution study commissioned by the Legislature concluded that the beat system was inefficient and, even then, recommended the unit system. Every study since has had the same results.

If there was any remaining doubt, it should have been nailed shut by Operation Pretense.

Is there any reason for bills to surface in any session of the Legislature to restore the beat system?

Mississippi citizens have savvy enough to figure out that someone stands to benefit, and it's not the taxpayers.

The lawmakers were right to kill this snake of a bill, in fact, they should be moving to require the unit system in all counties, not allowing supervisors to backslide.

The editorial captures well the essence of Operation Pretense. However, central purchasing is actually required for all counties as a result of the 1988 legislation, not just the unit counties. Also, a little over one-eighth, not one-quarter, of Mississippi's supervisors were convicted as a result of Pretense. No doubt the percentage of supervisors convicted would have been much greater had the undercover investigation covered all eighty-two counties rather than twenty-six. Because of the strain on the undercover agents and security concerns, the investigation was halted by the federal authorities when they had secured enough evidence to make an "Impact Statement" concerning the corrupt system. Local authorities were expected to pick up the ball and effect the necessary reforms.

Continued vigilance on the part of the honest citizens of Mississippi, like the Reverend John Burgess, is the only way that taxpayers can be protected from the reappearance of the conditions that necessitated Operation Pretense. Operation Pretense left in its wake devastated lives, lost political careers, significant reforms in county government, and changes in the day-to-day operations of county government. However, the reforms resulting from Pretense were far from perfect. A goal of the author was to document the important details of Operation Pretense and related matters in one place and to demonstrate that vigilance is necessary to prevent a similar scandal in the future. It is hoped that the book will serve as a reminder of the conditions that allowed corruption to flourish and that it will prod the citizens of Mississippi to continue the reforms that Operation Pretense spawned.

Appendix A

Counties and Their Officials Who Were Charged Under Operation Pretense, Indicted Highway Commissioners, and Vendors Charged in Operation Pretense—Disposition of the Cases

Counties

Attala (Chapter 14):
Belk, Colon—District Five
Pleaded guilty to one count. Sentenced to 18 months in prison and fined $1,000.
Ellard, Robert—District Three
Pleaded guilty to two counts. Sentenced to 18 months in prison, fined $2,000, and ordered to serve 3 years' probation.
Fancher, David—District Two
Pleaded guilty to one count. Sentenced to 18 months in prison, fined $500, and ordered to pay restitution of $370.

Claiborne (Chapter 5):
Burrell, Eddie—District One
Pleaded guilty to two counts. Sentenced to 5 years in prison with 4½ years suspended, fined $5,000, ordered to serve 5 years' probation, and ordered to pay restitution of $12,100.
Butler, Albert—District Four
Went to trial and found not guilty on all four charges.

Clarke (Chapter 17):
Becton, Lige—District Five
Pleaded guilty to two counts.

Sentenced to 5 years in prison with 4½ years suspended, fined $10,000, ordered to serve 5 years' probation, and ordered to pay $609 in restitution.
Spivey, Francis M.—District One
Pleaded guilty to three counts. Sentenced to 3 years in prison, fined $3,000, ordered to serve 5 years' probation, and ordered to pay restitution totaling $765.

Copiah (Chapter 18):
Berry, Barry "Ted"—District Five
Pleaded guilty to two counts. Sentenced to 3 years in prison, fined $5,000, ordered to serve 5 years' probation, and ordered to pay restitution of $2,753.
Heard, Thomas M.—District One
Pleaded guilty to two counts. Sentenced to 10 years in prison and ordered to serve 5 years' probation. Also sentenced to 16 years in prison on unrelated state charges.
Thompson, Sidney—District Three
Pleaded guilty to two counts. Sentenced to 5 years in prison with 3½ years suspended, fined $2,000, ordered to serve 5 years' probation,

and ordered to pay restitution on $1,474.65.

Covington (Chapter 18):
Wade, Wiley Tom—District Five
Pleaded guilty to one count.
Sentenced to 5 years with all but 3
months suspended, fined $5,000,
ordered to serve 5 years' probation,
and ordered to pay restitution of
$2,115.72.

Greene (Chapter 18):
Crocker, John M.—District Four
Pleaded guilty to two counts.
Sentenced to 3 years in prison, fined
$5,000, ordered to serve 5 years'
probation, and ordered to pay
restitution totaling $2,700.
Pierce, Lauvon—District Five
Pleaded guilty to one count.
Sentence suspended, ordered to
serve 5 years' probation, fined
$5,000, and ordered to pay
restitution of $730.
Smith, George Ivan—District Three
Pleaded guilty to two counts.
Sentenced to 2 years in prison, fined
$5,000, ordered to serve 5 years'
probation, and ordered to pay
restitution of $666.

Hancock (Chapter 19):
Courrege, Burt—District One
Pleaded guilty to one count.
Sentenced to 1 year in prison that
was suspended, fined $1,000, ordered
to serve 5 years' probation, and
ordered to pay $60 in restitution.
Ladner, Roger Dale—District Three
Pleaded guilty to two counts.
Sentenced to serve one year and one
day in prison, fined $2,000, ordered
to serve 5 years' probation, and

ordered to pay restitution of
$1,598.25.
Perniciaro, Sam J., Sr.—District Four
Pleaded guilty to two counts.
Sentenced to 3 years in prison with
all but 2 months suspended, fined
$5,000, ordered to serve 5 years'
probation, and ordered to pay
restitution of $946.12.
Travirca, James N.—District Five
Pleaded guilty to two counts.
Sentenced to 6 years in prison with
all but 6 months suspended, fined
$1,000, ordered to serve 5 years'
probation, and ordered to pay
restitution of $1,100.

Harrison (Chapter 19):
Moffat, Eddie—District Two
Pleaded guilty to two counts.
Sentenced to 1 year and a day in
prison, fined $2,000, ordered to
serve 5 years' probation, and ordered
to pay restitution of $950.

Jackson (Chapter 19):
Robinson, Fred, Jr.—District Two
Pleaded guilty to two counts.
Sentenced to 1 year and a day in
prison, fined $10,000, and ordered to
serve 5 years' probation.
Thompson, Maury (Road
Foreman)—District Two
Pleaded guilty to one count.
Sentenced to 5 years' probation and
ordered to pay fines and restitution
totaling $880.

Jasper (Chapter 17):
Graham, Rex L.—District Four
Pleaded guilty to two counts.
Sentenced to 5 years in prison, fined
$5,000, ordered to serve 5 years'
probation, and ordered to pay
restitution of $1,506.

Ulmer, John Robert—District Three
Pleaded guilty to two counts.
Sentenced to two years in prison
with the entire two years suspended,
ordered to serve five years'
probation, ordered to perform 400
hours of community service, fined
$5,000 and ordered to pay $892 in
restitution.

Lamar (Chapter 4):
Lott, Pascal—District One
Pleaded guilty to two counts.
Sentenced to 5 years in prison with
4½ years suspended, fined $5,000,
ordered to serve 5 years' probation,
and ordered to pay restitution of
$350.
Rayborn, Kermit—District Five
Went to trial and was convicted on 3
of 4 counts.
Sentenced to 6 years in prison, fined
$10,000, ordered to serve 5 years'
probation, and ordered to pay
restitution of $1,200.

Lauderdale (Chapter 15):
Brown, William (Rev.)—District Two
Pleaded guilty to two counts.
Sentenced to 1 year and 1 day in
prison, fined $2,000, ordered to
serve 5 years' probation, and ordered
to pay restitution of $1,516.15.
Harris, Billy Joe—District Four
Pleaded guilty to two counts.
Sentenced to 6 years in prison,
ordered to serve 5 years' probation,
fined $5,000, and ordered to pay
restitution of $4,400.

Leake (Chapter 14):
Freeny, James L.—District One
Pleaded guilty to two counts.
Sentenced to 5 years in prison, fined
$10,000, ordered to serve 5 years'

probation, and ordered to pay
restitution totaling $583.
Jones, Thomas Jack—District Five
Pleaded guilty to two counts.
Sentenced to 3 years in prison,
ordered to serve 5 years' probation,
fined $5,000, and ordered to pay
restitution totaling $1,839,98.
Myers, Deward Dean—District Three
Pleaded guilty to four counts.
Sentenced to 3 years in prison, fined
$5,000, and ordered to serve 5 years'
probation.

Lincoln (Chapter 18):
Britt, F. H.—District Five
Pleaded guilty to two counts.
Sentenced to 5 years in prison with
4½ years suspended, and fined
$3,000.

Marion (Chapter 7):
Moree, Sim Ed—District Two
Pleaded guilty to two counts of a
Pretense-related indictment.
Sentenced to 5 years in prison,
ordered to pay restitution of
$4,084.31, and ordered to serve 5
years' probation.
Went to trial and was convicted on
obstruction of justice charges.
Sentenced to 21 months in prison,
ordered to serve 3 years' probation,
and ordered to perform 400 hours of
community service.

Monroe (Chapter 13):
Cockerham, John Allen—District Three
Pleaded guilty to 1 count.
Sentenced to 2 years in prison, fined
$10,000, and ordered to pay
restitution of $15,100.
Faulkner, Leonard—District One
Pleaded guilty to two counts.
Sentenced to 18 months in prison,

ordered to serve two years' probation, fined $1,000, and ordered to pay restitution of $623.

Neshoba (Chapter 14):

Holly, John S.—District Five
Pleaded guilty to two counts.
Sentenced to 5 years in prison, ordered to serve 5 years' probation, fined $5,000, and ordered to pay restitution of $1,609.

Posey, Willard—District One
Pleaded guilty to two counts.
Sentenced to 2 years in prison, fined $5,000, and ordered to serve 5 years' probation.

Winstead, Arlo—District Three
Pleaded guilty to two counts.
Sentenced to 5 years in prison with 4½ years suspended, fined $10,000 and ordered to pay restitution of $421.

Newton (Chapter 15):

Edwards, William E.—District Five
Pleaded guilty to two counts.
Sentenced to 3 years in prison, and ordered to pay restitution totaling $1,630.

Hollingsworth, Harold—District One
Pleaded not guilty to 9 counts.
Died while under indictment; the charges were dismissed after his death.

Pinson, Durwood "Doc"—District Two
Pleaded guilty to two counts.
Sentenced to 5 years in prison with 4½ years suspended, ordered to serve 5 years' probation, fined $5,000, and ordered to pay restitution of $168.

Smith, Henry Mack—District Three
Pleaded guilty to two counts.
Sentenced to 3 years in prison, fined $1,000, ordered to serve 5 years' probation, and ordered to pay restitution totaling $3,023.

Panola (Chapter 13):

Mathews, Horace C.—District One
Pleaded guilty to one count.
Sentenced to 2 years in prison and fined $1,000.

Perry (Chapter 2):

Bowen, William F.—District Three
Charged with six counts.
Found mentally incompetent to stand trial.

Mixon, G. F.—District One
Pleaded guilty to two counts.
Sentenced to one year in prison, fined $20,000, ordered to serve 5 years' probation, and ordered to pay a total of $920 in restitution.
Died before serving any time.

Westmoreland, Trudie P.—District Four
Went to trial and was convicted on all six charges.
Sentenced to 9 years in prison (later reduced to 6 years), fined $10,000, and ordered to pay restitution totaling $2,003.

Pontotoc (Chapter 13):

Baker, Grady O.—District One
Pleaded guilty to three counts.
Sentenced to 2 years in prison and fined $3,000.

Baldwin, Theron—District Four
Pleaded guilty to three counts.
Sentenced to 2 years in prison and fined $3,000.

Finley, O. L.—District Three
Pleaded guilty to one count.
Sentenced to 18 months in prison and fined $1,000.

Nix, Talmage—District Two
Pleaded guilty to one count.
Sentenced to 2 years in prison and fined $500.

Stegall, Bobby—District Five

Pleaded guilty to one count.
Sentenced to 2 years in prison with
1½ years suspended and fined $1,000.

Rankin (Chapter 16):

Bridges, Kenneth—District Three
Pleaded guilty to state charges of
embezzlement and fraud committed
in public office.
Sentenced to 6 months in the Rankin
County jail with the sentence
suspended conditioned on good
behavior, resignation from office,
not seeking reelection for one year,
and not participating in the selection
of a successor.

Smith, Herbert—District One
Pleaded guilty to state charges of
embezzlement and fraud committed
in public office.
Sentenced to 6 months in the Rankin
County jail with the sentence
suspended conditioned on good
behavior, resignation from office,
not seeking reelection for one year,
not participating in the selection of a
successor, and continuing to
cooperate with the FBI as it might
request.
Note: The three other Rankin
County supervisors pleaded guilty to
non Pretense-related state charges of
violating bidding and purchasing
laws and were given sentences
similar to those of Bridges and
Smith. The other three supervisors
were Ralph H. Moore, Mike C.
Ponder, and Hilton R. Richardson.

Scott (Chapter 15):

Weems, Isaac, Jr.—District Five
Pleaded guilty to two counts.
Sentenced to a year and a day in
prison, fined $5,000, ordered to serve
5 years' probation, and ordered to
pay restitution totaling $230.

Smith (Chapter 17):

Blakeney, Charles "Hop"—District Two
Pleaded guilty to two counts.
Sentenced to 3 years in prison, fined
$5,000, ordered to serve 5 years'
probation, and pay restitution
totaling $2,340.

Wayne (Chapter 3):

Duvall, Jimmie T.—District Three
Went to trial and was convicted on 3
of 17 counts.
Sentenced to 6 years in prison, fined
$10,000, ordered to serve 5 years'
probation, and ordered to pay
restitution of $2,247.

Hutto, William H.—District Five
Went to trial and was convicted on
all six charges.
Sentenced to 6 years in prison, fined
$10,000, ordered to serve 5 years'
probation, and ordered to pay
restitution of $900.

Revette, Alfred Grant—District One
Went to trial and was convicted on 3
of 17 counts.
Sentenced to 7 years in prison, fined
$10,000, ordered to serve 5 years'
probation, and ordered to pay
restitution of $4,042.

Winston (Chapter 6):

Miller, Larry—District Four
Went to trial and was convicted of all
seven charges.
Sentenced to 6 years in prison,
ordered to serve 3 years' probation,
and ordered to pay restitution of
$1,051.40.

Joiner, Robert Earl (Bob)—Southern District Highway Commissioner

Pleaded guilty to two counts. Sentenced to 6 years in prison, fined $100,000, ordered to serve 5 years' probation, and ordered to pay all back taxes including fines and interest.

Waggoner, Sam—Central District Highway Commissioner

Pleaded guilty to 4 counts. Sentenced to 2 years in prison, and fined $100,000,

Vendors

Barrett, Gaston—President of Central Culvert and Supply Company (Chapter 20)

Pleaded guilty to two counts. Sentenced to 3 years in prison with 2½ years suspended, ordered to serve 3 years' probation, and fined $7,500.

Burt, Lee Hollis—Operator of Bull Mountain Gravel Company (Chapter 20)

Pleaded guilty to one count. Sentenced to 3 years in prison with 2½ years suspended. Burt cooperated extensively in the investigation.

Dacus, Pete—Salesman for Holiman Equipment Company (Chapter 20)

All charges were dismissed. Dacus cooperated extensively in the investigation.

Davis, Ray—President of Davis Chemicals (Chapter 20)

Pleaded guilty to two counts. Sentenced to 5 years' probation. Davis was "flipped" by the prosecutors and he provided much help in the investigation.

Dearman, Jarvis—Owner of Dearman Gulf Oil Products (Chapter 20)

Pleaded guilty to one count.

Sentenced to 3 months in prison and fined $5,000.

Gilbert, Max—Part owner of Holiman Equipment and owner of L & M Equipment (Chapter 20)

Pleaded guilty to one count. Sentenced to 3 years in prison with all but 4 months suspended, fined $5,000, and ordered to serve 5 years' probation.

Harrison, Billy Ray—Salesman for Mississippi Pipe & Oil Company (Chapter 20)

Pleaded guilty to two counts. Sentenced to 3 years in prison with all 3 years suspended, ordered to serve 3 years' probation, fined $5,000, and ordered to make restitution of $2,418.

Little, Bobby R.—President of North Mississippi Supply Company (Chapter 8)

Went to trial and was convicted on 241 of 264 counts. Sentenced to 6 years in prison, and fined $25,000. North Mississippi Supply Company also fined $50,000.

Lott, Billy Rex—Salesman for Puckett Machinery Company (Chapter 20)

Pleaded guilty to one count. Sentenced to 6 years in prison, fined

$5,000, and ordered to pay $10,800 in restitution.

Polk, William L., III—Salesman for Mississippi Pipe & Oil Company (Chapter 20)

Agreed to plead guilty to conspiracy charges.

All charges dismissed at the request of the U.S. Attorney.

Polk cooperated extensively in the investigation.

Smith, Jessie M.—Salesman for Consolidated Culvert and Supply Company (Chapter 20)

Pleaded guilty to 3 counts.

Sentenced to 5 years in prison, fined $10,000, and ordered to serve 5 years' probation.

Smith, Ray Dowell—Smith's Diesel Sales and Service (Chapter 20)

Pleaded guilty to one count.

Sentenced to 5 years in prison with all but 4 months suspended, fined $10,000, and ordered to serve 4 years and 8 months probation.

Williamson, Johnnie H.—Co-owner of Tubb-Williamson, Inc. (Chapter 20)

Pleaded guilty to one count.

Given a suspended sentence, ordered to live in a halfway house for 3 months, fined $10,000, and ordered to pay restitution totaling $8,900.

Appendix B

The Tale of the Tapes

The following are excerpts from transcripts of taped conversations between FBI agents and supervisors that took place during Operation Pretense. The transcripts were obtained by the author under the Freedom of Information Act. The taped conversations explain how the "drum-of-the-month club" worked, how "complimentary bids" were obtained, how invoices were "split" to avoid state law, and how supervisors were rewarded for bringing other supervisors into the undercover sting.

1. A conversation between a Copiah County supervisor and FBI special agent Jerry King (posing as Jerry Jacobs, salesman for Mid-State Pipe and Supply Company) that was taped December 19, 1995, explains how the "drum-of-the-month club" worked.

Agent: I'm gonna have to give 'em a deal like I'm giving some of my buddies in . . . I got this drum of the month lay-away program. (Laughs).
Supervisor: Uh-huh.
Agent: If anybody's interested.
Supervisor: Yeah.
Agent: What I do on that is uh . . . I do that at the (Mississippi Association of Supervisors) convention. Last year I did that quite a bit. Uh, guys, think that they need three hundred bucks, they're gonna give me an order. We don't write it up or nothin. They just say, "I want uh six drums in the next six months, give me a drum a month." And, so I give 'em three hundred dollars, that's fifty dollars a barrel. I give that up to 'em up front, and then I just . . . Now, if I don't deliver it, if they call me up the second month, and say, "I don't want this month." Then I owe them a hundred and fifty.
Supervisor: Uh-huh.
Agent: So, I get 'em fifty on the two hundred. See, so, that's how that works. And that's, that's been real good for me.

2. A conversation between FBI special agent Jerry King and Perry County district four supervisor Trudie Supervisor that was taped February 5, 1986, explains how "complementary bids" and "invoice splitting" were used to thwart state purchasing laws.

Supervisor: Uh, but, now you gonna have to bill these one one month and one the next month.

Agent: I gotcha. We'll take care of that. That comes in twelve and that's, uh, thirty-eight O eight a foot. Okay?

Supervisor: Okay.

Agent: Okay. That'll do it.

Supervisor: And we can put these together.

Agent: Yeah. That's a good whack for us. Okay. All right. Now you want those two, right?

Supervisor: Uh huh.

Agent: All right. Now are you going to need a second quote?

Supervisor: Yeah.

Agent: Okay (Agent was to secure the second "complementary" quote from a cooperating vendor). I, I can keep . . .

Supervisor: Anything over five hundred dollars you have to have two quotes, right?

Agent: Right. Now the only problem I can see running in here.

Supervisor: Yeah.

Agent: It's going to get over fifteen hundred dollars (which would require written bids).

Supervisor: With our sixty inch (culvert pipe).

Agent: I guarantee you. Thirty-eight . . .

Supervisor: Twenty-four foot of sixty, I know, I'm gonna need two of 'em now.

Agent: That's what I'm saying, see.

Supervisor: Well you just gonna have to bill 'em out differently now.

Agent: I know it. I know it. I will. Okay.

Supervisor: You gonna have to separate 'em.

Agent: All right. No problem. I mean as long . . .

Supervisor: Hell, long as you know how to figure it out.

Agent: Hey, I can do it. Now I'm good at that.

Supervisor: Now don't screw me up on my paperwork.

Agent: Naw. Naw. We're gonna get that straight. But see that is, uh, like I said that's, uh, thirty-eight, thirty-eight O eight, but I just went thirty-eight. Okay. Thirty-eight times . . . I tell you what I'm gonna do then. I can, I tell you what we, what, before I go on and start figuring all these up, on the grader blades . . .

Supervisor: Uh huh.

Agent: I'll also work, split with you on those if you, since you've got some on the yard, you know, and it's really, it's covered you know, those are throw away stuff anyway. I do that all the time. So you know, that way it's just flat and what I'm saying is on a couple of these invoices I might be able to fill in just a, a few, but, you know, on a blank . . .

Supervisor: Uh huh.

Agent: or two, you know, and add it in there and it'll still be under the fifteen hundred and, it'll be, or I can separate invoice it or whatever. And, you know, I'll just split that.

Supervisor: Okay.

Agent: So.

Supervisor: Sounds good.

Agent: All right. You want me to work a couple hundred up like that or a hundred

Supervisor: Be fine.

Agent: for you? What, okay. All right . . .

3. A Copiah County supervisor and FBI special agent Jerry King discuss busting invoices on weed killer in a conversation taped August 7, 1985.

Supervisor: That weed killer will work all right as long as you got enough stuff going through a company and all that can cover it up but, uh . . .

Agent: Yeah.

Supervisor: when you get somebody that ain't sending none to amount to much . . .

Agent: Yeah.

Supervisor: like you saying and all you don't know whether it's steam cleaner, soap, or Joy dishwashing liquid.

Agent: That's right. Well even if you got the right stuff in there, see, that, that barrel . . .

Supervisor: Yeah.

Agent: as long as you got a barrel of stuff there, I mean you could've bought three you, I mean you know . . .

Supervisor: Yeah.

Agent: There's no way, there's no problem with that stuff. That stuff goes for sixteen ninety-five a gallon and you can get thirty gallons and keep it at four hundred and ninety-five dollars (to avoid the two quote requirement). I figured all of this . . . I already got the price figured out and you don't even have to have a P.O. number on that keep it under five hundred (a signed invoice would do). And then that, uh, Permabond, pre-sealant patch, I don't know if you use it or not. That's not bad stuff. You just put it in those holes, you know cleaning it out, put it in those holes before you patch.

Supervisor: Well, can we do halves on that?

Agent: Yeah, I can do anything on that. Show you what we got. Let's see, see that's, uh, prepatch sealant, these are some of my, just ole notes here, uh, pressurematic, hydraulic oil six ninety-five a gallon, that comes in a drum. all comes in a drum.

Supervisor: Well what I trying to say to you now, do you bill us, do your, your company bill us or does, uh . . .

Agent: Naw, I bill you. I bill you.

Supervisor: What I was trying to say is and all I didn't know uh . . .

Agent: I can, you know, it, it doesn't make any difference. I've got, see I've got his damn order blanks, Davis Chemical over there out of Hattiesburg.

Supervisor: Well, what I'm trying to say though is say I got a fifty-gallon, I mean, uh, thirty-gallon drum of weed killer from you and, uh, it come to four hundred ninety-five dollars. All right then you'd bill me with your, yours and all and then you didn't buy it from that cat, what's it going to be then?

Agent: If I don't buy from Him?

Supervisor: Ye, in other words if they come audit you, y'all's company and y'all's company hadn't bought any from him to deliver to me . . .

Agent: Oh, he'll be, he'll deliver to me. He'll have paperwork. Don't worry about that. We've already got that worked out. He'll have the paperwork. That's what I got these things for. I can just write it for, I thought you were talking about just who, how I got my money.

Supervisor: Yeah.

Agent: I can bill you or, you know, if . . .

Supervisor: Well, what do you do? Just get a certain amount?

Agent: Yeah. I just split it, we just, we just, if, if it's, if we're gonna bust a gal, a barrel then we just, he and I split half, half of, we get a quarter a piece.

Supervisor: Yeah.

Agent: See. See. Just . . . that's better than nothing.

Supervisor: You damn right . . .

Agent: Hey, let . . .

Supervisor: (unintelligible).

Agent: . . . me tell you man and its better than that damn twenty percent, too. (unintelligible) work for just yourself, you know.

4. A conversation between FBI special agent Cliff Chatham (working undercover as Cliff Winters a salesman for Mid-State Pipe and Supply Company) and a Leake County supervisor taped March 4, 1985, depicts how supervisors would refer undercover agents to other supervisors who were willing to take kickbacks and how the referring supervisor would be paid for the referrals.

Agent: Let's make sure of that now. You wanted four fifteen inch lengths, twenty lengths, sixteen gauge, right. That's how y'all do it. It comes to four hundred ninety-six dollars there. Okay. You got one twenty-four.

Supervisor: Twenty-one.

Agent: Twenty-one inch that's thirty-four foot. It comes to thirty-four feet or eight fifty-two eighty-nine.

Supervisor: Now this is a state bid price.

Agent: Yes, sir.

Supervisor: Now I don't keep up with . . .

Agent: Yes, sir. I got it right here.

Supervisor: Just as long as state bid price, right. Cause when it comes in up there, if it's not state bid price, they just won't pay it no way.

Agent: I know that.

Supervisor: (unintelligible).

Agent: [blacked out] was supposed to call in the bid. See I got the State Auditor's number.

Supervisor: Pardon.

Agent: State Auditor's number. You got to have a State Auditor's number.

Supervisor: Okay.

Agent: I believe . . .

Supervisor: Okay. I, I don't really know. I'll talk to [blacked out] about it. Ah. Yeah. I think that's about it then.

Agent: (unintelligible).

Supervisor: Oh, yeah.

Agent: State Auditor's number is . . .

Agent: When we had these printed up, he had the wrong address, so I put 610. That's his number. You got my card, right?

Supervisor: Yeah.

Agent: Okay. And, ah, I think if there is anything else, there. That's about it.

Supervisor: (unintelligible).

Agent: Sir? Yes, sir.

Supervisor: (unintelligible).

Agent: Okay.

Supervisor: Alrighty:

Agent: Hey, [blacked out]. Hey. I don't want to embarrass you or nothing, but, you know, [blacked out] said you guys get ten percent now.

Supervisor: (unintelligible).

Agent: Or do you want . . . later . . .or

Supervisor: You know, that's, that's something between . . . breath that out or nothing . . .

Agent: Hey, Hey. I don't want that out.

Supervisor: You'll get me in trouble.

Agent: Okay. Oh, I realize that, but . . . I'll be honest with ya. I told him and said I need some business. And I was going to give you some, I was going to give you twelve percent. This is just between me and you.

Supervisor: You know, it's my word against your word, you know what I mean.

Agent: Exactly. Hey, look. I can't give this to everybody. Okay. I ain't gonna do it. Okay. But I'll tell you what I'll do too. Ah. If I can make a sale, I'll give you two percent of their first sale. (unintelligible).

Agent: But, ah, I can't give them twelve percent.

Supervisor: I understand.

Agent: But I'll give them ten. It's up to them now. If they don't want it. It's more money for me. I don't, you know. But I'm trying to get started and get a business going and ah, that's all I want to do. But, like I said. Just between me and you. Cause I don't want you go spreading around that, hey,

Supervisor: No.

Agent: He gave me twelve percent.

Supervisor: If going to do it right now (unintelligible).

Agent: You know what. I tell you what. I looked at that commission. I wonder who he represents cause I don't think he went to the country people. He's, ah . . . He done outsmarted himself really, but ah. Let me, ah, I'll just, you know. Just between me and you.

Supervisor: Okay. Fine.

Agent: Hey you know how that goes.

Supervisor: That's right. You know what I mean (unintelligible). Now the first one it's going to be my word against yours.

Agent: Yeah.

Supervisor: (unintelligible) you say. I'm going to say no I didn't.

Agent: You got that right. Twenty, forty, sixty, eighty, a hundred. I'm gonna go ahead like I said, there's ah, I'll give you a hundred on that.

Supervisor: (unintelligible).

Agent: But ah.

Supervisor: Man, just like I say now. This is bad business. I mean you get in trouble in a hurry.

Agent: Well

Supervisor: You get ourselves (unintelligible).

Agent: Hey.

Supervisor: (unintelligible).

Agent: Hey, we ain't going to say nothing to nobody.

Supervisor: All right, button your mouth.

Agent: I will. You can bet on that.

Supervisor: The one's that I can (unintelligible) around here. (unintelligible) you know I'll tell them you give ten percent.

Agent: Okay. But, ah, don't tell them I gave you twelve.

Supervisor: I'm not telling nothing.

Agent: Because, that cuts into my profit. Now, like I said. I wouldn't do it, if, ah, if I wasn't trying to get started . . .

Sources

Introduction

Newspapers:
Clarion-Ledger (Jackson)—July 30, 1987; November 4, 1999; March 5, 2000
Sun Herald (Biloxi)—December 17, 1987; January 8, 1988
Interviews:
Rev. John Burgess (July 14, 2000)
Former FBI Special Agent Jerry King (July 17, 2000)

Ray Mabus (November 3, 1997)
Former U.S. Attorney George Phillips (June 19, 2000)
Assistant U.S. Attorney James Tucker (June 29, 2000)
Other Sources:
Prosecution of Public Corruption Cases—Prosecution of Public Corruption Cases, U.S. Department of Justice

Chapter 1. A License to Steal

Newspapers:
Clarion-Ledger (Jackson)—February 13, 14, 1987; November 18, 1988; January 17, 1989
Northeast Mississippi Daily Journal (Tupelo)—August 11, 1987
Star-Herald (Kosciusko)—February 19, 1987
Other Publications:
Investigating and Prosecuting Public Corruption, U.S. Department of Justice (1992)

Interviews:
Rev. John Burgess (July 14, 2000)
Former Director of the Investigative Audit Division of the Department of Audit Louisa Dixon (June 5, 2000)
Former FBI Special Agent Jerry King (July 17, 2000)
Ray Mabus (November 3, 1997)
Former FBI Agent Keith Morgan (August 15, 2000)
Former U.S. Attorney George Phillips (June 19, 2000)
Assistant U.S. Attorney James Tucker (June 29, 2000)

Chapter 2. Perry County

Newspapers:

Clarion-Ledger (Jackson)—June 9, October 20, 1987; February 20, October 4, 1988

Clarion-Ledger/Jackson Daily News—August 22, September 26, December 12, 1987; March 24, December 3, 1988

Jackson Daily News—December 3, 1988

Hattiesburg American—March 12, June 1, 2, 3, 1987; March 24, 1988

Meridian Star—June 2, 3, 9, 10, 14, July 13, 1987

Vicksburg Evening Post—December 12, 1987

Richton Dispatch—March 19, April 4, 16, May 14, June 4, July 16, August 6, September 3, 1987

Other Publications:

U.S. v. Westmoreland, West Publishing Company (1988)

Internet:

www2.netdoor.com/~bfhenry/perry/perry.html

Court Records:

U.S. v. G. F. Mixon, Jr.

U.S. v. Trudie P. Westmoreland

Interviews:

Ray Mabus (November 3, 1987)

Former FBI Special Agent Jerry King (July 17, 2000)

Former U.S. Attorney George Phillips (June 19, 2000)

Assistant U.S. Attorney James Tucker (June 29, 2000)

Chapter 3. Wayne County

Newspapers:

Clarion-Ledger (Jackson)—March 15, 1987; July 22, 1987; August 4, 1987; September 19, 1987; November 18, 19, 20, 1987; January 9, 1988; May 9, 21, 1988; December 23, 1988

Hattiesburg American—July 23, 1987; August 11, 1987; May 9, 1988

Meridian Star—July 8, 23, 29, 30, 31, 1987; August 4, 5, 6, 10, 1987; May 13, 22, 1988

Northeast Mississippi Daily Journal—August 5, 1987

Other Publications:

United States of America v. Jimmy T. Duvall, West Publishing Company, Synopsis and Key Number Classifications

Court Records:

U.S. v. Jimmy T. Duvall and Alfred Grant Revette

U.S. vs. William H. Hutto, III

Internet:

www.allrednet.com/mscounty/counties/wayne.htm

Interview:

Former FBI Special Agent Jerry King (August 15, 2000)

Chapter 4. Lamar County

Newspapers:
Clarion-Ledger (Jackson)—May 24,
October 24, November 11, 1987;
March 23, 1988
Hattiesburg American—May 5, 8, 24,
25, 26, 27, 1987; March 23, 1988

Other Publications:
Mississippi Road Atlas, University
Press of Mississippi, Jackson (1997)
Court Records:
U.S. v. Pascal Lott
U.S. v. Kermit Rayborn

Chapter 5. Claiborne County

Newspapers:
Clarion Ledger (Jackson)—May 14,
15, June 11, 20, 21, 29, August 27, 1986;
September 12, November 4, 1987;
February 16, 17, 18, 19, September 19,
1988; December 29, 1989; June 8, 9,
13, 1991; November 23, 1995; January
14, 17, 18, May 14, 20, 21, 22, 23, June
6, 7, 29, 1997; April 14, 20, 26, May 14,
20, 1998
*Clarion-Ledger/Jackson Daily
News*—June 7, 1986
Hattiesburg American—February 19,
1988

Meridian Star—February 19, 1988
Natchez Democrat—February 20,
1988
Port Gibson Reveille—June 6, 20, 26,
1991; January 4, February 1, 29, April
4, 18, May 2, 16, June 20, July 4, 12,
19, 1996
Vicksburg Evening Post—May 16,
June 18, 1987; February 17, 19, 1988
Court Records:
U.S. v. Albert Butler
U.S. v. Eddie Burrell

Chapter 6. Winston County

Newspapers:
Clarion-Ledger (Jackson)—
December 13, 1970; April 14, July 31,
August 2, 1988
*Clarion-Ledger/Jackson Daily
News*—August 29, 1987
Meridian Star—February 21, 1987
Winston County Journal—March 21,
1958; April 7, 1966; February 18, 25,
March 18, August 12, 1987; April 20,
1988

Other Publications:
Mississippi Road Atlas, University
Press of Mississippi, Jackson (1997)
Mississippi State Park brochures
Internet:
www.allrednet.com/mscounty/
counties/winston.htm
Court Records:
U.S. v. Larry Miller

Chapter 7. Marion County

Newspapers:
 Clarion-Ledger (Jackson)—October 9, 14, December 9, 1987; January 6, 8, 9, May 18, 25, 1988; February 8, 1989
 Columbian-Progress—October 15, November 12, 1987; January 7, 14, March 17, April 8, 28, May 12, June 9, 14, July 28, 1988; February 9, 1989; September 30, 1995
 Hattiesburg American—March 11, 12, 1988
 Oxford Eagle—February 8, 1988
Other Publications:
 Mississippi Road Atlas, University Press of Mississippi, Jackson (1997)
West Publishing Company (1991)

Court Records:
 U.S. v. Sim Ed Moree
 U.S. v. Larkey William Broome and Donald Frank Gowen
Interviews:
 Employee of the Marion County Chancery Clerk's office—telephone (February 19, 1999)
 U.S. Probation Officer Ken Ferrell—telephone (August 15, 2000)
 Assistant U.S. Attorney James Tucker (June 29, 2000)

Chapter 8. A Vendor's Trial

Newspapers:
 Clarion Ledger—February 7, March 6, September 4, 13, 14, 15, 16, 1988
 Northeast Mississippi Daily Journal—September 16, 1988
 Oxford Eagle—September 16, 1988
 Daily Corinthian—November 20, 23, 1987; September 16, 1988

Other Publications:
 U.S. v. Little, West Publishing Company
Court Records:
 United States of America v. Bobby R. Little and North Mississippi Supply Company, Inc.

Chapter 9. The Auditors

Newspapers:
 Clarion-Ledger (Jackson)—July 24, December 18, 1983; September 9, 1984; January 15, 16, 19, 23, April 18, August 14, September 25, 29, October 23, 1988; January 11, 18, 22, 1990; February 9, 12, 17, November 2, 1995; July 23, 24, August 15, 16, 19, 20, 22, October 11, 17, 19, 20, 1996
 Enterprise-Journal (McComb)—January 19, 1989

 Meridian Star—February 17, June 11, 15, July 1, 25, August 23, 25, 26, 1987; May 8, 7, 24, July 22, September 26, 30, October 14, 19, 20, 1988; September 24, November 20, 1989
 Northeast Mississippi Daily Journal (Tupelo)—February 13, August 3, 13, December 1, 1987; May 19, October 6, 1988
 Oxford Eagle—January 5, July 22, September 1, October 5, 21, 24, 1988

Vicksburg Evening Post—November 5, December 16, 30, 1987; February 26, April 1, 12, November 12, 1988

Other Publications:

PEER report—A Management and Operational Review of the Mississippi State Department of Audit (December 8, 1983)

Other Materials:

Ray Mabus papers (reviewed at the University of Mississippi in the summer of 1998)

Interviews:

Former Director of the Investigative Audit Division of the Department of Audit Louisa Dixon (June 4, 2000)
Assistant U.S. Attorney John Hailman (June 29, 2000)
Ray Mabus (November 3, 1997)

Chapter 10. The Unit System

Newspapers:

Sun-Herald (Biloxi)—September 4, 5, 1998
Meridian Star—May 19, June 3, July 24, September 28, October 19, 1988
Times-Picayune (New Orleans)—December 22, 1961; April 13, 16, 1962; July 17, 1973
Commercial Appeal (Memphis)—June 26, August 16, 1973
Oxford Eagle—August 11; October 24, 1988
Clarion-Ledger (Jackson)—February 10, 1986; February 15, 1987; February 1, May 1, August 14, 17, 23; September 4, 25, 29, October 22, 30; November 10, 1988; September 24, November 30, 1989; January 11, 18, 1990; September 30, November 8, 1992; April 14, 20, 26, 1998
Northeast Mississippi Daily Journal (Tupelo)—June 10, October 6, 1988
Daily Times Leader (West Point)

Other Publications:

Brookings Institution—*Report on a Survey of the Organization and Administration of State and County Government in Mississippi* (1932)

William M. Wiseman—*Converting to the Unit System: The Neshoba County Experience—A Report by the Department of Political Science Mississippi State University and Government Services Division Research and Development* (1987)
William M. Wiseman, Katri Welford and Charles W. Washington, *The County Government Reorganization Act of 1988— An Informative Report*, John C. Stennis Institute of Government Mississippi State University (1988)
William M. Wiseman, *Summary Report of Research Conducted in Behalf of the Governor's County Unit Task Force*, John C. Stennis Institute of Government Mississippi State University (1992)
Mississippi Supervisor, Chancery Clerk and Tax Collector (November 1947)

Interviews:

Ray Mabus (November 3, 1987)
William M. Wiseman (summer 1998)

Court Records:

U.S. v. Eddie Moffat

Chapter 11. State Highway Commissioners

Newspapers:
Clarion-Ledger (Jackson)—May 6,
December 15, 16, 18, 21, 1987; January
5, March 11, 12, 18, May 5, 6, 7, 9, 10,
15, 27, December 22, 23, 1988;
February 9, March 7, 10, June 8,
November 9, 1989; April 20, October
6, 1990
Clarion-Ledger/Jackson Daily
News—December 27, 1987

Jackson Daily News—September 4,
1988
Northeast Mississippi News
Journal—December 31, 1987; April
28, December 22, 23, 1988
Vicksburg Evening Post—December
18, 19, 21, 1987; April 5, 7, 1988
Court Records:
U.S. v. Robert Earl (Bob) Joiner
U.S. v. Sam Waggoner, III

Chapter 12. Madison County

Newspapers:
Clarion-Ledger (Jackson)—June 12,
1996; January 1, 1997; October 10, 11,
12, 13, 14, 15, 16, 19, 22, November 12,
1998
Madison County Journal on the Web
(www.onlinemadison.com)
(numerous articles—specific dates of
publication generally not available)

Other Publications:
David Richardson, J. L. McCullough,
Karl Banks, J. S. Harris Jr.,
Individually, and in Their Capacity as
Supervisors of Madison County,
Mississippi; and Tubb-Williamson,
Inc. v. Canton Farm Equipment, Inc.;
West Group (1997)

Chapter 13. Action in North Mississippi

Panola County
Newspapers:
Clarion-Ledger (Jackson)—October
29, 1987; May 2, 3, 1989
Tate County Democrat
(Senatobia)—April 13, May 11, 1989
Panolian (Batesville)— November 4,
1987
Vicksburg Evening Post—April 23, 1988
Court Records:
U.S. v. Horace C. Mathews

Pontotoc County
Newspapers:
Clarion-Ledger (Jackson)—February
19, 27, March 13, 15, June 19, July 30,

August 27, 28, 30, September 5,
October 11, December 17, 1987;
September 13, October 1, 1988
Jackson Daily News—April 5, 1987
Meridian Star—February 19, June 26,
1987
Pontotoc Progress—February 19, 26,
March 5, April 9, June 25, July 9, 16,
30, August 13, 27, September 3, 10, 17,
October 8, November 12, December
3, 10, 17, 1987; January 7, June 9,
September, 29, 1988
Oxford Eagle—February 12, 13, 16, 19,
20, 1987
Northeast Mississippi Daily Journal
(Tupelo)—February 13, July 2, 9, 14,

15, 27, 28, 30, 31, August 2, September 1, 14, December 8, 17, 1987; September 16, October 1, 1988
Vicksburg Evening Post—April 23, 1988
Court Records:
United States of America v. Grady O. Backer
United States of America v. Theron Baldwin
United States of America v. Lee Hollis Burt
United States of America v. Ray Davis
United States of America v. Obern L. Finley
United States of America v. Max Gilbert
United States of America v. Bobby R. Little
United States of America v. Talmage M. Nix
United States of America v. Bobby Dean Stegall

Internet:
www.allred.com/county/
info.cfm?ID=58

Monroe County
Newspapers:
Clarion-Ledger (Jackson)—April 17, 19, 1999
Clarion-Ledger/Jackson Daily News—August 1, 1987; October 1, 1988
Hattiesburg American—August 1, 1987
Northeast Mississippi Daily Journal (Tupelo)—July 7, 1987; April 22, 1988; April 17, 1999
Other Publications:
Mississippi Road Atlas, University Press of Mississippi, Jackson (1997)
Court Records:
U.S. v. John Allan Cockerham
U.S. v. Leonard G. "Bud" Faulkner

Chapter 14. The Vortex of the Maelstrom

Attala County
Newspapers:
Clarion-Ledger (Jackson)—February 13, 14, 1987; June 5, July 30, August 3, and October 10, 1988
Clarion-Ledger/Jackson Daily News—June 4, 5, 1988
Northeast Mississippi Daily Journal (Tupelo)—February 12, 1987
Star-Herald (Kosciusko) February 19, 26, March 5, 6, 7, June 4, 16, 1987; March 24, April 24, August 4, September 8, 29, October 6, 13, November 4, 1988
Court Records:
U.S. v. Colon Belk
U.S. v. Robert C. Ellard
U.S. v. David Fancher
Jessie J. Fleming v. State of Mississippi

State of Mississippi v. Jesse J. Fleming
Interview:
Assistant U.S. Attorney John Hailman—June 26, 2000 (telephone)

Leake County
Newspapers:
Clarion- Ledger—December 30, 1987
Meridian Star—June 10, 28, 1987
Vicksburg Evening Post—August 29, 1987
Court Records:
U.S. v. James L. Freeny
U.S. v. Thomas Jack Jones
U.S. v. Deward Dean Myers
Internet:
www.allrednet.com/mscounty/counties/leake.htm

Neshoba County

Newspapers:

Clarion-Ledger (Jackson)—
September 15, October 16, November
17, 21, December 4, 18, 1987; February
1, 1988
Hattiesburg American—February 13,
1988
Meridian Star—February 12, 13,
March 11, May 24, June 5, September
12, 1988
Vicksburg Evening Post—February 13,
1988

Other Publications:

Mississippi Road Atlas, University
Press of Mississippi, Jackson (1997)
Willie Morris, *The Courting of*
Marcus Dupree, University Press of
Mississippi, Jackson (1992)
William M. Wiseman, *Converting to*
the Unit System: The Neshoba County
Experience, Mississippi State
University

Court Records:

U.S. v. John S. Holley
U.S. v. Willard Posey
U.S. v. Arlo Winstead

Other Records:

FBI transcripts obtained under the
Freedom of Information Act
Informal records maintained in the
Jackson by the U.S. Attorney's Office
of the Southern District of
Mississippi

Chapter 15. The I-20 East Corridor

Scott County

Newspapers:

Clarion-Ledger (Jackson)—August
19, October 11, 1987
Scott County Times (Forest)—June
17, August 5, 19, November 25, 1987

Internet:

www.allrednet.com/county/
info.cfm?ID + 62

Court Records:

U.S. vs Isaac Weems, Jr.

Interview:

Rev. John Burgess (July 14, 2000)

Newton County

Newspapers:

Clarion-Ledger (Jackson)—May 6,
July 28, December 22, 1987; January
13, February 25, 1988; March 30, 1989
Jackson Daily News—February 18,
1988
Meridian Star—April 27, May 3, 5, 14,
1987

Other Publications:

Mississippi Road Atlas, University Press
of Mississippi, Jackson (1997)

Court Records:

U.S. v. William E. Edwards
U.S. v. Harold Hollingsworth
U.S. v. Durwood Pinson
U.S. v. Henry Mack Smith

Other:

Telephone call to a Newton County
circuit court office employee (March
19, 1999)

Lauderdale County

Newspapers:

Clarion-Ledger
(Jackson)—November 19, 1987;
February 12, 1988
Hattiesburg American—April 9, 1987;
March 20, 1988
Jackson Daily News—September 10,
1988
Meridian Star—February 12, 13, 14,
15, 17, 20, 24, March 1, 4, April 8, 9,

10, 14, 16, 19, May 4, 10, 19, 21, June 15, 16, 18, July 10, 14, 16, 21, 28, August 1, 5, 7, 15, 22, 29. 1987; January 1, 24, February 9, 12, 18, 19, March 3, 29, April 5, May 17, June 11, July 10, 19, 23, September 10, October 18, 27, 30, November 9, 10, 1988

Internet:
www.allred.com/mscounty/counties/lauderdale.htm
Court Records:
U.S. v. William C. Brown
U.S. v. Billy Joe Harris

Chapter 16. Rankin County

Newspapers:
Clarion-Ledger (Jackson)—May 19, November 4, 5, 6, 11, 1987; January 5, 7, 15, February 2, 3, 5, 6, 9, 10, 12, 17, 23, 24, 25, 27, 29, March 1, 2, 3, 5, 9, 11, 12, 14, 15, 16, 17, 22, 30, April 4, 5, 6, 7, 12, 13, 14, 15, 16, 19, 20, 22, 23, 25, 28, 29, 30, May 6, 10, 11, 12, 13, 18, 19, 23, 24, 25, 26, 28, June 2, 7, 10, 11, 17, 23, 24, 25, 29, 30, July 1, 9, 30, August 16, 18, 20, 31, September 3, 12, 13, 14, 15, 16, 23, October 4, 8, November 9, 15, 21, 22, 29, December 5, 1988; January 31, February 22, March 28, April 22, 26, June 16, 28, August 3, 8, 10, October 3, December 19, 20, 23,

1989; March 8, 1990; February 20, June 25, 26, September 4, 5, 1991; October 8, 1991; April 16, 1992, June 19, 1993
Court Records:
State of Mississippi v. Joe Barlow
State of Mississippi v. Kenneth F. Bridges
State of Mississippi v. Ralph Moore, Herbert D. Smith, Hilton R. Richardson, Kenneth F. Bridges, and Mick C. Ponder
State of Mississippi v. Irl Dean Rhodes
County and Circuit Court Records involving Irl Dean Rhodes
State of Mississippi v. Herbert D. Smith

Chapter 17. Three Southern Counties

Smith County
Newspapers:
Clarion-Ledger/Jackson Daily News—December 12, 1987
Smith County Reformer (Raleigh)—March 18, July 8, December 16, 1987
Other Publications:
Mississippi Road Atlas, University Press of Mississippi, Jackson (1997)
Internet:
www.allrednet.com/county/info.cfm?ID = 65

Court Records:
U.S. v. Charles Blakeney

Jasper County
Newspapers:
Clarion-Ledger (Jackson)—March 30, 1988
Jasper County News (Bay Springs)—March 11, 18, April 8, 15, May 6, June 3, July 1, 22, 29, August 19, September 2, 23, November 25, 1987; March 30, 1988
Court Records:

U.S. v. L. Rex Graham
U.S. v. John Robert Ulmer

Clarke County
Newspapers:
Jackson Daily News—February 13, 1988
Meridian Star—June 12, July 9, 15, 1987

Other Publications:
Mississippi Road Atlas, University Press of Mississippi, Jackson (1997)
Court Records:
U.S. v. Lige Becton
U.S. v. Francis M. Spivey

Chapter 18. Big-Time Corruption

Copiah County
Newspapers:
Clarion-Ledger (Jackson)—February 13, July 31, August 14, October 15, 23, December 10, 11, 1987; March 17, April 8, 1988; May 11, July 7, 1989
Copiah County Courier—July 15, 22, August 5, 12, 19, September 2, October 14, 21, November 4, 11, 25, December 2, 16, 30, 1987
Meridian Star—May 2, 1987
Vicksburg Evening Post—November 8, 1987
Other Publications:
Mississippi Road Atlas, University Press of Mississippi, Jackson (1997)
Internet:
http://www.shs.starkville.k12.ms.us/mswm/MSWritersAndMusicians/writers/Henley. html
http://www.millsaps.edu?www/pubrel/magazine/summer98/story14.html
Court Records:
U.S. v. Barry B. "Ted" Berry
U.S. v. Thomas M. Heard
U.S. v. Sidney Thompson
Interview:
Former FBI Special Agent Jerry King (July 17, 2000)

Lincoln County
Newspapers:
Clarion-Ledger (Jackson)—June 13, 1987
Other Publications:
Mississippi Road Atlas, University Press of Jackson (1997)
Internet:
www.mscounties.com/info.cfm?ID = 43
Court Records:
U.S. v. F. H. Britt, Jr.

Covington County
Newspapers:
Clarion-Ledger (Jackson)—February 12, 1988
Jackson Daily News—April 2, 1988
Hattiesburg American—February 12, 1988
Other Publications:
Mississippi Road Atlas, University Press of Mississippi, Jackson (1997)
Internet:
www.allrednet.com/mscounty/counties/covingto.htm
Court Records:
U.S. v. Wiley Tom Wade

Greene County

Newspapers:
  Clarion-Ledger (Jackson)—March 11,
  June 8, October 10, November 27,
  1987; April 28, 1988
  Greene County Herald—February 19,
  March 12, 16, 19, April 9, 16, 27, May
  14, July 30, August 6, September 24,
  November 19, 1987
  Hattiesburg American—April 8, 9, 10,
  1987
Other Publications:
  Mississippi Road Atlas, University
  Press of Mississippi, Jackson (1997)
Internet:
  www.allrednet.com/mscounty/
  counties/greene.htm

Court Records:
  U.S. v. John M. Crocker, Jr.
  U.S. v. Lauvon Pierce
  U.S. v. George Ivan Smith
Other Records:
  Informal records maintained in
  Jackson by the U.S. Attorney's Office
  of the Southern District of
  Mississippi
Interviews:
  Former Director of the Investigative
  Audit Division of the Mississippi
  Department of Audit Louisa Dixon
  (June 5, 2000)
  Former FBI Special Agent Jerry King
  (July 17, 2000)
  Assistant U.S. Attorney James
  Tucker (June 29, 2000)

Chapter 19. Crime on the Coast

Hancock County

Newspapers:
  Clarion Ledger (Jackson)—July 10,
  August 13, December 5, 1987;
  February 21, June 10, July 31, 1988;
  March 11, 1989
  Sea Coast Echo (Bay St.
  Louis)—December 6, 1987
  Sun Herald (Biloxi)—March 12, July
  10, 11, August 6, 31, September 1,
  October 2, November 11, 14, 17, 18,
  December 5, 30, 1987; January 7,
  February 18, May 13, 21, June 10, July
  29, August 11, 1988; January 10, 14,
  March 12, April 13, May 12, 1989
Other Publications:
  Mississippi Road Atlas, University
  Press of Mississippi, Jackson (1997)
Court Records:
  U.S. v. Roger Dale Ladner
  U.S. v. Sam J. Perniciaro, Sr.
  U.S. v. James N. Travirca

Harrison County

Newspapers:
  Clarion-Ledger (Jackson)—
  September 8, 1988; March 22, July 8,
  September 30, December 18, 1989
  Jackson Daily News—September 4,
  1988
  Sun Herald (Biloxi)—January 5,
  February 12, 13, March 12, September
  3, 4, 7, 1988; March 22, 1989
  Vicksburg Evening Post—January 7,
  1988
Other Publications:
  Edward Hume, *Mississippi Mud*,
  Pocket Books, New York (1994)
  Mississippi Road Atlas, University
  Press of Mississippi, Jackson (1997)
Court Records:
  U.S. v. Eddie Moffat

Jackson County
Newspapers:
  Clarion-Ledger (Jackson)—March 19,
  April 8, June 20, 1987; August 17,
  November 2, 15, December 2, 31,
  1998; January 1, March 5, 7, 8, April
  22, 1999, June 15, 2001
  Hattiesburg American—November
  15, December 30, 1998; January 9,
  March 6, April 22, 1999
  Sun-Herald (Biloxi)—March 19,
  April 8, June 6, 18, 20, 30, July 7, 15,
  18, 1987; August 30, September 4, 5,
  October 20, 30, November 21, 25,
  December 1, 4, 6, 9, 27, 1998; April 18,
  24, May 6, 18, June 9, July 2, 7,
  August 25, September 18, October 5,
  6, 9, December 4, 1999; January 11,
  March 21, 31, April 4, 2000; March
  22, 23, April 19, 2001
  Vicksburg Evening Post—April 8, 1987
Other Publications:
  Mississippi Road Atlas, University
  Press of Mississippi, Jackson (1997)
Court Records:
  U.S. v. Maury G. Thompson
  U.S. v. Fred Robinson, Jr.

Chapter 20. The Vendors

Newspapers:
  Clarion-Ledger (Jackson)—March 15,
  June 18, July 4, November 20, 1987;
  February 25, March 19, April 15, 28,
  July 8, October 7, 1988; January 4,
  February 10, March 4, 1989
  *Clarion-Ledger/Jackson Daily
  News*—March 10, October 3, 1987;
  April 15, June 11, 1988
  Hattiesburg American—February 13,
  May 14, July 23, 1987; March 19, April
  16, 1988
  Jackson Daily News—September 3,
  1988
  Meridian Star—July 22, August 23,
  1987; February 25, September 4, 1988
  Pontotoc Progress—September 24,
  1987

Other Media:
  "The Preacher and the Sting
  Man"—*60 Minutes*, May 8, 1988
  (video)
Court Records:
  U.S. v. Gaston Barrett
  U.S. v. Ray Davis
  U.S. v. Pete Dacus
  U.S. v. Max Gilbert
  U.S. v. Billy Ray Harrison
  U.S. v. William Leslie Polk, III
  U.S. v. Jessie M. Smith
  U.S. v. Ray Dowell Smith
  U.S. v. Johnnie Williamson
Other Records:
  Informal records maintained in
  Jackson by the U.S. Attorney's Office
  the Southern District of Mississippi

Epilogue

Newspapers:

Clarion-Ledger (Jackson)—April 14, 20, 26, May 14, 20, September 26, October 23, 28, November 2, 12, 15, 1998; January 1, 1999

Hattiesburg American—October 22, 24, 27, November 15, 1998; January 9, 1999

Madison County Journal—August 27, October 22, 1998

Index